The Maastricht experiment

ANNEMIEKE KLIJN

The Maastricht experiment

On the challenges faced by a young university 1976–2016

Vantilt

Universities are institutions that embody 'structural dissent'. There is always an inherent tension between the professionals who would prefer to chart their own course, administrators of varying degrees of ambition and the expectations of society. Dissent is part of the very fabric of every university.
KARL DITTRICH, 2014

CONTENTS

INTRODUCTION 9

1 *Wynand Wijnen* WE NEED TO ABOLISH TEACHING AND BEGIN TO ORGANISE LEARNING 41

2 *Wim Brouwer* WITH ITS EMPHASIS ON PRIMARY HEALTH CARE AND GENERAL MEDICAL PRACTICE, THE BASIC PHILOSOPHY WAS HIGHLY MOTIVATING 55

3 *Marius Romme* PSYCHIATRIC ISSUES ARE THE RESULT OF PROBLEMS IN EVERYDAY LIFE 65

4 *Ine Kuppen* I WAS AT THE BIRTH OF IT ALL 77

5 *Coen Hemker* THE UNIVERSITY MUST CLAIM A PLACE ON THE SCIENTIFIC MAP. OTHERWISE, WE MAY AS WELL GIVE UP 83

6 *Geert Blijham* THE BASIC PHILOSOPHY WAS A FANTASTIC EXPERIMENT, BUT IF WE REALLY WANTED TO GET IN THE GAME WE WERE GOING TO NEED A FULLY-DEVELOPED HOSPITAL 97

7 *Hans Philipsen* SOCIAL HEALTH SCIENCE WAS THE FIRST, ALBEIT TENTATIVE, STEP TOWARDS A REAL UNIVERSITY 105

8 *Henk Schmidt* PROBLEM-BASED LEARNING IS MORE THAN A TEACHING METHOD – IT'S A TEACHING PHILOSOPHY 121

9 *Job Cohen* THE NEW APPROACH TO TEACHING LAW AIMED TO PRODUCE NOT BETTER BUT MORE MOTIVATED LEGAL PROFESSIONALS 131

10 *Ria Wolleswinkel* I WENT TO STUDY LAW IN MAASTRICHT WITH PAULO FREIRE-ESQUE IDEAS ABOUT THE PEDAGOGY OF THE OPPRESSED 151

11 *Joan Muysken* ECONOMICS IN MAASTRICHT HAD TO DEVELOP A RECOGNISABLE AND NEW IDENTITY OF ITS OWN 165

12 *Hein Schreuder* ECONOMICS IN MAASTRICHT HAD TO BE INTIMIDATINGLY DIFFERENT, MORE INTERNATIONAL AND BETTER 181

13 *Gerard de Vries* A SERIOUS UNIVERSITY NOT ONLY OFFERS CAREER TRAINING BUT ALSO CULTIVATES ACADEMIC THINKING AND CULTURE 193

14 *Wiel Kusters* WE WOULDN'T GET ANYWHERE WITHOUT SCIENCE, BUT WE'D BE NOWHERE WITHOUT THE ARTS 209

15 *Hans Peters* AS AN EXPERIMENTAL, TRANSNATIONAL DEGREE PROGRAMME, KNOWLEDGE ENGINEERING SERVED TO STRENGTHEN OUR SCIENCES EDUCATION 223

16 *Louis Boon* THE MOST INTERESTING THEMES ARE FOUND AT THE INTERFACE OF THE SOCIAL SCIENCES AND NATURAL SCIENCES 235

NOTES 257

LITERATURE AND SOURCES 276

PHOTO CREDITS 284

INDEX OF PERSONS 286

COLOPHON 288

INTRODUCTION

The State University of Limburg, today called Maastricht University, officially came into being in 1976 with what was referred to as 'the Maastricht experiment'. However, the 'real' birth year of the university is debatable. After all, thanks to skilful political manoeuvring, the Faculty of Medicine had already been founded two years prior, as an educational experiment with fifty 'course participants'. These participants were not called students as there was no legal basis to this adventure – despite Maastricht receiving backing from the government in The Hague. The founding of the faculty was initially legitimised as an experiment in educational reform. The legal side was formally addressed in December 1975 with the adoption of the *Wet Rijksuniversiteit Limburg* (Act on the State University of Limburg). This required a *lex specialis* – a first in the academic world – as by law a university had to have at least three faculties, and the State University of Limburg consisted of only two: a Faculty of Medicine and a General Faculty. The name of the latter was kept very vague on purpose, as there were no clearly-developed ideas about what it was to encompass. The formal opening of the State University of Limburg took place on 9 January 1976, which has since been considered Maastricht University's *dies natalis*.

The establishment of the university was the culmination of years of efforts by a Limburg lobby. The unusual name, State University of Limburg (rather than 'Maastricht'), underlined the extent to which Limburg's residents were concerned with the university and its development. The go-ahead for the establishment of the university had first been secured in 1969 on the strength of the following arguments: the spread of university education, compensation for the large-scale closure of mines in the province, and the need for a university in the German-French-Dutch cultural triangle. The arrival of the State University of Limburg transcended mere regional interests: it was expected to grow into a new type of university and contribute to the reform of higher education in the Netherlands as a whole. With its 'basic philosophy', the eighth Faculty of Medicine set itself apart from its counterparts elsewhere in the Netherlands. It sought to place an emphasis on, and also to incorporate social and behavioural sciences into, the study of primary health care. As far as the underlying educational philosophy was concerned, the emphasis was to be on problem orientation, autonomy, attitude development and a small-scale approach. The 'new-style' university would distinguish itself from the existing universities by its multidisciplinary and interdisciplinary approach, while, with its focus on social engagement, it would mount a response to some of the practical issues facing society. In addition, Maastricht's location offered cross-border opportunities, not only for research but also in the domain of education in the not-yet-united Europe.

The fact that Maastricht University was established *ex nihilo* – unlike all other post-war Dutch universities it had no immediate precursor – seemed to be an advantage: it was possible to start with a clean slate. Back in 1976, too, universities were seen as 'beacons of hope and expectation'.[1] So what were the problems in the academic world that the Maastricht experiment hoped to solve?[2] Since the 1950s, the universities had been confronted with a growing influx of students, many of whom dropped out partway through their degree programmes – the overcrowded lecture halls had a demotivating effect. Whereas for a long time academic life had more or less taken place in a bubble, in the 1960s the general increase in prosperity and the post-war baby boom brought unprecedented numbers of young people into the universities.[3] Among medical professionals, in particular, there was concern about 'the crisis in medical education' which coincided with an expansion of the medical field on all fronts. The 'information explosion' gave rise to the question of how students were to find their way around all the knowledge on offer. In addition, there was felt to be a lack of coherence in what was being taught, as each lecturer focused on his – or occasionally her – own niche area of expertise. Finally, there were a lot of complaints about the lack of connectivity between theory and teaching on the one hand, and professional practice on the other. How could that gap be bridged? Of course the Second World War and the cultural revolution of the 1960s had not left the academic world untouched. Was there a sufficient sense of social responsibility in universities? This is the type of questions that the universities found themselves confronted with. It was up to Maastricht University to show that a different way of doing things was possible; to carve out its own place as a 'new-style' university within the existing Dutch university system.

While, as a non-classical university, it was able to take up a special position in the Netherlands, similar new universities were being established in other European countries, which in many cases were clearly based on US academic culture and had a strong focus on socio-economic issues.[4] A number of universities established in Western Europe in the late 1960s/early 1970s, like the university in Maastricht, positioned themselves as innovators of educational reform, such as Stirling University (1967) in Scotland, Bielefeld University in Germany (1969), Roskilde University (1972) and Aalborg University (1974) in Denmark, and Linköping University (1973) in Sweden.[5]

Maastricht University was faced with the challenge of proving its right to exist, and from the very beginning focused on growth. If it was to be considered a fully-fledged university and avoid going under during the first round of austerity measures, broadening its base was essential. However, the other universities viewed this ambition with distrust – especially in light of the fact that the 1980s marked a turning point in the history of the Dutch universities.[6] From the 1980s onwards, the universities were increasingly required to justify their decisions and activities to the outside world, and achieve more with, relatively, less funds at their disposal. The number of students continued to rise, while the number of lecturers decreased proportionately by more than 10%.[7] From the mid-1980s, competition between the universities and the fight for scant resources increased. In this context it is unsurprising that, at the time, outside Limburg the Maastricht experiment was dubbed 'the Maastricht mistake'.[8] One of the key figures in the recent public debate about university education, Stefan Collini, points to the increasing political and economic pressure on universities to justify themselves in terms of their practical 'usefulness'.[9] Karl Dittrich, too, argues that the university as an institution no longer resembles an ivory tower so much as a 'glass house'. The university is required to meet impossible expectations. It is to be 'transparent' and universally accountable on all fronts. On the one hand, everyone is expected to be able to have a university education; on the other, students should be prevented from dropping out – without any compromises being made as far as the quality of the education is concerned.[10] In addition, research needs to be excellent and ground-breaking, as well as useful and quick and easy to apply in practical contexts.[11] This raises the question of how Maastricht University has attempted to position itself over time. As a young university especially, it found itself faced with this increasing political and economic pressure, while at the same time the burgeoning 'worldwide competition for talent' grew increasingly fierce.[12]

Maastricht University has successfully cultivated an inferiority complex for years, but it is time to let go of these feelings. By now, in 2016, it has grown into a university with more than 16,000 students, over half of whom are from outside the Netherlands. It holds a special position within the Dutch university system, and it has an interesting history. However, in its ongoing effort to focus on innovation and the future, it appears to have failed to give this history the attention it deserves. Almost everything that has been written about it to date has been in Dutch. To English speakers, the university's history has until now remained a closed book – which is striking given the fact that a university should be a champion of cultural continuity.[13] That is why it was high time for a retrospective. The fact that, at forty years old, Maastricht University is still a fairly young institution presents a unique opportunity for the historian to take a look back over its past in conjunction with those people who were instrumental in its inception. They carry with them stories that will disappear if they are not heard and recorded now. Indeed, a number of key figures from the university's early days have already passed away. This approach, unconventional among university historians (who usually opt for an overarching, institution-wide perspective), may in fact be highly fitting for a university which likes to describe itself as unorthodox.[14]

This book was born of curiosity about the 'pioneers' – with all the associations of heroic romanticism that term evokes – who were involved in the establishment and further expansion of Maastricht University. It enables the reader to go on a tour of the university's history, accompanied by sixteen 'protagonists'. What ideals and ambitions did they bring to Maastricht? To what extent did it turn out to be possible to really begin with a clean slate? Who stayed and who left? What challenges did they face in expanding the university? What strategies did they use – or did they tend to act in an ad hoc way, leaving things to chance? And how did they deal with the tension between seeking to establish an innovative new identity on the one hand, and the wish to be accepted by the 'other' universities on the other? In writing this book, the idea was to use interviews with various people involved in the university's inception as a way to gain more insight into how the institution fared as a community – something which would have been difficult to uncover from exclusively written sources such as policy documents and strategic plans.

The focus is primarily on the question of how the university positioned itself when it expanded. What obstacles did it come up against when embarking on new, uncharted courses? Was the development of this university a consciously managed process, or more of a contingent one?[15] In a perpetually changing social context, Maastricht University found itself constantly having to seek out the middle ground between two extremes. The protagonists in this story struggled with several classic conundrums at the same time. Is Maastricht University to focus on education or on research? Does it seek to provide generalist or specialist education? Should the emphasis be on the autonomous acquisition and development of knowledge, or on services to society and knowledge valorisation? Should the university seek to promote culture and science or should it be market-oriented? Is the number of graduates dependent on the absorption capacity of the labour market, or is there an 'elastic professional field', with the demand for graduates following supply? Should the university adopt a theoretical, discipline-based approach or a practical and problem-based one? With incoming and graduating students, is the emphasis on quantity or quality? To what extent does it seek to have a regional, national or international focus?[16] And is finding a balance between these extremes even possible?

The sixteen 'chosen ones' in this book each tell their own story of how they tried to leave their mark on Maastricht University – some with greater success than others. It cannot be denied that there was a certain degree of pragmatism at play in the selection of the interview subjects. To start with, the oral history approach, by its very nature, comes with the proviso that only those people who are able and willing to tell their story can do so – and not all who qualified, were willing. Not everyone was open to a dialogue about the past, even though the response was predominantly very positive. This book does not purport to be a comprehensive overview of the university's history, therefore, although it does cover the entire forty-year period of its existence. The focus throughout is on the genesis of a new initiative.[17] The interviewees were predominantly, but not only, professors. Since professors perform all of the university's core tasks, they are ideally positioned to play a role in the power games in the academic world. Incidentally, Maastricht University continued be a male-dominated 'old boys' network' for a relatively long time, which results in very few women being represented in this book. The glass ceiling remained in place over the years; unfortunately, history cannot be undone in this regard.[18] With the appointment of Law scholar Rianne Letschert as the first female Rector of the university in September 2016, the institution clearly nailed its colours to the mast as to its course for the future.[19] Because the practical 'now or never' consideration played a part in the selections for this book, the interviewees included not only Wynand Wijnen – one of the key leaders of educational reform, now sadly deceased – but also all the living members of the 'core group', i.e. the first professors who established the Faculty of Medicine and were expected to put the basic philosophy into practice: Wim Brouwer, who specialised in general medicine; the social psychiatrist Marius Romme; and the biochemist Coen Hemker. Geert Blijkham looks back on the basic philosophy from his perspective as both an idealistic champion of educational reform and a clinical specialist. Ine Kuppen shows how, as one of the first employees and as the secretary of founding dean Harmen Tiddens (†), she was asked to perform a variety of roles both during the pioneering period and thereafter.

The fact that the stories of this 'first generation' of staff members from the Medical Faculty make up a relatively large part of this book is also justified inasmuch as this faculty, with its basic philosophy, largely determined the credo that the subsequent faculties were expected to comply with. However, this book also focuses on a number of key players who made a contribution to the further development and expansion of the university. Many of them are people who went on to establish new faculties and degree programmes, such as the sociologist Hans Philipsen, who was instrumental in the establishment of the General Faculty, and the Social Health programme (later known as Health Sciences) in particular; Job Cohen, founder of the Faculty of Law; the philosopher of science Gerard de Vries, the first dean of the Faculty of General Sciences and the spiritual father of the Arts and Culture programme; and – last but not least – the philosopher of science and 'king of expansion' Louis Boon, the driving force behind the Faculty of Psychology, University College Maastricht, the Faculty of Humanities and Sciences, the Science College (which would later become known as the Science Programme) and University College Venlo. But this book does not restrict itself to the founders of new faculties alone. For example, Henk Schmidt is featured as well: he played a crucial role both within and beyond Maastricht University thanks to his contribution to the theory and dissemination of problem-based learning, an educational philosophy which also gained recognition outside the medical domain, and even in the academic world internationally. Ria Wolleswinkel was not a founding dean, but she was among the very first class of Law students and would go on to become Programme Director, which gives her a unique perspective in looking back on the discussions about education that took place in the Faculty of Law. Joan Muysken and Hein Schreuder were not founding deans either, but played a prominent role in the Faculty of Economics as, respectively, the first professor of General Economics and the first professor of Business Economics. Both sought to implement a new approach to, or 'an integrated presentation' of, their subjects. Literature professor Wiel Kusters was the first dean of the Faculty of Arts and Culture; as the son of a miner, he represents the university's roots in the Province of Limburg and its aim to branch out into the arts and humanities. Hans Peters's account shows how difficult it was to realise the university's deeply held wish to strengthen its science programmes, and reflects on the progress of knowledge engineering as an interdisciplinary and transnational degree.

The fact that this book deals with plans for expansion that have ended up coming to fruition may create the impression that it is intended as a 'success story', with the author having fallen into the trap of presentism. It happens to be a fact that all those plans to which the university committed in full did in fact lead to positive results. While it also had hopes of establishing degree programmes such as Chemistry, Policy Science, Leisure Studies and Literature, those plans never made it past the embryonic stage. Before coming up with detailed proposals, the university administrators put out feelers at an early stage in their interactions with the Ministry and provincial government to gauge whether these kinds of plans for expansion had any chance of succeeding. And their instincts tended to be right on the money, so that effort was only put into initiatives that stood a realistic chance of being achieved. Incidentally, the arrival of the disciplinary Psychology programme can be seen as a veritable 'Maastricht miracle'.[20]

The interviews paint a vivid picture of the machine of the university in action. When new degree programmes were established, especially, formal and informal pathways sometimes ran in parallel. For example, informal networks were important in recruiting new staff members. Indeed, sometimes it seemed that, when filling job openings, people just pulled out their Filofaxes and worked their way down their list of connections one by one. Some had an easier time making their way in this unstructured setting than others – with all the risks of imbalance in the development of a faculty's identity that this brought with it. The interviews also paint a picture of people who came to Maastricht with very different ambitions, each with their own agenda and their own 'baggage' – the university in fact did not start out with a clean slate at all – to make a contribution to a 'process of creation' in a 'pressure cooker', as Blijham put it. Every faculty or degree was based on a philosophy, a blueprint or at any rate an extensive policy document, which was used to legitimise the establishment of a new programme: with an unfailing emphasis on the 'experimental' and/or complementary character compared with degree programmes at other universities. The Maastricht experiment went hand in hand with a search for the 'blind spots' or 'niches' in higher education. Regardless of the detailed policy documents that may have been drawn up, it remained important to stay alert to opportunities that presented themselves, and to seize them – with, of course, the necessary opportunism; a skill in which Boon, in particular, excelled. The pioneering stage gave way to an episode in which – in somewhat simplified terms – some held on to the original ideals for reform in education and research, while others wasted no time to distance themselves from those ideals in order to fit in with more traditional university mores. After all, at the other, established universities they had to deal with people who were their colleagues in research. It is this tension between wanting and needing to find a different way of doing things on the one hand, but wanting to be accepted on the other, that is the leitmotif running through the history of this university.

The choice to focus on the actions of individuals means that the factor of coincidence and happenstance plays a significant role in this account of the university's history. This approach also makes it difficult to give unequivocal answers to the questions about the university's positioning that were raised above. Ultimately, discussions about the direction the university should go in are an inherent part of what a university is – a fairly chaotic and unwieldy organisation, with disparate and sometimes conflicting objectives.[21] For example, there was a great deal of debate about the Faculty of Medicine's basic philosophy, and concern that it might be overly focused on education and primary health care. To promote the acceptance and status of the Faculty of Medicine, would it not be better to have a real specialist hospital? Within the Health Sciences programme, there were discussions about unity and diversity and the question of how new research areas, such as nursing science, could be given a sound academic foundation. The staff members of the Faculty of Law soon found themselves discussing the pros and cons of problem-based learning: was this educational philosophy, and the experimental, thematic structure of the degree programme, a good fit for the discipline of Law? Over at the Faculty of Economics, the integration of General Economics and Business Economics – which was meant to be the hallmark of the study of Economics in Maastricht – had stalled; more and more, the emphasis was shifting to an international profile in order to attract enough students – which, in turn, gave rise to a new set of discussions. The Faculty of General Sciences failed to bring about the envisaged 'synergy' between philosophy, history, mathematics and information science. This faculty gave birth to the Arts and Culture programme, which was an interdisciplinary degree programme, although the boundaries between the different disciplines turned out to be more rigid than had been expected. The interdisciplinary Knowledge Engineering programme almost foundered because of differences of opinion, which had to do not only with clashing personalities, but also with profound, and profoundly underestimated, cultural differences with the Flemish colleagues, while the 'Leuven' power block was a strong opposing force. The issue also arose as to whether perhaps Knowledge Engineering, with its cooperation with the Limburg University Centre as a 'transnational degree programme', was a little *too* experimental. The Faculty of Psychology is a story in and of itself. Although the university consistently prided itself on its interdisciplinary ambitions, thanks to cross-faculty collaboration the Faculty of Psychology succeeded, after many trials and tribulations, in developing a predominantly monodisciplinary curriculum. Of course, this new degree programme distinguished itself from other Psychology programmes through its focus on cognitive psychology and biopsychology, but over time clinical psychology crept its way into the curriculum after all. The establishment of a number of University Colleges – inspired by the US model – not only brought about considerable conflict with the world outside, but was often dogged by internal squabbles, due to a fear of competition from within.

Although there are differences in emphasis and opinion between 'the sixteen', an image emerges of a university which, after four decades, has stayed remarkably true to its founding principles, even if realism has forced it to take a pragmatic approach to these principles. Friction between the ideal and the reality is inevitable: Maastricht University held on to the ideal and rhetoric of innovation on the one hand, while, on the other, having to make the necessary practical adjustments to daily operations. Over time it became a more and more 'normal' university, integrated into the Dutch university system; no longer the outsider it used to be. On the contrary: with problem-based learning, the university had found a winning formula which many other universities ended up implementing in their own ways. In this respect, Wijnen, Blijham and Schmidt's missionary work was certainly a resounding success. Of course, Maastricht University retains its special status in that it is not a classical, broad university with a Faculty of Literature and 'real' science degrees such as Mathematics and Physics – for now, that ambition has been put to rest. It has its own identity as a 'young university', but the other universities, too, are increasingly developing distinct identities of their own.[22] Maastricht University has grown into a university focused on social relevance and professional practice, which while no longer presenting itself as 'leading in learning' remains open to new developments in the field of education.[23] While the disciplinary reflexes may have tempered the original interdisciplinary ambitions, 'interdisciplinarity' has become a magic word used the world over as a way to win research projects. What has truly enabled Maastricht University to distinguish itself from other universities over the past few years is its international character and its regional ties in the areas of knowledge, technology and the business community. These cross-border ambitions were there from the start, but have become more important over time. The recent objective of becoming a trilingual university is fully in line with the tradition of this university, which is so acutely aware of its location at a cultural crossroads between the Netherlands, Belgium and Germany.

This book focuses on the challenges faced by the sixteen protagonists of this still-young university – not yet half a century old. The author faced her own set of challenges. Although every self-respecting university wants to have an account of its history, most university historians tend to maintain a certain distance from the very recent past, lest the present comes too close – with all the potential complications that might entail.[24] History is never finished. Accounts of recent history, in particular, are inextricably bound up with the positions, interests and perspectives of the various parties involved, who turn to 'their' history in search of something to hold on to, a sense of 'identity' that will enable them to face the future confidently. Although academic historiography has become a fully-fledged sub-discipline in its own right, at Maastricht University historiography remains linked to the idea of a celebratory publication to commemorate an anniversary. While that does not necessarily result in self-promotion on the part of the institution – the author has attempted to steer clear of this – it is easy for it to verge into this territory.[25]

Oral history, too, comes with its own share of challenges.[26] An advantage is that it honours the human element of history: the combination of *petite histoire* and the bigger picture can create a vivid image of the past. At the same time, it is an approach that makes irrefutably clear that every historical account can be interpreted in multiple ways.[27] Oral history is not so much about recording objective facts as such, but rather about discovering new, subjective perspectives: what do the protagonists remember of the past and what significance do they attribute to it? This puts the historian in the slightly paradoxical situation of enquiring about the past, but being presented with the present-day construction of it.[28] The oral source material comes about in dialogue with the historian, who not only asks the questions but also selects the information, interprets it and ultimately gives it its narrative structure. Now more than ever, in this digital era in which personal letters have become all but obsolete and the ephemerality of emails has become the new standard, oral history is a method for gaining insight into what motivated people in the past.

However, oral history does bring some considerable challenges, which will be discussed briefly here. We know that memory is selective – in fact, this is one of the interesting things about it. It is also unsurprising that people tell their life story in such a way as to invest it with meaning and justify their actions to themselves and the outside world – some with slightly bigger egos than others.[29] However, the main challenge was that not everyone had – or claimed to have – a sharp memory, and events were sometimes recollected in fragments, and were not always described consistently.[30] Some even took back things they had said before, which could make distilling a narrative like unpicking a Gordian knot for the author. Therefore, this book is not based solely on the interviews with 'the sixteen': many other people who were involved were consulted as well, along with additional literature and archival research, so as to not get lost in the tangle of history. Since, as stated, the intention was to take the reader on a journey into the history of Maastricht University, accompanied by and viewed from the unique perspective of 'the sixteen' (but also, admittedly, with some guidance by the author), each of the protagonists was given the opportunity to provide feedback on his or her draft chapter – not to authorise the text, but to enable them to make comments, provide additional information and answer follow-up questions – to see whether they could identify with the story that was emerging.

*

This book came about on the initiative of Maastricht University's Art and Heritage Commission, which considers it its duty to promote not only the institution's tangible heritage, but also its intangible heritage. Recording the stories of the men and women who helped give shape to this university can, in somewhat irreverent terms, be considered the cherishing of 'living heritage'. I would like to thank former chairman Rein de Wilde, as well as Ronald Wilmes and Mieke Derickx, for their constant support with this project, including during a difficult period. Incidentally, more portraits of university employees – from every level of the organisation – will appear on the Art and Heritage Commission homepage in the future, accompanied by photographic and video material. I would also like to thank the Executive Board and the Faculty of Arts and Social Sciences, who gave me the opportunity to write this book. I am also grateful that I was able to make use of the members of the supervisory committee. Rein de Wilde (professor of Science & Politics) and Harald Merckelbach (professor of Psychology & Law) were always quick to offer constructive feedback, while Leen Dorsman (professor of University History at Utrecht University), Hans Philipsen (former professor of Medical Sociology) and Luc Soete (former Rector and professor of International Economic Relations) all gave me very helpful feedback based on their own specific backgrounds and expertise.

It was great working with Jos Perry again in the form of a trialogue: he spontaneously offered to write the chapter on Wiel Kusters, which no one was better placed to do than Jos. I would also like to thank Myra Loog, who took upon herself the sometimes trying task of transcribing the interviews. She did this with great conscientiousness and good spirits throughout, and I very much enjoyed bouncing ideas back and forth with her while writing this book. I would also like to express special thanks to Gerard Korsten, who possesses a great deal of background knowledge on the expansion of the university, and who lent me items from his personal archive, allowing me to find a route into the subject matter in a very targeted way.

When looking for photographic material – of which plenty existed scattered in various locations, although thankfully most of the photos were in the university archive – I was able to count on the support of Meredith Bradt, Claire Bollen, Jean Franssen, Marion Janssens, Jean-Pierre Pielet, Menno Roosjen, Michel Saive, Willie Schipper and Ineke Stevens. Special thanks go to Franco Gori for making his stunning photographs available for this book.

I would like to thank all the people who were willing to share their memories with me. When writing this book on 'the sixteen', I was also able to draw on the memories of other people who were involved. To get a sense of the life of the university over the past forty years, I talked to Jeppe Balkema, Geert Blijham, Tannelie Blom, Louis Boon, Joost Bremer (†), Wim Brouwer, Job Cohen, Harry Crebolder, Karl Dittrich, Marijke Dzon, Cees Flinterman, René de Groot, Coen Hemker, Gerard Korsten, Sjeng Kremers, Ine Kuppen, Wiel Kusters, Ingrid Lathouwer, Ton van der Linden, Léon Lodewick, Gerard Majoor, Hans Peters, Henk Schmidt, Tiny Simon, Joan Muysken, Franz Palm, Hans Philipsen, Marius Romme, Rob Reneman, Hetty Snellen, Hein Schreuder, Anja Servais, Edward Steur, Loek Vredevoogd, Gerard de Vries, Frans van Wijmen, René Verspeek, Ria Wolleswinkel and Wynand Wijnen (†). These conversations will be incorporated into a story database, so that these voices of the past can be heard well into the future, too.

Finally, I would like to thank Linda Slangen and Brigitte Slangen for the smooth and creative cooperation that went into editing and designing this book. On to the next project!

THE MAASTRICHT EXPERIMENT

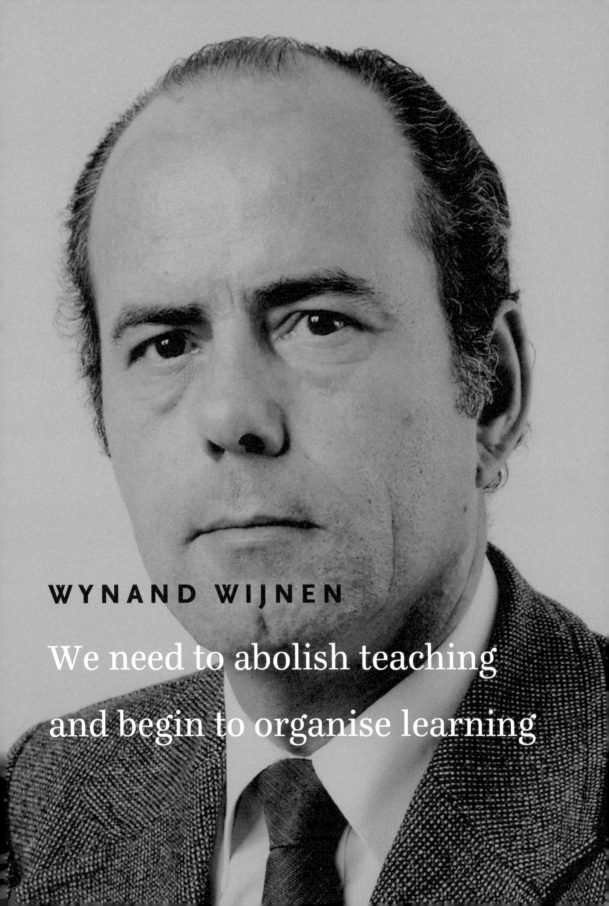

WIM BROUWER With its emphasis on primary health care and general medical practice, the basic philosophy was highly motivating

MARIUS ROMME Psychiatric issues are the result of problems in everyday life

INE KUPPEN

I was at
the birth
of it all

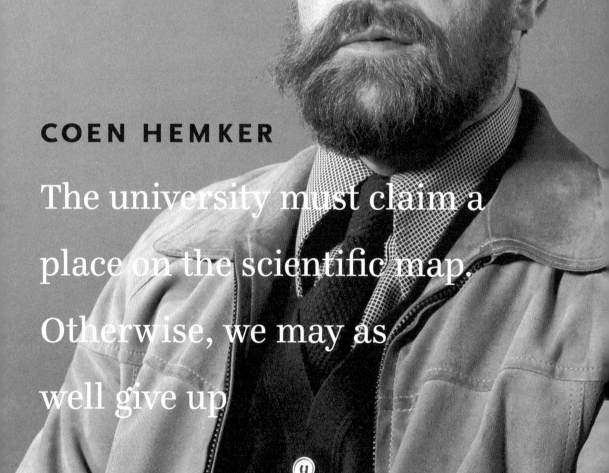

COEN HEMKER

The university must claim a place on the scientific map. Otherwise, we may as well give up

GEERT BLIJHAM

The
basic philosophy was a
fantastic experiment,
but if we really wanted to
get in the game
we were going
to need a fully-
developed hospital

HANS PHILIPSEN

Social health science was the first, albeit tentative, step towards a real university

HENK SCHMIDT Problem-based learning is more than a teaching method – it's a teaching philosophy

JOB COHEN The new approach to teaching law aimed to produce not better but more motivated legal professionals

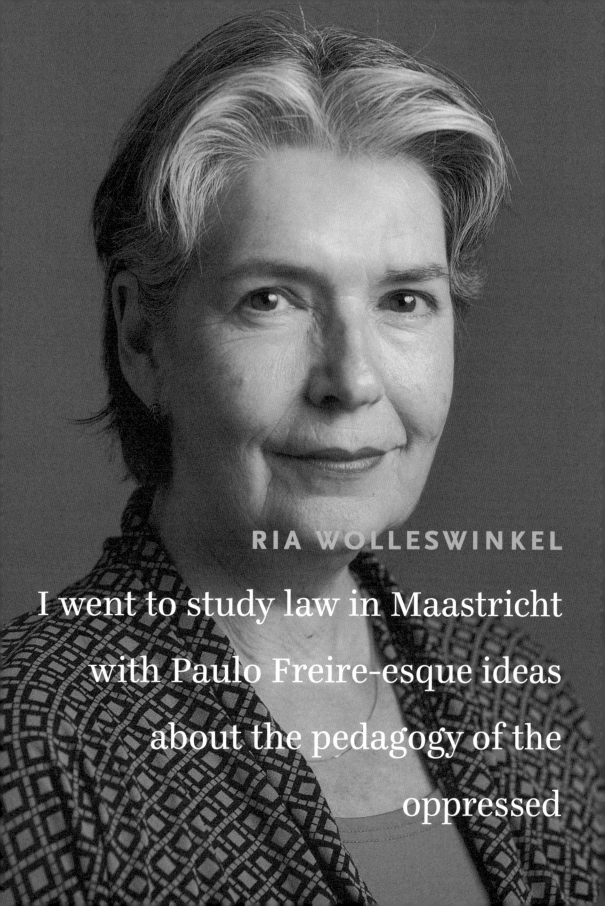

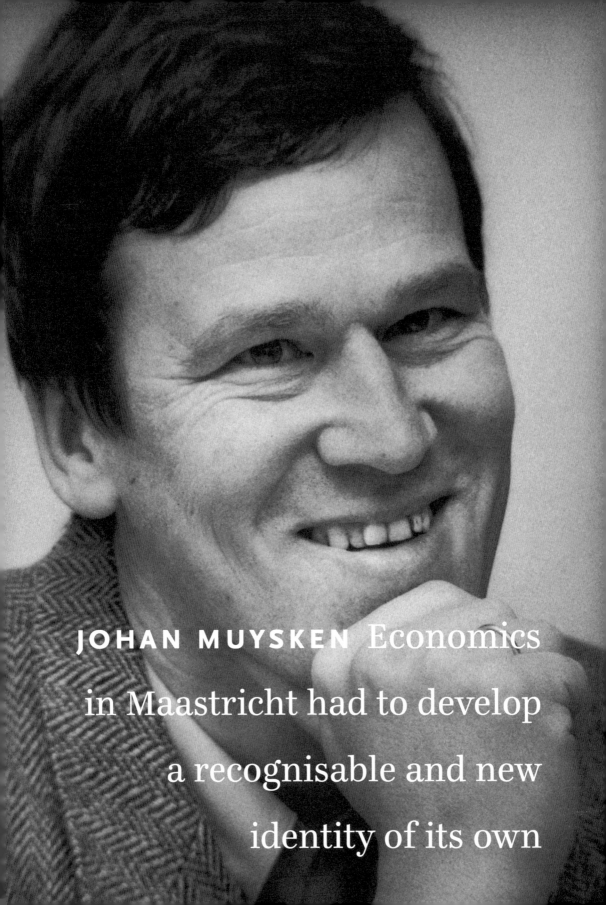

JOHAN MUYSKEN Economics in Maastricht had to develop a recognisable and new identity of its own

HEIN SCHREUDER

Economics in Maastricht had to be intimidatingly different, more international and better

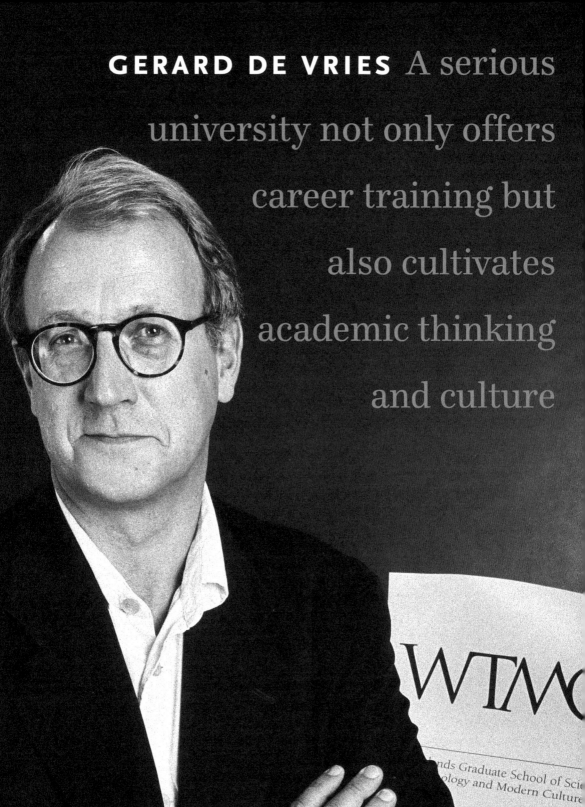

WIEL KUSTERS We wouldn't get anywhere without science, but we'd be nowhere without the arts

HANS PETERS As an experimental, transnational degree programme, knowledge engineering served to strengthen our sciences education

LOUIS BOON The most interesting themes are found at the interface of the social sciences and natural sciences

ON THE CHALLENGES FACED BY

A YOUNG UNIVERSITY 1976-2016

1 *Wynand Wijnen* WE NEED TO ABOLISH TEACHING AND BEGIN TO ORGANISE LEARNING

WIJNEN: FROM LIMBURG TO GRONINGEN From early on, educational innovation marked the life of Wynand Wijnen. His father, who was head of a Catholic primary school in the town of Hegelsom, in the north of the Province of Limburg, had already come up with a new curriculum aimed at reaching as many pupils as possible. In the morning they were taught arithmetic, reading and writing, while the afternoons were devoted to *heemgericht* teaching, which had a local focus: 'that would be about the farm or the heath or the town hall, things that were important to the children, who probably would never leave the area'. Wynand was born in 1934 and was raised in a large family of fourteen children. He was the second child and the oldest son. An education at the minor seminary of Rolduc was inevitable, followed by the seminary in Roermond where he studied to become a priest. It was there, at the age of 24, that he finally arrived at the conclusion, after a great deal of soul-searching, that that was not the path for him. In 1958 he decided to study Psychology and Sociology in Nijmegen. He finally chose to continue in Psychology and graduated specialising in – 'you won't believe it' Wijnen would later say in embarrassment – business psychology, after having completed an internship with the department of personnel research of the *Staatsmijnen* (the Dutch State Mining Company). He was asked to work with Jan Snijders, professor of Psychology in Groningen. After some hesitation – Wijnen was unfamiliar with the northern reaches of the Netherlands and the city was *very* far away indeed, according to his fiancée Mieke Fijten – he acquiesced. He began a study on the selection of medical students. The problem was that the medical faculties had great difficulty in coping with the large numbers of first-year students in the 1960s. Even the founding of a seventh medical faculty in 1966 in Rotterdam failed to alleviate matters. Perhaps somewhat surprisingly, Wijnen's research showed that using the final examination mark for Dutch was the best selection method. In particular, 'comprehensive reading' proved to have predictive power in establishing whether a student was suitable for studying Medicine. Be that as it may, very little was done with this finding.[1]

CRISIS IN MEDICAL EDUCATION With Snijders' support, Wijnen set up an education office: the Centre for Research and Development of Higher Education in Groningen. Similar offices already existed at other universities. The university educational system found itself under growing pressure due to the large numbers of students enrolling, many of them mature and discerning.[2] While university life had long tended to exist in relative isolation, now more and more young people chose a university education. How was teaching to be organised in what was referred to as a 'mass university'? And how could universities encourage a 'sense of social responsibility', which had been a legal requirement since 1960?[3] Wijnen focused on medical education in particular, with the medical faculties continuing to draw large numbers of students. In the national debate an eighth medical faculty was being discussed, since the future demand for doctors still seemed substantial. Wijnen joined the Interfaculty Committee of Researchers of Medical Education and soon became its chair; in 1972 the committee would be incorporated in the newly founded Dutch Association for Medical Education.[4] In these networks, medical faculties discussed 'the crisis in medical education'. Besides dealing with how to regulate student numbers, other issues existed. What kind of doctors were necessary for good health care? Should the curriculum not pay more attention to general medical practice? Was the need for training general practitioners (GPs) not greater than that for medical specialists? How could the changing demands of medical professional practice be addressed? How could the coherence of the medical curriculum be enhanced, when there was a concurrent explosion of knowledge and the number of medical specialties continued to rise?[5]

These circles brought Wijnen into contact with Paul Thung, professor of Medicine at Leiden University. Thung was strongly interested in reforming teaching – in particular medical teaching – and would later play an important role in founding the university in Maastricht. Wijnen also became acquainted with Harmen Tiddens, who was nearly ten years his elder, in whom he saw 'an inspired individual for the innovation of medical teaching'. Tiddens, originally a paediatrician, was professor in the 'methodology of teaching in medicine and paediatrics' and head of the Education Office of the Medical Faculty of Utrecht University. His interest in educational reform was raised in the mid-1960s in the United States and Canada, where he had encountered new forms of medical teaching. Students were not trained in individual subjects, but were confronted with practical problems that they had to solve themselves.

The aim was to bridge the gap between specialist medicine and 'general' health care. This problem orientation was well-suited to the ideal of *éducation permanente*: students needed to master active learning in order to provide patients with tailored care based on the continually increasing knowledge in their future professional practice. Tiddens also promoted 'personality moulding': students needed to develop a sense of responsibility and communication skills, a proper attitude 'towards patients, the community, team members of other disciplines and vis-à-vis the sciences'. According to Tiddens, the medical curriculum needed to pay more attention to psychology and sociology.

AN EIGHTH MEDICAL FACULTY It was Tiddens who would ask Wijnen in January 1970 to accompany him to a meeting at the Esso Motor hotel in Born at the invitation of the Limburg district of the Royal Dutch Medical Association (KNMG). There was great excitement among the doctors of Limburg. The eighth medical faculty was to go to Maastricht![6] Because a medical faculty on its own was considered to be onerous, the faculty was planned 'in the framework of a newly founded university'.[7] The decision was met with enthusiasm, although some KNMG members fell prey to uncertainty. What would the new faculty mean for the regional health care and what would its consequences be for the position of doctors and specialists in Limburg? Tiddens received ample opportunity to launch his ideas; as he recalled Wijnen was only there 'to help him a bit'. Tiddens made the case for how a new medical faculty would create an ideal opportunity for implementing educational innovation. According to him, it was 'very well possible' and 'indeed quite sensible' to create a university degree programme for medical doctors 'without a university hospital', referring to the medical faculty of Michigan State University that functioned well, supported entirely by health care in the area. This outlook was welcomed by senior KNMG officials in Limburg, who were already convinced that the new medical faculty should collaborate with existing regional health-care services. In any case, after the Born meeting, Wijnen was once again relegated to the sidelines with regard to developments concerning the 'eighth'. For quite some time, he heard 'nothing at all'.

THE 'WIJNEN METHOD' Wijnen gave priority to educational research. He was interested in systematically analysing test results; according to him assessments were often conducted in a way that was 'not rational, not reasonable, not logical'. De 1966 publication *Vijven en zessen* ('Fives and sixes') by Adriaan – 'A.D.' – de Groot, professor of Psychology and later Methodology at the University of Amsterdam, was an eye-opener for him: the study showed how arbitrarily the boundary was drawn between passing and failing. In his doctoral thesis *Onder of boven de maat* ('Insufficient or sufficient') – the title refers to that of De Groot – Wijnen argued in 1971 it was wrong to determine the boundary marks for passing and failing in advance, which was known as *absoluut normeren* (setting an absolute standard) – claiming that 'lecturers do not know how to set an absolute standard'. He made the case for 'setting a relative standard', which took into account 'both the level of students and the quality of the teaching'.[8] The aim was to determine the boundary between passing and failing 'in a rational manner'. 'And in that case', according to Wijnen, 'there are actually three things: First you have to establish what you want to compare the result of the individual student to. Do you want to compare it to the maximum score attainable that the lecturer has established in advance? Do you want to compare it to the average of that year's students? Do you want to compare it to an earlier performance on a previous test? You have to establish what your reference point is and then indicate whether you now want to think in entire questions, half-questions or quarter-questions, and then you have to determine how far off from that unit an answer is allowed to be. If you reason systematically from there on, you can base a method on this which basically says – very roughly speaking, because the details are a bit more accurate – that the average of the group minus one standard deviation is a reasonable boundary. You can hardly go wrong as a lecturer doing this. The margin is acceptable and it is easily defensible on theoretical grounds'.

Although Wijnen adhered to 'rational', 'logical' and 'systematic' thinking – and in any case was prone to using these words very often – he still knew how to enjoy himself during Dutch carnival celebrations. This attitude led him to plan his PhD ceremony in Groningen on the eleventh day of the eleventh month. This was 'a conscious choice', since Wijnen felt that 'PhD dissertations were bookcase fodder' as usually 'little was done with their contents'. In this case matters proved different. Although the relative assessment he suggested did not please everyone in 'the Dutch psychometric world', 'the Wijnen method' was implemented in many places.[9]

'WE NEED A UNIVERSITY' In the spring of 1973, Wijnen was suddenly summoned by Sjeng Tans for an introductory interview. Tans was the chair of the 'preparatory committee for the eighth medical faculty' which had been at work since March 1970 – although its solo approach, with little outside consultation, was not appreciated by all. Wijnen knew Tans by name. The Catholic socialist from Maastricht had gained national renown as the figurehead of the 'new progressive thinking' in the PvdA (Labour) party. In the 1950s he had seen his career as a teacher of Dutch at a Catholic secondary school thwarted because of his active role within the PvdA. He then switched to politics and managed to become the party's chairman and a prominent education specialist in the Dutch House of Representatives. He now wanted, whatever the cost, to see a university established in his 'own' city of birth. Tans was well acquainted with the political workings of The Hague and those of Limburg, and his political connections would prove invaluable.[10]

Wijnen noticed straight off during the initial meeting in Utrecht that Tans 'was a firm believer in the idea' that 'we need a university in Maastricht' and that it 'is more important right now that it is founded than what it should look like'. Tans brought Wijnen up to date on developments regarding 'the eighth' during the conversation. Tiddens had been roped in as adviser and Wijnen assumed that Tans had 'learned about him' from Tiddens. It became clear to Wijnen that the preparatory committee had already dealt with many challenges and would be facing many more in future. One of the points of discussion had been what the guiding principles of the new Medical Faculty should be. Should it specialise in biomedical sciences or indeed choose to focus on the social aspects of health care? And what should the university hospital look like? How would the collaboration with the existing Maastricht hospital St. Annadal be structured, and with the regional hospitals in neighbouring Heerlen and Sittard? Tans had to deal with local specialists who viewed the new medical faculty with distrust. In addition, opinion was divided on the construction of a new university hospital. Tans had wanted to build quickly, prior to establishing the Medical Faculty, and thus present The Hague with a *fait accompli*. However, new construction had been postponed, as had any prospective start date for the faculty. Government had to make cutbacks due to the faltering economy: in health care the need for reducing the number of hospital beds was discussed, while in political circles it was no longer thought that the training capacity for doctors needed to be expanded. Was 'the eighth' really necessary? This was the context that Tiddens was introduced to when the preparatory committee took him on board as an adviser. He felt that the new Medical Faculty could be easily justified if it were to distinguish itself from other medical faculties by embarking on an educational experiment. In August 1972 the *Basisfilosofie Achtste Medische Faculteit* ('Basic philosophy of the eighth Medical Faculty') was published in the *Medisch Contact* journal. The aim of the new faculty was to bridge the gap between specialist medicine and 'general' health care. Hence emphasis was laid on an active role for the new faculty in regional health care; in research and teaching the focus would be on primary health care. Other emphases would be on attitude development, problem orientation, self-motivation and progress evaluation. Shortly after the visit from Tans, Wijnen received a letter with an advertisement for a 'head of the Educational Development Office' of the 'future Maastricht Medical Faculty'.

FROM GRONINGEN TO LIMBURG Wijnen was appointed in August 1973 and four months later he moved with his family to Bunde. Thanks to deft political manoeuvring, the preparatory committee had managed to get the go-ahead for a possible early start in September 1974. The faculty would work with the regional hospitals in order to provide clinical training. Tans had immediately made his way to the Ministry of Education, Culture and Science when the cabinet led by Joop den Uyl (PvdA) came into power in May 1973, with its motto *Spreiding van kennis, macht en inkomen* ('Equitable spread of knowledge, power and income'). He had to deal with Minister Jos van Kemenade and State Secretary Ger Klein, both fellow party members and men he got along with quite well. The idea of conducting an educational experiment appealed to them. Klein did have a problem with the high cost involved, but Limburg was interesting to the PvdA from an electoral perspective; the economy of South Limburg was in dire straits after the mine closures. Wijnen recalled that Tans managed to play off 'the three major parties', the PvdA, the Liberals (VVD) and the Christian-Democrats (CDA) against one another in order to get his way. On 'several occasions' he witnessed Tans saying to someone in a conversation: '"Well, if you won't support this, we will go to so and so." And that would be the rival'. The preparatory committee made every effort to translate an early start into a point of no return for the project. Tiddens and Wijnen were firm believers in this idea: beginning the experiment as soon as possible in order to test the curriculum in practice and make any required adjustments. In the summer of 1973 funds were made available to appoint the first eight core staff members, the future professors. In addition to Tiddens, the other prospective professors were the internist Harry Hulsmans, social psychiatrist Marius Romme, general practitioner Wim Brouwer, surgeons Co Greep and Jos Lemmens, biochemist Coen Hemker and anatomical pathologist Roelof Willighagen. Tiddens became the core staff chair. He was promised an appointment to the Executive Board of the university, 'charged with educational affairs', and he would become the first Rector.[11] As future head of the Education Office, Wijnen did not formally belong to the core staff. He continued to work in close consultation with Tiddens, and 'that was not just restricted to the daytime. It went on into the night, it did! We actually enjoyed working those crazy hours, so to speak', to please Tiddens.

At the time the core staff members met once a fortnight; later they met once a week, on Fridays in Maastricht, to capture the curriculum in writing. 'There was a lot of talk about the number of beds, about the number of microscopes, and, well, researchers especially made themselves heard there', Wijnen would recall. The issue of teaching was always the last item on the meeting agenda. This 'was usually discussed with overcoats donned, and making mention of the train set to depart back to the western Netherlands', according to Wijnen. 'I think that less profound thought was devoted to teaching than in retrospect one would have liked.' In any case, according to Wijnen, most of the core staff members had a positive view of educational innovation. 'Someone strongly in favour was Wim Brouwer (professor of General Medical Practice), because it gave his discipline a positive drive. Marius Romme (professor of Social Psychiatry) was also quite positive, but for other reasons: psychiatry was always relegated to the sidelines, yet would now – social psychiatry that is – gain prominence. The ones less enchanted with educational innovation were those involved in truly basic subjects. Coen Hemker (professor of Biochemistry), for instance, was initially hardly enthusiastic, although later he would come round. Roelof Willighagen (professor of General Pathology) was compliant from the start.'

Tiddens introduced the core staff members to the didactics of problem-based learning. This educational approach was developed at McMaster University in Hamilton, in Canada, where they had already had four years' experience with such student-oriented education. Students received medical teaching in thematic format as a series of practical problems that they had to solve in small groups. Self-motivation and cooperation were both essential to the success of these groups. Passively listening to lectures had no part in it. Wijnen introduced block teaching from Groningen. The curriculum was divided into ten four-week periods, known as blocks. Each block had its own theme which was determined in consultation with the core staff members. It was Wijnen's idea to have the teaching blocks last four weeks, instead of the ten weeks that McMaster used. This would enable frequent assessment, and he also felt that it would encourage students to study regularly. In April 1974, Tiddens organised a trip to McMaster University. A number of civil servants from the Ministries of Education, Culture & Science and Public Health & Environmental Hygiene also went along; according to Wijnen the trip was primarily intended to raise enthusiasm among them for the new approach. Apparently it worked, because official permission was granted in late June 1974 to begin teaching experimentally, thus for the time being without any legal provisions. It was then, as Wijnen put it, 'all hands on deck' to prepare the course textbooks on time for the fifty students, officially referred to as *cursisten* (course participants), who would begin their Medical degree programme on 16 September 1974 in the former Jesuit monastery in Tongersestraat.

WIJNEN AND PROBLEM-ORIENTED LEARNING Wijnen had 'fond memories' of those first years: 'These were the true pioneering days that I thoroughly enjoyed'. It was a 'wonderful opportunity' to be able to start from scratch, 'since in existing institutions you always have to deal with the routine approach'. This was in any case what Wijnen and Tiddens had experienced in Groningen and in Utrecht, where the education offices 'were marginal entities' and educational innovation was difficult or impossible to implement. The motivation to make the most of the experience was widely shared by staff members and students. The 'community feeling' was strong and everyone was more than prepared to pitch in, wherever and whenever necessary. 'In those early days, formal rules and a strict division of duties' were less important. However, Wijnen was in favour of introducing an interpretation of problem-oriented learning that was as strict as possible, since he felt that a certain dilution or, more positively formulated, adjustment would inevitably develop. Since Wijnen held students personally responsible for how they fared in their degree programme, it mattered little, according to him, whether a tutorial group was supervised by an expert on the subject or not (supervisors were referred to as tutors). Students needed to be aware that 'you are responsible for your own future. You cannot push it away or wave it off by making someone else responsible'. According to him, a secretary could very well make an excellent tutor.[12] In the original plans, students would be able to consult an expert during tutorial group sessions by telephone if they were unable to resolve an issue themselves. Wijnen's conviction that a tutor need not necessarily be an expert on the subject to hand met with strong criticism from the start.

Perhaps Wijnen was overly optimistic in his outlook, given that he also felt that required attendance at all times was pointless in group teaching. Students thought otherwise and insisted on more structure and clarity. Henk Schmidt, who was hired in the autumn of 1974 to set up a skills lab, elaborated the so-called *zevensprong* (the Seven Steps method), in order to guide the study process and discussions in tutorial groups.[13] It also became apparent that in practice a four-week block was too short to delve into a theme. The block period was extended to six weeks as a result. It took a lot of hard work to be able to present the general outline of the third and fourth years of the degree programme in late 1975. This was shortly before the official opening of the Rijksuniversiteit Limburg (State University of Limburg) in Maastricht's St Servaas Church on 9 January 1976, a day Wijnen would later only recall for its 'pomp', with on the dais in the church 'many of the traditional Limburg administrators, such as the bishop, the mayor and the Queen's Commissioner', all of them 'individuals who were not actively involved in educational innovation …'.

The course exam created a problem for Wijnen. It turned out such an exam encouraged 'exam-focused studying', with students adjusting their study behaviour to the questions they expected in the course exams. This was at odds with the principle of problem-oriented learning, which was intended to encourage self-chosen study activities. 'That meant there was friction between the intended teaching structure and the manner of assessment that was chosen to go with it', according to Wijnen.[14] By inventing the progress test, Wijnen would make 'the most interesting and original contribution' to thinking on education, according to Schmidt.[15] Wijnen described the progress test as 'a random sample of questions, derived from the end point of the degree programme'. The test comprised some 150 to 200 questions covering the entire domain of medicine, and was compulsory for all medical students four times a year. This way the progress test not only provided insight into the level of individual students in relation to their peers, but also made it possible to compare the results of cohorts that had begun in different academic years. Apart from that, the test indicated the level of knowledge of students in various subjects, and this in turn provided information on whether the curriculum required improvement. Comparisons with other medical faculties were quickly drawn, and showed that the Maastricht Medical Faculty with its problem-oriented learning was doing a good job. The Maastricht degree programme was initially viewed with some reserve, said to be only capable of producing 'medical social workers'. It was the progress test that proved the key to 'the eighth' being accepted. The progress test would be copied over the years by various medical faculties in the Netherlands and abroad, as well as by other, non-medical faculties.[16] With the progress test, Wijnen cemented his reputation as an educational innovator with creative and practical solutions. In his work, he relied on people such as 'Schmidt, who tended towards the research side, and Peter Bouhuijs, who was more about teaching courses'. Hetty Snellen-Balendong, an experienced medical examiner, was recruited to design questions for the progress tests.[17]

In early 1977, Wijnen was appointed professor of Research and Development in Higher Education, with the Education Office continuing life as a separate department. This had been Wijnen's own work, since he wished to be taken 'seriously and as an equal'. 'Otherwise it was no use, I would get nowhere', he felt. Tans had already alluded to the prospect of a professorship. Even at the Maastricht Medical Faculty it was – and to this day remains – a struggle for the educational segment to get all the doctors on board, especially when putting together the curriculum. According to Snellen-Balendong, 'this was more difficult with the one fellow – it usually concerned a man – than with the other'.[18] Although not everyone was a firm advocate of problem-based learning, it was unthinkable that the faculty would ever relinquish educational innovation, its *raison d'être*. Wijnen played a very important role in the acceptance and dissemination of educational innovation. He was extremely convincing in person. According to Tiddens, Wijnen understood 'the art of having people believe what he thought they should believe. And the funny thing was that they would be convinced that they had come up with the idea themselves. This was a very efficient way of getting the doubters and opponents on your side'.[19] Schmidt also recalls this. 'He was a very ardent and also extremely intelligent person; he could simply talk circles around people. My colleague Peter Bouhuijs told me that he once went to Wynand, armed with conviction A, and that after a few of Wynand's Socratic questions, he left with conviction B.'[20] Wijnen would remain faithful to his educational principles, which he would continue to promote quite persuasively his entire life – he had something of an 'education guru' about him.[21]

A GENERAL FACULTY? Wijnen would no longer have time to conduct independent research after 1977, as he was appointed to various boards. According to Schmidt, he was the golden boy of the State University of Limburg in the 1970s. 'Nothing at all could happen, not the slightest event, without Wynand being involved ... You really can't imagine, but he would speak with students, chaired the Board of Studies, was in one meeting after the other, would consult with Harmen Tiddens sometimes three times a day. He was also on the Faculty Board, and yes, he was always being asked for advice, since he was really seen as the one who knew how things should be handled.' Directly after being appointed professor, Wijnen was selected to lead the movement towards *uitbouw* (expansion), as it was referred to. In order to become a 'real' university, the State University of Limburg needed at least one other faculty besides the medical one. The aim was to establish a 'General Faculty', and to then use this to develop new degree programmes. Neither the Ministry nor the other universities were in favour of such expansion, but Van Kemenade had suggested that 'Maastricht' set up a Social Health degree programme – although he refrained from making clear exactly what he meant by this.

In March 1977, a 'General Faculty working group' was created, headed by Wijnen. Other members included Tiddens, Thung and Hans Philipsen, professor of Medical Sociology at the Maastricht Medical Faculty. The remit of the General Faculty was the 'renewal of higher education'; it would focus on the interdisciplinary field of 'social health science' as well as seeking to collaborate with higher professional education. Social health science was given a rather unwieldy definition, as 'the science that studies the factors favouring and threatening a healthy existence, in addition to the possibilities for encouraging favourable circumstances eliminating threats'.[22] From the start, Wijnen focused on ensuring that the faculty would not become an extension of the Medical Faculty. 'The main fear was that if you were to make it social medicine, you would be immediately swallowed up by your big brother – and this has since happened [in the case of the establishment of the Faculty of Health, Medicine and Life Sciences in which the faculties of Medicine and Health Sciences were incorporated], which I find a real pity, to tell you the truth.' Wijnen was not so much concerned with the curriculum content as with the educational principles. He also saw to it that the General Faculty would put 'problem-oriented learning' into practice. In the summer of 1978, the State University of Limburg presented its plan to the Ministry of Education, Culture and Science. Van Kemenade had by now been replaced by VVD party member Arie Pais.[23] Pais's response was tardy. He had financial problems to deal with due to the economic crisis. There was little chance of establishing a new degree programme. As yet, the State University of Limburg was not granted permission and had to adjust its plans.[24]

'A FAIRLY DECISIVE TURNING POINT' In late 1978, Wijnen learned that Tiddens would be leaving. Long before his term as Rector was to end, on 1 January 1979 Tiddens moved to Tilburg to become professor of Health-care Organisation. He had seen the basic philosophy encountering strong opposition in practice: mistrust hindered cooperation between the faculty and regional health care, while little had yet been made of the intended focus on primary health care. But according to Tiddens the worst thing was that the call for a university hospital, 'setting the ideal of the day in stone', grew ever stronger.[25] Co Greep in particular – professor of Surgery and dean of the Medical Faculty since 1978 – had lobbied for a university hospital, preferably a top-of-the-line one. He mobilised political support by reiterating time and again that 'the eighth' would only be taken seriously together with a well-equipped university hospital; he also constantly emphasised the related employment opportunities. Tiddens's departure meant Wijnen losing his early compatriot. It was 'a fairly decisive turning point' in Wijnen's life. Philipsen, who was a member of the Executive Board, convinced Wijnen to succeed Tiddens. Wijnen considered this to be 'an emergency measure, because no-one else wanted to do so or was able to'. Wijnen found little enjoyment in the position of Rector, primarily because he felt that he 'was not a true administrator'. He struggled with a brimming schedule, since he also initially played a leading role in the Network of Community-Oriented Educational Institutions for Health Sciences. This international organisation had been founded in 1979 by some twenty medical faculties with an interest in educational innovation, at the behest of the World Health Organisation. The secretariat went to Maastricht.[26]

From an administrative point of view, expansion of the State University of Limburg had top priority. It was clear to Wijnen that for the time being the university would not have to worry about creating degree programmes in the cultural sphere. In order to encourage an academic climate of sorts, in 1979 he initiated a Studium Generale. The idea was to expand students' outlook to include other fields and developments in society. By making the Studium Generale activities free, he hoped to welcome people from the area too. Expansion looked to be tricky. Because of that, the university clung to the Deetman parliamentary motion of December 1978, in which the House of Representatives moved that the State University of Limburg should fully function as a university and have at least 6,000 students enrolled by 1990. The motion was in keeping with policy intended to stimulate the Limburg economy, which had the highest unemployment rate in the country. It was now the university's turn to act. The new degree programme in Social Health Science, set to begin in September 1980, was already a certainty. Wijnen had wanted to continue in his role as founding dean after 1980, combining it with his position of Rector, but to his dismay became embroiled in a conflict. He was accused of playing a 'double role' as Rector and as founding dean for the General Faculty. Indignation arose in the Medical Faculty, since Greep contended that the situation 'could only lead to the General Faculty being favoured and the Medical Faculty being disadvantaged'. Philipsen, 'one of those with true administrator's blood coursing through his veins', took over from Wijnen as founding dean, resigning from the Executive Board. The President of the Executive Board in particular, Rob van den Biggelaar, strategised to enable expansion. Pragmatism led to the choice of Law and Economics. The related degree programmes were relatively cheap – thus politically feasible – and attracted large numbers of students. As a member of the Executive Board, Wijnen became involved with the plans for a degree programme in Law. For a time in 1980, he chaired the 'Law degree programme preparatory committee', but would soon quit when the details of the degree programme needed to be fleshed out. Wijnen also chaired a committee charged with designing a development plan for the 1980–1990 period; suggestions were made to launch degree programmes in 'education and information focused sciences' and in philosophy.[27] Halfway through his term as Rector, Wijnen had the distinct feeling that he 'had lost every connection with regular staff members and students'. The University Council complained that it was not being heard sufficiently and accused the Board of lack of decisiveness in resolving internal organisational problems. In May 1981 the Executive Board even had to deal with a vote of no confidence. They were accused of 'ineffective management'; the third Board member, professor of Internal Medicine Harry Hulsmans, was even asked to step down outright. The Executive Board decided to remain in office, but for Wijnen, with his dislike of conflict, his term as Rector was – and would remain – an unsatisfying episode, 'in particular if you realise that you haven't been trained for it and would prefer to be doing something else with your time'.[28] To his mind, his work had mainly consisted of 'getting rid of huge stacks of paper' and 'then being allowed to go home'.

'AMBASSADOR OF EDUCATIONAL INNOVATION' On 8 January 1982, Wijnen handed over the office of Rector to Coen Hemker, professor of Biochemistry, and then took a sabbatical. He was assigned a small office in the library of a former monastery, the Bonnefantenklooster. He did not return to doing research and spent all of his time 'reading and discussing this and that' to bring his knowledge back up to speed. He returned to his department after this year and found that a lot had changed: 'I chaired the department for a number of years, but it had changed by then. Indeed, everything became more formal from then on – everything I had so enjoyed in the initial period was gone. Now things had to be set in rules much more often and many issues had to be addressed individually'. Yet the department would still remain his home base. He supervised many PhD students and whenever discussions cropped up at the university about problem-based learning[29], Wijnen would join in.

As a true 'ambassador of educational innovation', he focused his gaze primarily on the outside world. In addition to higher education, interest in his thinking also increased in secondary education circles – 'teaching is not primarily a transfer of knowledge from lecturer to student, but a type of knowledge acquisition by students themselves'. From the 1990s on, the Ministry of Education, Culture and Science increasingly requested his advice on issues related to 'quality' and 'feasibility'. Wijnen sat on many editorial boards, committees and other administrative bodies such as review committees, often chairing them. These included the executive board of the National Institute for Educational Measurement (CITO), the Advisory Council for Higher Education, the Feasibility Committee and the second-phase profile for secondary education steering group. His 1992 report *Te doen of niet te doen* ('To do or not to do') brought him fame; the so-called Wijnen catechism gave 83 dos and don'ts for getting students through their degree programmes as successfully as possible. He also became known for his advocacy of *het nieuwe leren* ('a new way of learning') when the *studiehuis* concept (independent study in the second stage of secondary education) was introduced. Wijnen remained unfazed by the criticism this educational innovation received, although he would admit, shortly before his death in 2012, that he was 'a bit disappointed'. According to him, there was always a 'pendulum movement': sometimes a 'step forward' was taken, sometimes a 'step back'. In retrospect he believed that 'many positive things' had occurred in the field of education during his lifetime. It was foolish to harbour unrealistic expectations in this regard. Major educational innovations always require 'a great deal of time and patience'.

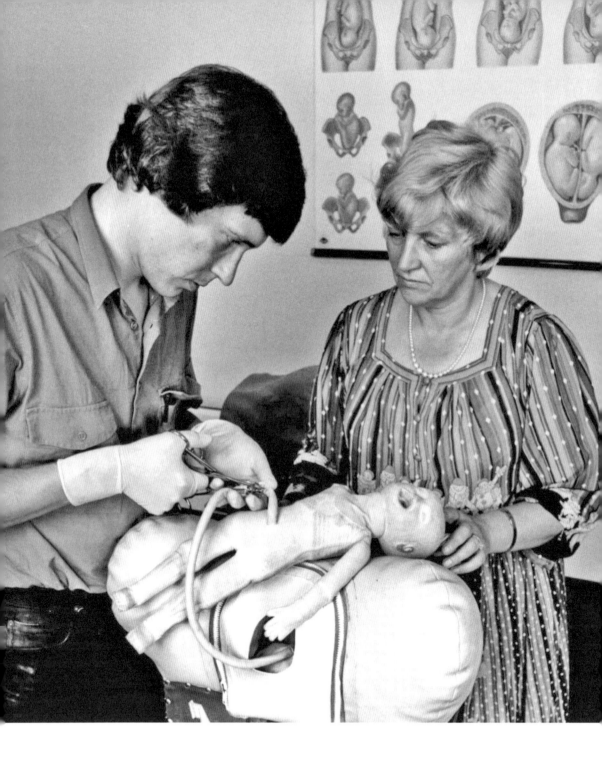

2 *Wim Brouwer* WITH ITS EMPHASIS ON PRIMARY HEALTH CARE AND GENERAL MEDICAL PRACTICE, THE BASIC PHILOSOPHY WAS HIGHLY MOTIVATING

BROUWER AND THE BASIC PHILOSOPHY As soon as *Basisfilosofie Achtste Medische Faculteit* ('Basic Philosophy of the Eighth Medical Faculty') was published in *Medisch Contact* in August 1972, Wim Brouwer announced his interest in the post of professor of General Medical Practice. Brouwer was immediately 'highly motivated'.[1] He saw this as a great opportunity to help build up the Maastricht faculty, which aimed to derive its goals from health care. According to this basic philosophy the main focus of attention would be training for and research on primary health care. The 'eighth faculty', as it was known, also wished to play an active role in the development of the health-care system in the region. In the projected curriculum the focus would be on problem-orientation and self-reliance – principles that Brouwer fully endorsed. By the start of the 1970s he had already gained extensive experience as a general practitioner. He was born in Genemuiden, in the Dutch 'Bible Belt', in 1924. After attending *gymnasium* (pre-university) secondary education in Kampen he immediately began studying Medicine in Groningen. In 1943, like many other students he interrupted his studies after refusing to sign the declaration of loyalty imposed by the German occupiers, and was conscripted for forced labour in Germany. After the liberation Brouwer completed his studies and in 1950 began work as a general practitioner in Emmeloord. In 1962 he earned his PhD with a dissertation entitled *Ervaringen met psychosocial-anamnetisch onderzoek als diagnostisch hulpmiddel in een huisartsenpraktijk* ('Experiences with psychosocial-anamnestic research as a diagnostic resource in a general medical practice') at the University of Groningen. Then he took up a post at the recently founded Dutch Institute of General Practitioners in Utrecht under the leadership of Jan van Es. In 1966 Van Es was appointed professor of General Medical Practice in Utrecht and thus held the first chair for general medical practice in the Netherlands – and only the second in the world.[2]

The central position of general medical practice in the 'basic philosophy' was related to the crisis in medicine that arose in the 1960s. Although some had already advocated the creation of general medical practice as a distinct subject of study in the 1930s, another thirty years passed before general medical practice really took off when, towards the end of the 1960s, criticism of the medical sector increased. Medical achievements were better than ever. But was modern medical technology not having a dehumanising effect? Criticism of the 'medical bulwark' was spurred on by publications such as *De dood op tafel* ('Death on the Table') by the Utrecht-based anaesthesiologist Bob Smalhout, whose contention that at least 200 patients died each year as a result of anaesthetics errors created a stir and drew strong media attention in 1972.[3] There was also dissatisfaction with the fact that, while the number of medical specialists was increasing rapidly, a shortage of general practitioners threatened. The realisation was growing that the ongoing development of (sub)specialties was drawing attention away from 'normal' medical problems – while these were by far the most common. General medical practice was and is only grudgingly considered a specialty: a general practitioner had to be and still has to be a generalist, and must learn to see his patient as 'a person with a history', as a 'psycho-socio-somatic unity'.[4] General medical practice was, in short, a 'young' specialty at the university at the time when Brouwer applied for the post in Maastricht. It was not until 1974 that it was formally decided that the training programme for general practitioners should last one year.[5] The fact that general medical practice still enjoyed low status in the medical world apparently did not bother Brouwer, who was averse to ostentation. Van Es was a member of the recruitment committee; he was a true networker who always did his best to promote general medical practice and to get good posts for his protégés. Shortly after his application interview Brouwer, who was 48 at the time, heard that he would be appointed professor of General Medical Practice: 'Well, not strictly appointed,' says Brouwer, who was initially advisor to the Minister, 'but we did already receive a professor's salary, up until the time that the university was actually awarded legal status'. At the end of 1973 he moved with his family to the town of Cadier en Keer, although his wife found it hard to get used to living in Limburg.

'TANS'S BRAIN TRUST' Brouwer was one of the six members of the core group who together were known as 'Tans's brain trust' and who had the task of developing the curriculum in more concrete terms.[6] Besides Brouwer himself and Harmen Tiddens, chairman of the core group, the 'brain trust' included social psychiatrist Marius Romme, anatomic pathologist Roelof Willighagen, biochemist Coen Hemker and surgeon Co Greep. At the start of 1974 Brouwer set out his vision for the role that general medical practice should play at the Faculty of Medicine.[7] His views aligned with those of

Wijnen, 'the education man', whom he greatly admired, and he advocated a curriculum in which theory and practice went hand in hand. Students should have to deal with health problems right from the start and at every stage of their studies, preferably 'in the field of extramural healthcare' such as in a GP's practice. Only in this way would the faculty be able to produce students who were well-prepared for professional practice. He put less emphasis on research, although he did see the value of research into the 'pre-medical period', i.e. the period in which the patient feels that something is wrong but has not yet consulted a doctor. In 1974 Brouwer said that it was very important for 'the faculty to participate in health care', but that he could 'still say little in concrete terms' about this because consultation with the general practitioners and other care providers had not yet begun at that point. Nonetheless, he had the impression, he stated optimistically, that 'collaboration between the primary and secondary health-care sectors, and especially between GPs and specialists, was good in Limburg. It was now up to the faculty to play a 'bridging role'.[8]

Brouwer looked forward to the task. However, the problem as it turned out was that the Faculty of Medicine itself was hanging by a thread, and Brouwer was worried that the whole project in Maastricht would be 'abandoned' due to 'all kinds of political rumours at that time concerning the faculties'. He was therefore relieved when Tans succeeded in persuading the national authorities to allow the Faculty of Medicine to begin on 'an experimental basis in 1974, instead of in 1975'. Tans's political acumen was 'a major advantage' according to Brouwer, because setting up a Faculty of Medicine was not only 'a medical but above all a political task'. Brouwer's motivation to take part in the Maastricht experiment was strengthened during his trip to the Faculty of Medicine of McMaster University in Canada in May 1974. At the urging of Tiddens, always an inspiring figure, he also visited the Faculty of Medicine of Queen's University in Kingston. There Brouwer first encountered a skills lab, where students could acquire skills such as reanimating a patient as part of clinical teaching. Moreover, during this trip Brouwer saw that regional cooperation in the health-care sector could be more difficult than expected. After a while he noticed something else, too. In the core group it was only Tiddens, Romme and himself who 'truly' embraced the basic philosophy; the other members tended to focus on 'their own thing'. He had particularly intensive contact with Tiddens when preparing the teaching programme for the first year: they often visited each other at home to discuss various issues.

PRIMARY ORIENTATION? It hardly needs to be stressed that Brouwer, as professor of General Medical Practice, occupied a key positon at the faculty in Maastricht. No other faculty of medicine in the Netherlands devoted so much attention to general medical practice as did the 'eighth faculty' in Maastricht. Although the status of general medical practice was, as mentioned, low in comparison to other specialties, the situation was different in Maastricht: Brouwer was an important 'power factor' within the faculty, says Geert Blijham, who trained there in internal medicine from 1975 onward.[9] During the first few years, Brouwer also acted as deputy for Tiddens, who had asked him to take on this role due to the latter's many trips abroad. The early start for the faculty meant that Brouwer had hardly any time for teaching activities. Not only did he develop the Orientation in Primary Health Care course, he also tried to bring the focus on primary health care closer to the students in the case histories presented to them. 'Of course, there was far too little time to prepare the whole thing, so it was a case of sink or swim in the first year. Once the first course was finished we had to race against the clock to make sure the second course was ready.' This involved 'lots of improvisation', says Brouwer, who recalls his role as tutor with mixed feelings – a role that he learned 'by trial and error'. He had to try hard to supress his tendency to act as an expert: after all, the students needed to be challenged to puzzle out the problems for themselves.

Brouwer was also involved in the very first beginnings of the skills lab, where students could acquire medical and social skills before applying these to 'real' patients in 'real' work. The 'eighth faculty' was the first in the Netherlands to set up a skills lab and this initiative was all the more important because it turned out that it was hard to organise sufficient internship positions for students at short notice. Neither the St. Annadal Hospital in Maastricht nor the other local hospitals nor the GP practices in the region proved particularly eager to provide guidance and supervision for students. But Brouwer did find Léon Lodewick, a young GP who worked in a Maastricht 'tandem practice': he was prepared to coordinate the Skills course on a half-time basis and to set up the skills lab. When putting these plans into practice, Lodewick received strong support from Tiddens, for whom he had 'huge respect due to his vision and drive'.[10] Looking back, Brouwer feels it is a pity that he did not devote greater attention to the skills lab. He would have liked to have used this facility for refresher training for established GPs, but this plan was shelved for financial reasons. He found that GPs preferred to receive refresher training from the pharmaceuticals industry, where they 'were provided with all kinds of stuff, meals and that sort of thing'. As a faculty, says Brouwer, it was 'not possible to compete with these disguised advertising activities'.

PRIMARY FIELD OF WORK FOR TEACHING (AND RESEARCH) Initially the General Medical Practice Department was provided with 'a few rooms with a desk and chairs, and that was it'. But if the faculty was to put its 'creed' regarding primary health care into practice, then more was needed.[11] Brouwer had the task not only of exploring the primary health-care sector for teaching and research, but claiming it as well – or indeed conquering it. Just like a biochemist needed a laboratory, so Brouwer could not do his work without the professional field of general medical practice. He had a greater affinity with teaching than with research. He felt that general medical practice 'had little to offer in the area of scientific research in the initial years. In order to conduct research in a GP's practice you need at the very least to have a "register of age and sex", meaning that you know the age and sex of all patients so that in the case of abnormalities you know whether these usually occur in this age group or in another group. But not a single GP had a register of age and sex. That would have amounted to an infernal amount of work, because there were no computers back then'.

Nonetheless, Brouwer was convinced that 'GPs had plenty to offer in the field of teaching' and he focused on this 'right from the very start'. Since the 1960s, many had begun to realise that the clinical internships in large (academic) hospitals did not sufficiently prepare the students for later professional practice. However, in the first years he had 'too little time' to properly build up contacts with the general practitioners in the region. 'We needed a huge amount of time to motivate these GPs' to supervise a student during his or her studies, even though they received 'decent remuneration for this'. There were terribly few GP practices that were prepared to collaborate with the faculty. Nevertheless, Brouwer did succeed in getting a few practices on board, such as that of the Maastricht GP Jan Meijers, also known as 'the red doctor' because of his membership of the PvdA (Labour) party. Thanks to this, students could already spend a few days accompanying a GP as part of the Orientation in Primary Health Care course. But Brouwer had to do a lot of travelling – he 'toured through South Limburg like a missionary' – in order to get more GPs interested. The new Faculty of Medicine generated little enthusiasm among most GPs. It was 'disconcerting' to see how they regarded the faculty as 'something far away and of no concern to them'. Moreover, he was faced with the problem that there were still few group practices at this time and it was hard for a GP in a one-man practice to find time for a student. The GPs regarded their own practices as 'personal kingdoms' over which they wished to maintain complete authority. Brouwer does not think that the fact he was a Protestant 'Hollander' made it even more difficult to establish productive contacts in the mostly Catholic south of the Netherlands, because problems like these occurred elsewhere in the Netherlands as well. Whatever the case, at the Faculty of Medicine Brouwer had a reputation as a 'conscientious' and slightly 'uncompromising guy' who probably 'couldn't be found sharing a nice glass of wine' with the local GPs and 'seemed a bit distant'.[12]

Despite these difficulties, Brouwer continued his quest for internship positions in the general practitioner sector. He was supported by Tiddens, who in his first Foundation Day speech, 'Practical Priorities', on 7 January 1977 referred to the 'specific identity' of general medical practice and strongly emphasised the importance of primary health care: it was 'absolutely vital' that Maastricht students should do a 'general practitioner internship'.[13] A course planning group then worked on putting the internship concept into practice and recruiting GP trainers. Brouwer still has lively memories of the major input provided by Tonja Mol, a psychologist and a 'very good member of staff' who did 'enormously useful work' to recruit GP trainers. In 1978 the 'practical medical education for general-practitioner practice' commenced, with the first 24 students gaining experience for three months in a GP's practice. This three-month period was unique: at other faculties of medicine an internship in a GP's practice lasted between two days and two weeks, or four weeks at the most.[14] The major advantage of this internship, says Brouwer, was that the student was forced to understand the feelings of the patient, to 'identify with them much more'; in a hospital setting, he says, students were far more prone to adopt the perspective of the specialist. The lengthy internships with GPs proved to be a success.[15] Moreover, the development of this internship programme led to a dissertation by Peter Bouhuijs, who earned his PhD on this topic in 1983, with Wynand Wijnen as supervisor and Brouwer as co-supervisor.

ACTIVE PARTICIPATION? As far as active participation by the faculty in contributing to 'the best possible health-care structure' goes, Brouwer was and is unhappy with developments: 'not a lot was delivered in this regard'. The biggest 'stumbling block' was that not only the GPs but also the specialists 'were really not interested in people from the university'. They all had 'their own shop and wanted to remain the boss in their own house'. When Brouwer first became acquainted with the situation in Maastricht in 1973, he noticed that the collaboration between GPs and specialists was based on 'personal relationships, characterised by mutual goodwill and trust'. The creation of the Faculty of Medicine disrupted this situation because a GP no longer knew which specialist, assistant or medical intern would be treating his patient.[16] In response Brouwer put forward two ideas – formulated during the time when he was still working for the Netherlands Institute of General Practitioners – that would enable the faculty to fulfil a 'bridging role' and thus to improve the relationship between specialists and GPs. He wanted to strengthen the primary health-care sector relative to the secondary sector by creating a 'middle course'. In order to reduce the number of referrals to clinical specialists, Brouwer gave GPs the opportunity to consult a specialist at a hospital if they felt this to be necessary. The advantage was that the patient could thus remain with their GP for as long as possible. However, Brouwer experienced that 'the specialists were actually very hostile' to this middle course because they did not wish to take responsibility for a patient whom they had not seen personally – a 'dogmatic standpoint' according to

Brouwer, which was not open to further discussion. Nonetheless, the ideal of bridging the gap between the primary and secondary sectors remained alive: from 1990 onward one of Brouwer's successors, Harry Crebolder, was to take part in training *kaderartsen* (staff doctors) who specialise in general medical practice and play a bridging role between the primary and secondary sectors. And some time after this, it became 'normal' in some GP practices to call in clinical specialists as consultants.[17]

Brouwer had more success with his second plan, which involved setting up a diagnostic centre as a bridge between the primary and secondary healthcare sectors: this diagnostic centre 'eventually achieved success'. In 1977 he had been able to get the backing of the Ministry of Public Health and Environmental Hygiene, as it was then called, for the creation of an experimental diagnostic centre in Maastricht. Utrecht was also given permission to set up a diagnostic centre. The aim was that GPs could have certain research activities, such as haematology tests or making an electrocardiogram, conducted by the diagnostic centre linked to the St. Annadal Hospital, and then consult with a clinical specialist about the results. The idea was that this approach could prevent unnecessary (and expensive) referrals to the secondary healthcare sector and also improve collaboration between GPs and specialists. However, Brouwer says that it took a long time after the opening of the centre before GPs began to make use of it because 'at the start they took a fairly suspicious view' of the centre.

CONFLICTS, NOTHING BUT CONFLICTS… Where Brouwer was already encountering resistance outside the faculty, with doctors in the region being unwilling to collaborate, he was now also increasingly confronted with tension and conflicts within the faculty. After the sudden departure of Tiddens to Tilburg on 1 January 1979, which came as a surprise to Brouwer as well, he had to continue the work alone. In the course of 1978 Tiddens had seen that those who were in favour of building a new, big 'classical' university hospital were gaining ground, while the plans for distributing academic functions over the various hospitals in the region were receiving insufficient support. In January 1978 Co Greep – a surgeon nicknamed 'the tank' or 'the bulldozer' – was appointed dean, and he showed himself to be a powerful advocate of the construction of a university hospital that should become 'the best hospital' in the Netherlands. Greep not only had the majority of the clinicians and pre-clinicians behind him but also the entire Limburg lobby, led by Sjeng Kremers, who had been the Queen's Commissioner in Limburg since 1977. It was now up to Brouwer to realise the primary health-care orientation of the 'eighth faculty', but he lacked the natural authority of Tiddens. He wisely remained on the sidelines of the debate about the ins and outs of the university hospital, but he was unable to avoid experiencing a 'hard, difficult time' with one conflict after another: 'I can't remember any phase of this period in which one could work on things in some kind of harmony'.

Together with Romme, Brouwer tried to establish the primary profile of the Faculty of Medicine and at the end of 1980 he organised a two-day conference on 'faculty and primary health care'. Joop van Londen, the director general of Public Health, agreed to open the event. He declared that strengthening primary health care was an important goal of his Ministry and that he expected the Maastricht faculty, in line with its basic philosophy, to play an important role in the 'Limburg test region', where he envisaged an 'academic health-care system' with 'a university hospital, an academised core of primary health care, outpatient mental health care and possibly basic health care'.[18] Many critical questions were asked during the conference but few concrete answers were presented. December 1980 saw the publication of the article 'Faculty of Medicine exit?' in *Medisch Contact*, in which the editor-in-chief wrote that the 'eighth faculty' would do well to finally put its basic philosophy, indeed its *raison d'être*, into practice.[19] In a reader's letter, Brouwer highlighted everything that had already been achieved with 'practical medical education in GP's practices,' but he also admitted that the faculty's participation in the primary sector needed to improve. He accused the faculty management of funding academisation of the hospitals but not of primary health care. It is hardly surprising that Brouwer had a hard time following this episode: some seemed to feel, says Brouwer, that he belonged to 'the fifth column'. He came into conflict with Greep, who wanted 'the biggest and the most specialised university hospital as possible,' an aim that was 'directly opposed to the primary health-care focus'. His colleague Hemker mocked the fact that research among the GPs was having difficulty getting off the ground. As far as he was concerned, it was not necessary either; under the pseudonym 'Karate Koentje' Hemker wrote: 'If they provide good teaching and train their assistants well, then in my view they are already achieving plenty. Why should they need to master two subjects? ... General practitioners are practically oriented doctors who can make use of science. They often think that they do not even need it. It is appalling to see them engaged in scientific activity'.[20]

TRIAL AND ERROR However frustrating this conflict may have been for Brouwer, it clearly showed that he had the backing of the national authorities where his aim to create a strong primary health-care orientation was concerned. And so the field of general medical practice continued to strive for the academisation of some GP's practices so that they could also do research into pathologies in the primary health-care sector. The first academised GP's practice was in the village of Geulle and was joined by a member of Brouwer's academic staff, Job Metsemakers.[21] Nonetheless it remained difficult to find GP's practices that were prepared to collaborate with the faculty – 'we always had to go cap-in-hand to get a place in the practical sector'.[22] The fact that this collaboration could promote knowledge intensification in general medical practice obviously did not present a sufficient benefit. On the other hand, this primary orientation continued to be favoured by the national authorities – so much so that in 1983 the Minister of Education, Culture and Science, Wim Deetman, launched the plan to make the 'eighth faculty' a primary faculty with St. Annadal as a teaching hospital based on the American model. However, he had also caused a major scare at the faculty by referring to plans to completely dissolve the 'eighth faculty'. But this proved infeasible in political terms. Policy now concentrated on 'division of tasks and concentration'. Brouwer felt that the faculty should be 'really happy' with this emphasis on teaching and research in the primary sector, even though he was well aware that this government policy had been prompted by spending cuts. The faculty, led by a pragmatic Greep, now focused on a two-track policy, i.e. on building a top-level university hospital as well as strengthening the primary health-care sector. Maastricht was even able to acquire substantial funding from the Innovation Fund to support the academisation of the primary sector.

Continuing this trend, shortly before his departure in 1986 Brouwer received reinforcement in the shape of Crebolder, who became coordinator for the primary health-care sector and was quickly appointed professor as well. According to Crebolder, an important step in the academisation process came with the introduction of computers in GP's practices: 'Nowadays we all see this as completely normal, but back then people really had to get used to computers'.[23] However, Brouwer himself now hardly found time to carry out research. He had invested much time and energy in teaching which, as he noted with some disappointment, lost status in comparison to research in the course of the 1980s. In his valedictory speech entitled *Vallen en opstaan* ('Trial and Error'), Brouwer said he regretted that he had been able to devote relatively little energy to his 'own specialist field, general medical practice'. Over all these years he had, 'with a degree of envy', watched the biomedics and clinicians carrying out research in the laboratory or clinic, while in practice he was struggling to create 'his own workplace'. He also advocated a 'systematic examination of the course of a disease' in order to verify the diagnosis and the corresponding therapy. He believed it was necessary for general medical practice to be based on epidemiological data and thus, ultimately, to be able to make protocol and work agreements – pointing to the need for what we now call evidence-informed medicine. In this context, Brouwer praised his young member of staff and later professor of General Medical Practice André Knottnerus, who would indeed make an important contribution to scientific research in general medical practice.[24] Following his departure, Brouwer did not sever all links with the State University of Limburg. He accepted the post of honorary professor of Medical Ethics and Medical Philosophy at the Faculty of Health Sciences that was set up in 1984.

3 *Marius Romme* PSYCHIATRIC ISSUES ARE THE RESULT OF PROBLEMS IN EVERYDAY LIFE

A REMARKABLE CHOICE It seemed like a 'remarkable choice', the appointment of Marius Romme, who was already nominated for the position of professor of Social Psychiatry in early 1973, thereby becoming part of 'Tans's brain trust'.[1] In those days, in the academic world, most professors of Psychiatry were *clinical* psychiatrists. But despite his background, Romme fit in well with the basic philosophy at 'the eighth', which had been instituted in 1972. More than was the case at other medical faculties, the faculty in Maastricht was working to expand the clinical perspective on illness by also focusing attention on the social aspects of disease. This meant that from the very beginning, the social sciences needed to be represented within the faculty as well. As early as the summer of 1970, Romme had come to the attention of the preparatory committee because of his role as an adviser to the Medical Inspectorate for Public Mental Health – in other words, long before the committee, headed up by Sjeng Tans, joined forces with Harmen Tiddens and embraced the basic philosophy.[2]

How did this come about? The increased attention for the social aspects of disease was in keeping with policies then in effect at the Ministry of Public Health, where the former professor of Psychiatry and World Health Organization (WHO) officer Pieter Baan had recently accepted a position as Chief Inspector for Public Mental Health. On his arrival in The Hague, Baan insisted that legislation concerning the work of the Regional Institutes for Outpatient Mental Health Care (RIAGG) be drafted quickly in an effort to reduce the number of psychiatric beds. Based on his time with the WHO, he knew that the Netherlands topped the European list in terms of the number of psychiatric beds – something he was keen to change in short order. In Romme – at that moment the only social psychiatrist in the Netherlands with a doctorate degree – Baan found himself an ally with the requisite expertise. In 1967,

Romme had completed his PhD work under Arie Querido, with research into the triage and admission procedures used by the Amsterdam Municipal Health Services' department of Mental Hygiene. In the process of writing his dissertation, he became steeped in the conviction that social circumstances profoundly influence the diagnosis and course of psychiatric conditions. Both Baan and Romme were working toward a more outpatient-based system of psychiatric care, and both men had high hopes for social psychiatry as well. It is easy to understand, then, why Baan suggested Romme when contacts in Maastricht asked him to propose candidates for the chair in Psychiatry.

It was in this same period that Baan became alarmed by what was going on in Maastricht. In August 1969, the construction of the Vijverdal Community Mental Hospital had begun – a large complex of buildings with a nine-storey, three-wing high-rise with beds for no fewer than 600 psychiatric patients. This was a very deliberate attempt to get in before the new legislation regulating the construction of hospitals and psychiatric hospitals was to take effect. And it was not just Baan; the State Secretary for Public Health was outraged, too. By that time, Romme had resigned his position as director of the Amsterdam-based Catholic Foundation for Mental Health Care and had been granted a temporary appointment with the Ministry as an adviser to the Medical Inspectorate for Public Mental Health, in anticipation of a potential professorship at the university. It was in that capacity that he was sent to Vijverdal to see whether it might still be possible to turn the tide.[3] In the summer of 1970, he issued a recommendation to all parties involved: the Inspectorate, the preparatory committee for the eighth medical faculty and the Vijverdal management.[4]

Romme did not manage to bring the construction to a halt. According to Romme, the general contractor Leon Melchior, from the Belgian town of Lanaken, who was known for his involvement in show jumping, was 'a very fast bricklayer'; the building works even included the construction of a five-metre-deep swimming pool. But he did manage to bring down the number of beds to a provisional 360. It was also agreed that Vijverdal would provide space for the Faculty of Medicine and the Foundation for Public Mental Health, an alliance of outpatient institutions for mental health care. Tans became involved in all this not only as the chairman of the preparatory committee, but also as a member of the Vijverdal board. As Tans naturally wished to avoid conflict with the government authorities in The Hague, he put pressure on the parties to accede to Romme's wishes after all.[5] Baan likewise supported Romme's recommendation. Baan saw the housing of the Foundation for Public Mental Health in the Vijverdal complex as an experiment in creating an integrated system of health-care services – an experiment that might serve as a prototype at the national level. In Baan's opinion, Romme would be just the person to make this integration a reality, 'down there' in the Catholic south of the Netherlands, if he were appointed professor of Social Psychiatry.

'A REASSURING BACKGROUND' It may have worked in Romme's favour that he had 'a reassuring background', as he described it. His father was the well-known Catholic politician and lawyer Carl Romme, who played a prominent role in Dutch politics both before and after the war. Carl Romme was the leader of the Catholic People's Party (KVP); a public figure who was one of the mainstays of the Dutch political sphere. According to Marius Romme, the fact that his father was well known in the Netherlands sometimes opened doors more quickly, making it 'easier for him to establish contacts'. But at other times it could also be a burden to go through life as 'the son of'. After graduating from secondary modern school with a focus on Science subjects, he decided to study Medicine in Amsterdam. This was a remarkable decision by the descendant of five generations of lawyers, a family 'devoted to the law', as Romme described it. The choice for Medicine stemmed from a 'very close relationship' with his former nanny, who had become seriously ill. This first gave him the idea 'of becoming a doctor instead of a solicitor'. Romme wanted to go to Amsterdam to join the Amsterdamsch Studenten Corps, the student association that his father had also been a member of. This was an elitist association, something which 'it would appear we took some pleasure in at the time', Romme says now. The awareness that his father was 'a figure of note in the country' fuelled his desire to be of importance to society, but he did not want to do the same thing as his father: he wanted to be 'a Romme in my own right'.[6]

Romme specialised in psychiatry, a decision in which he said his mother's depression later in life was a decisive factor. In the 1950s and 1960s, academic psychiatry was heavily focused on psychoanalysis; this was also true in Amsterdam.[7] In theory, the four-year degree programme for neurologists focused on both psychiatry and neurology, but in practice Romme just got the neurology side as a free bonus. That he went on to focus on social psychiatry should come as no surprise: psychoanalytically oriented psychiatry had a close connection to outpatient mental health care/mental hygiene and psychotherapy.[8] This choice reflects the example set by his father, not to mention that of his PhD supervisor Querido, who had shown Romme the importance of the social aspects of disease. In his dissertation, Romme argued that more extensive patient records should be kept, which could be used to more adequately plan health-care services, in particular psychiatric services.[9] As a matter of fact, from the mid-1960s, academic interest in social psychiatry rose significantly, although there were only very few professors of Social Psychiatry at the time. In 1968, the newly established Erasmus University Rotterdam hired Cees Trimbos as a professor of Social Psychiatry. Trimbos was the leading pioneer of Catholic mental health care, as well as being Romme's predecessor as director of the Catholic Foundation for Mental Health Care in Amsterdam. Romme was keen to become the fourth professor, as he found the position's combination of research and patient care highly appealing. Furthermore, he was nearing forty and, by his own account, was somewhat impatient.

TO MAASTRICHT? Romme found himself stuck in limbo for some time. Although the preparatory committee decided in January of 1972 that his appointment would be given priority, unexpected developments made the establishment of 'the eighth' more complicated than had been anticipated. At one point, it was even unclear whether the eighth faculty would end up being established at all. In the meantime, Romme continued his work as adviser to the Mental Health Inspectorate. In that capacity, in 1972, he visited eight mental health centres in the US on a scholarship from the WHO, all of which offered the whole range of mental health services for a given region.[10] Baan had tasked Romme with doing the groundwork for the legal requirements involved in establishing the Regional Institutes for Outpatient Mental Health Care in the Netherlands, and this trip was part of that mission.[11] Romme remembers being in the pleasant position during this period of acting as advisor to the three organisations that together were meant to make the establishment of the Regional Institutes for Outpatient Mental Health Care a reality. He not only served as advisor to the Medical Inspectorate for Public Mental Health, but also as advisor to both the National Health Insurance Council and the Netherlands Association for Outpatient Mental Health Care (NVAGG), of which he had been chairman since 1972.

Essentially, Romme was in perfect accord with the *Basisfilosofie Achtste Medische Faculteit* ('Basic Philosophy for the Eighth Faculty of Medicine') which had been drafted in the summer of 1972. As a social psychiatrist, he was sensitive to the importance of social factors in the emergence of psychiatric problems, and argued in favour of integrated mental health-care services. Harmen Tiddens still wanted to be certain that Romme agreed with the basic philosophy. After a meeting with Tans and Romme, he concluded that there was 'good potential for cooperation'.[12] Romme, in the meantime, came to feel that the basic philosophy was a 'sacred doctrine'. He was also an avid supporter of problem-oriented learning as an educational method, as it meant students were confronted with actual problems from health-care practice, rather than being taught on the basis of one specific scientific theory or discipline. Romme was predominantly drawn to this new way of working as he felt that in psychiatry people tended to set stock by an unscientific approach, whereby 'constructions of disease' were developed on the basis of the presenting problems without understanding the cause of those problems.

With the arrival of Den Uyl (of the PvdA (Labour) party) as the new Prime Minister in the spring of 1973, the tide turned in favour of 'the eighth'. Tans's strategic insight and political connections had enabled him to convince The Hague to let the eighth faculty get off to an early start, provided that this faculty was willing to enter into the educational experiment. By August, eight of the core faculty members, including Romme, had been appointed.[13] According to Romme, it was not a very extensive selection procedure, as things had been 'prepared so thoroughly by that point that you didn't feel like you were competing with a lot of other candidates'. Romme states there were 'no other social psychiatrists at the PhD level, and of course there weren't a lot of people who were willing to come out here in the first place'. Romme did move south, spending the first six months lodging with his colleague, the surgeon Co Greep, with whom he got on 'very well' initially. Greep 'didn't like to waste any time' and had been quick to purchase a large house. At first, Romme flew back and forth between Amsterdam and Maastricht twice a week. At the instigation of Tiddens, who had his pilot's licence and loved to fly, Romme took flying lessons to overcome his fear of flying. The idea was that the best way of getting rid of fear was to 'do what you're afraid of'. He remembered that, during one lesson, he had to turn off the engine to 'see what happens, find out what you need to do'. After some time the Romme family moved to a renovated farm in Bemelen, a village not far from Maastricht, where Romme had enough space to keep horses. Shortly before the move, he bought another house in Amsterdam, as he felt that he was emigrating to an 'underdeveloped area'. According to Romme, 'back then there really was nothing to do round here – I mean, going to a birthday party was pretty much the only available form of entertainment'.

PLANS As a member of the first group of professors, Romme was assigned the task of recruiting behavioural scientists for the faculty. Unsurprisingly, he was hoping the area of social and behavioural sciences would play a significant part. Now that it was becoming increasingly evident that psychosocial factors played a role not only in psychiatric but in all manner of somatic illnesses as well, Romme wished to emulate his mentor Querido by conducting further research into the influence of behavioural components and social background. In doing so, he expected to gain improved insight into the emergence and progression of diseases. Inspired in part by the influential epidemiologist John Cassell, Romme suggested conducting epidemiological research in Maastricht, aimed at investigating the influence of living conditions on the health patterns of the region's residents. Romme felt that greater attention should be paid in education to sociology, psychology, economics, ethics, law and ethology. In addition, he felt that the students in Maastricht should receive training in 'social skills such as learning to work as part of a team', not to mention 'learning to interact with patients'. He also felt it was important that students were not only trained in psychiatry, but also came into contact with mental health care in practice in order to learn communicative and therapeutic skills. Romme had ambitious plans, and envisioned a behavioural science portion of the Medical Faculty that would ultimately consist of 170 full-time staff members and 13 teaching commitments.[14] Looking back on those plans, Romme says: 'Well, sure, in hindsight that sounds quite ambitious'. It would eventually require a merger with the Faculty of Health Sciences, many years later, to achieve this goal.

BALANCING ACT For Romme, the early start in September 1974 had taken long enough. He had assumed that the faculty would get off the ground two years earlier, and had even quit his job at the Catholic Foundation for Mental Health Care in Amsterdam, enabling him to spend some time working for Baan. His new position in Maastricht brought with it all sorts of new responsibilities, which meant that he was sometimes forced to juggle academic ambition and his political and social commitments. For someone who, by his own account, prefers to focus on substance over structure and 'doesn't like playing a leadership role', combining all these roles was a tricky balancing act. From the very beginning, Romme was in charge of the academisation of Vijverdal and the Foundation for Mental Health Care, known from 1981 as the RIAGG, a task in which he soon received much-needed assistance in the form of a second professor, the social psychiatrist Mark Richartz, trained in Germany. Still, he had more than enough on his plate: Romme not only had responsibilities relating to education, research and management, but also maintained contacts with national organisations and soon found himself spending one day a week working for the RIAGG, where he treated patients and was involved in training psychotherapists and psychiatrists.[15] In addition, he played a role in the management of Vijverdal – 'although I didn't have to be very closely involved, thankfully, I did have to weigh in from time to time'.

At Vijverdal, there was little faith in the faculty's role in the process of academisation: while the 'eighth' requested and received access to the department for mood disorders, the Academic Centre for Axiety Disorders and the clinical therapy department, they steered clear of the departments housing chronically ill patients. This was in order to avoid demoralising the interns by exposing them to the 'hard cases' right away.[16] The academisation of the Foundation for Mental Health Care progressed more smoothly: the social psychiatric staff was expanded by creating workplaces for PhD candidates in Psychiatry and later, when it had become the RIAGG, with opportunities for Medical students to do their clinical rotations. According to Romme, one of the benefits of the educational system in Maastricht was that it was 'easy to combine research with all sorts of other posts, as, while I had to be there to prepare the course reader, I wasn't required to actually teach the curriculum myself'. For example, Romme contributed to the 'Out of Your Mind/Into Your Head' module, but he did not teach it very often. By his own account, he 'didn't like it all that much, and wasn't very good at it either': 'I tend to do too much of the thinking for people, because at the end of the day I'm not patient enough to let students figure it out for themselves'.

Be that as it was, Romme managed to produce three textbooks on social psychiatry. In 1976, together with Dorine Bauduin, he published *Psychiatrische epidemiologie. Over onderzoek naar de spreiding van geestesziekten* ('Psychiatric Epidemiology – On Research into the Spread of Mental Illness'). Two years later, the manual *Voorzieningen in de Geestelijke Gezondheidszorg. Een gids voor consument en hulpverlener* ('Mental Health-Care Services – A Guide for Consumers and Health-Care Providers') was published, for which he served as editor. It was intended primarily for the training of various mental health-care professionals. In 1981, together with Herro Kraan and Rob Rotteveel, he published the textbook *Wat is sociale psychiatrie?* ('What is Social Psychiatry?'), which discusses the theory and practice of social psychiatry. According to the authors, social psychiatry is concerned with the relationship between society and psychiatry, but they did not give a concrete definition – which only makes sense: ultimately the domain of social psychiatry, with its broad culture-specific dimension, cannot be clearly demarcated.

These manuals were compilations of others' work rather than the result of his own empirical research. Romme unfortunately never got round to conducting the type of large-scale epidemiological research he had envisioned at the start. What he did do, was develop new educational programmes and attempt to attract funding to support PhD candidates in social psychiatry. As of 1980, on Romme's insistence, the Foundation for Mental Health Care (soon to be the RIAGG) started keeping a Mental Health Case Register, a practice which had long been customary in the English-speaking world. Romme had managed to secure funding for the enterprise thanks to his close ties with the Ministry of Public Health and Environmental Hygiene, where Joop van Londen was director general. A comparable case register had already been initiated in Groningen. The Ministry decided that having two such registers would undoubtedly be useful, as it would allow them to compare problems and outcomes. Like Romme, Van Londen was a kindred spirit of Baan, who had passed away by that time. Romme says that Baan had 'two sons': Van Londen 'to have clout within the Ministry', and 'me to hold sway in the education sector'. Like Baan and Romme, Van Londen advocated an 'academic health-care system', that is, a more intensive collaboration between teaching hospitals, primary care providers and the mental health-care sectors. Thanks to Romme's extensive network – he was 'constantly on the road' – funding was also made available by the National Health Insurance Council for PhD research into the relationship between the treatment method and the duration of patients' stays in psychiatric institutions.

THE 'CONSTRUCTION MORATORIUM' AND FACULTY UPROAR OVER A PHD DISSERTATION In the early 1980s, Romme was one of the instigators of the campaign for a 'Moratorium on the Construction of New Psychiatric Hospitals', together with a number of others including Trimbos.[17] The campaigners wanted to persuade the political sphere to put a stop to the new construction and renovation of psychiatric hospitals. They felt that it was necessary to first undertake a fundamental review of psychiatric policy. People were 'bandying anti-psychiatric rhetoric about' and suggesting that 'psychiatric hospitals were based on antiquated notions about how to treat those with psychological disturbances'. Psychiatry was seen as an instrument 'for defusing deviant behaviour'. Psychiatric institutions had traditionally served as 'internment facilities for the protection of society'; 'repression, lack of freedom and coercion', along with medication, set the tone and many patients, it was suggested, ended up becoming institutionalised.[18] The moratorium received a great deal of media attention[19] and even led to a motion in the Dutch House of Representatives which cautioned against the Minister's plans. Yet in the end, there was insufficient political support for the 'large-scale replacement of psychiatric beds with alternative facilities, such as sheltered housing and part-time treatment'.[20]

Within the faculty, the call for the moratorium rubbed some people up the wrong way. Romme remembers that while he was often in agreement with Brouwer, 'a good GP, a good organiser and a nice man', who was not hidebound by a traditional clinical perspective and was open to collaboration, his initial friendship with Greep became strained. Greep had been dean of the Faculty of Medicine since 1978, and his behaviour had been a source of boundless frustration for Romme. Greep, Romme recalls, often came across as 'unreasonable' or 'impulsive', and 'discretion' was not one of his strong suits: he was open about having two women in his life, his wife and his girlfriend. The three of them even went out together and, as Romme recalls, 'for a lot of people in Limburg, that was a little strange; even in the west of the country it raised eyebrows'. In the 1980s, Greep was on a path diametrically opposed to Romme's ideals: he was committed to creating a new, large, well-equipped university hospital and, according to Romme, was only capable of thinking from a clinical perspective. Incidentally, Romme did not publicly protest against the arrival of that hospital as 'there were so many clinicians – in terms of numbers, you were never going to be able to win everyone over'.

The friction increased – not only as a result of the moratorium campaign but also because, according to Romme, the findings of the research commissioned by the National Health Insurance Council posed a threat to the hospital world. 'It emerged – although of course we already knew this – that very little time was spent with patients residing in psychiatric hospitals: only two minutes a day on average ... which naturally touched on a sore spot of Greep's.'

Two of Romme's colleagues were planning to use this research to earn a joint doctorate: the 149-page dissertation *Langdurige opname of permanent verblijf?* ('Long-term admittance or permanent stay?') had been completed, the National Health Insurance Council was pleased with the result and the Supervisory Committee had issued their approval as well. But right before the scheduled joint PhD defence on 25 November 1983, things hit a snag. Rector Coen Hemkers hastily assembled the Board of Deans, on a Sunday no less, before summoning Romme the following day and informing him that the joint defence could not go ahead as a 'committee of experts' – outside the Supervisory Committee – had found the dissertation to be of insufficient merit for conferring the two PhDs. In particular, according to the committee, the dissertation had failed to observe the standards for obtaining and processing statistical data.[21] As the 'scientific conscience' of the State University of Limburg, Hemker considered it his duty to stop the joint PhD from being granted, as the university's academic reputation was at stake, and it was a time when the young university had to 'prove itself'. Romme was ultimately advised to consider the option of allowing one of the candidates to defend the research and take their doctoral degree.

Romme was surprised and bewildered. According to him, the rejection of the dissertation was a 'political matter', as the researchers had been critical of 'the role and effectiveness of psychiatric hospitals'.[22] Romme felt deeply insulted, especially by Greep, of whom he had the distinct impression that the man would hear no ill word spoken of hospitals, and who he suspected had set things in motion by asking a few of his fellow professors to take a second, more critical look at the manuscript.[23] The national press spoke at length about 'the affront to Romme'.[24] Looking back on the affair, Romme describes it as 'a highly lamentable intervention'. He still regrets not just walking out – 'I should have simply said, come off it, I'll see you all on Friday at the defence' – since, procedurally speaking, it was highly irregular. The two PhD candidates rejected the suggestion that only one of them be allowed to defend the dissertation; having begun work together, they viewed it as a matter of honour to finish together as well. In Romme's estimation, the incident haunted the candidates for the rest of their lives: neither of them ever dared submit a dissertation again.

THE FALL OF CO GREEP It was a conflict between clashing egos, but it also shows how easily things can get unbalanced in a fledgling organisation in which there is a lot of informal leeway. The conflict also highlighted existing tensions between the non-clinicians on the one hand and the clinicians and pre-clinicians on the other, with the latter having the advantage that they worked in more established domains of research boasting longer research traditions. For Romme, the conflict was all the more grating because the

PhD research had been conducted using *external* funding. Romme had long been irked by the fact that the faculty gave more financial support to 'blood clotting and immunology' than research relating to primary care and mental health care.[25]

Romme drew his own conclusions after what happened. Even more than before, he went his own way. Bremer describes Romme as a 'very independent man who didn't let anyone tell him what to do'.[26] And Romme also plotted his countermove. He prepared 'very calmly, starting well in advance'. He made sure he had 'enough supporters' onside in the Faculty Council to defeat Greep at the deanship vote in May 1985. According to Romme, Greep felt so invulnerable that he was oblivious to the growing dissatisfaction within the faculty about the way he would appoint professors without consultation. Romme still thinks back with 'pleasure' to the moment when Greep was 'shocked' to discover that it was not he but his rival, the epidemiologist Ferd Sturmans, who was to be the new dean. Greep's fall is associated in collective memory with 'Romme's coup', but the fact of the matter was that the majority of the Faculty of Medicine wanted to be rid of Greep.[27] Either way, the affair had repercussions for Romme's position within the faculty. By his own account, with this stunt he had 'kind of ruined things for himself' with the administration. Romme suspects that a rumour that he owed his appointment to the provincial superior of the Jesuits (who was said to have forced Romme – 'the son of …' – upon the preparatory committee because he feared the Catholic People's Party would not lend its support to 'the eighth' otherwise) had come from a wrathful Greep.[28] Within the faculty, according to Romme, there were 'street fights' all the time: 'that's par for the course at a university', where there are always clashes about 'manpower and money'.

LIVING WITH VOICES While, in the late 1980s, academic psychiatry began to embrace biological psychiatry more and more, Romme, the social critic, remained faithful to the notion that 'psychiatric problems are the result of problems in everyday life'. Romme shifted his attention to auditory hallucinations. According to him the phenomenon of 'hearing voices' has nothing to do with schizophrenia – 'the validity of the schizophrenia concept is zero' – but is an expression of emotions someone is unable to process, for example in the wake of sexual abuse. As a result of his experiences in psychiatric practice, Romme had become convinced that it was necessary to listen to the experiences of patients who were hearing voices – what kind of voices did they hear and why? According to Romme, hearing voices is not an illness. Therefore, the focus should not be on 'curing' the patient, but letting the patient learn to accept and deal with the significance of these voices. He developed this research line together with Sandra Escher, who had a background in journalism and was highly adept at conducting patient interviews. She also managed to garner interest for the subject in the world outside of academia, even landing a guest appearance on Sonja Barend's TV show – quite popular at the time – in March of 1987. On the show, one of their patients, Patsy Hage, discussed her experience of hearing voices. The feedback on the episode was overwhelming. Romme and Escher became the pioneers of the 'voice-hearer movement'. In the late 1980s, *Stichting Weerklank* (the Resonance Foundation) was established to bring people dealing with this issue together. Later, the international Intervoice network (the International Network for Training, Education and Research into Hearing Voices) was established, which today is active in no fewer than 29 different countries.[29] Although this movement was viewed with scepticism among the psychiatry establishment in the Netherlands, Romme feels that, scientifically speaking, it marked a great step forward. In the English-speaking world in particular, there is greater appreciation for research into hearing voices than has been the case in the Netherlands.

The new research line took up so much of Romme's attention that he became an infrequent visitor at his department in Maastricht. In addition, an increasing shift towards biological psychiatry was taking place within the Medical Faculty. The arrival of Herman van Praag in 1992 was an important moment in this context. This and other organisational changes resulted in Romme feeling less than welcome at the faculty – 'they were looking to get rid of me and I was eager to be rid of them'. He agreed to accept partial redundancy pay, 'which meant I was free to do what I felt I should be doing'. In 1999, he heartily enjoyed all the attention and appreciation he received during a farewell symposium organised by the RIAGG in his honour. To his great joy, Her Majesty the Queen of the Netherlands promoted him to Knight of the Order of the Netherlands Lion in appreciation for his academic work and for his 'international achievement in bringing positive attention to the Netherlands and Maastricht abroad', a token of recognition that brought Romme a great deal of satisfaction.[30] He regrets that those at Maastricht University lacked enthusiasm for a social-psychiatric approach to mental health issues and that the faculty tended to lean heavily on a reductionist biological perspective, although he feels a particular kinship with professor of Psychiatry Jim van Os, who seeks to abolish the gloomy public perception of such conditions as bipolar disorder, borderline and schizophrenia. According to Van Os, this pessimism stems from a pronounced biological slant in how we view psychoses. 'People,' says Romme, 'are much more varied and complex than the theories being developed about them would have us believe'.

4 *Ine Kuppen* I WAS AT THE BIRTH OF IT ALL

EMPLOYEE 007 In late 1973 Ine Kuppen, then 28 years old, arrived at Havenstraat 3 in Maastricht for a job interview. This address was home to the administrative office of the preparation committee for the soon-to-be-established eighth Dutch medical faculty. Kuppen was looking for a new challenge, and she had heard that a new university was to be established, something which definitely piqued her interest.[1] Across the table during her interview were Harmen Tiddens, the prospective dean of the Medical Faculty, and Tiny Simon, already employed as a secretary. A typing test was part of the interview process, and Kuppen made over 20 errors – 'the first time I used an electronic typewriter' – which made her fear the worst. She was hired all the same, because, she supposes, she 'got along' with 'professor Tiddens'. Kuppen continued to address Tiddens as 'professor Tiddens' until his death – he set great store by this title, and was 'a real professor'. Conversely, Tiddens always addressed Kuppen by her first name, 'Ine'. She started working on 1 January 1974. Being the seventh employee, she was nicknamed '007' – a fitting epithet, given that she was no stranger to adventure.

At this point, Kuppen had already experienced various walks of life. She was raised in the Maastricht district of Scharn, and hoped to study Economics after completing her secondary education with the Ursulines at Grote Gracht in Maastricht. However, her mother, an early widow, decided otherwise. Her three brothers did get to pursue a university education – 'that's the way things went back then'. Kuppen decided to take the secretarial course at Schoevers in Arnhem, after which she went 'out into the wide world': she lived in Italy for a year, near Torbole, where she worked as a tourist guide on Lake Garda, in the Dolomites and in Venice and Verona. After she returned she worked in a Citroën workshop for a while, and later at JC Bamford, a wholesaler in construction machinery. In the evenings, Kuppen studied for a teaching degree in French in Sittard, but this proved to be a bridge too far. She was excited to start as professor Tiddens' secretary, even if she found the manners prevailing in the early days a bit too formal: when Kuppen was told to address Tiny Simon, who was several years her junior, as 'miss Simon' she said: 'that's not going to happen'.

FROM JACK OF ALL TRADES TO HEAD OF THE RECTOR'S OFFICE The secretaries at Havenstraat were employed as jacks of all trades, getting sandwiches and sometimes beers 'for the gentlemen' from café 'In de Moriaan' in Stokstraat, some fifty metres from the office. This café, Kuppen recalls, often served as a venue for the meetings of core group members such as professor of Internal Medicine Harry Hulsmans, professor of Biochemistry Coen Hemker, professor of Pathology Roelof Willighagen, head of the Education Office Wynand Wijnen and Tiddens himself. Kuppens did not mind the fact that, in the early days, her position called for a lot of improvisation and hard work, often until after seven o'clock in the evening. In fact, she is rather nostalgic about those days. 'Everyone was ready to do everything, whatever their status. All of us together, including the professors, worked on the first course book; absolutely everyone joined in. You had to work till you dropped, but we got it done. There was no bureaucracy, and everyone was very involved.' The university community was 'one big family'. Kuppens operated the offset press to finish the course books for the first cohort of students in 1974 in time, and of course she also served as a 'patient' for the faculty's practical training programme in the skills laboratory, or skills lab for short. The skills lab was intended to allow students to gain practical experience without exposing actual patients to clumsy trainees. This type of education was pioneered in Canada; in the Netherlands, the 'eighth faculty' was the first medical faculty to introduce the skills lab in the curriculum. Kuppen was also asked by Wijnen to act as tutor in a tutorial group, but that was a step too far for her. 'I refused. My thought was – there's really no way I'm doing that.' Nevertheless, she developed a special bond with the first Medical students. She feels everyone in Maastricht was happy with the education system, and at the end of term the staff, including Kuppen herself, often joined the students for drinks. Outside Maastricht, she recalls, enthusiasm was less pronounced: the first graduates of the new faculty needed to work extra hard to prove their worth.

Kuppen was one of the organisers of the official opening of the State University of Limburg in Maastricht's St Servaas Church on 9 January 1976. She was running around the whole day and remembers little of the ceremony, although she recalls it was difficult to manoeuvre everyone into the right seat. Later, Tiddens became Rector of the university. Kuppen joined him as his secretary and became 'head of the Rector's Office', supervising one other secretary as well as a part-time member of staff. This, Kuppen claims, 'was really no big deal.' Nevertheless, she was soon faced with new challenges. She was asked, for instance, to draw up the regulations for PhD defence ceremonies, although she had never even attended such a ceremony herself. Unperturbed, she consulted with other universities and drew up the regulations on two sheets of paper in April 1976, describing the protocol for PhD defence ceremonies. This 'PhD defence protocol' was wholly in the style of the State University of Limburg: on the one hand, the new university wanted to take part in the hallowed university traditions; on the other hand, they wanted to show how 'playfully' they interpreted the old customs. To illustrate, the dress code in the protocol read as follows: 'Upon mutual consultation, the PhD candidate and his/her assistants dress according to their own preferences, i.e. black lounge, morning dress, white tie, national costume. The public is to wear black lounge. The members of the committee of the Board of Deans appointed for the ceremony (hereinafter: the committee) are to be dressed in gowns; this also holds for non-professors or lecturers who serve in the committee as examiners'.[2] On 7 May 1976, Peter Cuypers was the first candidate to attain his PhD from the State University of Limburg. In fact, Cuypers had conduced part of his research previously at Leiden University, where he had worked alongside his supervisor, biochemist Coen Hemker. At that time, there was 'no bureaucracy whatsoever' at the university, says Kuppen. When drafting the protocol, she thought: 'How am I ever going to manage this?'.

Rector Tiddens was often absent from the university. One of the reasons was his ongoing association with the Wilhelmina Children's Hospital in Utrecht, where he still occasionally saw patients. In addition, he was a real globe trotter. He was not only active in the European Society of Paediatric Nephrology, which he had co-founded in 1967, but also in the World Health Organization (WHO), where he promoted the notion of a 'community-oriented health system', a health-care system focusing on 'ordinary', i.e. common health-care needs. Because of these activities Tiddens was rarely seen at the St. Annadal Hospital, and he increasingly lost touch with the university organisation. From the start, he had not taken up many clinical tasks in Maastricht, and now he ceased doing so altogether. Kuppen considered Tiddens to be a 'lone wolf' and, in her experience, 'a bit of a sphinx': he was 'very good content-wise', but not very 'outspoken', rather 'modest and not particularly decisive'. He also failed to tell her about the serious disagreements between him and professor of Surgery Co Greep, who, serving as dean from 1978, was not enthusiastic about collaboration with the hospitals in the periphery and, contrary to the ideas that made up the basic philosophy, strove for the construction of a large new university hospital. Tiddens's position was particularly difficult, Kuppen thinks, because he also had to deal with Sjeng Tans, President of the Executive Board, who was a dominant personality and, like Greep, a strident proponent of a newly-built university hospital. When Tiddens announced, in late 1978, that he was resigning to move to Tilburg as professor of Health-care Organisation, this came as a complete surprise to Kuppen. 'He did not even see the first cohort of students graduate', she remembers.

For a while, Kuppen continued to work for Tiddens's successor, Wynand Wijnen, who served as professor of Research and Development of Higher Education from early 1977. Unlike Tiddens, Wijnen did not insist on formalities and was happy to be addressed by his first name. He was also considerably less of a traveller than Tiddens, and tried to be involved in education as much as possible. Wijnen, too, did not always have an easy time of it, Kuppen recalls. He was 'a really nice man', 'modest', 'a true Limburger', who sometimes had a hard time standing up to the other professors at the Medical Faculty, many of whom hailed from 'the west of the country'. Still, Wijnen was extraordinarily intelligent, Kuppen says, and just kept focusing on the thing he, in the end, cared most about: education.

THE 'NETWORK' Through Wijnen, Kuppen became involved in the Network of Community Oriented Educational Institutions for Health Sciences, which established its administrative office in Maastricht in 1980. Initially, this office was associated with Wijnen's Rector's Office, but it was later claimed by the Medical Faculty, as the Network focused on the latest developments in medical education.[3] Professor Greep took control of the Network and became its first Secretary General. However, since Greep knew little about education, he asked Henk Schmidt, who worked as an educational psychologist in Wijnen's department, for support. Kuppen set up the administrative office. Supported by the WHO, the Network grew quickly and contributed a great deal to the State University of Limburg's international stature. At workshop-like conventions around the world, issues such as the development of the medical curriculum, problem-based learning and community-oriented health care were addressed. Kuppen greatly enjoyed accompanying Greep on his many travels, which took her to Cuba, Egypt and Thailand. Greep was quite in his element at these conventions, and in fact so was Kuppen: 'With Co you got to travel everywhere; it was really an adventure'. She remembers the convention in Havana in 1983, which was opened by Fidel Castro with an interminable speech. It turned out Castro was interested in health-care reform, and he wanted to talk to Greep. Kuppen did not budge from Greep's side. 'I stayed close to Greep, of course. Fidel was surrounded by forty security gorillas, and I got to shake his hand... an impressive man.'

Kuppen referred to Greep as 'the tank', because he could not be stopped by anything or anyone, he got to go everywhere and always got his way. Medicine was a man's world, and surgery especially so; here, tough talk was the standard. There were few women at the Medical Faculty, and even fewer female professors. Riet Drop, professor of Medical Sociology, was appointed as the first – and for the time being only – female professor in 1980. According to Kuppen she was a 'tough lady', who could 'teach some of the men a thing or two'. Kuppen herself was by no means docile towards Greep: 'I could come across as a fishmonger's wife from time to time, but he could handle that very well.'

COMMUNICATION After working for Greep for about a decade, Kuppen took a new step in her career in the early 1990s, when she moved to the Communications Department. Her role was to serve as a liaison for employees in the city centre who had to be relocated to the new campus at Randwijck. Her office: a wooden shack under the chestnut trees on Universiteitssingel. Every now and again, small groups of people would enter to find out where they would end up. Kuppen would enthusiastically show them where their new workspaces would be and so on, but noticed that few employees were happy about moving to Randwijck, a suburb where hardly anything had been built yet and very little was going on. In fact she herself 'really disliked' the building on Universiteitssingel 50, which housed the hospital, but tried to keep this to herself. She felt it was a 'cold building', a kind of 'box' built to house 'a lot of people'. Kuppen had grown accustomed to the old Jesuit monastery at Tongersestraat 53, where everyone and everything could be found, including the skills lab, the Anatomy Department and the Centre for Test Animals. Clearly, she thought, 'no women' had been involved in the design of the new building. The long hallways were colourless, there were no windows in the rooms or in the clinics. 'It all missed a woman's touch', Kuppen says, even if she admits that the idea to house all staff and services in a single location was 'essentially the right one'. When the new hospital opened, Kuppen noticed there was no clock in the lobby, although patients and visitors wanted to check the time to know, for example, when to catch a bus. When she inquired she was told the architect was against a clock, because it 'wouldn't look good'.

Setting up a 'Business Contact Point' in the Communications Department turned out to be a mission impossible, Kuppen found out. The aim was to establish a central inventory of all contacts between the university and the business sector. The contact point failed to materialise, however, because 'not a single faculty was willing to cooperate.' The Medical Faculty's research institutes simply refused to share their data. There was 'too much resistance' within the university against such attempts at centralisation. As a result, Kuppen started looking for a 'new challenge'.

ALUMNI It had puzzled Kuppen for a long time that the university had no alumni policy, even though alumni are really the main ambassadors for the institution. She had also strongly sympathised with the first generation of

Medical students, who had such a hard time in gaining the recognition of the medical profession at first. Kuppen brought up the issue with President of the Board Karl Dittrich – 'Karl was a very approachable person' – and he turned out to be 'very alumni-minded'. '"*Gaank diech dat mèr doen*" – you go ahead and do that', he said in Maastricht dialect. For Kuppen, the 'alumni business' was an 'article of faith', and from 2001 she worked at the Student Service Centre as the alumni coordinator to establish closer ties with the university's former students. Again, Kuppen turned to other universities for advice. She noticed that they had entire offices set up for alumni affairs, while 'I was just messing around on my own'. Not everyone at Maastricht University cared about alumni, Kuppen says, recalling that the Law Faculty in particular did not care to get involved at first. Now, however, she notes 'with pride' that there are 12 UM alumni circles in the Netherlands and 18 abroad.

DOORS OPEN AND CLOSED Looking back on the 38 years she worked for the university, Kuppen believes that the increasing formality within the organisation is the most noticeable development. It became 'more and more difficult to get things done', because at a certain point 'directors became managers and managers became managers who were no longer supposed to be called managers'. From the third floor of the administrative building at Minderbroedersberg, where she worked, she would look down and be astonished to see that many managers were hidden behind closed doors. 'There was never an open door to be seen, even of the Executive Board, never'. All in all, Kuppen considers herself to be of the old school, someone who felt more at home at a young university than at a mature one, with all its rules and regulations.

5 *Coen Hemker* THE UNIVERSITY MUST CLAIM A PLACE ON THE SCIENTIFIC MAP. OTHERWISE, WE MAY AS WELL GIVE UP

AN UNCERTAIN ADVENTURE Towards the end of 1972, Coen Hemker, aged 38, had arrived at a crossroads. Which career path should he take? A lector in the biochemistry of cardiovascular diseases at Leiden University, Hemker had already gained international recognition for his research into the mechanism behind blood coagulation. Four choices presented themselves. He could stay in Leiden, with the prospect of a professorial appointment in due time. But he had a good shot at a professorship in haematology at VU Amsterdam, too. Also, he was still in the running for a job at a renowned biomedical research institute in Basel. And, lastly, he was 'deliberating the real possibility of Maastricht', where he was engaged in talks about a professorship at the nascent Medical Faculty – 'something of an uncertain adventure'.[1] Hemker vaguely remembers being approached by Harry Hulsmans, professor of Internal Medicine in Rotterdam and a member of Maastricht's preparatory committee, who had been pegged as the new faculty's future dean. Hemker and Hulsmans knew each other well from their PhD research days, back at the University of Amsterdam.

Already, Hemker boasted a long list of accomplishments. Young Hendrik Coenraad grew up in a 'non-academic household' in Amsterdam. Neither of his parents had attended secondary school, but both possessed 'shrewd minds' and his father had a boundless interest in the 'fascinating world at the cusp of biology and medicine'. This interest manifested itself in a bona fide laboratory in their small four-room house.[2] The family's five sons – there were no daughters – were simply expected to make room. Coen caught his father's scientific enthusiasm and, after secondary school, enrolled at the University of Amsterdam, where he studied Medicine and later did research at the university's biochemistry lab. Hemker's original plan after obtaining his PhD in 1962 was to become a paediatrician, but he soon realised that he lacked the

crucial bedside manner. He was only interested in the more unusual patients; when faced with 'routine cases', his attention tended to drift. Thinking back, Hemker recalls a ward with 24 patients where he was only taking care of the four who were deathly ill, 'but the two scheduled for release the next day completely slipped my mind'.

After becoming 'incurably infected with the research virus', Hemker transferred to Leiden, where he would conduct research into thrombosis as a lector in the Biochemistry of Cardiovascular Diseases.[3] The biochemical research being conducted there was aimed at such goals as the identification of preparations to treat haemophilia patients. But 'what really got Hemker's pulse racing' – according to Fredi Loeliger, his boss in Leiden – 'was the thought of enzyme kinetics'.[4] The freedom to conduct experimental research into the complicated mechanism by which blood clots were formed was in no way wasted on Hemker: he quickly garnered international recognition by discovering the influence of PIVKA (proteins induced by vitamin K absence) on the clotting process.[5] In 1968 he was awarded the *Prix Européen Ganassini* in recognition of the clinical implications of this fundamental research. Hemker also worked in Paris for six months, in the laboratory of haematologist Jean-Pierre Soulier, and spent a few weeks in the lab of Scottish haematologist Robert Gwyn Macfarlane in Oxford as well. His career was taking off. Starting in 1972, he taught medical students as a part-time visiting professor of Pathological Chemistry at the Vrije Universiteit Brussel. At the time Hemker entered into talks with Maastricht, he had already supervised a handful of PhD candidates and had dozens of publications to his name. He was a member of editorial boards and served as editor-in-chief of *Haemostasis*, a well-respected journal. In short, as a pivotal figure among a growing team of mathematicians, physicists and chemists conducting multidisciplinary research with direct relevance for health care, Hemker was an appealing candidate for Maastricht.[6]

A TRUE UNIVERSITY CONDUCTS RESEARCH It should come as no surprise that the preparatory committee was eager to see Hemker settled in Maastricht. The surprise, rather, was that Hemker himself was willing to come. He was, in his own words, a bit adventurous by nature and thought, 'if we can get a real university going there, we have a chance to build something great'. He found the prospect of creating something out of nothing, of establishing something new, to be an exciting one. The experiment in Maastricht undoubtedly appealed to Hemker's drive. The announcement of cutbacks in Leiden became another factor at work in his decision. Initial contact between Hemker and Maastricht had gone through Hulsmans, but in 1972, according to Hemker, Hulsmans stepped down without protest in favour of Harmen Tiddens, who – along with Wynand Wijnen – had been responsible for introducing the new basic philosophy. In the course of discussing that basic philosophy, Hemker noted that the chair of the preparatory committee, Sjeng Tans, appeared to have a blatant disregard for research: 'research was not even a word in Tans's vocabulary, so as far as that goes he did not have anything against it'. From the very beginning, Hemker insisted that a true university must also establish an individual reputation through research. And if that was not in the cards, he was not coming to Maastricht. While it was true that Tiddens's main interest, in light of the basic philosophy, was the enhancement of primary health care, the university elected to move forward with Hemker's appointment. Not only did he have clinical experience, but more importantly, it was hoped he would be able to bridge the gap between primary health care and research. In other words, he could unite the preclinical and clinical aspects, which was another principle of the basic philosophy.

In late August of 1973, Hemker's appointment as member of the core staff was a fact. Notably, among the staff he was the only one with any real research experience. According to Hemker, there were only two people there who had ever seen the inside of a laboratory: 'the anatomic pathologist, Roelof Willighagen, and myself'. During the negotiations leading up to his appointment, Hemker had specified that 17 people from Leiden – practically the whole Leiden group – as well as the entire contents of his laboratory be brought to Maastricht 'no questions asked, lock stock and barrel'. He had naturally also insisted that a proper lab be prepared in Maastricht. Initially, he expected to have found a partner in Willighagen, who would join him in developing the biomedical courses. Hemker would conduct research into blood clotting, as he planned to continue the research he had done in Leiden here in Maastricht, while Willighagen would concentrate on the ageing process of the immunological system. It soon became clear to Hemker, however, that Willighagen did not feel the need to conduct research and was more interested in teaching. Gerard Majoor, who worked under Willighagen as a biologist in pathology/immunology from March 1974, recalls that his boss had little enthusiasm for research and was a 'fervent supporter of educational innovation'. Willighagen was course coordinator for the Structure and Function of the Human Body I course and faced an additional obstacle of being denied access to the St. Annadal Hospital. The anatomic pathologist who worked there refused to allow Willighagen and his students into the dissecting room unless he was bought out. As a result, Willighagen was forced to have post-mortem material brought in from Leiden and, for the first few years, make do in the classroom with pig's hearts.[7] In September 1976, Willighagen – at Tiddens's insistence – was made dean, meaning he was drawn into the convoluted workings of faculty administration. At the time of the faculty's inception, Hemker was therefore more or less alone in his strong focus on research – which proved to have not only drawbacks, but also advantages in terms of Hemker's ambitions.

PROBLEM-BASED LEARNING The thought of enzyme kinetics may have made Hemker's heart race, but he was somewhat less enthusiastic about teaching. While he subscribed wholeheartedly to the problem-oriented principles of the basic philosophy, 'that whole dogmatic problem-based learning thing' sometimes rubbed him the wrong way.[8] He served as a tutor on a handful of occasions and concluded that, lacking the necessary patience, he simply was not cut out for the role. According to Hemker, two possibilities came up in the group's meetings: 'either I was to be bored stiff, or I could resort to giving a lecture. And after that, two more possibilities presented themselves: either the group would put up with it, or they would not'. It was typical of Maastricht, Hemker says, 'that I was not allowed to teach my own subject, even if I put a problem-based spin on it'. Time and again, Wynand Wijnen would show up to explain how that was not really what they were after. Hemker had no trouble responding to Wijnen with arguments of his own. By prioritising problems from clinical practice in the curriculum, Hemker argued, they were running the risk that students would gain insufficient insight into the role of science within the medical field. The attention to basics was indeed rather meagre in those early years; anatomy was offered only marginally, for example. Hemker suggested to Wijnen that first-year students be taught a bit about how biological molecules interact with one another.[9] The idea was rejected without mercy. Wijnen informed Hemker that simple problems must be taught before the more complicated issues: in other words, first the psychological and then the molecular problems. It was clear to Hemker that he and Wijnen were 'diametrically opposed' on this point. He himself always considered psychology to be much more complex than biochemistry. 'The molecules I am dealing with react the same every single time, are highly calculable, are straightforward – they are simply a bit more abstract.'

Hemker's criticism did not end there. Since too little attention was being paid to science in the problem-driven curriculum, any tutor eager to impart more knowledge to students, but who was under no circumstances allowed to teach, quickly lost his or her enthusiasm for education – Hemker's own experience told him as much. This system also denied students the opportunity to be inspired by passionate lecturer-scientists; after all, according to 'the school of thought', tutors were supposed to support the learning process as non-experts on the content. According to Hemker, the lack of opportunity for forming productive master/apprentice relationships was a shortcoming of problem-based learning. Wijnen was undeterred by this sort of criticism. He was 'quite tenacious' in maintaining efforts towards educational innovation. Hemker thought of him as a bulldog, or 'maybe more of a terrier, really', and eventually stopped engaging him in debate. He minimised his own involvement with the educational aspect and settled into conducting 'quiet research'. There were plenty of employees in his department to whom he could leave the educational tasks, and they 'enjoyed doing it, too'.

A BIT OF A FREE-FOR-ALL EVERY NOW AND THEN, BUT NOT REALLY ALL
THAT BAD Hemker had managed to negotiate a strong starting position when he was appointed. After that, the challenge was to actually develop biomedical research at the fledgling faculty, where problem-based learning, primary health care and psychosocial research took pride of place and the exact sciences were apparently considered a 'necessary evil'.[10] First among his demands was, of course, a laboratory. Hemker calculated precisely 'how much floor space he needed for each lab area' and set about involving himself intensively in designing the space 'down to the very last beaker'. It was up to 'Majoor and his associates' to place orders for the 'refrigerators, test tubes, centrifuges' and various and sundry other things.[11] In the fall of 1974, a temporary building on Beeldsnijdersdreef behind the St. Annadal Hospital became available for use. The building was quickly renovated and expanded to house a large, modern laboratory facility. It goes without saying that the new biomedical facility needed to be up to Hemker's standards, as he abundantly made clear: 'no laboratory, no Hemker'. It was only after the lab was opened that his staff from Leiden made the move south. Among them was Peter Cuypers, the first person to earn a PhD degree at the university on 7 May 1976, on the basis of work he began in Leiden. Hemker served as his PhD supervisor. The blood-red togas they donned for the first time that day were his idea. To give the academic ceremony a further bit of class, the professors wore traditional black togas. While some of Hemker's new colleagues would have preferred to dispense with the custom of academic dress entirely, for others this was a bridge too far.[12]

Hemker's research ambitions initially found scant support, but he encountered little in the way of resistance either. Scientific research was 'viewed as a hobby indulged in by a few devotees, far removed from the central events taking place in problem-based learning and primary health care'.[13] He did, however, find an ally in a professor of Physiology who, like Hemker, hailed from Amsterdam and joined the core staff in 1974: Rob Reneman. Hemker was 'very pleased' with the physiologist, as Reneman demonstrated a natural affinity for research into cardiovascular disease. 'There was practically no stopping' Reneman when it came to getting something done. Hemker and Reneman would prove an unbeatable duo in that regard. Like Hemker, Reneman had past clinical experience – something Tiddens in particular saw as being of vital importance. Initially, Reneman had planned to pursue a career in anaesthesiology, but he later switched to research in physiology and bioengineering. He headed the Life Sciences department at Janssen Pharmaceutica in Beers and by 1973 had already come into contact with Maastricht. The challenge of setting up 'something completely new here' proved the deciding factor behind his making the move in 1974, according to Reneman.[14] He revealed himself to be an extraordinarily effective organiser whom the department 'really enjoyed having aboard', says Hemker.

Reneman quickly became a managerial force to be reckoned with and was soon appointed Research Committee chair. He successfully convinced his colleagues – notably Tiddens – to adopt a project-based approach to their research. Although programme funding in a university setting was a completely new concept at the time, Reneman had grown accustomed to the practice with his previous employer in the industrial sector. This meant that rather than distributing research funding equally among the professorships or departments, the university would allocate funds to a select a handful of research projects. The objective was to facilitate teams of multidisciplinary researchers working together in order to explore specific themes. This decision was a major one, and could only be taken by an organisation starting from scratch and as yet unburdened by the detritus of established interests. Hemker thought this was a fantastic idea; together with Reneman, he took on a major role in Cardiovascular Diseases, one of the five research projects launched by the faculty. This project benefited enormously from the new approach.[15] Reneman and Hemker were abuzz with plans for new research and secured a great deal of funding from both internal and external sources, while 'other' researcher groups were unsuccessful at getting their projects off to such a quick start. The pair therefore encountered little in the way of opposition.[16] As dean, Willighagen's mild character did not allow him to put up much resistance; he was disappointed to note that the basic philosophy was slipping away. The idealistic 'founding father' of the university decided to leave Maastricht in 1977.[17] It was, as Hemker says, 'a bit of a free-for-all every now and then, but not really all that bad, because they were not terribly interested. It cost them some money, and so long as we were happy with it' things went along smoothly. And so it was in an atmosphere of 'benign neglect', according to Hemker, that he was able to continue his research. In the early 1980s he had amassed a research group of 25 individuals. The Cardiovascular Diseases research project was going well – thriving, in fact. After a while, there were sufficient means available to allow them to attract 'good people', like cardiologist Hein Wellens, pharmacologist Harry Struyker Boudier, physiologist Vic Bonke and biochemist Rob Zwaal. As early as the mid-1970s, the first building blocks were laid for the School for Cardiovascular Diseases in Maastricht (CARIM, founded in 1988), which developed into a successful research institute.[18]

THE UNIVERSITY'S 'SCIENTIFIC CONSCIENCE' Undoubtedly, Hemker found the great passion of his life in the laboratory. His research into blood clotting – what role does thrombin play in the interaction between blood and vascular wall, and why does blood sometimes clot too quickly, and at other times not quickly enough? – was a source of endless fascination for him. Yet he was no narrow-minded savant. In 1978, for instance, he published a cookbook with professional cook Jacques Zeguers, entitled *De verstandige keuken* ('The Sensible Kitchen'), full of recipes for both healthy *and* delicious eating. A few years after that, he was named the best amateur cook in the Netherlands.[19] Hemker additionally was very much aware of the importance of gaining societal legitimacy for university research. He regularly pointed out that thrombosis kills more people than cancer and accidents combined. At the State University of Limburg, in Hemker's opinion, the balance between education and research was poor, and he felt it was his duty to set things straight. In 1982, he became Rector. It was not only the thought of being the 'scientific conscience' of the university that pleased Hemker. He also felt it was high time – after Tiddens and Wijnen, both education-oriented Rectors – to start putting the State University of Limburg 'on the scientific map', as otherwise the university was 'done for' in that regard. That the incumbent Board members had not been in favour of Hemker's appointment as Rector only strengthened his conviction that research at the university was getting the short end of the stick.[20] And at that point in the early 1980s, precisely when the budget was under pressure, the ability of the State University of Limburg to compete in the scientific arena was a matter of life and death. He had heard that a 'bunch of civil servants' within the Ministry of Education, Culture and Science were advising the Minister to disband the university in Maastricht, arguing that little was being done there in the way of research and the school was turning out only 'barefoot doctors'. Hemker received support from Co Greep, dean of the Medical Faculty, and Hans Philipsen, dean of the General Faculty. Given the political circumstances, the State University of Limburg sorely needed precisely that kind of strong personality: a Rector who was not afraid to go toe-to-toe with the Dutch government – even though, by his own admission, he was not always the picture of diplomacy.

In accepting the position as Rector, Hemker hoped to combine the new responsibilities with his work in the laboratory. He remembers thinking: 'the first six months I'll put some hard work into my position as Rector; then after that I'll combine the Rectorship with biochemistry for two years; then in the final half-year, I'll shift back over into administrative mode, and then everyone will think they had a top-notch Rector for the duration'. The reality did not quite go to plan. While he did manage to combine being Rector with conducting his own research, it came at a price: 70 and 80-hour working weeks. When handing over the Rectorship during the university's sixth Foundation Day on 8 January 1982, departing Rector Wijnen emphasised the State University of Limburg's duty to make a contribution to resolving educational issues in the coming decades. Coming man Hemker, on the other hand, asserted that the university – on this, its sixth birthday – had to leave the 'rather protected environment of early childhood' behind, as it was now time to 'go to big-kid school' where an objectively determined standard of performance would be expected. This also implied that the university, like every primary-school pupil, would need to learn to write: to write in the academic sense, to communicate the results of its education innovations, for example. Where education was concerned, the State University of Limburg now needed to navigate the delicate balance between rigidity and dilution – and to Hemker's great joy, the teaching there began to gradually discard 'its sacred belief in a sole, sanctifying recipe for success'. Since Hemker had announced it was his personal objective as Rector to help research at the State University of Limburg attain credibility – social acceptance, if you will – in the scientific community, he proceeded to address the matter in great detail. The economic recession forced the university to prove itself capable of applying its research time both usefully and efficiently. Useful research did not equal socially relevant research, but was primarily taken to mean fundamental research. Either way, defining relevance in a scientific debate is never a simple matter. Then, as now, good research is always socially relevant. The university recognised a social responsibility to enhance the economy – in other words, the knowledge industry – by conducting high-quality research.

EXPANSION? While Hemker had been prepared for the university to face tough times in the 1980s, he did not foresee what a 'difficult episode' his time as Rector would turn out to be. The 1980s were a time of economic stagnation, stringent cost-cutting measures and government intervention. The academic community faced challenges from an increased demand for accountability. It was the start of a tense era for the State University of Limburg. How would it survive? So far, the basis of its existence had been rather narrow. At the time of Hemker's appointment as Rector, the university consisted of only two faculties, the Faculty of Medicine and the Faculty of General Sciences, which employed fewer than 1,000 people and taught fewer than 1,000 students. The likelihood of the Deetman motion seemed distant; after all, Dutch parliament had voted in favour of a fully-developed university in Limburg in December 1978 (with a target enrolment of at least 6,000 students in 1990). The State University of Limburg had received the go-ahead for a study programme in Law in 1980 and, in 1981, for offering a study programme in Economics as well. When Hemker took the reins, the founding deans – Job Cohen for Law and Wil Albeda for Economics – had already begun preparations for the start of their faculties, which would be inaugurated in 1982 and 1984 respectively.

Various plans for other new study programmes circulated at the State University of Limburg; pedagogical science, philosophy, media & communications and history were all considered. Hemker was dismissive of what he called 'fashionable programmes' and set his sights on providing a wider range of traditional disciplines in the Humanities and Sciences.[21] He was the one who suggested offering a study programme in Chemistry in Maastricht. To the frustration of all, permission to begin new study programmes was denied.

Hemker was particularly indignant that plans for a History programme had been discarded, especially since it was the Ministry of Education, Culture and Science itself that had insisted on the elaboration of plans for that programme. Subsequently, Hemker did not let an opportunity to point out the Ministry's 'wasteful compulsion to meddle' pass him by.[22] In connection with the current need to reduce costs, would it not be wise, he asked, to dismiss half of the employees in civil service? After all, government Ministries were 'populated with an abundance of social-science types'. Still, those at the fledgling university did not lose heart. The idea to begin a Liberal Arts study programme was raised: a broad course of study in keeping with the goal of becoming a fully-developed university, designed to train students to become intellectuals with a well-rounded perspective on scientific and cultural matters. As the existing study programmes and faculties at the State University of Limburg 'were among the most vocation-oriented study programmes available in a university setting', Hemker was in full support of this new plan. He viewed Liberal Arts as a study of 'Being Generally Clever' that involved gaining a 'reasonable knowledge of humanities, exact and social sciences, without becoming an expert in any one of those things'.[23] It was also Hemker who invited biologist and poet Leo Vroman and his wife Tineke Vroman, a creative and erudite pair of polymaths, to join him in further developing the idea. The Vromans had been living in New York for some time and drew the inspiration for their multidisciplinary design of the proposal from the Liberal Arts programmes at American universities. But this plan failed as well. Hemker informed Vroman that the Minister 'might not be mad or foolish, or maybe not even both at the same time', but that he took 'mad, or even foolish decisions from time to time', such as rejecting the proposal for Liberal Arts in Maastricht.[24] Apart from that, in 1983 the State University of Limburg did receive permission to launch a core unit for Philosophy.

CREATING DISTINCT PROFILES The *State University of Limburg* needed to respond effectively to the policies of Wim Deetman, who had been appointed Minister of Education, Culture and Science in May of 1982 under the 'no nonsense' cabinet of the CDA (Christian-Democrat) and VVD (Liberal) parties. In order to improve the efficiency and quality of higher education, Deetman introduced the idea of delegating tasks at the national level; he also implemented what became known as conditional financing in academic research. The crux of the matter was an unprecedented cost-cutting operation that reduced the budget for higher education by 285 million guilders in the 1983–1987 period. This news caused quite a commotion in the academic world. From now on, the universities would be obliged to create distinct individual profiles, and this obligation was to go hand-in-hand with an increasing need to compete with one another as well.

While its limited basis was a liability, the State University of Limburg also had an advantage over the traditional universities: each of its degree programmes already had its own distinct profile. Problem-based learning alone was enough to set Maastricht apart from other institutions. Hemker realised now more than ever that the education system they had adopted was a 'highly advantageous selling point, politically speaking'. Indeed, the return on their investment was so good that Maastricht became an example to all other universities in the Netherlands. A fundamental discussion on the merits of problem-based learning was no longer in order – although Hemker remained wary of 'rigidity' in matters of education.

The act of delegating tasks also posed a risk, at least from the perspective of the Faculty of Medicine – and even more so for Hemker himself. Deetman placed pressure on the faculty to adhere to the basic philosophy: once again, rumours circulated that the faculty might be closing. In other words, their research should focus on the primary aspects and, in Deetman's view, a small general hospital would suffice. But to Hemker's mind, a primary faculty was just another way of saying second-rate faculty. He saw Deetman's plan as being catastrophic for the university: Limburg would remain excluded from the ranks of 'true universities' and would have to settle for being a 'highly advanced vocational school'. That was naturally not the kind of university Hemker considered 'fully developed', and not the kind of place where students and staff would have the opportunity to practise science at the highest levels.[25] In the spring of 1983, on 31 March and 14 April – at exactly the opportune moment – NRC Handelsblad newspaper published a list of the top 100 most-cited medical professors in the Netherlands. An impressive six professors from Maastricht made the list, all of them researchers from the Cardiovascular Diseases group.[26] At around the same time, the Advisory Council on Scientific Policy issued a positive evaluation of the departments of Cardiology and Biochemistry in Maastricht. These tokens of recognition were 'extremely lucky' for Hemker, as they served to illustrate the State University of Limburg's fully developed participation in the area of research. Deetman no longer had the necessary leverage to carry out his plans. To Hemker, these events demonstrated that the State University of Limburg could, and must, demonstrate a unique scientific identity in order to survive.[27] The 'unique approach to the programme funding of research in Maastricht' placed the State University of Limburg firmly on the path to success. And although Hemker vehemently opposed governmental interference in the university's research agenda, he was satisfied with having to select a number of themes based on the limited budget: the way he saw it, difficult choices gave rise to competition and would eventually yield better research. 'The good ones will make it, the bad ones will be eliminated', he noted to the *Observant* – Hemker always enjoyed giving provocative soundbites.[28]

LIMBURG SCIENTIFIC INDUSTRY The economic crisis of the 1980s was accompanied by growing demands on the Dutch universities. People looked to the universities for contributions to resolving not only economic issues, but broader societal ones as well. While he was no proponent of 'socially relevant' research as defined by politicians in The Hague, Hemker was an advocate for research conducted in collaboration with the business community. This allowed the university to not only keep its head above water, financially speaking, but also to promote economic growth and success in the region.[29] Referring to its 'fertile soil, the region of Limburg', he proposed that the State University of Limburg establish a *Wetenschaps Industrie Limburg*, or W.I.L. ('Limburg Scientific Industry'), as cooperation with the business community would offer 'great advantages and new opportunities'.[30] During his speech on the occasion of the university's seventh Foundation Day, on 14 January 1983, he speculated on a procurement agency for applied research and a Science Park where entrepreneurs and scientists could work together designing valuable initiatives – as long as both the university and businesses performed well in terms of effective research. Hemker parried the question of whether his vision would be 'prostituting the scientific community' by replying that the initiative was more a 'marriage of convenience'.[31] Hemker stated that he himself 'never felt' as if the business community directed his research. It was more the other way around: he 'disguised' his 'curiosity driven research' as 'useful research' and then explained to outsiders that they were 'in dire need of it'. In advocating for a W.I.L, he focused primarily on his own Medical Faculty. According to Hemker, the social sciences have a more difficult time maintaining their scientific independence while conducting contract research. In fact, social science must be 'much more difficult than exact science', because 'while they have thousands of students enrolled, their Einstein has yet to come along'.

ON THE SCIENTIFIC MAP Following his time as Rector, Hemker was relieved to be able to resume his research. Although Roel in 't Veld, director general of the Ministry of Education, Culture and Science, had asked Hemker to consider serving as President of the Executive Board, Hemker had little interest in such a position. He did, however, ask In 't Veld whether, *if* he were to accept the presidency, the State University of Limburg might also receive a Faculty of Mathematics and Physics. Unfortunately, this proved too great a request. His colleague Bonke succeeded Hemker as Rector in 1985. Bonke's appointment instilled confidence in Hemker that the Rector after him would continue to serve as 'the scientific conscience of the institution'. For his part, he returned to the laboratory. He wished to effectively bridge the gap between biochemical research and clinical practice; it was an old goal, dating all the way to back his time in Leiden. He spent his sabbatical in a clinical research laboratory in Paris, where he conducted research into the physiology of clotting in patients together with biomedical researcher Suzette Béguin. Béguin earned her PhD in Maastricht in 1987 and later received a professorship in Milan. Their research led to the development of the thrombogram, a diagnostic test used to gain a picture of the complete clotting mechanism – vital information, in light of the prevalence of cardiovascular disease. Completely in line with the goals of W.I.L., Hemker founded a company called Synapse B.V. that became a link between the university and the medical business community. Synapse also brought a diagnostic test used to measure thrombin generation to market.

Hemker was among the pioneers of 'Tans's brain trust', which put the fledgling university on the map of the scientific community. He published a great deal, won various awards and supervised more than 70 PhD candidates. He once described himself as 'an expansive narcissist who indulges that vice on the academic stage'.[32] Hemker was a great wit and had a reputation for his occasionally sharp tongue. Rumour has it that his staff once took their revenge with a joke of their own, yelling: 'Phone call for Mr Hemker, we have Stockholm on the line!', at which point he came running to take the receiver, absolutely delighted. Be that as it may, Hemker was present from the very beginning of the vigorous Cardiovascular Diseases research line in Maastricht, which today belongs to the internationally renowned research institution CARIM. When asked what the most important characteristic is for a good researcher, his answer is short and sweet: imagination. A researcher has to 'invent something new' time and time again as he or she searches for explanations. Even after his retirement from the university, he was unable to give up his research entirely. To this day, he still has scientific goals he would like to accomplish, such as developing a 'very simple little device that will measure thrombin generation in the blood using a finger prick'. As far as his inability to stop doing research is concerned, he says, 'that goes on the same way it always has, nothing I can do about it'. Hemker continues to present the results of his research to a wider audience as well. In 2013, he published a book entitled *Thrombin*, dedicated 'to S.B.', which has since been translated into several languages. The book deals with the role of thrombin in regard to both clotting and the development of thrombosis, as the technique for measuring thrombin generation had not yet gained wide application in medical practice.[33] *Thrombin* features a foreword by Vroman (who was 99 years old at the time he wrote it) and also contains humorous and, obviously, imaginative pen-and-ink drawings by Hemker's own hand.

6 *Geert Blijham* WHILE THE BASIC PHILOSOPHY WAS A FANTASTIC EXPERIMENT, IF WE REALLY WANTED TO GET IN THE GAME WE WERE GOING TO NEED A FULLY DEVELOPED HOSPITAL

EDUCATIONAL INNOVATION, MANAGEMENT AND EXPERIMENTS WITH RABBITS 'Would you be prepared to consider pursuing your studies in internal medicine in Limburg, while helping us develop a curriculum at the same time?'[1] This was the question posed by Wynand Wijnen to 29-year-old Geert Harmannus Blijham (1946) at the start of 1974. Wijnen and Blijham were already acquainted with one another, having met previously in Groningen. As a Medical student, in 1968, Blijham had been a member of the Supervisory Board of Groningen University's Centre for Research during the wave of democratisation that swept through the Dutch universities during that period. Wijnen was director of the Centre for Research at the time. Their shared affinity for education created a bond between the two. The Groningen-born Blijham had begun his study of Medicine at the University of Groningen in 1964. During the 1960s he was a member of the Groningen Student Council, a representative body that consulted with the university administration and negotiated with them on behalf of the students. The PvdA (Labour) party was popular among the student body. Future PvdA politician Jacques Wallage was chair of the Student Council, for instance, and Job Cohen – who later became founding dean of the Faculty of Law in Maastricht – was a member as well. As Council Board member, Blijham was responsible for the education portfolio. He had shown an interest in education and management from an early age. According to Blijham, it was a 'phenomenal time' in his life, which revolved around lively evenings of debate in front of packed halls and student participation in academic affairs. In 1971, as a member of academic staff, he began his PhD research project on immune response and white blood cells. More specifically, his research concerned the question of why transplants are rejected by some patients' immune systems. This research resulted in the dissertation *Histofysiologie van het helper T cellen systeem in het konijn*

('Histophysiology of the helper T-cell system in rabbits') (1975). The research involved the use of rabbits as test subjects, 'no humans and fortunately no Labradors either...'. Meanwhile, he also participated in the University Council, a group of around twenty individuals that met with the Executive Board 'to deliberate about things like the price of coffee'. It was a 'great time' for him, like 'some sort of exciting boys' book'.

Still, Blijham could not see himself 'messing about with those rabbits' until his retirement; he realised he lacked the 'internal passion' for that kind of scientific research. By his own admission, he needed external pressure to really keep him going. The idea formed in his mind of pursuing an academic clinical career after all, and then translating that into fundamental research. He applied for an internship in internal medicine in Groningen, but was rejected under the argument that he had shown himself to be perhaps a bit too 'socially engaged' during his involvement with the University Council. The letter of rejection stated that, due to 'the general sentiment towards him present in the Internal Medicine Department', it seemed unwise to admit him to their programme. It was a major disappointment. The offer from Wijnen, who had heard about the rejection, therefore came at precisely the right moment.

FROM GRONINGEN TO MAASTRICHT Blijham stepped into his Citroën Deux Chevaux at a very early hour and headed south; he did not want to be late for his meeting with Wijnen at noon. Wijnen immediately invited him to lunch with him at a restaurant located in Tongersestraat, around the corner from the faculty. For someone from Groningen, conducting a professional interview over lunch was 'completely unthinkable', and then the menu arrived featuring *steak au poivre* – a dish Blijham had never even heard of. The agreement was quickly struck. In the fall of 1975, Blijham began working for Wijnen as senior lecturer. From January 1976 he combined a faculty appointment with a traineeship under Jef Coenegracht, head of Internal Medicine at the St. Annadal Hospital. Blijham was enthusiastic about the basic philosophy from the very beginning. He was assigned to help set out a curriculum for the third and fourth academic years. Blijham has fond memories of this period. He came into contact with all manner of inspiring people: Wijnen, of course, but also Henk Schmidt, Hetty Snellen, Peter Bouhuijs and the dean, Roelof Willighagen – who hosted gatherings to discuss the curriculum at his home in the evenings. According to Blijham, each of these men was creative and able to think outside the box. He experienced this period as one long process of creation, free from bureaucratic red tape. They were involved in organising medical education very differently than in other places: the patient complaints heard by doctors provided a direct basis for the problem-driven curriculum. Not everyone in the faculty was on board with this new set-up. Coen Hemker asserted that the new system was not teaching students enough about the basic subjects – the scientific foundation of medicine, in his view – and withdrew from teaching in order to concentrate on expanding his own line of research whenever possible. In the early stages, says Blijham, a kind of informal playing field was in effect: an environment in which not everyone felt equally at home.

IDEOLOGY OR PRACTICAL SYSTEM? Harmen Tiddens and Wijnen were the godfathers of the basic philosophy. Both men tried to adhere strictly to its chief principles, as they shared a conviction that the philosophy's best chance of practical success would lie in being applied as faithfully as possible. During one day of general consultations, Blijham was given to understand that Tiddens wanted to put off re-evaluation of the basic philosophy for the first five years. The message was: give the philosophy at least five years' time, so we have a chance to find out how well it works. Initially, Tiddens even suggested that the faculty could do without a professor of Anatomy. It was as if, Blijham recalls, the need for Medical students to first grasp how the body is put together was a matter of no importance. The faculty was quickly subjected to so much criticism, however, that they yielded and appointed a professor of Anatomy in 1978. Tiddens considered this a concession by any measure. He and Wijnen wanted to keep a tight rein on the faculty with regard to problem-based learning as well. They saw to it that not a single lecture hall was present in the entire former monastery on Tongersestraat, the building that housed the faculty in its early days. The best way to prevent lectures from being taught was to ensure that no lecture halls were available; 'that is all we need to do', was the reasoning. Giving an inaugural lecture was considered beyond the pale. Edmond Marres, professor of Otorhinolaryngology (ENT), was the first to deliver an inaugural lecture, on 22 January 1982. Tiddens had already left Maastricht by then.

One thing that Wijnen kept a particularly close eye on was the progress test.[2] This test did not measure a student's proficiency in a particular subject, but rather indicated how much the student had left to go in becoming the 'ideal doctor': someone with a broad knowledge of the practice of medicine. In that sense, the progress test was an essential element of the basic philosophy. The test was an invention of Wijnen's and was 'so revolutionary', according to Blijham, 'that it sent a shudder of revulsion through the Dutch medical community'. Years would pass before the test became common practice at other medical faculties. Quite a few lecturers, however, were unable to stomach the fact that they could not administer examinations in their own subject; there were no course examinations in the beginning, either. In Maastricht, where the preconditions for educational innovation were unusually favourable, resistance to the basic philosophy gradually increased. Some individuals even likened the basic philosophy to Chairman Mao's little red book: 'it began to feel like a kind of dogma, like some biblical edict'. This perception was connected with the expansion of the faculty as well. Although new employees were still being asked to embrace the basic philosophy, its ideological nature was tempered somewhat from the mid-1980s onward. The 'new folks' took a more pragmatic approach to problem-based learning, in Blijham's estimation. People like Ton van der Linden – who had had an orthopaedic practice of his own in Annadal before being appointed professor of Orthopaedics in 1979 – took very little pleasure in tutoring students. Van der Linden accepted the role only to see 'what it was like' and subsequently left the teaching duties to his assistants.[3]

THE ACADEMISATION OF ST. ANNADAL HOSPITAL? Blijham first entered St. Annadal in early 1976. He started work there as a faculty staff member under the supervision of Harry Hulsmans, the faculty's founding father and professor of Internal Medicine, while also working as a PhD candidate under Jef Coenegracht. The intention was to bridge the gap between the faculty and the local hospital, St. Annadal. The faculty had yet to acquire an academic workplace of its own. After all, it had been founded without a university hospital 'of its own' as well. A university hospital was not considered a priority under the basic philosophy. Cooperation within the region was proposed, the idea being that the faculty might secure an academic *pied à terre* at the regional hospitals. All kinds of ideas circulated, for instance in connection with the construction of a Regional Medical Centre in collaboration with the hospitals of Heerlen, Maastricht and Sittard.[4] Any attempt to distribute the academic functions across the regional health-care system failed, however, bogged down in endless meetings – much to the disappointment of the basic philosophy's proponents, including Blijham. As a result, the faculty's clinicians became even more dependent on St. Annadal. At the hospital, this 'academisation' was handled differently in every department, depending on the position taken by the head of department in question. The integration proceeded fairly smoothly in the Surgery department. There was an explanation for this: in consultation with Co Greep, one of the surgeons in residence was named a professor of the university in order to serve as a bridgehead between the two.

In his own department, Internal Medicine, Blijham was forced to acknowledge that academisation was proving an extraordinarily difficult challenge.[5] Initially, Hulsmans was simply barred from entering the hospital. Later, he was allowed to treat only a few patients in outpatient care. While Coenegracht had a reputation as a highly competent internist, he was also a difficult man who was in no way inclined to share power in his personal kingdom. He was used to doing things the way he himself saw fit: he conducted rounds of his patients only when he felt like it, for example. As someone born and bred in Maastricht, he also felt little affinity for the 'Hollanders' from the coastal provinces who had joined the faculty.[6] And the department of Internal Medicine was not the only one where the faculty encountered resistance.[7] Anaesthesiology proved a true disaster in Blijham's view: the professor of Anaesthesiology, Jan Lelkens, never made it further than the Biomedical Centre; his office was located right next to the bridge connecting the building to St. Annadal, and yet he was consistently denied access to the hospital.

The majority of specialists at St. Annadal were not inclined to just give up their territory without a fight. What they found particularly irritating was the arrogance of the new arrivals, who emphatically proclaimed it was 'high time to throw open the windows of St. Annadal and let in some fresh air'.[8] Still, the commotion surrounding the buyout amounts was a far more serious problem. While it was true that a contract on a buyout arrangement between St. Annadal and the Dutch government had been in place since the summer of 1975, approved at the time by then-Minister of Education, Culture and Science Jos van Kemenade, the subsequent Minister, VVD (Liberal) party member Arie Pais, found the settlements too high. The faculty was likewise indignant over the 'disgraceful buyout arrangement'. The St. Annadal specialists were publicly made out to be money-grubbing mercenaries, at a time when it was already fashionable to criticise the medical establishment for all manner of things.[9] The friction increased to such a degree that it threatened the very future of the faculty, which now dangled by a thread, as the St. Annadal specialists prepared for battle (and found they had a strong legal position). The case of professor Hein Wellens in particular, Blijham recalls, led to an uproar. At Co Greep's instigation, Wellens – an internationally renowned cardiologist – was appointed to the university staff in Maastricht. Greep wanted to enhance the specialties, in this case the treatment of complex arrhythmias and cardiac surgery, by lifting them to a higher scientific plane. He saw Wellens's appointment as a useful first step on the path to reaching that goal. His objective was to, in a way, force the hospital's evolution into a fully-developed university hospital. Wellens wasted no time making himself at home in St. Annadal, immediately and unceremoniously claiming beds in the clinic for his own work. Although, according to Blijham, he may not have been 'the greatest tactician on earth', in the end he did manage to win the battle with the cardiologists in residence at St. Annadal. All of this served as a learning process for Blijham: he noted that it took real managerial skill to weigh one's options and then consistently take the best course of action, 'even when it hurts'. It was not until 1982 that tensions in St. Annadal began to ease, when the parties in the conflict were able to resolve their differences through a settlement proposal. The Internal Medicine Department, where Blijham worked, turned out to be the last department to be academised: the step proved possible only after Coenegracht's departure.

GREEP, HOUSTON, KREMERS AND THE HOSPITAL ISSUE There was one person who was like a fish in water during this pioneering era, with its attendant lack of fully crystallised bureaucratic guidelines. This person was Co Greep, who became dean in January of 1978. Greep, says Blijham, 'thundered through the hospital' and was 'exactly the right man in the right place at the right time'. Greep had an enormous ego and, while his manners may have been rough at times, there was – according to Blijham – a great deal more to the man. In his opinion, Greep had a 'fantastic ability to allocate his ego to others, and he was an exceptionally gifted organiser'. In that regard, Blijham continues to admire Greep to this very day. It was also Greep who, out of the blue one Saturday morning, in the lift at St. Annadal, turned to him and asked: 'So, Blijham, how would you like to go to America?' Greep was the kind of man who, according to Blijham, stopped at nothing when it came to promoting someone whom he felt showed potential. It was thanks to Greep's mediation that Blijham was able to accept a year-long fellowship in Houston at the M.D. Anderson Cancer Center, the largest cancer treatment centre in the world. He used the fellowship in Texas to train as a haematologist and oncologist. The experience marked a turning point in Blijham's views on the basic philosophy. While he had been a 'hard-core basic philosopher' prior to leaving for the US, he assumed a more balanced position upon his return to the Netherlands. Blijham had discovered how 'exciting and enjoyable' it was to work in an environment where not only could he involve patients in clinical and experimental research, but patients with rare or complicated conditions also received the highest level of care. And it was undeniably true that this type of academic medicine developed best at a single location, within the confines of a single hospital with an adequate infrastructure, such as an excellent intensive care facility: 'you can't conduct bone-marrow transplants in one place and pancreatic transplants in another place and perform cardiac surgery at a third location'.

The prospects for that kind of university hospital, complete with highly specialised functions, seemed favourable when Blijham returned to Maastricht. This was because, in November of 1979, the Limburg lobby had succeeded in gaining government permission to build the new hospital. Crucial roles in the lobby's success were played by Greep and, even more so in terms of politics, by the energetic Sjeng Kremers, who had been appointed Queen's Commissioner for Limburg in 1977. Kremers had applied all of his considerable ingenuity to winning approval for the construction – a remarkable feat given the fact that the Ministry of Education, Culture and Science was struggling with a budgetary deficit at the time.[10] When he took office as the Queen's Commissioner, Kremers had vowed to make the elimination of unemployment in Limburg his personal goal.[11] To that end, the 1978 *Perspectievennota Zuid-Limburg* ('Memorandum on the Prospects for South Limburg') was drafted, in which agreements were established between the national and regional governments in order to, around 1990, bring unemployment in Limburg back in line with the national average. For the purposes of this policy, the university was seen as an engine driving the region's economy. The faculty breathed a collective sigh of relief. Nevertheless, a few years later, in 1983, the hospital issue was once again an item on the political agenda. The then Minister of Education, Culture and Science, Christian Democrat (CDA) Wim Deetman, wanted 'the eighth faculty' to retain its focus on primary health care, for which he considered a university hospital without hyperspecialisation to be sufficient. The faculty, however, found such a second-rate hospital unacceptable. Not only the clinicians, Blijham emphasises, but also the researchers in the Biomedical Centre wished for a full-blown hospital in order to fully participate within the academic medical community. Once again, the Limburg lobby sprang into action and, once again, Kremers came to the faculty's aid. The mandate for construction of a new 'fully developed' university hospital was now secured, and the builders were to start in 1984.[12]

ACADEMISATION OF INTERNAL MEDICINE At the time of Coenegracht's departure in 1982, the academisation of the Department of Internal Medicine had yet to truly begin. It was up to Guus Flendrig, the new professor of Internal Medicine and head of the department, to oversee and guide this process. 'Founding father' Hulsmans was put on the sidelines. According to Blijham, Flendrig was 'a nicer version of Greep' with strong managerial qualities, which came in handy in helping the various subspecialist areas come into their own within a single organisational context, i.e. general internal medicine.[13] His goal was to not only combine academic excellence with organisational efficiency, says Blijham, but also to create a consolidated power block at the faculty. In the first few years, efforts on all fronts were centred on growth and setting up operations, as internal medicine had some catching up to do. Blijham focused his energies on developing the Haematology and Oncology Departments and establishing their respective profiles. An 'outpatient oncology clinic, an outpatient haematology clinic and a good laboratory' were installed; the latter was considered 'extremely important for haematology, for examining all those blood cells, and for evaluating bone marrow samples'. The early years were 'very, very exciting, thoroughly enjoyable and we also managed to establish a regional network, so that certain difficult-to-treat cancer patients could be referred elsewhere', according to Blijham. In the summer of 1986 – made possible by the expertise Blijham had gained in Houston – the first experimental autologous bone marrow transplant took place in the old St. Annadal Hospital. In addition to patient care and education, Blijham also concentrated on oncology research and obtaining subsidies from secondary sources (government agencies) and funding from contract research. He additionally sat on various governing bodies, was offered a position in the Queen Wilhelmina Fund (KWF) and the Organisation for the Research and Treatment of Cancer, became a member of the faculty research committee and shortly thereafter joined the Faculty Board. In light of those activities, it should come as no surprise that he was appointed professor 'of Internal Medicine, in particular of Medical Oncology' in 1987.[14] More surprising, perhaps, is that Blijham decided to leave Maastricht in 1991.

THE MAASTRICHT EXAMPLE As Blijham remembers it, sometime around 1990, the Department of Internal Medicine in Maastricht was on the cusp of a phase of consolidation. He began to notice 'it was all a bit too much of the same old thing', and that he was not cut out to simply 'mind the store'. He furthermore felt himself being pulled in different directions: sometimes more in the direction of research and sometimes more towards governance matters. His administrative insight and sober, clear sense of perspective in combination with a basically positive attitude had apparently also drawn attention elsewhere. He was offered the opportunity to both conduct research and participate in governing the university in Utrecht. There, in 1992, he became a professor of Internal Medicine specialising in Oncology, while at the same time serving as medical manager of the internal medicine division in the university hospital: like Maastricht's own Flendrig, but then in Utrecht.[15] Six years later he once again stood at a crossroads. This time he chose administration. He became chair of the Executive Board of the University Medical Center Utrecht, the organisation created by the merger of the Academic Hospital Utrecht, the Wilhelmina Children's Hospital and the Faculty of Medicine. Did he bring anything from the Maastricht ideology with him to this new position? First of all, Rob Reneman's idea of thinking not in courses, but in content-based key points, which requires taking difficult decisions on the research lines one will explore. Moreover, when it came to education, Maastricht had been truly 'exemplary'. As an administrator, Blijham dedicated himself to innovating education in Utrecht – no easy feat in an organisation with a long history of tradition – taking problem-based learning as his source of inspiration. The previous discipline-oriented curriculum in Utrecht was replaced by a more patient-oriented version. This meant that the ideas of Harmen Tiddens, who had left Utrecht to come to Maastricht in 1973, finally came full circle and were implemented at his old university after an elaborate detour. In Blijham's opinion, everyone 'in Maastricht should feel incredibly proud'. 'When I was abroad, visiting other universities, and the conversation turned to the Netherlands, then they were naturally aware that there was a university in Amsterdam, and sometimes they knew there was a university in Utrecht as well – but every one of them had heard of Maastricht.'[16]

7 *Hans Philipsen* SOCIAL HEALTH SCIENCE WAS THE FIRST, ALBEIT TENTATIVE, STEP TOWARDS A REAL UNIVERSITY

PIONEERS AT THE COUNTRY'S FRONTIER In late 1973, 38-year-old Hans Philipsen (1935) had been a professor of Social Science Research Methods and Techniques at Leiden University for more than six years when Harmen Tiddens contacted him. Tiddens invited him to join the appointments committee for the first professors of Medical Sociology, Medical Psychology and Health Economics. According to the basic philosophy, the new Faculty of Medicine's developing curriculum required substantial input from the social sciences. Good doctors, particularly those working in primary health care, needed to be able to view illness and health from a broad, and not purely medical, perspective. The seven-strong core group had been working since the summer of 1973. Philipsen knew of Tiddens only through publications. Halfway through the procedure, Tiddens suddenly asked Philipsen if he himself would not like to be a professor of Medical Sociology in Maastricht. Philipsen was open to the idea, as he was ready 'to make a move' after six years:[1] he did not relish the thought of being a permanent fixture in Leiden for years to come. He was ready to start something from scratch, being a pioneer on 'the country's frontier', where there were possibilities for experimenting with new forms of education and research.

MATHEMATICS PLUS HISTORY, DIVIDED BY TWO, GIVES SOCIOLOGY That Philipsen would become a professor at such a young age was never a foregone conclusion. He was born into a working-class family that had been hit by unemployment in the wake of the economic crisis of the 1930s, and grew up in the working-class area of Laakkwartier in The Hague. His parents were members of the socialist movement, commonly referred to as 'the red family'. They were strict adherents to the movement's philosophy and read the socialist

daily *Het Vrije Volk*, listened to the VARA socialist broadcasting association and were active members of the Social Democratic Workers Party (SDAP), the forerunner of the PvdA (Labour) party.[2] Driven by a longing for emancipation, 'elevation and progress', this was an environment that greatly valued broad development. Young Hans was encouraged to visit the library, where he devoured books on art and culture. However, his Hague accent was not considered to be conducive to 'social elevation', so he learned to express himself using standard Dutch and went to high school, where he 'could keep up well enough'; he wanted to prove himself by obtaining good grades. He graduated, and left holding a *gymnasium-b* diploma (for pre-university education with an emphasis on the exact sciences). But what to do next? He was in two minds: should he study Mathematics or should he choose History?

Applying the formula 'mathematics plus history divided by two', he settled on Sociology at the Political Sociology Faculty of the University of Amsterdam.[3] During his studies, the development of courses in methods and techniques had barely begun at Dutch universities. In Amsterdam, Sociology was very much a discipline of literature and philosophy. Philipsen turned to American textbooks to teach himself the 'new' research methods, such as surveys and statistics. After graduating he went to work for the Netherlands Institute for Preventive Medicine/TNO.[4] He conducted research into absenteeism based on TNO's national absenteeism statistics. In 1968 he earned his PhD at the University of Amsterdam for his dissertation *Afwezigheid wegens ziekte: een onderzoek naar oorzaken van verschillen in ziekte*verzuim tussen 38 middelgrote bedrijven ('Absence due to illness: a study into the causes of differences in absenteeism between 38 medium-sized companies'), in which absenteeism was seen more as an indication of an organisation in trouble than of an ill employee. Soon afterwards, he was appointed professor of Methods and Techniques at Leiden University, which was straining under the 'enormous growth in student numbers' and was hiring young staff in great haste. In the progressive climate that characterised those years, the focus of students and young academic staff was more on improving the world than on study and research, according to Philipsen. In the hope that, as a young professor, Philipsen 'would be able to navigate his way through the entire carry-on involving councils, consultations and employee participation', he was asked to become dean of the Faculty of Social and Behavioural Sciences effective early 1973. Owing to his unifying qualities, he was expected to be a dean who 'wouldn't be arguing with students every day'. And indeed he was passionate about promoting democratisation. Looking back, Philipsen says that this episode in which he was elevated 'by accident' to the position of dean at such a young age did not exactly benefit his own academic development. Tiddens's proposal to come to work as a professor of Medical Sociology in Maastricht and contribute to the new Faculty of Medicine came at an opportune moment.

GOING DOWN SOUTH As early as the spring of 1974, Philipsen knew he could become professor of Medical Sociology at the Netherlands' eighth medical faculty. Philipsen was unique among his colleagues: he was the only one of their number who already had professorial experience in a 'high student pressure' environment and with university governance. He was appointed chair of the Medical Sociology Department and, after some time, was able to convince several Leiden University staff, such as Jos Diederiks, Jan Joosten and Riet Drop, to also head south. Medical Sociology found a home at the Vijverdal Community Mental Hospital, where the Departments for Social Psychiatry (Marius Romme), General Medical Practice (Wim Brouwer), Health Economics (Wim Groot) and Medical Psychology (Joost Bremer) could also be found.

Both the new didactic principles and the drive towards multidisciplinary cooperation were welcomed by the medical sociologists. For example, Philipsen served as a tutor in the first Introduction to the Study of Medicine course, which was coordinated by Wynand Wijnen. This course began with problem-orientation training and went on to also examine the relationships between Medicine and other academic disciplines. Philipsen also appreciated the thematic approach of the research, insofar as there was time for research in those early years. Nevertheless, the Medical Sociology Department started research into the impact of social and cultural phenomena on illness and health and on the organisation of health care as a sociological issue. In due course the 'structure and performance of the health-care sector' research project was launched. This period also saw the emergence of the epidemiology and statistics fields of study, allowing further refinement of education in methods and techniques.

A 'BOYHOOD DREAM' According to the basic philosophy, the faculty's aim was to interface seamlessly with existing primary and secondary health care in such a way that it would make a classic university hospital superfluous. 'That made sense in those anti-authoritarian days', says Philipsen. It was the task of the Medical Regional Centre, an overarching body, to promote such cooperation between the Faculty of Medicine and the regional health-care sector. Philipsen participated in the process, but had to admit that nothing came from this ideal. Actually, he never really believed in it. According to Philipsen, the idea of having specialists from the region play a role at the faculty acted 'like a time bomb' under the basic philosophy. After all, they were 'totally uninterested in problem-based learning' and were far more inclined to nominate fellow specialists with PhDs from the region for a professorship via their medical specialist association. Nevertheless, Philipsen resisted the urge of immediately advocating the idea of establishing a university hospital. For a while he and Tiddens believed in a middle way: 'enhancing' the existing hospital with a limited number of academic wards, with the other hospitals in the region being allocated the remaining academic functions. 'It's a shame we never tried that', Philipsen says, but 'the distribution of academic functions across the region came up against routine opposition'. It was 'a kind of boyhood dream': 'the actual decision-makers didn't want it, and in the end neither did The Hague'. The civil servants, however, really liked the idea, 'but what really mattered was whether you could get the medical world to feel the same way. After six months we realised that it would never work. It could only have worked if political decisions had been taken on the question of university hospitals, and that never happened'. Continuing to advocate the distribution of academic functions across multiple hospitals in the region was 'absolutely flogging a dead horse, but a horse that had not yet disappeared; that's what made it so difficult to let it go. If we had acted differently, the university would have had far fewer problems in the early days'.

MANAGEMENT From the very beginning, Philipsen was astounded by how the university was managed initially. The Executive Board President was Sjeng Tans, a former Dutch teacher from Maastricht, a combative Catholic socialist and a PvdA politician with an enormous drive for education in general and 'his' State University of Limburg in particular. The Vice-president was the business-like Antoine (Ton) Rottier, a conservative Catholic, economist and former president-director of the State Mining Company. Tiddens was Rector, professor of Paediatrics and 'basic philosopher': he was often away and enjoyed flying around the world to attend international congresses on educational reform. It was obvious, according to Philipsen, that this triumvirate had no experience managing a university. He remembers how Tans imperiously sought to run the university as if it were some kind of secondary school, complete with the occasional reprimand. The fact that it was a professional organisation staffed by many highly qualified professionals working independently seemed lost on him. Moreover, the Executive Board worryingly appeared to have zero notion of the 1972 *Wet op het Universitaire Bestuur* (University Governance Act, WUB). Responding to calls for participation during the student protests of the late 1960s, the Minister of Education, Culture and Science, Gerard Veringa, had implemented far-reaching democratisation of the administrative structures. The WUB granted consultation and participation rights to all branches of the university community. The Executive Board was ultimately answerable to the University Council, which co-decided on the institution's budget and policy. During his tenure as dean in Leiden, Philipsen had gained experience of the WUB, but he soon realised that Tans, Rottier and Tiddens had little idea of what this Act implied. Tans felt that they were 'special' and largely ignored the Act. But in Philipsen's view, it was crucially important to arrange everything properly from the start, so that institution-staff relationships could be formalised and faculty structures set down, for example. As there was no one else who sensed the urgency of the situation, Philipsen decided to 'jump in at the deep end', as he remembers 'with false immodesty'. He devoted himself to establishing a well-run University Council and was appointed its first chair in 1976. One of his first acts in that role was to argue for the appointment of women to more senior positions. The position of women at the State University of Limburg was appalling: there were no women on the University Council, the proportion of women among academic personnel was below 10% and there were no female professors.[5] Despite this appeal, the university would long remain a male bastion. Nevertheless, the University Council brought Philipsen close to the centre of power. In order to exercise 'reasonable influence on the process', he attended the Executive Board meetings, where his presence was not immediately appreciated. Philipsen remembers being locked out of a meeting between Tans and Rottier. In January 1978, Philipsen was appointed member of the Executive Board.

GENERAL FACULTY One of the topics of the Executive Board meetings that piqued Philipsen's interest was the development of the General Faculty. According to the Act, a university had to have at least two faculties. While the Faculty of Medicine was under construction, work was underway on designing that second faculty as well. Wynand Wijnen took on the role of founding dean. The name of this faculty was deliberately vague, as it was not clear which subject area or areas it would be devoted to. Its statutory tasks were also formulated rather broadly. The faculty was expected to contribute to educational reform, cooperate with institutions of higher professional education in the area of health care, develop new degree programmes and establish an experimental General Education programme.[6] This task description allowed for a great deal of flexibility. The Executive Board initially envisioned a degree programme that would produce versatile generalists who would go on to fill management positions. Ever since the 1960s, Tans had been pleading for a university that did not train narrow specialists and founding dean Wijnen considered expanding into an area other than health care, in order to give the State University of Limburg a somewhat broader foundation.

But the Minister of Education, Culture and Science, Jos van Kemenade, took a dim view of these Maastricht plans. In the summer of 1976, van Kemenade put forward the idea of social health, suggesting that the General Faculty establish an experimental degree programme focusing on social and organisational issues surrounding health and illness. According to Van Kemenade, the health-care sector urgently needed staff and policy officers, to work on cost reduction, quality improvement and more effective assistance. Health-care expenditures were rising rapidly as a result of the economic growth in the 1960s and the expansion of the social insurance system. Supply and demand were racing against each other. However, the Netherlands fell into an economic slump following the 1973 oil crisis, and controlling health-care costs rose high on the political agenda.[7] Moreover, Van Kemenade argued that the advantage of a Social Health degree programme was that the State University of Limburg could set up a new course of study in that area using a portion of its existing personnel – a reiteration of the cost control argument.

SOCIAL HEALTH? It was now up to the Executive Board to flesh out this idea. The first question they had to tackle was how exactly to interpret and delineate the notion of social health. Van Kemenade never provided an exact description of what such a degree programme should entail. Together with Wijnen, Philipsen put his stamp on the memorandum *Ontwikkelingen voor de Algemene Faculteit van de Rijksuniversiteit Limburg* ('Developments for the General Faculty of the State University of Limburg'), published in late 1976, which discussed the phenomenon of 'social health'. The memorandum stated that those entering this discipline would be 'studying social phenomena and their consequences and implications for health and disease'.[8] It suggested three 'key areas'. First, it would be possible to study health and disease in relation to social phenomena, with a focus on issues such as absenteeism, euthanasia and the ageing population. Second, students could focus on social structures and social phenomena in relation to health by studying environment, diet and high-risk lifestyles, for example. Third, students could study social structures and social phenomena, on the one hand, and health and disease, on the other. In the latter case, the focus could lie, for instance, on preventing health problems, 'teaching health-promoting behaviour' and the 'relative costs of health care in the context of social services'. The three key areas unmistakably reflect the optimism of the ideal of social engineering of the late 1960s/early 1970s. In order to meet all of the government's wishes, the General Faculty, like the Medical Faculty, would take a problem-oriented approach and seek close cooperation with higher professional education.

POLITICAL COMPLICATIONS The Developments for the General Faculty memorandum sketched the contours of a Social Health degree programme. While the Act provided for the General Faculty, according to Philipsen 'the rest of the Netherlands could have done without it'. Though the State University of Limburg had permission to flesh out the plans, it was by no means a foregone conclusion. The Ministry of Public Health and Environmental Hygiene bombarded 'Maastricht' with critical questions. Should 'social health', with its multidisciplinary dimensions, not be part of the Faculty of Medicine?

Surely such an approach would be in perfect alignment with the basic philosophy. From the very outset, however, Philipsen was a staunch advocate of the Social Health degree programme developing outside the Faculty of Medicine. He put forward two arguments. Launching this degree programme at the General Faculty had a major advantage in that it would mean the State University of Limburg would satisfy the statutory requirement of a second faculty in the short term; since the field of social health could profit from the expertise available at the Faculty of Medicine, costs would not quickly spiral out of control. Moreover, Philipsen expressly wanted the new Social Health degree programme to develop outside the Medical Faculty in order to give it a chance 'to prove itself'. Philipsen believed that this would be virtually impossible within the Medical Faculty because doctors were simply more focused on cure rather than on care.

Philipsen had an influential voice in the working group chaired by Wijnen, which, after many objections, presented the report *Sociale gezondheidkunde* ('Social Health Science') in May 1978.[9] It was an attempt to meet 'all of the Minister's proposals'. While the previous memorandum referred to 'social health', this report spoke about 'social health science' – a concept broadly defined as the interdisciplinary science 'that studies the benefits of and threats to a healthy existence, as well as the options for producing those benefits and eliminating those threats'.[10] The degree programme would have three graduation tracks: social-health science research, health facilities planning and management, and health education. By the time that Maastricht was ready to consult with The Hague on the planned commencement of the Social Health Science degree programme in September 1979, the political wind had changed. VVD (Liberal) party member Arie Pais, the new Minister of Education, Culture and Science, was less favourably disposed towards the State University of Limburg than his predecessor. Philipsen was convinced that Pais wanted nothing less than to completely shut down the State University of Limburg, as that 'would take care of his budget cuts all at once'. What was more, the Ministry of Public Health and Environmental Hygiene continued to ask critical questions. However, it was impossible for Pais to ignore the Brinkhorst (D66, Liberal Democrats) motion that was carried in December 1978, which argued for the degree programme in Social Health Science at the State University of Limburg to be launched in September 1980. This motion was an extension of the Deetman motion, which advocated a fully-fledged university. Parliamentary support for the State University of Limburg was, according to Philipsen, mainly down to Limburg lobbying as a united front in The Hague. A key figure was 'the energetic Sjeng Kremers, who used his influence to play a crucial role in expanding the university'.

Nevertheless, Pais did not immediately approve the proposed Social Health Science degree programme. To Philipsen's amazement, the Minister had a surprise in store in early 1979: he granted permission for the experimental degree programme in Social Health Science to commence, on condition that the State University of Limburg dropped the Social Health Science research graduation track and replaced it with Nursing Science. By doing so, he was complying with the wish of his fellow party member Els Veder-Smit, the State Secretary for Public Health and Environmental Hygiene. Philipsen thinks that the State Secretary saw the new General Faculty as an opportunity to make 'nursing' a subject of academic study and training, as was already the case in the United States. Yet again, the State University of Limburg found itself compelled to coordinate its expansion plans with ideas from The Hague. The university was tasked with detailing a curriculum for Social Health Science in consultation with the two Ministries involved and the field. Time was running out. The universities in Rotterdam and Utrecht were working on similar plans. In Maastricht there was a fear that their plans would never come to fruition if they did not act fast. Philipsen remembers that 'a large number of conferences with people from the field' were organised under enormous time pressure in the hope of still being able to launch in September 1979.

DESIGN FOR A SOCIAL HEALTH SCIENCE DEGREE PROGRAMME In August 1979, Pais received the *Ontwerp voor een studierichting Sociale Gezondheidkunde aan de Rijksuniversiteit* Limburg ('Design for a Social Health Science degree programme at the State University of Limburg'). The document had been drawn up under the responsibility of the Board of the General Faculty. Wijnen, Philipsen and Paul Thung, especially, had been hard at work again. Thung was a professor of Medicine from Leiden and also worked at the State University of Limburg to advise on education. Social Health Science was to have a joint one-year propaedeutic phase and a three-year doctoral phase, with three different programmes: Nursing Science, Health-care Facilities Policy and Management, and Health Education. What did Nursing Science entail? According to the authors of the document, this was an academic discipline in development and it was still to be seen whether it would ever become an independent discipline with 'its own' theories and research methods. The idea was to give nursing practice a scientific foundation and to match developments abroad. Nursing Science, as it was presented in the design, was a compromise in Philipsen's view. He would have preferred a more experimental degree programme that was given the possibility of teaching both the theory and practice of nursing with, for example, four years of theory and two years of practice. But that was 'never permitted for purely financial reasons'.

The Health-care Facilities Policy and Management graduation track was intended to respond to issues in the health-care sector. How could health-care costs be brought under control? How could health-care quality and efficiency be measured and improved? The third graduation track, Health Education, focused on preventive medicine, which was also important from the perspective of cost control. There was a desire to better understand the connection between certain behaviour (such as smoking) and the probability of contracting diseases. With the help of the Medical Faculty and working according to the same education principles, Social Health Science aimed to offer 'problem-oriented', thematic, course-based education.[11] The university in Maastricht was optimistic about the employment perspectives; the study programme was socially relevant, practically focused and, therefore, useful. Those involved worked hard, but 1979 was no longer feasible. In early 1980, Pais approved the 'experimental degree programme': Social Health Science was able to start in September 1980 with 100 students. There was a strong interest in the degree programme. The first information day, held in October 1979, was attended by 1,600 people.

YEARS OF WORKING LONG HOURS In the meantime, a change of the guard had taken place in the upper administrative echelons of the State University of Limburg following the departure of Tiddens as Rector in 1979. Philipsen thought Tiddens's departure to be a 'wondrous move, to put it nicely'. From a basic philosophy perspective, 'everything was going well except for that hospital'; apparently the 'medical mafia' had been too much for him. And so Tiddens was gone before the first doctor had graduated. Wijnen succeeded him and also wished to remain as the founding dean of the General Faculty. However, it was impossible to combine the two positions. In early 1980, Philipsen stepped down from the Executive Board in order to take over the deanship from Wijnen – 'though not without some struggle'. Not only did he already know the ropes, in Leiden he had earned a reputation as a troubleshooter. This change at the top resulted in a 'historic moment' from an emancipatory point of view. Philipsen's department welcomed a new professor of Medical Sociology: on 6 June 1980, Riet Drop became the first female professor at the State University of Limburg.[12]

For Philipsen, the following years were characterised by hard work during the build-up phase of Social Health Science. The first urgent problem was how to recruit 'sufficient master's degree graduates' in the short term who could take teaching positions. This was no easy task, since there were few candidates to be found with specific expertise. Social health science was of course a new area and the new degree programme was an experiment. This was a unique situation in the Netherlands, brought about by the dominant influence of the social sciences. For some candidates, it was the first time they had even heard of the discipline. However, the biggest problem by far, Philipsen remembers, was recruiting good professors. When Social Health Science was launched in September 1980, none of the three specialisations yet had Crown-appointed professors. And no candidate at all had applied for a position in Nursing Science. However, Philipsen was able to recruit Wilhelmina Rouwenhorst in the summer of 1981: she became the first professor of Health Education in the Netherlands at the age of 65. Fred Vorst was appointed professor of Health-care Facilities Policy and Management. Incidentally, Vorst, when he still worked at the Ministry of Public Health and Environmental Hygiene, had been critical of the Social Health Science degree programme organised outside the Faculty of Medicine.

During his hunt for professors, Philipsen discovered that the people involved in social health were overwhelmingly practical in nature, with typically little interest in research. Nevertheless, Rouwenhorst and Vorst were beneficial to the faculty, as not only did they make it acceptable to the field, but their connections throughout the country would also come in very handy for grant applications. The new staff had to deal with a heavy teaching load, but they could rely on the support and expertise of the Faculty of Medicine; in principle, all departments of the Faculty of Medicine were able to contribute to the new degree programme. However, the question was to what extent Social Health Science should copy the problem-based learning[13] of the Faculty of Medicine. Though the students were certainly enthusiastic about the tutorial groups, they also desired other teaching methods. This was an issue in which Philipsen took an unorthodox position. He distanced himself from Wijnen with the ironic comment that the Faculty of Medicine considered lectures 'even more objectionable than mixed swimming'. He saw the basic philosophy, with its principles of education, 'as an attractive ideal, an inviting guide', but felt that the expansion 'had no place for absolutist ideologues for whom the crusade does not end before the divine Jerusalem has been conquered'.[14] Indeed, Social Health Science soon saw the introduction of supplementary teaching methods, such as Q&A sessions and lectures aimed at quickly familiarising students with a certain theme.

PHILIPSEN'S TRIANGLE The Social Health Science degree programme turned out to be enormously popular.[15] Nevertheless, what social health science actually entailed was hotly debated.[16] Was this a separate field of science or was it simply three specialisations without a common body of knowledge? Philipsen was not surprised by the chaos surrounding the theory of this new multidisciplinary field of study.[17] Indeed, he found little agreement on the new definitions of problems and theoretical and methodological approaches. In his view, health sciences was not a science in itself but a scientific orientation. Elaborating on the ideas of Jan Piet Kuiper, professor of Social Medicine at VU Amsterdam, he presented a diagram in the shape of a triangle, which would go down in history as 'Philipsen's triangle'. This allowed him to create a framework for social health science. What set social health science apart was that its research focused on the relationship between healthy living, threatening or favourable factors, and intervention. Social health science focused in particular on the care factor in health care. According to Philipsen, health sciences covered a broader domain and included cure-focused medicine. This philosophy allowed for social health science to be expanded into health sciences: a wide range of specialisations which interfaced not so much on the basis of common theoretical principles, but rather by virtue of common problems within Philipsen's triangle.

To strengthen the faculty, and therefore the university, collaboration was again sought with the Faculty of Medicine during the course of 1982 and 1983 to develop another four degree programmes: Mental Health Sciences, Health Sciences Theory, Movement Sciences and Biological Medicine. The latter two variants took a more biological, hard science-based approach. Philipsen's triangle was referred to in the ideological section of the memorandum *Gezondheidswetenschappen in Maastricht* ('Health Sciences in Maastricht').[18] Philipsen was present during the consultations on the expansion with the Ministry of Education, Culture and Science. He was seized by an 'almost disagreeable sense of joy' when approval was granted to start all four degree programmes in 1984. Maastricht had counted on getting no more than one or two. To this day Philipsen does not understand why Deetman took that decision. The only explanation he can give is 'that they liked the idea. They also said that we would have to do it with the same funding, so why should they have cared if we had seven degree programmes. It was the university's problem to arrange the details. Though it was rather irresponsible to start four new degree programmes, we could hardly have said: never mind'.[19] In 1984, the new Faculty of Health Sciences was launched with seven degree programmes. Yet the problem of unity and diversity did not diminish.[20]

NURSING SCIENCE After six years of 'relatively full-time development and administrative work' Philipsen thought it was time to call it a day in the spring of 1982. Not wanting to become fully entangled in administrative roles and still harbouring ambitions to amount to something in the scientific world, Philipsen knew it was high time – he was now 46 years old – to return full-time to research. After all, he had transferred from Leiden to Maastricht to get away from administrative work, though he had also transferred because he enjoyed the idea of joining a university in its infancy. Moreover, the increased pressure to publish made the return to research even more necessary. A further complication was that no professor of Nursing Science had been found. Philipsen decided to combine his Medical Sociology professorship with chairing the Nursing Science Department, with the objective of getting empirical research in this virtually uncharted territory off the ground. He had been impressed with the high level of nursing science he had encountered during a study trip to the United States in 1981. He was also attracted by the emancipatory factor: the field's academisation went hand in hand with a strengthening of the professional identity of nurses. In the Netherlands, nursing science was still in its infancy.

It was no easy ask to get empirical research into nursing practice going. Philipsen found it difficult to get nurses in the field to conduct 'sound research': 'while they did wish to increase their grounding in science, they tended to opt for a social-pedagogical rather than an empirical approach as was common in English-speaking countries. Nursing staff more often followed their hearts rather than their heads. Thick tomes existed on all aspects of nursing patients, but there was no empirical research into the practice of nursing'. Anneke Van den Bergh-Braam, who was part of that social-pedagogical approach, was appointed to the first chair in Nursing Science in the Netherlands in 1986. She belonged to 'the nursing elite' and had had a long career, first as a nurse and later as a nursing lecturer. In 1984 she defended her PhD dissertation titled *De hoofdverpleegkundige in het ziekenhuis* ('The Head Nurse in the Hospital'). In her inaugural lecture, Van den Bergh-Braam criticised the power structures in the health-care sector which she claimed led to 'de-personalisation and de-humanisation'. She then argued for more 'people-friendly structures' and more attention for the patient as a full person in the health-care sector.[21] She showed little affinity with Philipsen's empirical approach and he, for his part, considered her philosophical longing for holism 'completely moralistic'. It was of course difficult to deny that many students starting the Nursing programme could do without empirical research. They often had a nursing background and Philipsen believed they enrolled in the university Nursing programme in order to advance their careers and later hold positions such as nursing staff director or something similar. Philipsen thinks that scientific research in nursing got off the ground thanks to 'the boys and girls' who immediately enrolled in Nursing Science following secondary school, and who were not hindered by 'a built-in resistance to change'.

Philipsen set himself the goal of promoting research into the aspect of care in the health-care sector. He thought that the study of care processes had been stuck on a 'back burner' for far too long because 'the average doctor who wanted to cure operated on the front lines and did not return every day to inspect the wound'. Philipsen focused mainly on the continuity of care, which needed to be strengthened based on new scientific insights. The coordination of care was often lacking: in the 1980s, for example, patients might sometimes be driven home in an ambulance without any further arrangements being made for their care at home. But new knowledge was also needed to answer questions such as, 'How do you deal with patients with diabetes, heart failure or bedsores?' This type of research did sometimes encounter scepticism, such as when the question was put to Philipsen whether something such as 'academic bum washing' actually existed, to which the answer was that it was indeed extremely important to know how one washed bums.[22]

By the end of the 1980s, the field of Nursing Science had grown in popularity: newly established part-time and full-time degree programmes in Utrecht and Groningen were attracting students in droves. At Philipsen's initiative, the three universities that offered the degree programmes in this field started collaborating closely. This did not work out for the State University of Limburg: halfway through the 1990s the degree programme went under for lack of interest. Many Nursing Science students chose Utrecht over the long journey to the South, while students leaving secondary school preferred other areas within the health sciences. Yet Philipsen is not dissatisfied with how Nursing Science developed in Maastricht: 'we certainly saw around 100 PhD theses, many of which came about under my leadership'. He also looks back with satisfaction to the period around 1985, when the part-time degree programme enjoyed a high degree of success and 'produced 1,000 graduates in a couple of years' time'.

RETURN TO MANAGEMENT After years dedicated to Social Health Science (later Health Sciences), Philipsen faced a dilemma. He had always tried to juggle two balls, by combining scientific research and administrative duties. He concluded that the management game held a strong attraction for him and that he was 'pretty good at it'. For Philipsen, what mattered was 'the big picture'. In 1990 he considered the rectorship, but abandoned this ambition at the last moment in favour of Job Cohen: 'he would be an asset for the university'. Moreover, Philipsen had heard from his research group that people would rather not lose him, and that was the end of the matter as far as he was concerned. Three years later, the opportunity presented itself again when Cohen became State Secretary for Education, Culture and Science – with the guarantee that he would be able to return to Maastricht.[23] It was now or never, and Philipsen decided to become Rector until Cohen took over again in 1995. While still interested in medical sociology, from that point his primary focus was on university governance. Up to two years before his departure in 2000, Philipsen was a member of the Executive Board, first as Rector and later as a third member 'who was allowed to bear the title of Vice-Rector for internationalisation'; Cohen was often absent owing to his PvdA commitments. In the 1990s, Philipsen, Cohen and Karl Dittrich, who became an Executive Board member in 1986 and President in 1994, attempted to bring 'relative calm' to the various branches of the university, which was growing rapidly in those years; Philipsen and his two colleagues 'had no intention to launch any special initiatives, we just wanted to sustain the momentum'. As third member, Philipsen was responsible for personnel and organisation. He pursued a single university personnel policy. That was not always an easy task following the introduction of the *Wet modernisering universitaire bestuursorgansisatie* (University Government Modernisation Act, MUB) in 1997, which provided for greater autonomy for deans formulating policy. As an executive officer, he tried to keep the big picture – the final objective – in mind during conflicts in order to prevent escalation. His ability to cope with stress often served him well.[24] Furthermore, Philipsen wanted to promote bilingualism at the university as well as, more generally, internationalisation, given that the pursuit of science is international by nature. Internationalisation was already underway at several faculties, due in part to the need to attract students from outside the Netherlands. Philipsen advocated changing the name from 'Rijksuniversiteit Limburg' to 'Universiteit Maastricht', a decision that was formally made in 1996.[25] One 'of the few things that I can probably chalk up to myself is that name change', Philipsen says years later. Through his work, and that of many others, for the Faculties of Medicine and Health Sciences, he made an important contribution to the development of education and research focused on human health. In the end, he supervised a total of over 60 PhD candidates. At his departure in 2000, he assumed that these faculties would eventually merge.[26] The discussion on the fundamental question of whether health sciences and medicine belong together or not had not yet ended. But that merger did finally take place with the establishment of the Faculty of Health, Medicine and Life Sciences. It seems that after around 30 years, the health sciences were emancipated enough not to experience a merger with medicine as a threat. It was especially that yearning for emancipation that had concerned Philipsen ever since his younger years. During his farewell ceremony, he recalled the emancipation struggle of his social-democratic parents who had enabled him to embark on 'the social, cultural and intellectual journey' which he would continue after saying farewell to the university.

8 *Henk Schmidt* PROBLEM-BASED LEARNING IS MORE THAN A TEACHING METHOD – IT'S A TEACHING PHILOSOPHY

THE HILLS OF LIMBURG Henk Schmidt was still working on his Psychology degree at Utrecht University when, in 1974, he was approached by Wynand Wijnen via his mentor Don Mellenbergh and invited to join the State University of Limburg's Education Office in Maastricht. The idea appealed to Schmidt. During his degree he had come to 'focus on the methodology and statistics of scientific research'. He now made an effort to graduate as quickly as possible so that he could get that job in Maastricht. At the time, behaviourism was the dominant theoretical paradigm in psychology, but he did not set a lot of stock by it: 'it was a fairly primitive theory on human behaviour'.[1] Mellenbergh was a specialist in designing and analysing exams. Like Wijnen, he was strongly influenced by the work of Adriaan de Groot on ways to select and assess students.[2] It therefore came as no surprise that Mellenbergh advised Schmidt to apply for a job in Maastricht. Schmidt had been born in Limburg and, from his home on the tenth floor of a high-rise in Utrecht's Kanaleneiland district, he imagined him and his wife – whom he had met at school in Heerlen – returning to 'the hills of Limburg and going for walks in the beautiful countryside'. The interview with Wijnen took place in August 1974, and Schmidt was hired on the spot. Wijnen felt that Schmidt would be able to support him in his views and initiatives relating to examinations. It turned out that they got along very well. Wijnen had a great sense of humour, spoke with the gentle accent typical to those from Limburg's central region, and was the driving force behind the *Narren Universiteit Limburg* (NUL), the 'Jesters' University of Limburg' – an organisation that parodied the State University of Limburg, at which he would do a comedy act during carnival about all the wacky things that had been going on at the university.

THE STAGE OR UNIVERSITY? Hendricus Gerard Schmidt was born at the *Vroedvrouwenschool* (midwife school) near Heerlen in 1947. His grandparents had come to Limburg in the early 20th century. Schmidt's father was a public servant who worked at the Limburg head office of the State Mining Company, in Heerlen. The family was Reformed Protestant. While most children in Limburg went to schools like St Bernardinus or St Clara, Henk went to the Queen Wilhelmina School, and later on the Grotius College, the only co-ed secondary school in Heerlen. There he found himself among pupils whose families were also from 'Holland', as Limburg natives called it. Although Schmidt 'always identified with Limburg and its residents', he grew up in what he viewed as a kind of cultural isolation. He did not kneel down when Catholic processions marched through the streets and did not have a Limburg accent. Schmidt completed the *gymnasium* level of secondary school (i.e. pre-university education with classical languages), with a science-focused profile, though he had to repeat two of the grades. There was a specific reason for that: as a teenager, he preferred doing theatre and stand-up over doing his homework. For years, he was in all the school plays. He initially wanted to become a stage actor, but ultimately realised he did not quite have what it took to make it in the world of professional theatre. And so he ended up enrolling in a Psychology degree. He hoped to combine his studies with his interest in theatre. In the first year of his degree, he took part in the Camaretten Festival, a competition for young stand-up comedians. The first prize went to stand-up group Don Quishocking, with the second prize going to the comedy duo Bram Vermeulen and Freek de Jonge, both of whom would go on to be stand-up comedians of national renown. Schmidt et al. finished last, which 'was the end of his ambitions for the stage'. After that, he focused on his studies. He soon found he was able to make use of his acting talents as a student assistant, teaching statistics to large groups of students.

FLOWER POWER IN MAASTRICHT In the autumn of 1974, Schmidt started working at Wijnen's Education Office. He moved to Mheer, a picturesque village in the hills with plenty of opportunities for long walks in the surrounding countryside. Initially he knew very little about educational theory, but Wijnen soon caught him up on the basics. He also got to know another founding father of the basic philosophy: Harmen Tiddens, the dean of the Faculty of Medicine, which had started on an experimental basis in September. Schmidt remembers Tiddens as a charismatic man, somewhat sphinx-like, with twinkling eyes. He always 'looked very alert and pensive, he didn't say very much and had little to do with the day-to-day realities of education'. Meetings often took place in Tiddens's office – if, that is, he was not on the road as part of his work for the WHO. Tiddens and Wijnen embraced problem orientation – a key component of the basic philosophy – for different reasons. For Tiddens, it was an important tool because it offered the opportunity to put the core health problems that afflicted society at the heart of the curriculum, while Wijnen's main feeling was that it was important to promote autonomy on the part of students. For Tiddens, the reform of medical education had a mainly *social* goal, while Wijnen primarily had an *educational* goal in mind. They complemented each other perfectly.

Schmidt was joined at Wijnen's Education Office by a number of others including Peter Bouhuijs, Tjaart Imbos, Maarten Verwijnen, Hetty Snellen, and – a little later – Jos Moust. Schmidt's first move was to help to establish the skills lab.[3] But soon, alternating with the biologist Gerard Majoor, he became the coordinator of the first module: Studying at the Faculty of Medicine in Maastricht, in which students were introduced to the new educational principles. He made a series of films, sometimes with Gerard Majoor, to show students and tutors how tutorials work. One of these movies is pure comedy.[4] He acted as a tutor in the medical modules, such as Infection and Inflammation. According to the prevailing philosophy, the tutor was not necessarily required to have specific expertise on the subject matter – it was considered sufficient to play a facilitating role, providing support with the learning process. Schmidt initially found the approach to education in Maastricht to be 'rather exotic'. It reminded him of the flower power era of the late 1960s, which had had a similar emphasis on working in groups. The students would sit together in small groups smoking and debating problems. 'A few little ideas about a medical issue' would emerge from these gatherings, after which the students would diligently pore over textbooks looking up the way in which they might address the problem. According to Schmidt, the first few years were rather shambolic. 'The tutors didn't really understand what they were supposed to be doing, so they were rather at sea too. Often the learning objectives that the students pursued tended to be focused mainly on professional practice. They asked themselves: what does a GP do when someone has the flu? rather than asking: what actually is the biological process that causes flu? What type of virus is this and what does it do inside the body? Very often they would divide the work among themselves – you do this, you do that – to then spend half a day looking into the issue and sum up their findings in five minutes during the next tutorial. Of course, that didn't work.'

THE TUTORIAL SYSTEM AND THE SEVEN-STEP APPROACH During its first two years, the degree programme lacked a clear structure: the students and the tutors were not always sure what was expected of them. Every now and then, there would be an upwelling of unrest among the student body, with students writing protest letters to the Education Committee. One of the bones of contention was that, from 1974, students received 'a sort of sensitivity training' to prepare them and lay down a foundation for their work in tutorial groups. This training was very much in the spirit of the times, and was organised by the Canadian psychiatrist Norman Bell, who had been recruited on the recommendation of social psychiatrist Marius Romme. Bell was psychoanalytically oriented and, Schmidt recalls, had students evaluate each other along the lines of 'You seem fairly arrogant to me; I don't know why, but that's the feeling I've got about you'. The students thought all this was pointless waffle – they wanted to get on with it and study medicine. The training was dropped after one year. Although McMaster University in Hamilton, the birthplace of problem-based learning, did not offer specific training for tutors, there was a clear need in Maastricht for more structure to serve as guidance for the classroom.

In August 1975, Joost Bremer, professor of Medical Psychology, took the initiative of drawing up a *Handleiding voor tutoren (= begeleiders van onderwijsgroepen)* ('Manual for Tutors (= Tutorial Supervisors)').[5] That autumn, he offered a one-off training session, which he taught in tandem with Wijnen. The manual elaborated on the importance of problem-oriented learning: independent learning encouraged students to 'make use of all the options at their disposal for the acquisition of knowledge and insight, skills, as well as inventiveness and creativity'. Meanwhile, in the first module Schmidt also experimented with a training session for the students, teaching them how to engage in collaborative learning. The first experience was disappointing. Only 60% of the staff members and students who had been invited turned up – and they clearly viewed the training session as a chore. There was a distinct lack of enthusiasm for taking part. People were also frustrated with the high workload, which did not help matters.

In 1976 Schmidt became the coordinator of the Tutorial System project group, which also included Bouhuijs and Bremer. In the summer of 1977, Schmidt and Bouhuijs published the booklet *Het tutorensysteem* ('The Tutorial System') which aimed to 'provide information about the practicalities of a problem-oriented educational system'. Among other things, it discussed the types of behaviour students might display, and how the tutor should respond to them. Drawings by Chris Voskamp illustrated archetypes such as 'the quiet one', 'the criticaster', 'the talker' and 'the class clown'.[6] The Maastricht approach had come to deviate from that of McMaster University. Where at McMaster University the tutor also played the role of moderator or discussion leader – albeit one that encouraged the students to engage in independent study using the Socratic method – in Maastricht the tutor retreated more into the background, monitoring the group dynamic and the learning process from the sidelines. In Limburg, it was the students that played the role of moderator and minute-taker as a way to develop social skills in a team setting. In Maastricht there was also a heavy emphasis on the 'seven-step approach', a working strategy which had been developed by Schmidt in 1976 to better structure the learning process in the tutorials. The seven-step approach was piloted in Maastricht, but would end up being used all over the world, partly thanks to the Summer Course on Problem-Based Learning that was launched in the early 1980s and brought hundreds of university lecturers from all over the globe to Maastricht. The method consists – unsurprisingly – of seven steps: 'Step 1: Clarify unfamiliar terms. Step 2: Define the problem. Step 3: Analyse the problem. Step 4: Systematically review the different explanations that emerged during step 3. Step 5: Formulate learning objectives. Step 6: Look for additional information outside the group, for example in the library. Step 7: Synthesise and test the new information'. According to Schmidt, the idea behind the introduction of the seven-step procedure was to create order in the tutorial sessions, which until that point had often been a little chaotic. The students could use the procedure to learn how to acquire new knowledge step by step while working in groups of no more than ten participants. With the publication of the booklet *Onderwijs in taakgerichte groepen* ('Education in Task-Oriented Groups') in 1980, the seven-step approach became widely known, including outside Maastricht, and many reprints were to follow. The publisher had stated a preference for the phrase 'task-oriented groups', as he considered it unwise from a marketing perspective to have 'something with problems' in the title.[7]

PROGRESS TESTING Wijnen's primary interests lay in the field of examination. The assessment of student performance was the domain in which he exhibited great creativity. Schmidt still speaks with great admiration about Wijnen's idea of introducing a 'progress test'. This test (initially called 'screening test') consisted of 200 questions about general medicine; 10 questions on physiology, 10 on anatomy, cardiology, and so on. From 1977, all students took this test (which was continually adapted) four times a year. The progress they were making could be inferred from their successive scores on the test. What was special about the progress test was that the only way that students could prepare for it was to study regularly and diligently. Wijnen believed that this would result in a shift away from an exam-oriented approach to studying, and give students more space to explore their own interests within the subject matter. Medical specialists who may have had doubts as to what the students were learning within their particular area of expertise (a frequent issue during the first few years) could see from the results of the progress test that the students were, in fact, progressing year by year. The progress test was also used by way of an experiment at other faculties of medicine. On the whole, the knowledge level of the students in Maastricht turned out to be on a par with that of students who were being educated at conventional faculties of medicine.[8] However, the academic success rate of the eighth faculty of medicine was considerably higher from the start – evidently, small-scale problem-based learning had a singularly motivating effect.[9]

PROBLEM-ORIENTED OR PROBLEM-BASED LEARNING? However, Schmidt did not agree with Wijnen on everything. For example, he was sceptical about the intrinsic desire for independent study that Wijnen attributed to students. Schmidt felt that, while students were perfectly willing to work hard, they would benefit from some guidance in the process. In his view, the quality of the problems with which they were presented played a central role in this. They needed to be problems that would guide the learning process in the right direction. According to Schmidt, this problem-based way of working was the distinctive characteristic of the Maastricht approach, and set it apart from other types of problem-oriented education, such as project-based learning. Therefore, in 1979 he made a case for the adoption of the term 'problem-based learning' to describe the Maastricht approach.[10] In the same publication, he pointed out that not all the problems used in education needed to be derived from professional practice, and suggested that some theoretical problems of the kind that crop up in some of the many scientific disciplines that do not have an explicit professional practice as such should also be included. In his view, problem-based learning was not primarily about 'solving' problems but, more than anything, about 'understanding' problems in terms of their underlying principles and ideas. Schmidt's suggestion allowed for an expansion in the types of degree programmes in which the problem-based approach could be introduced. New programmes that were more focused on conceptual and theoretical problems than the Medical degree programme was, liked the term problem-based learning. The term came to be commonly accepted in the Netherlands, in part due to the promotional work undertaken by the State University of Limburg in the 1980s on the initiative of Rector Vic Bonke, which involved large advertisements in the national newspapers.

Schmidt also had his own views on the question of how proficient educators needed to be regarding the content of a module in order to be effective as tutors. Studies undertaken in the Faculty of Health Sciences, comparing the academic performance of students supervised by tutors who were experts on the subject matter, tutors who were not experts on the subject matter and student tutors, revealed that in the first year in particular, students benefited from the presence of expert tutors, without this getting in the way of their ability to work independently.[11]

THE ACTIVATION OF PRIOR KNOWLEDGE AND ELABORATION After Wijnen became Rector in early 1979, Schmidt succeeded him as chair of the Educational Development and Educational Research Department, the next incarnation of the Education Office. In addition, Schmidt was coordinator of the Task Force on Problem-Based Learning that formed part of the Network of Community-Oriented Educational Institutions for Health Sciences, an organisation in which he would later serve as Associate Secretary General.[12] In other words, he was active not only within the university, but also outside it. For example, between 1979 and 1984 he and Peter Bouhuijs helped to establish a new problem-based medical curriculum for the Suez Canal University in Ismailia, Egypt. As a researcher, he was a part of international research networks – for example, he regularly published with Vic Neufeld and Geoff Norman, two early McMaster staff members.[13]

In the late 1970s, Schmidt asked himself the following question: what is it that students do in those small groups? He started to 'seriously read up on the matter' and came upon literature from cognitive psychology, in which the role of prior knowledge and the integration of new and existing knowledge were described as prerequisites for 'deep learning'. In 1982, with Wijnen as his supervisor, Schmidt earned his PhD with a dissertation entitled *Activatie van voorkennis, intrinsieke motivatie en de verwerking van tekst. Studies in probleemgestuurd onderwijs*' ('The Activation of Prior Knowledge, Intrinsic Motivation and Text Comprehension. Studies in Problem-Based Learning'), a collection of six articles. This dissertation was based to a large extent on empirical research, drawing on the practical experiences with problem-based learning in Maastricht. Schmidt demonstrated how essential the role of prior knowledge is in understanding, retaining and applying new information. This conclusion implied, he argued, that differentiation and individualisation of education were not just 'buzzwords bandied about by proponents of educational reform', but were a necessity because of how the cognitive system works. Since no two people are the same, education had to be able to respond to each student's individual prior knowledge and experience. Schmidt concluded that problem-based learning, with its seven-step model as an educational method, was able to activate that prior knowledge in a way that benefited the learning process.[14]

In later publications, Schmidt went into greater detail about problem-based learning as a 'technique for elaboration'. It was already known that the brain is not capable of storing information for longer periods of time if such information is not called upon. For example, an audience is unable to concentrate on a lecture for more than ten consecutive minutes, and will forget its content soon afterwards; the learning effect of passively listening to new material is small. This is because the storing of new information requires 'elaborative attention': the brain can only store new information if it is actively processed in some way. In Schmidt's words, the brain has to 'do something with information from the surroundings before that information can be stored as a memory'. That is exactly what happens in problem-based learning during a tutorial. By systematically analysing a problem in groups, students activate their prior knowledge; this gives them a relevant context into which the new information can be coherently integrated.[15] This means that, in the tutorial, it is necessary to make students aware of the relationships between prior knowledge and the new learning task with which they are confronted. Repeated knowledge activation is the way to get new knowledge to stick.[16]

RECOGNITION The fact that the value of problem-based learning came to be increasingly recognised was partly as a result of Schmidt's scientific research. Incidentally, he had already emphasised in his dissertation that there were, undoubtedly, other educational methods out there that also focused on the activation and restructuring of prior knowledge. Recognition of the value of problem-based learning tended to come more from abroad than from within the Netherlands. The Network of Community-Oriented Educational Institutions for Health Sciences played an important role in this context. From 1987 onwards, even the medical programme at Harvard began experimenting with problem-based learning. The first quality assurance assessments that took place in the early 1990s revealed that the Maastricht Faculty of Medicine was doing well. The small-scale approach appealed to students, and the dropout rate was relatively low. In the early 1990s, the internist Geert Blijham, who had studied in Maastricht, would even take the Maastricht approach to Utrecht, where he became the driving force behind a new curriculum at the Utrecht Faculty of Medicine which was grounded in problem-based learning.[17]

In the course of the 1980s, people became increasingly interested in educational reform, as the universities were called upon to deliver greater 'quality' and 'returns' with less money per student at their disposal. The dropout rate at the midway point of the degree programme was still too high. Schmidt feels that the Educational Development and Educational Research Department did not get a lot of appreciation within the Faculty of Medicine for the work it was doing. 'Those education people' – many of whom did not come from the medical field – were not held in high regard. After Wijnen retired from his post as Rector – he would go on to turn most of his focus outside the university – Schmidt was confident that he would eventually get the opportunity to become professor. However, according to Co Greep, dean of the Faculty of Medicine, the clinicians within the faculty would not countenance the appointment of a second professor from a non-medical background. Schmidt set out for McMaster and McGill University in Canada for a year (which meant foregoing his Maastricht salary; at the time, sabbaticals did not yet exist at Dutch universities) to broaden his perspective. The Network of Community-Oriented Educational Institutions for Health Sciences was not happy with his departure for Canada, and proceeded to put pressure on Rector Vic Bonke, who was quick to take action. He came up with the idea of appointing Schmidt for the Tans rotating chair in 1987, which had been established to stimulate educational reform. In 1988, Schmidt joined the Faculty of Health Sciences, where in 1990 he became professor of Educational Methodology in

Health Sciences. Louis Boon, professor of Health Care Ethics and Philosophy, had at that time just become dean of the Faculty of Health Sciences, and he and Schmidt became good friends. They had similar interests: the quality of education, Apple computers and the great outdoors – although Boon was an animal lover and Schmidt was more interested in hiking. Schmidt soon joined the Faculty Board and was given responsibility for the Educational Affairs portfolio. In 1993, he succeeded Boon as dean and, together with Boon, helped to establish the Faculty of Psychology, where he became professor of Cognitive Psychology. However, shortly after the new faculty had been established, Schmidt and the other professors became embroiled in a conflict with Boon.[18] According to Schmidt, this conflict did not stem so much from differences of opinion as from Boon's 'abrasive management style' as dean.

DATA FROM ROTTERDAM AND MAASTRICHT In 2001, Schmidt moved on to Erasmus University Rotterdam, where he was given the opportunity to establish a new Psychology degree programme based on 'classical' problem-based learning. He accepted the challenge because he believes he performs best in pioneering roles. In addition, Maastricht had come to have an increasingly lackadaisical approach to things like safeguarding the small size of tutorial groups. According to Schmidt, the foundation of problem-based learning was at risk of caving in if its essential building blocks were removed. Schmidt soon became dean of the Faculty of Social Sciences at Rotterdam, and between 2009 and 2013 served as Rector. He did not miss the hills of Limburg as much as he had expected. He did remain faithful to problem-based learning though, and helped to implement the 'Maastricht system' in three different faculties in Rotterdam. Rotterdam had brought him in as an 'education guru'. However, he prefers to be known as the person who gave problem-based learning its empirical foundation. He is one of the most-cited academics in the world in the field of research into medical education.[19]

From Rotterdam, he continued to publish on the basis of the Maastricht data. He demonstrated that the competencies that Maastricht alumni had developed during their studies (such as writing skills, working under time pressure, various social skills, and working independently) stood them in very good stead in their professional practice as doctors, and they were more successful in these areas than Rotterdam alumni. He found that, looking back, Maastricht alumni had a positive view of problem-based learning, in particular because it gave them the opportunity to practise the competencies that would turn out to be so relevant in their later work.[20]

Problem-based learning is an international success story – Schmidt can rightly make that claim nowadays.[21] But to what extent is its success contingent on the field in which this educational method was developed, i.e. medicine? In his research, Schmidt's main focus has been on the effectiveness of problem-based learning in medical programmes. The question therefore remains as to the extent to which this educational approach can be 'translated' for use in non-medical programmes, such as Law and Economics.

9 *Job Cohen* THE NEW APPROACH TO TEACHING LAW AIMED TO PRODUCE NOT BETTER BUT MORE MOTIVATED LEGAL PROFESSIONALS

MAASTRICHT AND THE LEIDEN CONNECTION A few years on from the start of the Maastricht experiment, what were the findings? In the early 1980s, problem-based learning was still viewed with a fair amount of scepticism, though people were beginning to be curious about how this new approach had worked in practice so far. There had been interest in educational reform at Leiden University since the late 1960s. On the 10-year anniversary of the Leiden Bureau of Educational Research in 1978, one of its employees, lawyer Job Cohen, declared: 'How about we celebrate this occasion by doing something? How about we go to Maastricht? They seem to be doing something special over there'.[1] The director of the Bureau, Hans Crombag – who had studied Psychology in Nijmegen – thought this was an excellent idea. Crombag was a friend of Paul Thung, a lecturer in Medicine who was interested in educational reform in Leiden and one of the driving forces behind discussions and initiatives about innovation in education, and medical education in particular.[2] Thung was advising the Executive Board of the State University of Limburg on how best to structure the General Faculty. He was curious as to whether problem-based learning could also be applied in the context of a Law degree.[3]

Crombag and Cohen were not only close to Thung, but also to their colleague Wynand Wijnen, who at that time was the Rector at the State University of Limburg. Before long they had set a date for the excursion to Maastricht. And this is how, in early 1978, a number of employees from the oldest university of the Netherlands (established in 1575) found themselves on the doorstep of the newly established State University of Limburg. The Faculty of Medicine was the only part of the university that was fully operational at the time. The Leiden delegation got the opportunity to experience problem-based learning up close in the old Jesuit monastery on Tongersestraat, where

the Faculty of Medicine was based back then. They returned home 'tired but satisfied'. On the way back, Cohen was full of ideas about the Maastricht experiment, which 'completely fascinated' him. Together with Crombag, Cohen went on to write an article, *De nieuwe medische faculteit in Maastricht en de juridische opleiding* ('The new Faculty of Medicine in Maastricht and the Law degree programme'), which was published in *Nederlands Juristenblad* (the Dutch lawyers' journal). Cohen sent a copy to Wijnen to show him what their visit had yielded. Down in Maastricht, the article was read with rapt attention. The authors claimed that problem-based learning could be a good way to structure a Law degree programme. This was an audacious statement. Problem-based learning had originally been developed within the context of medical training, and until that point it had not been used outside of this context anywhere in the world. Was it really suited to a Law degree programme? Were legal professionals not known for their attachment to traditions and conventions? Cohen was invited to a follow-up meeting in Maastricht to discuss the possibility of establishing a Law degree programme. Who was this lawyer who was willing to entertain the thought of conceiving of 'a Limburg-style Law degree programme'?[4]

AN UNORTHODOX LAWYER Marius Job Cohen was born in 1947 and grew up in a non-Orthodox Jewish household in Haarlem. He had been familiar with the academic world since childhood: both of his parents had a History degree. His parental home was open-minded and politically progressive. His parents felt at home in the PvdA (Labour) party, which had been established in 1946 and aimed to bring together all progressive forces in the country. After secondary school, in 1966, Cohen went to Groningen to study Law – not because he was particularly motivated by the subject, but because he did not know what else to study. He never regretted his decision: he 'learned a great deal' – even if he 'wasn't a particularly diligent student'. At the age of eighteen, Cohen joined the PvdA, and he experienced the cultural revolution of the 1960s as being 'a very exciting time'. He was active in the student movement – not in the radical wing, incidentally – and became the first student to join the Faculty Board. In Groningen, he not only met his future wife Lidie Lodeweges, but he also became close friends with fellow student Jeppe Balkema, who would later go with him to Maastricht. During his studies he also met Hans Crombag, who gave a lecture in Groningen about his doctoral dissertation, which explored the extent to which students who belonged to a student association were more successful in their studies than those who did not. Cohen considered Crombag to be 'an interesting person, a cool guy', and someone who was not afraid of polemics. Shortly before his graduation, Cohen stumbled upon a job advertisement in a newsletter published by the Leiden Faculty of Law. Crombag was looking for 'an unorthodox lawyer, capable of thinking out of the box' for his bureau in Leiden. Cohen did not hesitate for a second. He applied for the position and was hired after an interview. He could start the job in 1971.

The Bureau of Educational Research, headed up by Crombag, had been established to research education, with the goal of course of bringing about improvements in teaching. There was great interest in new educational methods at the Faculty of Law in particular, as relatively many students dropped out partway through their degree programmes due to insufficient motivation. The faculty was also somewhat at a loss as to how to cope with the large numbers of new students who were enrolling. The idea was that the emphasis in the Law degree programme should come to be more on the acquisition of skills and analytical ability than on obtaining factual knowledge. It was up to Cohen to review the Law degree programme. He did evaluative research and reflected on the question of how legal and academic skills could be prioritised more within the degree programme.[5] As part of this effort, a new practical, Legal Methods and Techniques, was developed. After a number of years, Cohen started working on a doctoral dissertation about the legal position of students. He was 'under no obligation' to complete a PhD, but he felt compelled to address this topic, which had cropped up directly in his own life. His wife Lidie was taking a long time in getting her degree, because the supervision and evaluation of her PhD dissertation were fraught with unexpected delays.

Cohen was still in the middle of his doctoral research when, after publication of the article in *Nederlands Juristenblad*, he was invited to give a follow-up lecture on it in Maastricht. He was drawn to Maastricht. In a way, his father Dolf Cohen, professor of Medieval History at Leiden University, had played a part in the State University of Limburg's inception. As the head of the Board of Rectors, Cohen Senior had given a speech on 9 January 1976 to welcome the 'youngest sister'. On this occasion, he had emphasised the idiosyncratic nature of the State University of Limburg, which because of its location offered 'opportunities that transcended boundaries' – not only as far as research was concerned, but also in terms of education 'in our not-yet-united Europe'. He also spoke about the General Faculty in development, which could serve as a 'testing ground for what higher education could look like in the future'.[6] Of course, he could not have anticipated at the time that his son Job Cohen would come to play a role in this.

EXPANSION AND A FIRST OUTLINE The discussion about how best to structure the General Faculty was in full swing when Cohen and Crombag's article was published in May 1978. At the State University of Limburg, plans were underway for a Social Health Science degree programme, but in early 1978 there was no consensus about how the university was to grow further. Sjeng

Kremers, the Queen's Commissioner for Limburg, had a clear vision. During a meeting with President of the Executive Board Rob van den Biggelaar and grand old man Sjeng Tans – though when exactly this took place can no longer be established – Kremers, by his own account, dismissed the suggested option of a Policy Studies degree programme. Given the unfavourable economic climate, he urgently recommended that they focus on degree programmes that drew large numbers of students and had low overheads: Law and Economics.[7] Van den Biggelaar and Tans allowed themselves to be convinced. The article by Cohen and Crombag was more than welcome in all this. From that moment onwards, the Limburg lobby was able to present a united front towards The Hague, with, in the first instance, the goal of establishing a Law degree programme. In the course of 1978, they ratcheted up the political pressure on Minister of Education, Culture and Science Arie Pais (from the VVD liberal party) to get the go-ahead for the expansion of the State University of Limburg.

The famous Deetman motion in late 1978 marked a turning point. The State University of Limburg now had the support of the House of Representatives in moving towards further expansion.[8] In the summer of 1979, a first *Schets van een juridische studierichting aan de Rijksuniversiteit Limburg* ('Outline for a Law degree programme at the State University of Limburg') was published. Cohen and Crombag had contributed to this document, but according to Cohen, Thung – 'a great man with a broad vision' – had provided the primary effort behind it. The authors wanted the Law degree programme to be housed within the General Faculty for now, as the establishment of a third faculty would require a time-consuming change in legislation. The idea was that the new Law degree programme would be based on the same educational principles as those of the Faculty of Medicine. In order to have a distinct identity 'of its own', the programme had to be both vocationally oriented and problem-based. The first question was: what professions did Law graduates end up practising? Research revealed that only a minority ended up in the courtroom. Many legal professionals worked in settings where expertise relating to law and regulations came in handy, but there were also many Law graduates whose subsequent job was not directly related to their studies at all.

If 'Maastricht' wanted to produce Law graduates who were well-equipped for professional practice, according to the *Outline* it was necessary for them to be confronted with concrete issues – as was also the case in the Medical degree programme. In addition, the students had to come to understand that Law was not a standalone discipline, but was part of a broader social, political, economic and cultural context. The degree programme should not be structured according to different branches of law, but by the thematic fields that Law graduates would encounter in professional practice, such as 'housing', 'forms of cohabitation' and 'freedom and coercion'. The outline was very much focused on 'skills' – with language skills being a key area of focus – again with the objective of preparing Law students for their future roles in society. The Maastricht Law degree programme would distinguish itself from existing Law programmes by employing the experimental approach and an emphasis on 'social relevance'.[9] At the same time, the challenge was to find a middle ground and not be too 'out there'. The curriculum had to be credible in the eyes of the outside world, which meant that it had to be compatible with the existing University Statute and meet the requirements of the *Wet op de rechterlijke organisatie* (Judiciary (Organisation) Act) and the *Advocatenwet* (Counsel Act).[10]

LAW IN MAASTRICHT: A FUNDAMENTALLY NEW APPROACH The 'Outline for a Law degree programme at the State University of Limburg' was the first step. How would this document be received by the Minister and the other universities? The feedback from the Ministry was positive. They appreciated the thematic approach, and felt that the establishment of a Law degree programme in Maastricht might also help relieve the nationwide shortage of study places in Law programmes: there seemed to be no end to the number of students applying to study Law. Most universities were also enthusiastic about the thematic approach, though some more so than others. Leiden University was particularly excited: in the autumn of 1979, they made clear they were keen to be involved in further developing the plans being made in Maastricht. Only Nijmegen and Tilburg expressed criticism: they urged Maastricht to undertake an evaluative study of problem-based learning at the Faculty of Medicine before introducing this method in the context of a Law degree programme. Also, they added, they were willing to expand their own programmes in order to address the national capacity issues. In November 1979, Maastricht received good news. In a meeting between the Dutch cabinet and the provincial government, Prime Minister Dries van Agt (CDA, Christian-Democrats) revealed that the cabinet had agreed in principle to the establishment of a Law degree programme at the State University of Limburg.

In early 1980, they started the search for 'a Tiddens in the legal domain': a charismatic personality with infectious enthusiasm for educational reform. The Board asked Crombag for suggestions, but no names came immediately to mind for him.[11] Unlike when the Social Health Science degree programme was established, this time around the university had to call in expertise from outside. The university did not have many lawyers at this point. For this reason, Van den Biggelaar went on a tour of all the faculties of law in the Netherlands to find the right people for the 'preparatory committee for the Law degree programme in Maastricht'. Of course, he was looking to get 'the bigger names' onside: the committee would need a sufficient air of authority in the legal world.[12] Only from Nijmegen did Van den Biggelaar return empty-handed. The final make-up of the preparatory committee included more than ten legal experts from all over the country, as well as several employees from the State University of Limburg. The Leiden connection was especially striking. Cohen ended up having an impact on the establishment of the committee, which included both his friend Balkema – who at the time was senior lecturer in Criminal Law at the University of Groningen – and his PhD supervisor, professor of Constitutional Law Tim Koopmans from Leiden, who had a special interest in educational reform. Cees Flinterman, who at the time was working for the Ministry of Foreign Affairs, was also involved. Cohen had previously worked together with Flinterman, Koopmans and Karl Dittrich (a university lecturer in Political Science) to introduce the new subject of Dutch Government and Politics in Leiden – an interdisciplinary admixture of constitutional law and political science. At 32, Cohen was the youngest member of the committee and the only one who had not yet obtained his PhD.

The preparatory committee, headed up by Thung, worked fast: the commencement of the Law degree programme was scheduled for 1982. According to Flinterman, the committee only convened two or three times. The members were received hospitably, with sumptuous lunches and fancy dinners at a posh restaurant.[13] There was a positive atmosphere: the committee members had the sense that getting the go-ahead for the new Law programme was essentially a done deal, and everyone on the committee was on board with the problem-based learning approach. After three months, in late 1980, the committee presented the report, *Rechten in Maastricht. Plan voor een juridische studierichting aan de Rijksuniversiteit Limburg te Maastricht* ('Law in Maastricht. Plan for a Law degree programme at the State University of Limburg in Maastricht'). This document was essentially a continuation of the previously made outline. The central objective of the degree programme became to 'produce good lawyers', i.e. 'people who are capable of recognising the problems presented to them and, where necessary, coming up with solutions that are both legally and socially relevant'.[14] According to the authors, there were three educational advantages to the new thematic approach: knowledge that was subsequently put into practice tended to be retained; learning by discovery helped students get an idea of lay of the land in professional practice; and knowledge that was clearly anchored in reality invited them to explore new areas of expertise. The problems to be studied needed to cover all the core branches of Law, so the students would be moved from the initial social reality towards legal expertise and understanding. *Rechten in Maastricht* devoted considerable attention to skills training, especially language skills, while also emphasising the importance of practicals, such as the 'Methods and Techniques' practical that had been established in Leiden, and a moot court. Maastricht wanted to produce well-rounded professionals who were aware of the social context of law and capable of practising law in a wide range of different contexts.

Although the new Law programme hoped to break through traditional boundaries, there was no getting around the fact that the building blocks of the curriculum had to come from the traditional sub-disciplines. After all, this was how the study of law was organised. The suggestion was made of establishing departments for the fields of private law, constitutional and administrative law, criminal law, international law and the interdisciplinary study of law (auxiliary sciences such as legal history, philosophy of law and legal psychology). Thung was adamant that they start recruiting a core faculty team and Crown-appointed professors as soon as possible, so that everything would be ready in time to receive the first 100 Law students in 1982. Things were rolling along nicely. Within six months, all the procedural hurdles had been cleared; the Academic Council, too, gave Maastricht the go-ahead. Minister of Education, Culture and Science Arie Pais gave his approval on 19 June 1981.

THE TRAILBLAZERS Confident that it would be a success, Thung had previously asked Cohen to be in charge of the Maastricht experiment. Cohen was a committed proponent of problem-based learning, which he felt was 'inspiring and beautiful'. After having worked at the Leiden Bureau of Educational Research for over a decade – and being situated somewhat on the outskirts of the university – he was also ready for the next stage in his life. Cohen thought it was 'fantastic' that he was getting the opportunity, at such a young age, to play the role of 'trailblazer' in establishing a Law degree programme. Nine days before Pais gave the definitive go-ahead, Cohen successfully defended his PhD dissertation on *Studierechten in het wetenschappelijk onderwijs* ('Study Entitlements in Academic Higher Education') in Leiden, with Koopmans as his supervisor. As the chair of the General Faculty's Dutch Law Committee, he was now able to devote all of his energy to the Maastricht adventure. It did take him a while to find his feet in Maastricht. In the first few weeks, he was too afraid 'to open his mouth' in shops, instead just pointing at what he wanted to buy. After that, he began to 'fall increasingly in love' with his new life.

In September 1981, Cohen, together with Dittrich, entered the former Jesuit monastery on Tongersestraat. Dittrich had accompanied him to Maastricht because the plan was that the new Law degree programme would be placing a great deal of emphasis on the social context of law. After obtaining his PhD in 1978, Dittrich had worked on a scholarship in Florence for a year, but this seemed like a good time for him to return to his hometown of Maastricht. He still harboured the dream of one day becoming chairman of the local football club, MVV Maastricht.[15] Cohen remembers the pair of them walking into their office to be welcomed by secretary Victor Rutgers, who had been appointed some time prior, and had until that point held a different position at the General Faculty. Some time later, Balkema joined them, followed by four other employees – most of whom were still young: Alma van Bers, Hans Lensing, Gerard Mols and Jan Willems.[16] Flinterman, René de Groot and Wim Beurskens arrived in early 1982.[17] These nine men and one woman were given twelve months to prepare the first year of the programme. No one had had any prior experience with this, but there was great enthusiasm for educational reform among the team. According to Cohen, they 'talked endlessly about problem-based learning'. According to Dittrich, the entire endeavour was 'completely insane', as they lacked even something as elementary as a library.[18] Thanks to De Groot's research work, they soon discovered that the 250,000-volume library in the old Jesuit monastery included a fantastic collection of legal publications. De Groot saved the books in the nick of time from being relocated to a damp basement.[19]

The trailblazers were trained in problem-based learning by the Education Office, i.e. 'Wijnen's club'. Henk Schmidt, Peter Bouhuijs and Jos Moust – the latter went on to work at the Faculty of Law as an educational expert – assisted in the implementation of problem-based learning, making use of their own experience. The new employees had to read the basic philosophy from A to Z, even though it was focused on teaching medicine. They were expected to have this core text by their side at all times: 'on your bedside table and under your pillow'.[20] Cohen remembers that the lecturers gained experience by practicing with Medical students. He was also a huge proponent of progress tests. 'I was all about the ideology. I felt that was how we were supposed to do things. I considered it a great, clear system.' However, it turned out not everyone was as enthusiastic about the progress tests. The outline of the curriculum was simply copied from the Faculty of Medicine and the Social Health Science degree programme that had begun in 1980. In addition to six 6-week modules on topics such as regulations, agreements, unlawful behaviour and law enforcement, there were practicals such as Case Studies and Moot Court. The case studies used for this purpose in Leiden were copied 'wholesale'.[21]

When putting together the module readers, heated discussions would sometimes break out about the role of law in society. After all, the way lawyers think is very much driven by norms and standards.[22] Should law be taught through the lens of issues about law and justice, tying into the philosophy of law, sociology and criminology – i.e. broader social developments – in order to encourage a critical attitude towards the legal system – as Mols and Van Bers, with their sociocritical perspective, felt? Or, as Balkema argued, should the primary focus be on the system of law, on the formal laws and regulations in place – exactly because justice was at stake?[23] In these types of discussions, Cohen tended to be more on Balkema's side, but he felt that the most important thing was that these debates should be happening. The discussion should never end, as in an educational setting it was essential that people learned to deal with uncertainties.[24]

PROFESSOR OF LAW, IN PARTICULAR... In 1982, Cohen was the head of the Dutch Law Committee, but he was not a professor. He had, however, drawn up a 'Crown-appointed professor plan' for the appointment of five professors of Constitutional Law, Criminal Law, Private Law, International Law and Administrative Law. According to Cohen, the idea was that he himself would become professor of Constitutional Law, but the sister faculties blocked this from happening. Rightly so, he felt in retrospect; after all, he had 'never before worked in the area of constitutional law'. Incidentally, in Maastricht, the appointment of professors whose field of study was explicitly stated was viewed as 'an anachronism'. Just as in the US, all lecturers – regardless of their rank – were tasked first and foremost with 'teaching law', followed by a specification.

The idea had been to appoint Flinterman as 'professor of Law, in particular International Law'. However, the opportunity suddenly emerged to put Theo van Boven up for this post. Van Boven had lost his job as head of the United Nations Human Rights Committee because of his open criticism of the dictatorial regimes in South America. The countries in question, which were UN member states, had used their influence to remove Van Boven. Flinterman was excited to welcome Van Boven to Maastricht, as the latter had already gained the reputation of being a heavyweight, while the founding fathers of the Law degree programme were not yet very well-known at this stage.[25] They found a solution for Flinterman by appointing him 'professor of Law, in particular Constitutional and International Law'. Soon afterwards, Balkema was appointed 'professor of Law, in particular Criminal Law'. Cohen was kept waiting for some time. A new chair with a long title was created for him. In September 1983, he became 'professor of Law, in particular Legal Methods and Techniques for Developing Legal Education'. According to Cohen, this appointment was ultimately 'circumstantial': he was required to be a professor in order to become dean of the Faculty of Law, established in 1984.[26] Around the time that Cohen was appointed professor of Law, Twan Tak became 'professor of Law, in particular Administrative Law', while Jacques Elders became 'professor of Law, in particular Private Law'. Twak and Elders were both slightly older, and had already established reputations for themselves in the legal world. This was not insignificant, as the new degree programme was subject to critical external scrutiny. In keeping with Wijnen's ideas, none of the professors gave inaugural addresses. After all, the Law degree programme did not use the lecture format either and, according to Flinterman, the professors – all of whom, incidentally, were men – wanted to truly live according to the tenets of problem-based learning.[27]

A DIFFERENT APPROACH At the commencement of the degree programme in September 1982, all of the nearly 100 first-year Law students received a copy of the booklet *Onderwijs in taakgerichte groepen* ('Education in Task-Oriented Groups') by Schmidt and Bouhuijs, with a preface by Wijnen. After the first few months, the degree programme moved from Tongersestraat to De Nieuwenhof, a former monastery which had been refurbished especially for the purpose. The lecturers were possibly even more nervous about the first tutorials than the students. Cohen thought things had got off to a fantastic start: the first batch of students turned out to be very engaged. He considered it an advantage that a relatively large proportion of the student body were older students from Limburg who were seizing the opportunity of undertaking a university degree. These older students had already gained social experience out in the world and understood what it was all about. According to Cohen, the first practical experiences were 'not bad at all'. The students were very much aware that they were part of 'the experiment' and that their progress was being closely monitored by the lecturers. The students and the faculty members were very close. The tutorials never involved more than 10 students, while the numbers for the practicals never exceeded 25. The lecturers met every Wednesday morning to discuss the problems they had come up against in practice. The role of tutor was found to be challenging: tutors who were experts on the subject at hand had a hard time taking a hands-off approach to teaching, while those who were not experts felt insecure.

In the course of that first year, it already became apparent that the thematic approach came with its share of challenges and complications. Approaching legal issues thematically made it difficult for students to structure their knowledge. The required reading tended to be subject-based. Another problem that soon presented itself concerned all the essays that the students were required to write every term. According to Cohen, this aspect of the curriculum revealed a 'refreshing naiveté'. In practice, it turned out the students spent so much time on these essays – which largely determined their grade – that they ended up not having enough time to study the course material. This meant that the required essay-writing inadvertently promoted a focus on exams, which ran completely counter to the principles of problem-based learning. After the first year, the decision was made to reduce the number of essays that students were required to write.

ONWARDS AND UPWARDS An educational experiment, by definition, requires a willingness to make adjustments further down the line, where necessary, based on practical experience. The new approach sparked a great deal of debate among the faculty members. There was a growing need for a root-and-branch review as the number of students increased (with 300 first-years enrolling every year from 1984), the pressure rose and staff numbers increased.

Some of the new employees did not share the same educational ideals that had brought the first influx to Maastricht. In early 1985, Cohen made an initial attempt to jumpstart a discussion about education in the faculty. He did not shy away from critical questions about the thematic structure of the curriculum, the skills-based approach and the effectiveness of the tutorials.[28] Some faculty members and students were 'over the moon' about the degree programme, while others were 'deeply unhappy' with the state of affairs.[29]

As a professor of Legal Methods and Techniques and the Development of Legal Education, Cohen played a linchpin role in the discussion about the shape of the curriculum. He felt there was still a lot of enthusiasm for the Maastricht approach to education among the lecturers and – not least importantly – the students, but some doubt had begun to creep in too. Was this 'challenging educational concept' successful in reality? Were the students learning enough? Did the degree programme succeed in producing lawyers with sufficient skills and expertise to function in the courtroom setting, if that was what the students desired? The outside world had originally regarded the unconventional Maastricht degree programme, 'run by all those PvdA guys', with a fair amount of suspicion. People wondered if the programme was essentially just a training school for 'legal aid lawyers'.[30] These sorts of questions all went into 'the large-scale educational debate' that was held in 1986.

Together with Flinterman and Mols, among others, Cohen contributed to the discussion paper with the 'great title' *Doorgaan, maar beter* ('Onwards and Upwards'), which was published in the spring of 1986. The title alone made clear that the authors were not advocating the abolition of 'the system' – a move for which there was ultimately little enthusiasm in the faculty. Least of all from Cohen, who felt problem-based learning was a 'great concept that the faculty should carry on putting into practice'.[31] According to Flinterman, no one wanted to jettison problem-based learning altogether. It had also turned out that, among the small pilot group, this approach appeared to be successful in keeping students motivated: the dropout rate among Law students in Maastricht was relatively low. Only a few people – like Nico Roos, who since 1985 had been a professor of Interdisciplinary Law – felt that 'the Maastricht system' was not suitable for all lecturers or students. He argued in favour of two groups of students: one group consisting of students who had deliberately chosen to study according to the Maastricht model, and another made up of those who would be taught in the traditional way. However, Roos was alone in advocating this approach.

In the spring of 1986, the entire faculty went on a retreat to an estate near Lanaken in Belgium. They debated 'until they dropped' about the issues that had been outlined in *Doorgaan, maar beter*.[32] Cohen, who had initially been a 'purist', was now open to a less dogmatic approach. The Education Committee felt the curriculum lacked a content-based structure. They wanted to stick to the original principles without getting too hung up on them. Of course, getting all the faculty members to agree was going to be a mission impossible; the faculty was, after all, full of 'idiosyncratic individualists'. The thematic approach was the most hotly-debated topic during the course of the retreat. Critics argued that the curriculum was overfull and disorganised, leaving students unable to see the wood for the trees. Most felt that theme-based education could not yet be called a success. A few people even felt that it should be abolished altogether, arguing that the students were alarmingly unclear as to the structure and systems underlying the individual classical areas of law. That fear resulted in 'separatist behaviour from lecturers', i.e. tutors essentially giving mini-lectures. It had also proved tricky to teach the subjects that formed part of the interdisciplinary study of law as part of the thematic approach. In the absence of a broader context, chunks of legal history or philosophy of law were scattered 'piecemeal' across the different modules. The proposed solution was to stick with the thematic approach, but to reduce the number of disciplines included in each thematic module. The subjects that formed part of the interdisciplinary study of law, meanwhile, should be taught in lectures. Experiences with the teaching of 'legal skills' were largely positive. Maastricht's focus on professional practice entailed an emphasis on text analysis and a methodical approach to case studies. Moot court had got off to a rough start, but plans for a new approach were already underway. There was also broad support for the idea of setting up a Legal Aid Clinic following the American example: a form of practice-based learning that enabled students to practice law in professional settings, under the supervision of qualified lawyers.

Opinions about the effectiveness of the tutorials varied. The students were motivated by problem-based learning as a didactic principle, but it turned out some were frustrated by the exclusive focus on the 'seven-step approach'. This educational method assumed that activating existing knowledge was important when acquiring and retaining new knowledge. However, there were serious doubts about this basic idea. Various faculty members believed that the students had no existing knowledge to draw on and that the seven-step approach was too unwieldy. The idea was to encourage experiments with other types of assignments: discussions, strategic tasks and more traditional study assignments. There was also the issue of 'passive students' in the tutorials. When faced with this problem, a number of tutors had the tendency to focus at length on their own specialism. The faculty members had extensive discussions about how actively tutors should guide students, and how much of an expert on the subject matter at hand they were required to be. Cohen himself did not believe that tutors should necessarily be experts on the topics they were teaching, but he did feel that, for some students, a certain degree of proactive guidance was necessary. Co-founding father Flinterman, on the other hand, was a strong proponent of having tutors in place who were experts in the relevant discipline. It was suggested that they settle on a middle ground: students would be given the opportunity to put any questions their tutor was unable to answer to an expert during a weekly 'question time' session.

The lecturers also struggled with Wynand Wijnen's invention: the progress test. This test was based on the notion that problem-based learning should put an end to an exam-oriented approach to studying.[33] After all, you could not prepare for the progress test. After doing away with the essays students were required to submit after each module, the faculty had begun administering module examinations instead, which ran counter to the ideal of a non-exam-oriented approach to learning. For this reason, Cohen was unhappy about this move. He was a firm believer in the merits of the progress test. Although not everyone was a fan, they decided for the time being not to dispense with it – after all, according to Cohen, ultimately it was 'so integral to the Maastricht approach that it was impossible to make a real case against it'. The decision was made to carry on with the module exams as well. Most employees were happy with a pragmatic way forward and 'toning down the overly dogmatic elements of the curriculum'.[34] One of the members of the original team, lecturer in Criminal Law Hans Lensing, was disappointed with the Maastricht approach. He felt the faculty had failed to address the issue of the heavy workload. His suggestion was to replace the tutorials with 30-student working groups focused on ensuring the students would get a firm grasp of the basics of law. Lensing was unable to bring his colleagues on board with the idea. Later, he would leave his post in Maastricht for a job at Radboud University Nijmegen.

STEADFAST, BUT FLEXIBLE AND WITH MODERATION... The Education Committee responded to the 'large-scale educational debate' by making an effort to better prepare lecturers for their role, offering more training sessions and devoting greater attention to the roles of tutor and practical teacher. Under the motto 'steadfast, but flexible and with moderation' – as Wim Beurskens, lecturer in Civil Law, who was involved in the restructuring, put it – a 'more moderate version of theme-based education' was established. The new curriculum was more geared towards giving students an understanding of the structure and internal coherence of the classical areas of law. Each module tended to focus on just two areas, or three at the most, so that the students were less likely to get confused and overwhelmed. However, settling on an approach to the subjects that formed part of the interdisciplinary study of law continued to be tricky. For legal history, they 'went back to a lecture format'. Another problem was that individual teachers in the graduation phase of the programme continued to offer courses which tended to be highly specialised, with no fewer than 60 electives on the curriculum.[35] What was typical at Maastricht was that skills training played an essential role. Now, the practicals became even more important. According to Cohen, the number of practicals in the areas of legal, social and academic skills was 'considerable'. Several new practicals had been added to the curriculum, such as practicals in negotiation and in conversational skills, as well as an elective module on Legal Practice at the State University of Limburg, which was a follow-up course to the District Court Nieuwenhof moot court, a type of testing ground for solving legal problems. While these practicals were very attractive to students, they turned out to be extremely labour-intensive for the lecturers. Whereas a small-scale approach to teaching came naturally to their 'brothers at the Faculty of Medicine', the only way for this to work at the Faculty of Law was for there to be a better student-faculty ratio, according to Cohen. He came to the conclusion that, if the budgetary means at their disposal remained the same, they would have to cut down on the range of courses on offer.[36] Cohen's 'mentor', Crombag, who in 1987 had become professor of Legal Psychology at Maastricht, completely agreed with this point of view.[37] There were more and more complaints among the faculty members about the workload resulting from 'the Maastricht system'. In the late 1980s, the faculty had in excess of 1,000 students, and the 'academic success rate' was on the decline. Some faculty members complained that they did not have enough time to do research, while expectations in that area were only increasing from the mid-1980s onwards.

THE MAASTRICHT CHALLENGE One of the founding fathers, Cohen's friend Balkema, also grew disillusioned with 'the Maastricht challenge'. In late 1987, Balkema left to accept a post as a justice at the Arnhem Court of Appeal. This was a milestone, prompting Flinterman to think: 'Gosh, we're a proper faculty now: we not only have people coming, but also people going'.[38] Balkema felt the programme had come to be too focused on 'what' instead of 'how' the students were learning. The original objective of producing well-rounded graduates, 'which there was a tremendous need for in the professional world', had given way to the 'temptations of specialisation'. In addition, lecturers tended increasingly to stick to their own specialisms. Balkema felt that the Faculty of Law, with its distinct educational philosophy, should acknowledge that it was primarily a faculty of education.[39] He felt that the experiment could have been allowed to go on for longer without the compromises that had been made further down the line. Balkema himself enjoyed teaching much more than developing research programmes. However, the pressure to contribute research to the field kept increasing. The faculty had several research projects already, such as Human Rights, Legislation and Local Politics, but according to Cohen the research still had a very individualistic focus. For Cohen, Balkema's departure was a tremendous loss. The times of being 'one big family' were over. Also, Cohen ultimately 'wasn't all that interested' in doing research. He does not remember having done a lot of it. 'I did publish all sorts of things, but I lost nearly all of them.' In those days, Cohen recalls, professors could still 'get away with that'.

A MANAGEMENT ROLE IS OK Cohen did not hesitate long when, in early 1989, he once again had the opportunity to become dean. Crombag's first, short-lived stint as dean had not proved a success. After a conflict on the Board, he had quit.[40] Cohen was on sabbatical at the time, but he was happy to accept the deanship a second time. He quite enjoyed being in a management role. His relaxed approach to the position reflected this. During meetings, he often sat back in his chair, listening attentively. Although he was not keen on poring over reams of paperwork, he was capable of getting to the heart of complex issues at lightning speed. In debates, he had an air of intellectual gravitas and authority and could also enjoy being ironic and, at times, sarcastic.[41] But more than anything, he was known as 'a harmonious being', a diplomatic builder of bridges who – even then – always tried to hold things together. Those were the qualities the faculty needed from him, because there was a great deal of debate about the workload of the degree programme, the new Tax Law degree programme that was to begin in 1990, and whether or not further internationalisation was desirable. Since the mid-1980s, students had been encouraged to spend one or two course periods abroad on an Erasmus scholarship, for example in Lancaster, Trier, Trento, Nancy, Dublin, Salamanca or Brussels. Around 1990, the question arose as to whether Europe and European law should be more prominently featured in the degree programme. Together with De Groot and Flinterman, Cohen organised an international conference in Maastricht to discuss the future of the degree programme. It was at this conference, held in 1991, that De Groot made the suggestion of establishing a European Law School, in which it would be the *ius commune Europaeum*, rather than the national legal system, that would be the core focus of the curriculum.[42] Cohen opened the conference, but he was no longer dean by then. After a curious appointment procedure, in the summer of 1990 he had – to this own surprise as well – become Rector of the university.[43] He succeeded the physiologist Vic Bonke, who had been Rector for six years. On the Executive Board, he met Loek Vredevoogd, an economist who had been President since the spring of 1987, and his companion Dittrich, who had been the third member since early 1986. When Vredevoogd asked him about his ambitions as Rector, he replied: 'I don't really want all that much. I want the people within the university to be able to do their jobs'. He mainly saw himself playing the role of a 'servant rector'. He went on to play a constructive role by, as he put it, 'oiling the machine'.

RECTOR WITH A NEW STRATEGIC DIRECTION? Although he was the first non-physician to become Rector, Cohen did not intend to break with the strategic direction set by his predecessor – even if he felt that Bonke was very different from himself. Bonke thought in terms of market forces: his ideal was a fully-privatised university with autonomous, financially independent faculties. He felt this would enable the university to strengthen its competitive edge over other universities and be more 'enterprising' in responding to the market. According to Cohen, however, higher education was a fundamental part of the public sector. He feared that a network of privatised universities would jeopardise 'culture and history, the accessibility of education and fundamental research'. While Cohen did agree that, given social developments, contacts and contracts between the business community and the university may be necessary – the days of 'the ivory tower' were past – the university had nonetheless to remain alert to the dangers inherent in this partnership: it should not be dependent on contract research or corporate stakeholders. Cohen saw the relationship between the university and the market as 'the result of a balancing act that could never be in a perfect state of equilibrium'.[44] Nevertheless, in his role as Rector, from 11 January 1991 onwards Cohen continued to strive to find a balance between the university's various roles and responsibilities.

LOOKING FOR BALANCE IN RESEARCH AND EDUCATION Born on 18 October, Cohen considers himself to be 'a true Libra': a reserved relativist, always weighing up the scales – 'after all, there are at least two sides to every issue', looking for the right balance.[45] In his view, the Executive Board should play a facilitative and supporting role towards the faculties. He, in turn, hoped to be the go-between between the faculties and the Board.[46] As the Rector, he was responsible for the university's education and research portfolio. Within the Faculty of Law he was known as the 'educational conscience', and as Rector, too, he continued to be a staunch advocate of problem-based learning. But he was always open to discussion. In the late 1980s, he had taken part in an institution-wide debate on the university's basic philosophy. This had resulted in a working group comprised of faculty members, which undertook a closer review of the educational system and, in late 1990, published the memorandum *Leren te leren* ('Learning to Learn'). In the conclusion, Cohen stated that there were five core conditions that had to be met for the university's approach to qualify as problem-based learning. The learning had to take place in small groups, be problem-based, promote student autonomy, be highly focused on skills training, and, finally, incorporate progress tests.[47] Incidentally, as soon as Cohen had become Rector, his 'own' faculty abolished the progress test – 'those bastards', as Cohen laughed years later. He did not want to play the role of 'educational police', but abolishing problem-based learning was inconceivable for him: it formed part of the university's strategic profile. However, the various faculties were given greater scope to put problem-based learning into practice in their own ways. Cohen pulled off a similar balancing act on the issue of internationalisation. He was a proponent of a greater focus on international relations – in a report published in 1990 by the Wiardi Beckman Foundation, a think-tank linked to the PvdA, he made a case for the internationalisation of several Dutch universities – but it was up to the faculties to set their own pace in this regard.[48]

In the early 1990s, the State University of Limburg was still primarily an education-oriented university, but the pressure to also establish a reputation for research was increasing. Up to a certain degree, Cohen tried to counterbalance the 'rationalisation' of research. The government assumed that a structure modelled on the business world, whereby universities comprised different research schools and research institutes, would bring greater focus, more visible 'output', more competition and 'therefore' better quality. Cohen thought this rationale was 'beneficial to a degree', but he also made sure to direct attention to the other side of the coin. He defended 'academic mavericks', emphasising the importance of academic freedom and of fundamental and independent research. When dealing with these issues, Cohen kept seeking to balance different interests, always looking for the middle ground. At the end of the day, he himself was more passionate about education than research. In retrospect he acknowledges that, in his post as Rector, he should have focused more on research. The State University of Limburg had only limited success in obtaining funding from the national research funds.

THE EXPANSION OF THE UNIVERSITY When he took up his post as Rector, Cohen, along with the other members of the Executive Board, saw the expansion of the State University of Limburg as being by far the greatest challenge. While the university had reached its target number of 6,000 students in 1990, its four faculties – Medicine, Health Science, Law and Economy – provided a fairly one-sided focus. Since the arrival of Vredevoogd in the spring of 1987, expansion had been high on the university's agenda. According to Vredevoogd, the State University of Limburg could perfectly well be a fully-fledged university without subscribing to the Humboldtian model of higher education, according to which all classical faculties are represented within one university.[49] They were looking to achieve expansion in 'new areas', such as culture and technology, and to increase the number of degree programmes within each of the disciplines that the university already offered. According to Cohen, Vredevoogd was the person on the Executive Board who was the most dogged, and the driving force behind the expansion. Vredevoogd had, for a spell, acted as deputy director general at the Ministry of Education, Culture and Science. He had excellent contacts in The Hague and was up-to-date on the interests at play there. In 1991, the Faculty of General Sciences began a degree programme in Arts and Culture and, one year later, another in Knowledge Engineering. In addition, there were plans to establish a new Psychology degree programme. All these plans not only struck nervousness and even ire into the other universities; tensions were also increasing at Maastricht, Cohen realised. In the summer of 1993, he found himself faced with the university's new Psychology programme while acting in an entirely different role. After the forced departure of Roel in 't Veld, Cohen became State Secretary for Education, Culture and Science in the third Lubbers cabinet. In 1994, when the cabinet was already governing in a caretaker capacity, Cohen gave the green light for programmes in European law and fiscal economics, following positive advice from the Advisory Committee on the Provision of Study Programmes. Greenlighting the Psychology programme was ultimately more Minister of Education, Culture and Science Jo Ritzen's responsibility. In the summer of 1995, Cohen returned to Maastricht. He turned down the offer to become the Minister of Education, Culture and Science in the first Kok cabinet for personal reasons. His wife wanted to resume her work in Maastricht and his children were going to secondary school there – Cohen did not want to miss out on that stage of their lives. However, he continued to be drawn to the political sphere. He eventually joined the Dutch Senate and the committee responsible for the PvdA's election programme.

SECOND ROUND AND GOODBYE In Maastricht, he picked up where he had left off. He had a guaranteed right of return as a professor. Presented with a choice between Philipsen, who had replaced Cohen as Rector, and Cohen, the Board of Deans chose Cohen by a narrow majority. Since he was also on the Senate – first as a 'regular' member, but soon as group chairman of the PvdA, Philipsen became vice-chair and responsible for the internationalisation portfolio. For Cohen, his second spell as Rector was entirely different from the first. Whereas in the early 1990s he had had to 'fight' to expand the State University of Limburg, after 1995 the institution was no longer the 'underdog'. With the increased range of programmes on offer, it had become a serious competitor with other universities, with 9,000 students and 2,000 members of staff. While the State University of Limburg – which in 1998 changed its name to Universiteit Maastricht – 'lacked' natural sciences and humanities, according to Cohen it would simply not make sense to seek to introduce these disciplines at the university as long as there was no demand for them. The university no longer represented an 'interesting potential source of cost savings'; it had become a significant presence in Dutch higher education. Cohen had also become a different type of Rector. He had become more outward-looking, and liked to get involved in the national debate about higher education. He gave lectures on the increasingly high expectations universities were required to meet, about the feasibility of degree programmes, vouchers and academic education – dealing with setbacks was a part of that too – as well as on more general academic policy. In 1997, he announced that he wanted to resign from the position. 'The paradox of the post of Rector is that as time goes by you become worse, rather than better at it. That's because, inevitably, the Rector increasingly grows into the role of administrator, rather than researcher and lecturer, as a result of which he is less able to identify with the group from which he came, i.e. the professors.'[50] According to Cohen, he had been a 'cog' in the machine, rather than a driving force: 'there are only a few things that can be directly attributed to me'.[51] He said goodbye in January 1998. He had made clear earlier on that he was interested in returning to politics. He had 'loved' his year as State Secretary. In the summer of 1998, he became State Secretary for Justice in the second Kok cabinet, tasked with the policy on asylum seekers. Later on, he would become the mayor of Amsterdam and go on to return to the national political area, this time as leader of the PvdA.

10 *Ria Wolleswinkel* I WENT TO STUDY LAW IN MAASTRICHT WITH PAULO FREIRE-ESQUE IDEAS ABOUT THE PEDAGOGY OF THE OPPRESSED

A NEW START Ria Wolleswinkel was one of the 98 students who started the Law degree programme in Maastricht in early September 1982. With its thematic approach and problem-based structure, this degree programme was a didactic experiment. Wolleswinkel had to hurry to be at the official opening on time. There had been no end of problems: the invitation had not arrived on time and – 'so unemancipated' – it had also been wrongly addressed in the name of her husband, while she had continued to use her own surname following her marriage.[1] She only heard where she had to go at the very last minute: the church behind the station. Wolleswinkel entered in a somewhat irritated state just as Karl Dittrich was speaking. Dittrich, a political scientist whose task was to place law in a broader context, spoke in an 'agreeable and convivial' voice. His recurring mantra was: 'Here we train generalists!'. That sounded just fine, and with a voice like his Wolleswinkel expected many jokes. Dittrich, however, turned out to be quite strict: students were expected to work and be available for 40 hours a week. 'But how am I going to manage that with my one-year-old son?', Wolleswinkel wondered. Dittrich was followed by Job Cohen, lawyer, chairman of the preparatory committee for Dutch Law and the main driving force behind the degree programme. Cohen spoke with 'a beautiful voice and diction'. He said: 'Here we don't train better lawyers than anywhere else in the country, we just train them differently'. That message came as a disappointment for Wolleswinkel, however. Had she moved from Amsterdam to Maastricht for that?

Wolleswinkel had consciously chosen Maastricht for the problem-based approach to learning, an approach which had for several years been increasingly gaining recognition in the medical world. She associated problem-based learning with 'Paulo Freire-esque ideas' and an education project in Amsterdam run by Co van Calcar.[2] The critical Brazilian philosopher and educator

was known for his work *Pedagogy of the Oppressed* (1970). Education should be geared to students' direct perception of the environment as closely as possible, according to Freire, who saw education as a means of emancipating the poor and oppressed. He believed that political liberation was only possible if the oppressed themselves assumed responsibility for acquiring knowledge.[3] Wolleswinkel recognised elements of Freire's philosophy in problem-based learning with its emphasis on self-motivation. The State University of Limburg was founded in a region facing problems after the closure of the local mining industry. There was an emancipatory aspect to this that appealed to her. 'Why shouldn't consciousness-raising start in Limburg?', she thought. And it was indeed striking how many Limburgers, and especially how many somewhat older Limburgers, enrolled in the Law degree programme. The university was clearly attempting to gain academic recognition. Wolleswinkel suspects that the average age of the students – 28 – was even somewhat higher than that of the lecturers. She herself was 29. In 1982, Wolleswinkel already had an entire career under her belt and there were a number of reasons why she was ready for 'a new start'.

MARIA WILLEMINA Ria (1953) was born in Renswoude, an enclave in the Dutch 'Bible Belt' between Utrecht and Arnhem, where her parents had a farm. She grew up in a Protestant household marked by memories of the Second World War, but where the religious atmosphere was not especially solemn. Ria was named after her grandmother. Her parents were proud of the Dutch name of Willemina, i.e. not Wilhelmina, the more common spelling. Both at the beginning of the war and during liberation, fighting in the Gelderland countryside had been fierce. Her parents were forced to flee twice and they lost a young son. Yet they were thankful that they had survived. For Wolleswinkel, the war served as a kind of moral yardstick. 'What would I have done and would I have had the courage?'. As a young girl, she cycled a couple of times to the war victims commemoration ceremony on her own. Attending the ceremony was too difficult for her parents. This was a household in which education was viewed as essential and, like her brothers, Ria attended secondary modern school (economics option). University, however, did not feature in her aspirations. She wanted to go to journalism school. She enjoyed writing compositions and put her 'entire soul' into them. However, because of the lottery system she failed to get a place and was advised to enrol in a university degree programme. She chose to study Sociology in Utrecht. Wolleswinkel was thrilled to live in student rooms and plunged headfirst into student life, including two theatre groups. During her studies there was much discussion about the *Frankfurter Schule* and the need for 'consciousness-raising of the working class'. But this was all too theoretical for Wolleswinkel. She wanted to discover the real world, and left university after 18 months to do temporary agency work. A chance encounter led to the idea of attending a social academy. She decided on Nijenburgh in Baarn, which had been founded shortly after the war on orthodox reformed principles. In the 1970s, Nijenburgh was full of left-wing do-gooders and hippies; it was a culture in which she felt right at home. While a lot of work was 'done on ethics', the degree programme was mainly practically oriented.

Wolleswinkel quickly departed for Amsterdam to do a work placement under major Bosshardt of the Salvation Army. She experienced Bosshardt as an inspiring woman who approached people in need with openness and without prejudice. Averse to status or outward appearance, Bosshardt went about her work purposefully. She even managed to get a home for the elderly constructed in the city centre of Amsterdam. All of this left an impression on Wolleswinkel: she visited everyone on the waiting list and heard many stories about the occupation in the city, the deportations of Jews, the round-ups and the Dutch famine of 1944 – 1945. In 1976 she started as a social worker in the Duin en Bosch psychiatric hospital in Castricum, where she first heard about anti-psychiatry, a movement which criticised psychiatry as a medical disciplinary instrument used for social control. At the academy, she had already read the bestseller by anti-psychiatrist Jan Foudraine *Wie is van hout... Een gang door de psychiatrie* ('Not Made of Wood: Psychiatrist Discovers His Own Profession', 1st edition in 1971), which had already gone into its 25th edition in 1976. The anti-psychiatric movement voiced strong criticism of the large psychiatric institutions in remote locations where chronic patients were only 'institutionalised'. The Duin en Bosch hospital, which was built in 1909, had a poor reputation as regards accommodation.[4] In a job that was new for the institution, Wolleswinkel became a social worker on a number of wards for chronic patients. A sheltered accommodation project was launched, in which patients' opinions were sought about the design of their new, small-scale social housing. This led to Wolleswinkel coming to surprising insights 'simply by talking to people'.

Wolleswinkel was confronted by issues which often had a legal angle, mostly relating to contacts between family and patients. She was amazed by the civil servants of the province – Duin en Bosch was a provincial hospital – many of whom were legal experts and tended to respond in terms of procedures. Those procedures often had such an impact on people's lives ('especially those procedures that extend and delay admission while nothing happens in the meantime') that she thought: 'I have to study Law'. Maastricht became an option because her husband could do epidemiology there and it had just launched a new Law programme. The university's practice-oriented, problem-based learning dovetailed with what she had experienced at the social academy. In the summer of 1982, the couple moved to De Heeg in Maastricht. They loved it there: it seemed as though they were abroad with all those hills! It became a summer to remember in 'a house with front and back garden and a place in the daycare centre' for her young son.

LAW IN MAASTRICHT That first cohort of Law students was infected by 'an idea of emancipation'. The students overwhelmingly came from Limburg and included relatively many mature students, such as a mother who had enrolled to study Law together with her son. Most spoke with 'pleasant Limburg timbres'; indeed, the 'standard Dutch' of the university staff stood out. Wolleswinkel remembers how secretary Victor Rutgers welcomed her with: 'So, you come from Amsterdam'. He told her how pleased they were that someone from Amsterdam had decided to study Law in Maastricht. The first students probably started the degree programme with the same level of enthusiasm and motivation as the first members of staff. That created a bond and a strong feeling of community. It was a busy time: the student-edited faculty paper *Caracas* was very soon being published and the student association 'Ouranos' was founded in 1983.

The students liked being taught in small groups. Wolleswinkel did notice that a number of lecturers would immediately question students, which for her was something 'from a very distant past'. This especially happened during practicals, whenever the 20 or so students failed to get a discussion going spontaneously. Wolleswinkel tackled Cohen about this, who responded with surprise and openness, but who subsequently continued the practice. In any case, the lecturers were extremely interested in the experiences of the students, who were constantly bombarded with questionnaires and evaluation forms.[5] Wolleswinkel remembers Jeppe Balkema as one of the most enthusiastic staff members, but Cees Flinterman and René de Groot also seemed to derive great pleasure from their work. The first staff members had of course been recruited on account of their positive attitude towards problem-based learning.

Wolleswinkel felt closest to the socio-critical 'non-conformists', such as Criminal Law lecturer Gerard Mols, Legal Theory lecturer Alma van Bers and Public Law lecturer Loes Brünott. Mols was her first tutor and mentor. His appearance was defined by unkempt hair and a torn leather jacket. He was 'non-governmental' and a member of a team of lawyers defending suspects associated with the *Rote Armee Fraktion*. Wolleswinkel also has animated memories of Van Bers, who would ask the students about their ideas of justice. Van Bers initiated 'The Salon'; a small study group in which both students and staff participated. The group met at a different member's house each time to discuss esoteric books and articles by Fjodor Dostojevski, Michel Foucault and Jürgen Habermas, for example. Brünott was a feminist from Rotterdam with an 'impressive international network for those days'. She was involved in the adoption of the UN Convention on the Elimination of All Forms of Discrimination Against Women (1979). The Netherlands only ratified this convention in the early 1990s, after it had already come into force in 1981. Brünott was one of the initiators of *Nemesis*, a journal launched in 1984 and named after the Greek god of retribution and justice, which focused on 'women and the law'. As a student, Wolleswinkel thought Van Bers and Brünott had 'huge added value', but neither would stay long at the faculty. While they 'perhaps had trouble settling in Limburg', they probably did not feel very much at home at the faculty either.

THEMATIC EDUCATION For Wolleswinkel, the main question remains, which group had more trouble with thematic education: the students or the lecturers? The students quickly became confused if a course handled various areas of law. For example, the Representation module dealt with private law, criminal law, and constitutional and administrative law. Wolleswinkel realised that the lecturers, who themselves had been traditionally trained, found compiling a course textbook a complicated task: how much should be included from one area of law and how much from the other? This was further complicated by the fact that the outside world responded sceptically to that cross-border approach, which itself formed a risk for students hoping for a career in the courtroom. Cohen, Balkema and Flinterman therefore travelled several times to The Hague to explain the Maastricht approach to the interest group representing the court system and the legal profession. The exact amount of criminal law, private law and constitutional and administrative law that the curriculum would contain was formally established. As these requirements clashed with the thematic structure of the programme, it was decided that the thematic approach would be handled 'somewhat more cautiously'.

Moreover, Wolleswinkel observed how 'embarrassingly tricky' it was for several tutors in tutorials to admit ignorance about something: an unavoidable consequence of thematic education. Even if according to 'the theory' tutors were not expected to impart knowledge – after all, the students themselves were responsible for their learning process – tutors were sometimes clearly confused and embarrassed when in unfamiliar territory.[6] Furthermore, there were students who enjoyed needling tutors about their lack of expertise. Wolleswinkel's year group included students who had experience in business as entrepreneurs, and some of them enjoyed teasing 'all those PvdA (Labour) party supporters', whose number among the first staff members was indeed considerable. Wolleswinkel recalls how a visibly nervous tutor went red in the face when the subject of company accounts was broached in the Company course and one of the students burst out laughing.

And so the thematic approach of the degree programme came under pressure from a number of different corners, and according to Wolleswinkel the tendency towards specialisation only grew stronger as the degree programme progressed. Indeed, in the third and fourth years, students chose elective courses, which were often subject-oriented modules designed by tutors with the relevant expertise. These tutors tended to turn to their expertise rather quickly when the need arose. Wolleswinkel says that students would then be confronted with 'stares or, even worse, cries of disbelief if they did not properly understand a key concept'. And to think that these same students 'were told on commencing the degree programme in 1982 that it was no big deal' if they were 'still learning new things' in the fourth year. At that time, the degree programme was presented as a kind of jigsaw puzzle: the missing pieces would fall into the right places faster at the end than at the beginning.[7] Wolleswinkel got the impression that particularly the lecturers were uncertain about whether the students were capable of completing that puzzle. 'The Maastricht experiment' was of course viewed with suspicion by the legal community.

YOU LEARN FROM TRYING From the outset, the Law degree programme in Maastricht focused on fostering strong writing skills. This is why, as mentioned previously, Cohen spoke about the importance of a lawyer being able to 'juggle language'. Wolleswinkel welcomed the writing assignments that came at the end of the six blocks every time, as she had always enjoyed writing in secondary school. She noticed that the other students' assignments adhered fairly closely to the curriculum, with essay titles often referring to 'recommended reading'. Efforts on her part to find literature with 'a different voice' out of 'academic curiosity' were not always appreciated. The exception was De Groot, who was pleased when she found something new, whatever its source. Wolleswinkel and other students felt they learned a lot from those writing assignments thanks to the feedback that they received. However, the lecturers thought that the writing work took up so much of the students' attention that the tutorial group was being adversely affected. Of course, they also found providing feedback a fairly time-consuming task. It was not long before the lecturers decided to reduce the number of assignments and introduce a course exam, on the assumption that this would serve to deepen the students' understanding of the material.

Wolleswinkel, however, viewed the course exam as an admission of weakness. The lecturers were in the habit of criticising the students' studying methods without reflecting on their own 'behaviour as tutors'. Those lecturers appointed after 1982, in particular, rarely acted in her opinion as real tutors working to stimulate their students' self-motivation. In the meantime, the students became increasingly ciritical: some did far too little, others focused purely on the code of law and case law, while others again read too much of other material to the detriment of the code of law. Shortly after graduating, Wolleswinkel was quite dismissive about the course exam: it was a 'hotchpotch of learning by rote, case-solving questions and in-depth theoretical questions'.[8] In her opinion, the course exam simply resembled a high-school test. This was not without an effect on the students: towards the end the students in the tutorial groups seemed 'photocopier crazed'. But the lecturers, too, were affected, such as when they, out of sheer powerlessness, threatened a poorly performing group with the course exam. Wolleswinkel feared that the relationship between staff and students would revert to something more traditional: the independence of the students had been compromised. With all the criticism of the course exam, she realised that the progress test was not without its flaws either: the further she progressed through the study programme, the more difficult it became to confidently mark a question as correct or incorrect. Yet despite these criticisms, Wolleswinkel looks back positively to her studies. She believes that the practical training sessions, such as the Negotiations practical and the Moot Court (though that was still being developed in her time), proved that the Maastricht system worked: 'that you learn from trying'. Moreover, after a couple of years, good contacts were established with a number of law firms in the region that offered work placements. The clearly practice-oriented character of the study programme motivated Wolleswinkel, and, together with Mols, she established the Law and Practice working group. This interdisciplinary working group turned its attention, for example, to the legal aspects of the contamination of the Meuse by French and Belgian industries; efforts which, incidentally, later produced a dedicated line of research. Wolleswinkel experienced the study programme's alternating focus on theory and practice as 'extraordinarily stimulating'. She also has good memories of her personal contacts with the lecturers. The education principles underlying the Maastricht system worked to promote contact between staff and students, though Wolleswinkel felt that the informality during the start-up phase of the Law degree programme sometimes went too far – 'at the end of the day, you are in a position of dependence'. She remembers, for example, declining an invitation to attend the birthday party of the course coordinator.

WOMEN AND LAW Wolleswinkel graduated with 75 fellow students in late 1986. She was one of three students to be presented their degree certificate with the designation *cum laude* by Mols, the chairman of the Examination Board. Balkema was so enthusiastic about her final paper on juvenile law that he suggested she write a dissertation on the subject. She had never even considered it! But the idea of doing PhD research now stuck in her mind. Being able to start immediately as a lecturer in the Criminal Law and Criminology department, she used that year to write a research proposal on the re-socialisation of women ex-convicts. Through Brünott, she later secured a 'Pais position': a post financed for 25% by the Ministry of Education, Culture and Science in order to stimulate women's studies.

Remaining based in the Criminal Law and Criminology department, Wolleswinkel became a part-time university lecturer with the intention of simultaneously working to obtain her PhD. She became involved with the internationally oriented Women and Law research project, which Brünott had set up in 1986. As a fervent feminist active both in the Netherlands and abroad, Brünott critically examined the relationship between women and the law. The dominant view at the faculty was that the theme of women and the law only interested women. Brünott felt great disdain for the 'male bastion' where 'the gentlemen held the key positions' and she kept it no secret – within the faculty she could only count on the support of Cees Flinterman and Theo van Boven from the 'men's side'.[9] In due course, the old boys' network offended Brünott so strongly that she left the faculty, and she would not be the only one of the faculty's first women to come to that decision.

The place to be for the old boys' network was Café Tribunal, where problems could sometimes be resolved over lunch and a bottle of wine.[10] Known for its cheerful tuck-ins, Café Tribunal became a 'kind of annex of the faculty': the home of the faculty's informal power base. It would be 16 years before the Law Faculty appointed its first female professor: Ties Prakken was appointed professor of Criminal and Procedural Law only in 1998. It was a milestone that Brünott would not live to see: she died suddenly in 1991.

Wolleswinkel had a very busy schedule, particularly given her part-time appointment. Not only did she have to complete her dissertation and coordinate the women and law research project, she was also expected to integrate 'women and law' subjects into the existing curriculum, take over the Negotiations elective practical and participate in a host of committees such as the State University of Limburg Women's Emancipation Committee, the Inter-faculty Women's Studies Consultative Body (later) and the national Legal Consultative Body on Women's Studies; in 1998, she became a member of the Centre for Gender and Diversity, which was established in that year, and of the supervisory committee of the *Opzij* chair[11]. Also, as a former student with experience of problem-based learning to draw from, Wolleswinkel became involved with a 'lecturer professionalisation' working group. Together with Cohen, Wendelien Elzinga of Private Law and Huub Spoormans of Metalegal Studies and others, she published a number of articles and brochures, including *Tips voor tutoren* ('Tips for Tutors'), in 1989. Drawing from 17 situations in the tutorial group, this brochure zoomed in on the problems and difficulties that could arise in practice.

She spent much of her time 'screening the entire curriculum for women-and-law subjects'. Wolleswinkel was able to come to a final agreement with Cohen – the Negotiations practical launched by Cohen had apparently been successful – about her receiving support for one half day a week from Jenny Goldschmidt, a specialist in the field of women and law who had been seconded from Utrecht University as a consultant. Wolleswinkel attempted to integrate 'women and law' subjects into the curriculum in various ways, such as explicitly introducing 'women and law' themes in courses and including role-breaking examples in the teaching material. For example, a violent criminal was given the name 'Ali' – a man or a woman? – to make students aware of gender-specific conceptualisation.

From 1989, Wolleswinkel also became coordinator of Women and Law, an elective course that drew from a number of legal areas to examine what the equality principle, anchored in the Constitution since 1983, meant for women in practice, also in the context of developments in international and European law. According to Wolleswinkel, the course sparked a fundamental discussion on the dual role of the law: to what extent should the law safeguard social stability and to what extent is it an instrument for changing existing, unequal, relationships? As interesting as these questions were, after a few years this course failed to attract enough students (but for one exception, male students avoided it completely) and it was eventually discontinued in 1993. For Wolleswinkel, however, emancipation remained a key driver. A more integrated approach became the new strategy. Wolleswinkel was the driving force behind a number of new elective courses, such as Emancipation as an Issue of Division, The Principle of Equality, Division of Labour, Income and Time, and Victims and Criminal Law, the last of which she fully developed herself; after 2000, she was a member of the planning group of The Principle of Equality and of the Implementation of International Women's Rights at the Domestic Level, later Human Rights of Women. She also designed an Introduction to Law for University College Maastricht. The titles of the courses alone reflected the faculty's increasingly international profile.[12]

IMPRISONED IN MOTHERHOOD: LAW IN ACTION It was no simple task for Wolleswinkel to strike a balance between her teaching and research duties, and her PhD research often had to make way for other priorities. Moreover, a culture of research barely existed in the legal world of the 1980s. In fact, Law professors who did not hold doctorates were not at all uncommon in the mid-1970s. Staff members with doctorates soon became eligible for professorships. On the same day as his PhD ceremony in late October 1988, De Groot was appointed professor of Comparative Law and International Private Law, something that would be almost inconceivable today, even if De Groot had established a reputation as a researcher.[13] From the 1990s, requirements on research, including research by lawyers, increased: there was to be more control, greater competition and more output. Wolleswinkel was interested in the fate of women who had been in prison. How did they fare after release? She wanted to take an interdisciplinary approach to the study into the resocialisation of women ex-convicts that had an empirical basis in interviews and follow-up interviews. The faculty's response to her intended research was extremely discouraging, however, as it lacked any expertise with this type of social scientific research. Wolleswinkel consulted Riet Drop, professor of Medical Sociology and experienced in the field of empirical research, but she was unable to help.

Eventually, Wolleswinkel opted for a 'purely' legal angle by focusing on the legal position of imprisoned mothers. She was supported by her supervisor Mols, as well as by her co-supervisor Peter Bal, senior lecturer in Criminal Law and Procedural Law, who had himself conducted empirical research and was well-grounded in criminology and legal theory. In May 1997, Wolleswinkel obtained her PhD with a dissertation titled *Gevangen in moederschap. Gedetineerde vrouwen en het recht op family life* ('Imprisoned in Motherhood. Women in custody and the right to family life'), a substantial book of more than 400 pages. It examined questions such as: what is the relationship between the interests of imprisoned mothers and that of their children in the light of human rights, and what role does the government play? Wolleswinkel believed that, in this question, the interest of the child should be the guiding principle. Her position on the co-detention of children was 'extremely reserved'.[14] She also showed that a prison sentence placed an additional burden on mothers because a woman's identity was largely bound up with her role as a woman and a mother. Wolleswinkel therefore argued for a gender-specific approach to childcare, vocational training for women and social activities outside the institution to allow women to prepare for life after prison. The Netherlands' most popular legal journal, *Nederlands Juristenblad*, hailed the dissertation as a great contribution to penological research.[15]

Her passion to be socially engaged had inspired Wolleswinkel to try her hand at writing a 'real law-in-action book' that was practically relevant – and she succeeded. She was able to draw the attention of the academic world and beyond to the plight of imprisoned women and their children. A slew of publications, lectures and committee appointments followed. In 1998, she was appointed senior lecturer. Wolleswinkel focused more and more on the rights of children of imprisoned parents. She was one of the initiators of the European Action Research Committee on Children of Imprisoned Parents, the European network for children of imprisoned parents, which she chaired from 2000 to 2005.[16] Through her research, she found within 'the cluster of gender, diversity and vulnerable groups' a link with the Human Rights research school established at the instigation of Flinterman in 1995 and in which the universities of Maastricht, Rotterdam and Utrecht participated. In the same year, the universities of Maastricht, Leuven and Utrecht established Ius Commune, a research school dedicated to researching international and transnational legal issues.[17]

INTERNATIONALISATION AND HUMAN RIGHTS In this way, Wolleswinkel was able to keep up with the trend towards internationalisation. Internationalisation was not only important in order to continue attracting sufficient numbers of students – Limburg had finally secured academic recognition – but was an obvious direction for the university given Maastricht's location and the increasing importance of Europe, especially in the area of the law. The pressure on universities to promote themselves increased after the mid-1990s. To some extent, this pressure was easier on the State University of Limburg (known as 'Universiteit Maastricht' from 1996 and, since 2008, as 'Maastricht University' also in Dutch), given the cross-border opportunities that were already obvious when the university was founded.[18] Moreover, key figures associated with the faculty such as Van Boven, Flinterman and De Groot had been strongly internationally oriented from the beginning. It was also the intention of the Bologna Declaration of 1999 and the introduction of the Bachelor's/Master's system to stimulate cooperation in higher education and student mobility.[19] Wolleswinkel found links with other universities in the area of human rights. On behalf of Maastricht University, she was appointed director in 2004 of the the European Inter-University Centre for Human Rights and Democratisation (EIUC) in Venice, which offers a European Master's programme in Human Rights and Democratisation (E.MA).[20] A total of 41 universities now participate in this degree programme. She not only contributed to its curriculum, in 2013 she was also elected chairperson of the E.MA Council, the Executive Committee and the Academic Curriculum Group, Her working time factor was increased by 0.1 to 0.7 FTE. Wolleswinkel was now a senior lecturer in Law, Gender and Legal Education. According to Wolleswinkel, the advantage of this position is that it offers her sufficient opportunity to be socially active on a number of different fronts.

WHAT ARE WE TRAINING GRADUATES TO DO? Wolleswinkel came to Maastricht with Paolo-Freire-esque ideas in 1982. She remained faithful to her original ideals. Then and now, her main interest lies in the emancipatory dimensions of law and, inextricably linked to that, of education. Rather than clinging to rigid ideals, she wanted to continue developing. Consequently, she integrated the theme of women and law into the larger context of human rights and worked with Raymond Schlössels and Jaap Hage on editing a handbook entitled *Recht, vaardig en zeker. Een inleiding in het recht* ('Law, skilful and dependable. An introduction to the law') (2001).[21] This handbook dovetailed with the programme's initial course, Introduction to the Law, and aimed to offer metalegal studies combined with knowledge on positive law. From the perspective of the degree programme's original education principles, writing such a handbook is of course unforgiveable. But problem-based learning had come under pressure in the 1990s, and not only at the Faculty of Law. The university had to train increasing numbers of students at ever lower cost, while education's status faded compared to research. It was difficult to reconcile the inherent tendency of research towards specialisation with the thematic approach with which the faculty had wished to stand out. The tutorial groups had also grown larger.[22] Moreover, with increasing internationalisation, the call for 'more lectures' grew louder. On the one hand, critics spoke about the 'watering down of problem-based learning', while on the other, the pioneers of the first cohort were viewed as 'missionaries'. What is important, however, is for the discussion on education to continue unabated and to remain open to new education methods. It is not surprising that, with her experience with problem-based learning, she was appointed programme director in 2005, even though the Executive Board did have to consider the appointment carefully, since programme directors are normally professors. Wolleswinkel's task is now to safeguard the quality of *all* programmes. In the light of what the past decades have taught us, her point of departure is a flexible application of problem-based learning. The Maastricht degree programme recognises the importance of acquiring skills: as part of 'the importance of lifelong learning', students need to know how they can keep their usable knowledge up to date.[23]

Wolleswinkel supports the original objective of training generalists, though now from a more international perspective: the degree programme seeks to train lawyers who are able to place the law in a broader social context and to move around the European labour market flexibly. Law at Maastricht University is now firmly established; its outsider image is fading. Wolleswinkel thinks that while the Law degree programme at Maastricht has probably become 'more normal', other faculties have also 'copied more from us'.

11 *Joan Muysken* ECONOMICS IN MAASTRICHT HAD TO DEVELOP A RECOGNISABLE AND NEW IDENTITY OF ITS OWN

THE LIFE OF RILEY... Joan Muysken was 'leading the life of Riley'. A senior staff member at the Faculty of Economics of the University of Groningen, he was on a sabbatical at the State University of New York at Buffalo with his family in 1983 when he got a phone call from his boss, professor of Macroeconomics Simon Kuipers, who advised him to apply for a job in Maastricht.[1] There was an opening for a professor of General Economics at the State University of Limburg. Muysken was 34 at the time, so he was still quite young to take up a post as a professor of Economics, and he was not particularly eager to become a professor at the time. He also had another sabbatical planned in Vienna. However, he allowed himself to be persuaded. After all, these kinds of opportunities did not present themselves very often, and Muysken thought it would be 'an interesting challenge'. Moreover, he had managed to accumulate 'a fair number of publications'. So after some hemming and hawing, he applied for the job and was invited for an interview. The interview took place in Utrecht, inside the Hoog Catharijne shopping centre, where he was received by Wil Albeda, the chair of the Selection Board. At the time Albeda, an economist who died in 2014, had just started as founding dean at the Faculty of Economics in Maastricht. A Reformed Protestant, Albeda was a well-known politician with the Dutch centre-right CDA (Christian-Democrat) party, who as the Minister of Social Affairs had been the figurehead for social engagement in the first Van Agt cabinet (1977–1981). In addition to Albeda, the Selection Board included Jaap van Duijn, professor of General Economics at Delft University of Technology's Graduate School of Management, and Wim Driehuis, professor of Economics at the University of Amsterdam. At the end of the interview, Driehuis wanted to know whether perhaps Muysken was only applying for the job as a way to demonstrate his market value. Muysken's wife ran her own GP practice in Zuidhorn, and Driehuis assumed she would be unwilling to move to Maastricht with him. Muysken was a little irked by the question, replying: 'I'm applying for the job because I *want* the job'. Muysken soon got the news that he was, indeed, getting the job. He was 'quite taken aback: I suddenly found myself becoming a professor at the tender age of 34', being expected to help give shape to a faculty that was only just starting out.

LIMBURG AND GRONINGEN AND VICE VERSA Muysken considered himself at home in Groningen, where he had gone to university, but he knew Limburg – or at least the mining region in the east of the province – well. Joan was born in Delft in December 1948. He is the scion of a Protestant family of mechanical engineers from 'the Delft upper crust'. Joan Muyskenweg, a road in Amsterdam, was named after his great-grandfather. After the Muysken family had spent five years living in Bolivia and Peru, his father got a job at the *Staatsmijnen* (State Mining Company) in Limburg. That is how, as a child, Joan 'ended up dropped like a Protestant parachutist into a Catholic environment', one with which he 'did not engage socially' – that is what things were like at the time, when society was very much divided along socio-political lines. He attended the only Protestant secondary school in the Limburg province: the Grotius College. Although it was expected that Joan, too, would go on to study in Delft, he decided to read Economics in Groningen, as he thought this would broaden his range of options for a future career. Muysken was drawn to an exact approach to economics. Right after graduating in 1972, he began working for the internationally renowned professor of Economics Frits de Jong, although Muysken was known as a 'left-wing whippersnapper'. One great advantage of the job was that it provided him with a 'declaration of indispensability', exempting him from military service. In the spring of 1979, he obtained his PhD with a dissertation on the concept of aggregate production function, drawing on empirical data from cotton mills in Japan. Muysken had obtained this data from a Japanese man who had 'sent him a massive box full of punch cards via the North Pole'. He went on to publish various reports and articles on labour, the labour market and unemployment in quick succession, working with academics in the field such as Kuipers and his immediate colleague Chris de Neubourg, who would go on to join him in Maastricht. Muysken's international experience, and his interest in research topics related to technology and labour, made him a good fit for Albeda's plans for the Faculty of Economics in Maastricht. When, on 1 April 1984, Muysken started his job in Maastricht 'as the first professor to be officially appointed after Albeda had been appointed as founding dean', the development of the new faculty was already in full swing.

ECONOMICS IN MAASTRICHT The idea of establishing a degree programme in Economics at the State University of Limburg had existed since early in 1978. Sjeng Kremers, the Queen's Commissioner for the Province of Limburg, had recommended that the Executive Board establish not only a Law programme, but also an Economics programme. These degree programmes were expected to draw significant numbers of students and give the university a more solid foundation. Kremers thought an Economics programme, in particular, would be of great significance to the region: it would provide an impetus for the regional economy, especially if it led to links with the local business community. The Minister of Education, Arie Pais (from the liberal VVD party), who like Albeda made up part of the first Van Agt cabinet, was, it turned out, receptive to the ambitions harboured in Limburg, and asked the State University of Limburg to come up with a plan. Since there was a shortage of economic expertise within the existing faculty, he proposed that the well-known professor Arnold Heertje from the University of Amsterdam be tasked with preparing a proposal. Together with two employees from the Leiden Bureau of Educational Research, Koen van der Drift and Hans Crombag, Heertje wrote the memorandum *De contouren van een economische studierichting aan de Rijksuniversiteit Limburg* ('Outline for a degree programme in Economics at the State University of Limburg'). Crombag had previously played a key role in establishing the Law degree programme in Maastricht, and was familiar with the use of the Maastricht approach to education outside the context of medical education. The Academic Council's section of Economics rejected the proposal, as they felt that the profile for the proposed programme in Maastricht was too similar to what was already on offer at the five existing faculties of economics in the Netherlands. In addition, they were unsure as to whether the 'Maastricht model' was suitable for an Economics degree programme. But Pais persevered. In May 1981, shortly before a rally held by his party in Heerlen, he announced that he had 'the greatest level of enthusiasm' about the prospect of a Faculty of Economics in Maastricht, and would 'do everything in [his] power' to promote its establishment.[2] Rob van den Biggelaar, President of the Executive Board, promised that a bust would be erected in Pais' honour if everything were to work out. Maybe this tipped the scales in Maastricht's favour, maybe not – at any rate, even though by then he was already an outgoing minister, Pais still let the Academic Council know that the State University of Limburg would be submitting a revised version of the proposal.

WIL ALBEDA The fact that, in the summer of 1982, the Executive Board managed to get Albeda for the post of founding dean was 'a brilliant move'.[3] He had been professor of Socio-Economic Policy at the Netherlands School of Economics in Rotterdam, and, as a former Minister and former International

Secretary of the Christian Dutch Trade Union (CNV) he had access to an extensive network, both nationally and internationally. He had a great interest in international issues in particular. With Albeda, Maastricht had managed to bring an impressive figurehead on board for the planned Faculty of Economics: he was a highly-regarded politician and unionist, someone with a good sense of humour who often managed to achieve his goals in a very likeable way – a Frisian, a little shy, but tenacious.[4] Albeda was tasked with developing an Economics curriculum that was to be 'complementary' to the existing degree programmes. He found himself faced with the same dilemma as Cohen: on the one hand, the new degree programme would need to have a distinct identity of its own, yet on the other it could not be too drastically different from similar degree programmes elsewhere in the country if it was to be taken seriously by the other universities. Immediately after his appointment, Albeda went on the road in Limburg: he met for talks with various potential stakeholders such as Kremers, the unions and a number of companies based in the province. He wanted to give the new faculty a clear place in South Limburg: the Economics degree programme should provide a boost for the region, which had been hit hard by the economic crisis. From the outset, Albeda saw Maastricht as an excellent location from which to build international partnerships with the universities of Aachen, Hasselt and Leuven.[5] He was also hoping to establish partnerships with the European Institute of Public Administration, which had been established in 1981, and the Dutch Open University, which was to welcome its first students in September 1984.

Albeda received support from the Economics Committee at the State University of Limburg, which included Cees Flinterman (professor of Constitutional and International Law), Frans Rutten (professor of Health Economics), Paul Thung (professor of Medicine and the driving force behind initiatives promoting educational reform, who advised the State University of Limburg on its expansion plans), René Verspeek (who would later go on to be director of the Faculty but who at the time – after having dropped out of an Economics degree – was working at Studium Generale) and Wynand Wijnen (the founding father of 'the Maastricht approach to education') – in other words, very few economists. The economic expertise was provided by an external group of consultants which included Jaap van Duijn, Piet Keizer (academic staff member in Macroeconomics at the University of Groningen), Karel Mulder (professor of Business Economics at Delft University of Technology) and Frans van Winden (academic staff member at Utrecht University). Albeda worked fast. By early 1983, he was able to present the report *Economie in Maastricht. Plan voor een studierichting economie aan de Rijksuniversiteit Limburg te Maastricht* ('Economics in Maastricht. Plan for an Economics degree programme at the State University of Limburg in Maastricht'). This outline was well-received, both within the university and beyond. Wim Deetman, Minister of Education and Science in the first Lubbers cabinet (CDA and VVD), supported the initiative; in the spring of 1983 he gave the official green light for the new degree programme, which distinguished itself from the existing Economics degree programmes in a number of key ways.

ITS OWN IDENTITY The Economics degree programme had to have 'a clear identity of its own'.[6] The decision to employ problem-based learning – which initially still included the progress test – was, alone, sufficient grounds to call the degree programme experimental in nature: there was after all no other Economics degree programme anywhere in the world that used this educational method. However, problem-based learning seemed ill-suited to subjects like mathematics, statistics and accounting; the preferred approach for these subjects was more task-based, with students receiving instruction as to what exactly they were meant to find out. But in terms of the content of the curriculum, too, the programme had its own focus. It was intended to be a bridge between General Economics and Business Economics. Albeda believed it was important that a dialogue be established between these two disciplines, as he felt general economists and business economists lived in their own separate worlds. In the US, to his horror, these two subjects were sometimes taught at two separate faculties. Breaking down the boundaries between Business Economics and General Economics also sat well with the overall aim of interdisciplinarity with which the State University of Limburg had sought to legitimise itself from its inception. In addition, according to Albeda, a 'good economist' had to be mindful of the wider social context in which economic decisions were made. For this reason, the social sciences – 'sociology, law and management science in particular' – were given a prominent role in the curriculum.

In addition, the Economics degree programme in Maastricht had to distinguish itself from 'ossified curriculums' elsewhere, in Albeda's phrase. Albeda had made a significant mark on the report by explicitly concentrating on three new areas of focus.[7] The idea was for the degree programme to respond to the needs of modern society. In his view, the Maastricht Faculty of Economics, like the Faculty of Medicine, would do well to focus on certain specific areas. The first he had in mind was the economics of technological development, as the role of technology within economics was only set to become more important. The rise of microelectronics alone, he stated, constituted a technological revolution, which gave rise to new economic questions. Why was technology being used in the way it was? And what were the implications of these technological developments for the organisation of production, and for economic trends and structural developments? Albeda emphasised that technology was one of the response variables relevant to economics. He had derived this idea from his contacts with the universities of Warwick and Sussex in England, and Stirling in Scotland. Like the State University of

Limburg, the University of Stirling was a new university, established in a 'depressed area' partly with a view to providing a boost to the local economy. The second area of focus was labour economics. This was a topic Albeda was personally interested in. How does labour function within an economy? What economic mechanisms govern the supply of, and demand for labour? How are wages determined? Given the economic crisis of the 1980s, Albeda considered labour to be a key factor in the economic process. The third and final area for Maastricht to focus on was economics and government. According to Albeda, the economy was shaped more by the state budget than by market forces. Economists should ask themselves how this had come to be. Albeda talked about 'economic political science': for example, how could economics be used to explain voter behaviour and the functioning of bureaucracy?

All in all, the Economics degree programme in Maastricht had to 'make a new contribution to the academic world'. However, in recruiting staff members – with the exception of professors and senior lecturers – Maastricht had a hard time competing with the corporate world. Recruiting high-calibre business economists, in particular, turned out to be difficult, as higher salaries awaited them in the corporate world.[8] Meanwhile, the plan was for the programme to kick off in September 1984 with a first cohort of 100 students.

In late 1983, Muysken started working as a consultant to the Economics Department.[9] On 1 April 1984 he was appointed professor of General Economics. Soon after, Hein Schreuder was appointed professor of Business Economics, which was followed by Paul van Loon's appointment as professor of Business Economics with a special focus on Finance. In Maastricht, Muysken found a group of predominantly young trailblazers who were yet to obtain their PhDs and who, under the direction of Piet Keizer, were hard at work developing the curriculum: Tom van Veen, Dirk Tempelaar, Mark Ten Hove, Paul Kunst, Hans Peters, Jo Soeters and Geert Woltjer. They had been hired because of their enthusiasm for problem-based learning and were 'working together very closely and with full commitment' to design the curriculum.

FRONT OFFICE Albeda did not tend to get closely involved in academic matters, such as the content of the curriculum. He acted as a kind of father figure within the faculty and, according to Muysken, was mainly there 'for the front office': with his 'extensive network' he was a 'very valuable asset' and managed to get a lot of things done. For example, as early as 1984 Albeda, together with Kremers and with the support of Minister Deetman, made the first steps toward bringing a research institute of the United Nations University (UNU) – a worldwide network of research institutes coordinated by the United Nations – to Maastricht. The United Nations University had initially planned to establish this institute in Helsinki, but Kremers was undeterred by that, and flew to Brazil under his own steam to set about changing the UNU Council's mind.[10]

Luc Soete was appointed in 1985 as professor of International Economic Relations, and soon afterwards established the Maastricht Economic Research Institute on Innovation and Technology (MERIT), of which he became director. On coming to Maastricht he managed to obtain a prime piece of real estate for the institute. 'Luc's little palace', as it came to be referred to, was situated near the faculty's main building on Tongersestraat. MERIT fitted in perfectly with Albeda's plan for *Economics in Maastricht*. The institute started out in 1987 with the help of seed grants from the central and provincial government; in addition, MERIT focused on establishing relationships with external clients. Soete had modelled MERIT on the Science Policy Research Unit at the University of Sussex, where he had spent some time working with the internationally acclaimed Christopher Freeman, an expert on the economics of technology. The institute became part of the Faculty of Economics as a foundation. Partly due to Soete's academic talent and entrepreneurial savvy – he created a sound financial footing for the institute by buying and selling Hungarian forints at just the right time – MERIT achieved an excellent international reputation.[11] More than twenty years later, MERIT would merge with the Maastricht-based UNU institute and continue under the name UNU-MERIT.

Albeda's ties with the Ministry of Education and Science – and with director general Roel in 't Veld in particular – also brought the Research Centre for Education and the Labor Market (ROA) to Maastricht. The research undertaken by this institute is aimed at improving the connection between education and professional practice, based on the notion that the better that connection is, the more effective education can be in contributing to economic growth. The question of how education could get the economy back on its feet was high on the agenda during the economic crisis of the 1980s, a period with worryingly high unemployment rates, including among highly educated professionals. The ROA, too, fitted in perfectly with the plan for *Economics in Maastricht*. Incidentally, by the time all these institutes actually got off the ground, Albeda had already left his position as founding dean. While he continued to work for the university as professor by special appointment, from the spring of 1985 his primary occupation was that of President of the WRR Scientific Council for Government Policy.

Johan Muysken

BACK OFFICE According to Muysken, it was up to the 'back office' to devise a curriculum based on problem-based learning. He was a little put out to learn just how much headway the young trailblazers had made with their plans in his absence: it was not going to be easy for him to still make a clear mark on the first curriculum. Since most of these trailblazers were general economists, the first curriculum was skewed more towards their discipline, much to the displeasure of the business economists. In the end they did manage to carve out some space for their discipline in the curriculum. In spite of these trials and tribulations, Muysken experienced this pioneering era as 'an incredible time', mainly because of the sense of community there was: 'we were all keen to get the faculty off the ground'. He remembers the staff members 'driving through the country in Volkswagen vans with loudspeakers to promote the faculty to the public'.

Although Muysken agreed with the educational principles behind problem-based learning, he was somewhat taken aback by the initially dogmatic approach that its proponents took to 'the faith'. He was given a copy of the booklet *Onderwijs in taakgerichte groepen* ('Education in Task-Oriented Groups') by Henk Schmidt and Peter Bouhuijs: 'We were expected to live by that Bible and be real religious zealots about it'. Muysken learned 'Schmidt and Bouhuijs' by heart in its entirety. 'We were heavily indoctrinated by these two "apostles" from the medical field, and it took us a great deal of effort to notice that later on and distance ourselves from their views. We wanted to do things their way, but we found that it simply didn't work.' For example, the multidisciplinary approach turned out not to be viable in educational practice.

Just as with the Law degree programme, initially the idea was for the Economics curriculum to be taught not according to the disciplinary canon, but with 'the reality' forming the point of departure, in the hopes that this didactic approach would produce more practice-oriented economists. For example, course modules were developed on topics such as production, market, money and management. However, this led to confusion on the part of both students and lecturers. Muysken, at any rate, hated having to be a tutor on subjects that he did not know anything about or was not interested in, such as marketing and organisation. An additional complicating factor was that Maastricht worked with the same subject-specific textbooks that were used elsewhere in the country. No alternatives seemed to be available. Maastricht also did not try to write any textbooks or course readers that dealt with economic issues using an integrated, multidisciplinary approach. Quite the opposite: the lecturers kept making reference to the tried-and-true textbooks on the curriculum in order to demonstrate to the outside world that the Economics students in Maastricht were given the same intellectual foundation as students elsewhere.

Maastricht had to consider its reputation and be credible in the eyes of other universities. Tilburg University even threatened to refuse entry to students who had done the first year of their degree programme in Maastricht. According to Muysken, all this meant that 'fairly soon, we switched to bi-disciplinary modules, bringing together two subjects at most – and preferably ones that were already interrelated organically in some way. Just that was hard enough, if it was even possible at all'. After a while, a discussion arose about the use of the progress test, which proved to be untenable and ended up being abolished after a few years. A progress test can only work if the things that graduates need to know and be capable of have first been clearly established. Meanwhile, the faculty was under pressure from the Executive Board to attract as many students as possible, but it proved difficult to maintain the expensive, 'labour-intensive' system with an influx of hundreds of students every year, while the requirements for scientific 'output' were on the increase. More and more the lecture format began to sneak its way into the curriculum after all for reasons of efficiency.

Looking back, Muysken concludes that, in practice, the problem-based approach to education soon found itself drifting from its ideals on certain points. However, part of experimentation is the willingness to 'acknowledge that the experiment doesn't always work in every respect'. Making the interdisciplinary ambitions a reality; integrating economics, sociology and psychology – all of that turned out to be more difficult than had been anticipated, to the disappointment of people like Keizer, who decided to leave Maastricht.[12] Incidentally, more than twenty years later, the cross-fertilisation between economics and psychology, in particular, would end up getting off the ground after all, in the context of the Human Decision Science Master's programme. Over the years, it turned out to be difficult to break through the 'old' disciplinary boundaries: as they advanced in their studies, students increasingly specialised along disciplinary lines. Muysken does not feel there was a tension between theory and the reality of the evolving programme. On the contrary; he feels that it was the process of shaking off the shackles of dogmatism that made it possible for the 'workable system of problem-based learning that exists today', with groups of 14 students and a heavy emphasis on skills, to come into being. The Maastricht model turned out to be a 'recipe for success': other universities ended up incorporating elements of it into their own Economics degree programmes – even, eventually, Tilburg University.

UNITY IN DIVERSITY? What was particularly unique about the Maastricht Economics programme was the intention to build a bridge between General Economics and Business Economics. After all, the degree programme had to be 'complementary' to the existing degree programmes for it to have a right to exist. A close cooperation between Muysken and Schreuder, therefore, was the first prerequisite. The fact that both of them formed part of, and headed up, their 'own' departments made that integration difficult from the start, even though they were both definitely open to it. Both of them were 'fairly young and ambitious, so that was exciting', Muysken recalls. According to him, the general economists and business economists did not compete with each other, but they did tend to look down somewhat on each other's discipline. The academic status of the general economists, who 'published prolifically', was higher than that of the business economists. Business economists were not interested in research 'as a matter of course', but the field was on the rise and drew the most students. According to Muysken, they were 'two worlds that communicated only very little', especially in Groningen, and 'one of the exciting things about Maastricht' was that he got to talk to more business economists than he ever had before. He found himself having to get used to the idea that business economists could be 'pretty smart'. In Groningen, it was the 'slightly less clever ones' that chose to study business economics – at least, that was how Muysken had viewed it at the time. That idea was dispelled altogether in Maastricht: it 'took some getting used to' to come round to the fact that there were also 'smart business economists' – he was 'quite floored by that at first'.

Muysken and Schreuder looked for links between General Economics and Business Economics. In the introduction to an essay collection they co-authored entitled *Economische wetenschappen: eenheid in verscheidenheid?* ('The Economic Sciences: Unity in Diversity?'), they used the metaphor of a living apart together relationship between an older and a younger partner: 'General Economics considers itself the more mature personality of the two and is worried that Business Economics, in its youthful arrogance, will mess things up. After all, Business Economics considers it part of its duty to advise on practical issues, and is also willing to do so even if no theories are available yet that are capable of meeting the strict requirements related to General Economics'.[13] In the conclusion, Muysken and Schreuder were of the view that there was a wide range of different opinions on the issue. The two of them held their inaugural speech on the same day, 6 September 1985, one after the other. By doing this, they wanted to clearly communicate to the outside world that they were aiming to establish a close collaboration between the two disciplines, even if the general economists tended to focus on more theoretical issues than the practice-oriented business economists.

Muysken's speech was entitled 'How general is General Economics?' The question was to what extent General Economics was capable of incorporating microeconomics and macroeconomics, and the relationship between the two, in its analyses.[14] In this context, the question was also whether a Hicksian approach could be reconciled with a Marshallian approach.[15] The economist John Hicks used a deductive method, based on the notion of the 'representative consumer' who focuses on maximising profit and utility, while Alfred Marshall advocated an inductive approach and wanted to arrive at generalisations only through empirical observation.

Where the business economists tended to emulate Marshall, the general economists were more inspired by Hicks's deductive approach. Muysken's speech sought an economic theory that could be used by both the general economists and the business economists. It is unsurprising that there was no ready-made answer to be found, although he did say that he hoped to be able to learn a lot from the business economists. This theoretical reflection was mainly aimed at his colleagues elsewhere in the country, and, indirectly, at the Economics students in Maastricht. He wanted to demonstrate that what was going on in Maastricht was 'up to par academically'.

The ambition to integrate General Economics and Business Economics was undeniably innovative, but led to disappointment. In addition to the division into individual departments, a certain degree of competition between the two men also did not help matters. According to Muysken, he and Schreuder made a good team, 'but at the same time, from the start we were also arch rivals who were stuck with each other – let's say we were arch rivals who were very good at joining forces'. Incidentally, that rivalry was not just due to the fact that they were both young, ambitious professors who were keen to advance their careers, but also stemmed from the imbalance that, as mentioned before, soon came about within the faculty. Friction arose between the two disciplines. The general economists were very focused on accumulating academic publications. On arrival, Muysken had immediately told the trailblazers who had not yet obtained their PhDs that they had to get on with doing so as soon as possible. But the business economists were the buoy that kept the faculty afloat; by far the most students – up to 80% or 90% – chose to specialise in Business Economics. This meant a significant workload for the faculty members working in this discipline, who as a result had less time left to do research. In addition, business economists were drawn to the practice-oriented corporate world due to the more attractive job prospects and higher salaries compared to the public sector. This meant that the faculty found it increasingly difficult to fill vacancies for Business Economics. This alone made it tricky to give students the opportunity to specialise at an early stage in their studies, but irrespective of this problem there was a fundamental desire to provide first-year students with a broad foundation, even if most of them would go on to specialise in Business Economics after that. These frictions increasingly squeezed General Economics to the margins of the curriculum, while the business economists felt they were getting insufficient academic recognition. Now and then, the question was even raised as to whether it would not be better if the general economists and the business economists were to go their separate ways. However, a split of this kind would cause irreparable damage to the image of the Maastricht Economics programme. It was partly the mediating efforts of Franz Palm – who became professor of Quantitative Economics in 1985 and also got his own department – that managed to prevent this rift. As a 'neutral party', Palm became dean multiple times. The faculty did change its name on a number of occasions – with such changes revealing the shifts in direction that were taking place. Where it started out as the Faculty of Economics, the name was later changed to Faculty of Economic and Business Sciences, followed by Faculty of Economics

Johan Muysken

and Business Administration and – recently – School of Business and Economics. According to Muysken, it was something of a surprise that the word 'economics' was allowed to remain a part of its name at all.

SCALE AND LANGUAGE The faculty grew quickly, sometimes even too quickly for the Faculty Board's liking. Faculty Director Verspeek feared that Economics may just have been 'in fashion' and that students' interest in the subject was just as likely to wane at any moment, with all the consequences this would entail. In addition, by Maastricht standards the academic success rate for the degree programme was not exactly high.[16] Nevertheless, the Executive Board put pressure on the Faculty of Economics to keep growing. And it was successful: by 1990, the faculty had nearly 2,000 students.[17] As it expanded, there was a growing need for differentiation and specialisation. New majors and specialisations were added – with others disappearing or being given new names – such as International Management, Econometrics, International Business Administration, International Economic Studies, Fiscal Economics and Infonomics. Currently the School of Business and Economics offers four bachelor's programmes and nineteen master's programmes, with only two master's programmes being taught in Dutch. According to Muysken, the most striking changes that took place in the course of his career related to 'scale and language'. He recalls how, back in the faculty's heyday, the demographic changes that were taking place gave rise to concerns about the fact that only few students from outside Limburg were coming to Maastricht to study Economics. The faculty consequently turned its attention to prospective students in Germany. The Business Economics department already had a relatively large number of Germans on the staff, such as professor Jürgen Backhaus and lecturers Peter de Gijsel and Thomas Ziesemer, who utilised their networks in Germany. They thought there were bound to be German students who would be interested in doing an English-taught degree in the Netherlands, and would be drawn to the small-scale educational system in Maastricht.

Plans to launch an English-taught degree programme were on the table as early as 1985. The Faculty Board tasked Willem Molle, director of the Netherlands Economic Institute in Rotterdam and professor by special appointment of European Integration, with exploring the possibilities. Molle came up with the idea of launching an 'interfaculty' degree programme in Business Administration and Management together with the Faculty of Law. The latter, however, was not very enthusiastic about this idea. In the meantime, the Faculty of Economics had appointed the organisational psychologist Geert Hofstede, who held a special chair partly funded by the Limburg University Fund (SWOL).[18] Hofstede was supposed to investigate the possibility of establishing a new specialisation in Business Economics at the Faculty of Economic Sciences. In October 1985, Hofstede began developing the International Management track, in which the universities of Liège and Aachen were also involved as part of the so-called ALMA cooperation network. International Management was launched three years later, in 1998, and immediately drew large numbers of students. However, an internal faculty committee considered the programme to be too lightweight and not 'economic' enough. Hofstede was not there at the time, and felt that envy and animosity on the part of the general economists had played a role in this assessment. He resigned, and at his departure ceremony in 1993, Muysken, acting as dean, apologised on behalf of the faculty for the inelegant way in which the matter had been dealt with.[19] In spite of all this, internationalisation gave a new impetus to the faculty, Muysken recounts. Building on the success of the International Management track, efforts commenced to establish a new, independent International Business Studies programme, taught entirely in English, which was to be launched in 1993 and replace International Management. That same year, at the initiative of De Neubourg and De Gijsel, the specialisation in International Economic Studies was introduced within the existing Economics degree programme.[20] The internationalisation of the faculty continued steadily in this way, and at some point 'we became completely Anglicised – there's not a Dutch sign left in the building'. According to Muysken, internationalisation was 'our salvation', as it enabled the faculty to keep innovating and ultimately develop a distinct character of its own.

INCREASING PRESSURE ON RESEARCH OUTPUT In the late 1970s and early 1980s, there was not a lot of pressure on academics to publish, says Muysken, who remembers that the economists at the University of Groningen in fact had rather a superabundance of academic freedom: if an economist wanted to observe the behaviour of frogs, according to the standards that prevailed at the time they should be allowed to do so.[21] Muysken happened to become a professor right at the time when the government began to curtail the universities' autonomy. The academic world was confronted with funding being subject to certain conditions, and, some time later, with the necessity of establishing research schools. According to Muysken, compared to other faculties of economics, the Faculty of Economics in Maastricht was in the fortunate position of being able to attract – predominantly young – staff members with demonstrable research expertise. One of the first things Muysken did was to establish the Netherlands Network of Quantitative Economics (NAKE) in conjunction with other universities, for the benefit of his PhD students. He would end up acting as PhD supervisor to more than twenty students. In Maastricht, research programmes were established focusing on three core topics: labour, technological innovation and governmental behaviour. Later on, the METEOR research school – the Maastricht Research School of Economics of Technology and Organisations – was established, which was recognised by the Royal Netherlands Academy of Arts (KNAW) and Sciences in 1997 and is now called the Graduate School of Business and Economics. By his own account, Muysken has always had a 'love-hate relationship' with METEOR. Where research topics were concerned, he did not want to be straitjacketed. In practice, he felt METEOR was little more than a mailbox: 'You throw in a parcel, and it comes out with a "METEOR" stamp on it'.

Muysken did not like structuring his research. By his own account, his approach to research was 'flighty': he was quick to jump from one topic to the other, and even left articles unfinished sometimes if he found another subject that drew his attention: 'I have too many interests'. According to him, this is partly related to his fondness for working with others. His PhD dissertation, and the other publications related to his PhD research, were the only things he wrote by himself. Muysken often found himself getting engaged in a discussion with colleagues, becoming enthusiastic and curious, and before he knew it they were 'sitting down together to write a piece', with consultations preferably taking place over lunch at work rather than via email. So when irreconcilable differences of opinion over HR policy – whether or not to assume a 'stringent and hard-line culture' – led to his department being broken up into General Economics 1 and General Economics 2, with him continuing to be the director for the latter group, he felt bitterness that it should have come to this.

While Muysken would not call himself a top researcher, his research career has been incredibly productive, with a list of over a 100 publications to his name – and that list is only set to continue to grow in the future.[22] The majority of his research focused on labour economics, the economics of technological change and the monetary economy. Since the banking crisis, he has become more and more interested in the monetary policy of the European Central Bank. Muysken's research is very much informed by his social engagement: he is acutely aware of problems caused by high unemployment. In this context it is not only the economic crisis of the 1980s, which he himself experienced, but the Great Depression, too, that is in the back of his mind. Jobs are not only important from a financial point of view, but also on a social level. One of his best-known works is *Full Employment Abandoned. Shifting Sands and Policy Failures* (2008), a book he co-authored with William Mitchell, professor of Econometrics at the University of Newcastle in Australia. Muysken got to know Mitchell, 'a radical economist with left-wing views', when he spent several months as a guest lecturer in Maastricht around 1990. Mitchell made Muysken realise that he had drifted somewhat from his 'Groningen roots' and acquired 'a Keynesian slant', although he had remained a member of the PvdA (Labour) party. Muysken was so inspired by Mitchell that he, in his turn, ended up going to Australia for some time. They have been visiting each other almost every year ever since. This is how *Full Employment Abandoned* came about, in which the authors make a case for the introduction of employment guarantees. Based on a theoretical analysis of the nature and causes of unemployment over the last 150 years, they criticised the neoliberal ideology that national governments have used to justify the abandonment of full employment as a goal. The authors stated that governments should, in fact, help to create additional jobs and offer job guarantees, and that this would benefit the economy. In his farewell speech on 29 November 2013, too, Muysken argued in favour of active government intervention, criticising the government's fixation on deficit reduction and cutting public spending. Drawing on an analysis of the global financial crisis of 2008, Muysken made a case for a more stimulatory budgetary policy, preferably using monetary finance, i.e. printing more money.[23] He also criticised the transformation of the welfare state into a 'participatory' society. This so-called civil society went hand in hand with the 'flexibilisation' of labour, which for individual employees often amounted to temporary or permanent unemployment. Muysken again advocated the introduction of employment guarantees.

He also referred back to his inaugural address, in which he had sought a bridge between the Marshallian and the Hicksian approaches. Thirty years later, he felt he had found that middle ground in stock-flow consistent modelling. Following on from his previous research, Muysken explained how the current weakness of the Dutch economy (like that of the 1970s and 1980s) is caused by a structural lack of investment and a lack of balance-sheet equilibrium, especially in the banking industry and in private households. The key idea here is that equity and debt (including that related to home-ownership) are the decisive factors in explaining the behaviour of businesses and consumers. This model is based on a fundamentally different conception of behavioural economics. Where neo-Keynesian economics assumes that businesses and consumers plan ahead far into the future, Muysken's model is based on the more realistic assumption that the future behaviour of consumers tends to be more or less the same as that of today and yesterday. It also differs from the neo-Keynesian approach in that it is aggregate demand (rather than aggregate supply) that forms the starting point. Muysken feels that the stock-flow consistent model can not only help Economics to get ahead as a scientific discipline, but that it can also help to find a way to overcome the weaknesses of the current economic system. When he retired from his position, he vowed to continue to explore this research area. He stated that, given the unexplored territory that lay ahead in this field, he was extremely reluctant to retire.

12 *Hein Schreuder* ECONOMICS IN MAASTRICHT HAD TO BE INTIMIDATINGLY DIFFERENT, MORE INTERNATIONAL AND BETTER

A LOST LETTER In his quest for a professor of Business Economics, founding dean Wil Albeda went to great lengths to track down Hein Schreuder.[1] Albeda had sent Schreuder a letter asking him to apply for a job in Maastricht, but the letter never arrived. In 1983, Schreuder was enjoying a sabbatical and working at the University of Washington's Graduate School of Business in Seattle as a visiting scholar. It was a case of crossed wires: the invitation to apply for a post as professor in Maastricht had ended up with another Schreuder, the biologist Paul Schreuder, who promptly sent a polite reply saying that he was not looking to change his discipline just then. It was not until after he had returned to the Netherlands that Hein Schreuder finally got to see Albeda's letter. Just to be sure, Albeda had sent a copy to Schreuder's house in Nieuwkoop. By that point, the letter had already been sitting on his doormat for two or three months but, since his curiosity was piqued, he rang Albeda asking if there was still any point in applying for the position. A number of staff members had been appointed by then, such as Joan Muysken as professor of General Economics and Paul van Loon – who came from a finance background – as professor of Business Economics. Schreuder had initially focused on finance and accounting, but during his sabbatical his emphasis had shifted more towards strategy and organisation as he had grown interested in economic organisation theory. According to Schreuder, at the time marketing was still 'kind of seen as the poor relative of Business Economics'.

Albeda was keen to meet. The young Schreuder seemed like a promising candidate: he was already accomplished in his field, with a considerable number of publications to his name. By then he was already in the Dutch Economists Top 40, an annual ranking based on publications in journals which was dominated by general and quantitative economists. The Selection Board was swiftly convened so that a meeting with Schreuder could be arranged after all. The interview took place at the parliamentary building in The Hague, the Binnenhof, where Albeda had managed to book 'a massive room'. Schreuder remembers it well, because he was impressed by the whole entourage. He was received by 'a full committee in which all the faculties of economics were represented, because, naturally, everyone wanted to be in the know about what was going on in Maastricht'. He remembers that Tilburg University, in particular, was nervous about the plans that were being hatched at the time in Maastricht. The Selection Board also included representatives from the business community, such as Hans van Liemt, CEO of Dutch multinational Royal DSM. The interview went well; after a spirited conversation, Schreuder was told immediately that they were keen to hire him as professor of Business Economics. He had just turned 32 and had previously established a research institute in Amsterdam. He had already received offers for a part-time position as professor from both Leiden and Utrecht. However, he was very much drawn to the idea of building something new in Maastricht: 'I'm a builder'. He thought this would be the last opportunity to establish a new faculty of economics in the Netherlands. He was also drawn to the fact that this was not to be a mere simulacrum of all the other faculties, but would be putting a new educational system into practice: 'There was a need for something new'.

JAKARTA, HONG KONG, SINGAPORE, MELBOURNE, SCHEVENINGEN, ROTTERDAM, AMSTERDAM AND MAASTRICHT One of the things that probably made Hein Schreuder an interesting candidate in Albeda's eyes was his international background. In his report *Economics in Maastricht* (1983), Albeda had pointed out the opportunities presented by the Maastricht location for establishing partnerships with the universities of Hasselt, Leuven and Aachen. The contacts he had made there were 'promising'. This outline document already suggested the possibility of establishing a specialisation in international management within the Business Economics discipline.[2] Schreuder had already lived in a number of different countries because of his father's job. He had been born in Jakarta in 1951. After being a POW in a Japanese internment camp and a long period of recuperation in the Netherlands, his father had worked his way up and become an executive of Internatio, a large multinational based in Rotterdam that traded in a wide range of products (rubber, cocoa, cotton, coffee) and which went on to merge with the shipping company Müller. Schreuder's father had managed to take over all sorts of companies in Asia and Australia, becoming CEO in the first few years following the takeovers. His entrepreneurial spirit meant that the family ended up moving every two years or so: from Jakarta to Hong Kong, from Hong Kong to Singapore and from Singapore to Melbourne. Hein had no siblings, which meant it was up to him to make new contacts at the various schools he went to, and make new friends time and again. He had gone to elementary school in Melbourne. By his own account, he received a good education there, although he also remembers the approach to education being very authoritarian. When, at recess, he accidentally smashed a window with a cricket ball, he was hit on his hands with a belt by his teacher in front of his classmates. Schreuder says that his experiences with a wide range of different cultures gave him 'a sociologist's perspective': 'looking from the outside in and assessing social situations, sometimes with some degree of surprise'.

By the time he moved to Scheveningen with his parents, at the age of eight, in what was to be a permanent return to the Netherlands, he spoke fluent English, albeit with an Australian accent. In 1969, he graduated from the Eerste Vrijzinnig-Christelijk Lyceum (First Liberal Christian Lyceum) secondary school in The Hague, with a science-focused subject package that included classical languages. After some deliberating – Law or Economics? – he decided to study Economics in Rotterdam. He had discovered in a series of summer jobs that he was drawn to the corporate world. He became a research assistant with the Finance Department – 'a very talented group of people, many of whom would go on to become professors' – and at the tender age of 20 was already being asked to teach Q&A sessions to hundreds of first-year students. By his own account, it was here that he became 'infected with the academic virus'. His fascination with academia grew and his desire to move on to the corporate world waned. Schreuder graduated in 1976, majoring in Business Economics with a specialisation in Finance, but he was also interested in public values – for example, businesses' corporate social responsibility with respect to the environment. Schreuder had been very impressed by *The Limits to Growth* (1972) by the Club of Rome, a group of scientists from all over the world who had outlined a doomsday scenario for the future of the world by establishing a link between economic growth and the disastrous consequences of it for the environment. The report had a tremendous impact, generating fervent debate.[3]

Schreuder found his first job at the Netherlands Economic Institute, which formed part of Erasmus University Rotterdam. At the time, it was known as 'Tinbergen's institute', and conducted economic research for developing countries, often commissioned by external parties.[4] However, it had other departments too, and Schreuder became a junior researcher in the Business Economics Department. Among other things, he studied the merger of the Amsterdam and Rotterdam insurance exchanges and 'the extent of fraud in the construction industry'. The latter research took him to Limburg for the first time. Schreuder remembers well a tax inspector explaining to him that in Limburg people built houses for each other, and that could not be classified as fraud.

Before long, he moved on to VU Amsterdam's Economic and Social Institute, where he started out as head of Business Economic Research, subsequently becoming director of the institute in 1981. This institute was one-quarter funded by the university and otherwise dependent on externally contracted research. That same year, Schreuder had obtained his PhD under Bob Goudzwaard, professor of General Economics at VU Amsterdam and a well-known politician with the CDA (Christian-Democrat) party, who was one of the party's progressive wing. His co-supervisor was professor of Business Economics Lou Traas. Schreuder found Goudzwaard's enthusiasm and Traas's practical approach to be a good combination. Working with the two of them was also one of the first things that sparked his desire to build a bridge between General Economics and Business Economics. Schreuder's PhD dissertation was entitled *Maatschappelijke verantwoordelijkheid en maatschappelijke berichtgeving van ondernemingen* ('Corporate Social Responsibility and Corporate Social Reporting').

As part of his research, Schreuder found himself delving into sociology and psychology. His research also fed into the debate on 'welfare economics', at the core of which lay the question of whether the term 'welfare' should in fact be expanded. Could economics be reduced down to no more than market variables? Schreuder stated that businesses had more than simply the responsibility to make a profit, but had, in addition, an 'overall responsibility', i.e. a *social* responsibility for their impact on people – their workforce in particular – and the surroundings, especially in terms of the environment. This responsibility could be summed up by the 'triple bottom line': people, planet and profit. This concept would go on to become widespread across the corporate world, with the TBL framework being central to the approach of Royal DSM, the company Schreuder would go on to work for. Schreuder's dissertation chimed with both Goudzwaard and Albeda's views. It is therefore unsurprising that Schreuder – with everything he had managed to achieve, and at a fairly young age at that – should have been earmarked for a professorial post in Maastricht. During Schreuder's time there, VU Amsterdam's Economic and Social Institute had tripled in size, from ten to thirty staff members. Schreuder's decision to go to Maastricht yielded another unexpected advantage. At his farewell party, he managed to get Franz Palm, then professor of Econometrics at VU Amsterdam, interested in Maastricht. Palm was originally from Büllingen, a German-language municipality in the Belgian province of Liège, and liked the idea of a return south. In 1985, he was appointed professor of Quantitative Economics at the State University of Limburg.

TENSIONS On his arrival in Maastricht in March 1984, Schreuder, like his colleague Joan Muysken (who had just been appointed professor of General Economics), was enthusiastic about problem-based learning. He was keen to give it a try, and did not feel 'the slightest hesitation'. He was especially drawn to the idea of 'learning to learn', as he felt that this skill was one of the hallmarks of an academic mind. He also felt that an emphasis on skills, such as learning to work as part of a team, was important. He was hoping that the interdisciplinary approach would teach students to reflect on the role of economists and economics in a broader social context.[5] He did feel that the approach was being put into practice in a rather dogmatic way. The 'educationalists surrounding Wynand Wijnen were very proactive', keeping a close eye on the economists to ensure they stayed true to the tenets of problem-based learning. Schreuder remembers discussions with Wijnen about the issue of how students could learn statistics in a problem-based way. Schreuder felt that it was necessary to first provide them with a certain body of knowledge. He recalls that, over time, the economists made adjustments to the strict application of the problem-based approach to education. For example, they introduced lectures and began to enable students to do practical assignments with companies; innovations which, according to Schreuder, the students actually liked. Nevertheless, in Schreuder's view problem-based learning continued to be the core method. Incidentally, he feels the business economists had an easier time of it than the general and quantitative economists, as Business Economics is a practice-oriented field that can fairly easily be placed within the framework of problem-based learning. In the beginning, he was deeply immersed in his activities as a tutor, but after some time he shifted his focus towards management and research. Where there was already tension between the theory and practice of the problem-based method, within the Faculty of Economics there was also a conflict – at least as significant – between General Economics and Business Economics/Business Administration. The Academic Charter stipulated that a core faculty of economics had to have four professors of General Economics, four professors of Business Economics and two professors of Quantitative Economics. This, however, created an imbalance in Maastricht, as it turned out that only 10% of the students ended up specialising in General Economics. As already became apparent in the chapter on Muysken, the majority of students preferred Business Economics over General Economics. Many of the first faculty members, however, were general economists, so that the emphasis in the curriculum was initially on this discipline. This early imbalance ended up working in Schreuder's favour, as it enabled him to get his 'own type of business economists' on board – people who were internationally minded and highly interested in research.

ECONOMICS IN MAASTRICHT: A POLITICALLY SHREWD DOCUMENT

According to Schreuder, with *Economics in Maastricht* Albeda and his advisors had written a politically shrewd document, as it presented the new degree programme in Maastricht as complementary to the existing economics programmes in the Netherlands. Schreuder remembers Albeda as an erudite economist with a strong sense of social engagement; originally a unionist, he went on to become a 'true politician'. Schreuder got on well with him, although he found him 'difficult to fathom' at first. According to Schreuder, Albeda had 'found a politically clever way to carve out a niche for the Faculty of Economics in Maastricht'. The focus areas of labour, technology and the public sector were, however, typical choices from a General Economics perspective. A business economist might also opt for technology and would, in Schreuder's words, 'be able to make something of "labour" – and we did'. However, the topic of 'the public sector' was not something a business economist would be able to do much with. Schreuder felt it was predictable that most students would choose to specialise in Business Economics and Business Administration, as elsewhere in the Netherlands, too, most students preferred these disciplines. Shortly after his arrival in Maastricht, Schreuder came to the conclusion that 'the environment' – i.e. the leading politicians and industrialists of Limburg – would have preferred a Business School or a Business Administration and/or Management degree programme, while Albeda's outline was based on the idea of a 'fully-fledged Faculty of Economics'. Schreuder soon saw 'friction emerge between the original intentions expressed in this outline document and the needs of society and the student body'.

A BUSINESS SCHOOL? According to Schreuder, Albeda, too, quickly became aware of this friction. Schreuder had not yet been in Maastricht for three months when, in the autumn of 1984, he and Albeda sat down with various stakeholders to explore the possibility of founding a Business School. Talks were held with the Queen's Commissioner for the Province of Limburg, Sjeng Kremers (who was always keen to promote Limburg in any way possible), the Limburg University Fund (SWOL) and representatives from the business community. Schreuder was told they felt it was a shame that no Business School had been established in Maastricht, as Limburg had a greater need for business economists than general economists. Couldn't the Faculty of Economics be turned into a Faculty of Economic and Business Sciences? According to Schreuder, the Executive Board even toyed with the idea of establishing a new Business School in addition to the Faculty of Economics to preempt any competition from the outside.

It was Albeda who concluded that, within the Academic Council's Department of Economics, there was a growing conviction that a Business School could only exist as part of the Faculty of Economics. Albeda considered it unwise to establish a 'business track' in the short term. He thought that the faculty should get through the first four years first, and that they should wait and see how the 'Molle plan' would work out.[6] This referred to the plans of Willem Molle, professor appointed to the endowed chair for European Integration, who at the request of the Faculty Board was working on developing an internationally oriented programme at the interface of management, management science and business administration. The idea was for this programme to be taught jointly by the Faculty of Economics and the Faculty of Law.[7] Molle and Schreuder knew each other well and exchanged thoughts in this period. They had been colleagues at the Netherlands Economic Institute, and Molle was director of the institute while the talks on the expansion of the Faculty of Economics were underway. In consultation with Albeda, President of the Executive Board Rob van den Biggelaar, Rector Vic Bonke and Kremers, in the spring of 1985 Schreuder also began to explore the possibilities for a major in Management, Business Administration and Public Administration 'on a confidential basis' – in other words, to take the first steps towards a Business School within the Faculty of Economics.[8]

Schreuder suggested that Geert Hofstede be contacted and asked to help get the new Business Administration programme off the ground. They knew each other from the early 1980s, when they had both been working at the European Institute for Advanced Studies in Management, based in Brussels. Since the publication of the book *Culture's Consequences* (1980) Hofstede, according to Schreuder, had come to be known as 'the great culture guru in the field of Business Administration': 'Geert was a big name in the field of comparative cultural studies.' The fact that Hofstede was willing to come to Maastricht represented an 'incredible opportunity'. In late October 1985, the Limburg University Fund earmarked 400,000 guilders to appoint Hofstede as the 'driving force' behind a new specialisation in Management, Business Administration and Public Administration. Schreuder managed to convince Hofstede's previous employer, IBM, to also make 'a sum of money' available to the Limburg University Fund. Hofstede went on to combine a 'regular' post as professor with an endowed chair, and immediately titled the new specialisation 'International Management'.[9]

This essentially meant that two initiatives to expand the Faculty of Economics were taking place in tandem: Molle's and Hofstede's. Looking back, Schreuder explains this slightly odd approach: 'In those exciting, turbulent first years of the faculty, various formal and informal pathways were running in parallel and crisscrossing one another'.[10] Ultimately, the faculty would end up going with the programme developed by Hofstede, to be taught entirely in English: in 1988, the International Management programme was launched, a course which, according to Schreuder, became a 'resounding success' thanks to its internationalist approach – with an exchange programme in place between Aachen, Liège and Maastricht – and drew a lot of students.[11] This gave the Faculty of Economics a new, international profile. Schreuder: 'Yes, the region wanted it, the students wanted it, and – let's be honest – though not everyone was keen on the idea, and it involved quite a battle within the faculty, I wanted it too. The idea was right up my street. We had to do something different, distinguish ourselves from the other faculties of economics –

focus not on the Netherlands, but turn our attention beyond Dutch borders. Moreover, we had to start teaching in English'.

According to Schreuder, with the launch of the International Management programme the tensions the *Economics in Maastricht* report had previously aroused were relegated to the background: 'within a year, we were focused on something different'. Paul van Loon, who had succeeded Albeda as dean, found this difficult to accept: 'it didn't work out' with Van Loon, who ended up deciding to go back to Tilburg. Unlike what was going on in Rotterdam, for example, in Maastricht General Economics and Business Economics continued to be housed within the same faculty, in spite of the 'labour pains' this brought with it. According to Schreuder, there were also some general economists in the department who did consider internationalisation to be important. Muysken was interested in it. And someone like Luc Soete, who was also a general economist and the founder of MERIT, was 'always looking for ways to innovate': a 'true cosmopolitan' with 'an international perspective'.[13]

ECONOMICS (AND) BUSINESS According to Schreuder, the *Economics in Maastricht* report – which was actually meant to legitimise the new faculty – had a built-in 'structural defect' which created, or exacerbated, tensions between the general economists and the business economists. Despite of that, Muysken and Schreuder were quite willing to work together. They held their inaugural addresses on the same day, 6 September 1985. Muysken's inaugural speech discussed the question of 'How general is general economics?'[13], while Schreuder's was titled 'Economics (and) business. On business economics as a challenging, exciting and idiosyncratic component of the economic sciences'.[14] Schreuder recalls that they had shown each other their drafts in advance and given each other feedback. They had even dedicated 'a little conference' to this. In his speech, Schreuder stated that the discipline of Business Economics could be approached from multiple angles: as a sub-discipline of Economics; as a more or less separate discipline which focused on business problems in a very practical way; and as a fairly independent discipline that, starting from an economic angle, sought to integrate insights from other disciplines in the social sciences in order to examine business problems. It should come as no surprise that Schreuder preferred the third perspective. This take on Business Economics also implied that he thought it was an illusion to believe that it was possible to dissolve the tensions within the field between a focus on economic theory and a focus on practice – although he agreed with Muysken that the general economists and the business economists could benefit from each other's theoretical insights. The point was that the business economists had a different object of study; for example, they were interested in management issues, planning and control and the different behavioural aspects of alternative approaches.

THAT MAY WORK IN PRACTICE, BUT IT DOESN'T WORK IN THEORY As a scientific discipline, Business Economics was still relatively young. It had started out not as an offshoot of General Economics, but as an answer to the need for practical knowledge. The academisation of Business Economics had taken place only fairly recently. Only in 1921 had the University of Amsterdam (known at the time as the Municipal University) been the first in the Netherlands to get a 'Faculty of Trade'.[15] According to Schreuder, business economists are by nature interested in the realm of the practical, which did not change the fact that he was always looking for economic theories (including organisational theories) and approaches from other disciplines that could be helpful to him. For example, he became interested in behavioural economics, an interdisciplinary area of research at the crossroads of psychology and economics, with research taking into account the psychological factors that play a role in economic decision-making. Focusing on the impact that psychological, social, cognitive and emotional factors had on economic decisions made by individuals and institutions, this field had first emerged in the early 1980s. What made it difficult for the business economists to undertake research was that their teaching workload was relatively heavy. They also found themselves having to combat the image of them held by the general economists: the notion that Business Economics was 'unsophisticated', insufficiently grounded in theory and too practice-oriented. Schreuder jokingly sums up this attitude with the adage 'that may work in practice, but it doesn't work in theory'.

Schreuder was therefore keen to become chair of the Science Committee. He wanted to ensure that 'the internal criteria for the allocation of research funds were balanced, such that different research methods were given the opportunity to flourish, rather than certain approaches monopolising all the funding'. Schreuder felt that too much of the research funding at other faculties of economics was given to the general and quantitative economists. As the chair of the Science Committee, he saw it as his duty to ensure that the business economists did not just end up teaching, but were also given the time to do research. The research group surrounding Schreuder was mainly focused on organisational issues. Many of the young people in this group who had been present at the faculty's inception went on to become professors, such as Anne-Wil Harzing, Sjoerd Romme, Arndt Sorge, Arjen van Witteloostuijn and Mariëlle Heijltjes, who in 2006 was the first woman to become professor at the Maastricht Faculty of Economics. In addition, from 1985 Schreuder was first member, and later president, of the Foundation for the Promotion of Economic Research (ECOZOEK), the economic branch of the Netherlands Organisation for Scientific Research (NWO). According to Schreuder, his appointment was rather exceptional, as business economists were barely given any say within the NOW in those days. His own research focus was 'strategy and organisation'. For example, he co-edited the book *In-*

terdisciplinary Perspectives on Organizational Studies with Siegwart Lindenberg (a sociologist and supporter of rational choice theory), and together with Sytse Douma, professor of Business Administration at Tilburg University, he published *Economic Approaches to Organizations,* a handbook on economic approaches to the study of management and organisations. Schreuder had gained inspiration for this book before coming to Maastricht, during his stay as a visiting scholar at the University of Washington in Seattle. He did not find the time to write the book until a later sabbatical in 1990, when he stayed at the Netherlands Institute for Advanced Studies and the Harvard Business School. The book was first published in 1991, has since been translated into six different languages, and is now on its sixth reprint.[16] Schreuder was a prolific writer: during his relatively brief spell as professor at the State University of Limburg, he published a wide range of articles and reports in both English and Dutch – in addition to the books mentioned above. He covered various topics, preferably topics with a clear practical impact, such as leadership and organisational culture, corporate strategy and the reporting and use of information. However, Schreuder had a keen entrepreneurial spirit and ambitions that ranged beyond just establishing a broad line of research.

ENTERPRISING Schreuder founded LIBER: the Limburg Institute for Business and Economic Research. He modelled the institute, established in 1986, on VU Amsterdam's Economic and Social Institute, of which he had – as mentioned previously – been director. Initially, there was a fair amount of opposition to these plans at the State University of Limburg. But Schreuder's argument that Maastricht 'couldn't lag behind' other universities in Amsterdam, Tilburg and Groningen, turned out to be persuasive.[17] LIBER was – and remains – the central body affiliated with the Faculty of Economics through which contract research is won and undertaken. Schreuder succeeded in giving LIBER its own legal personality so that it was able to enter into contracts independently, enabling the institute to be 'more flexible and agile' in responding to the market. The staff were employed by the university and seconded to LIBER to undertake project research. The idea was that LIBER would undertake research for the business community – especially the local business community in Limburg – but according to Schreuder, people also tried to do things the other way around, i.e. research projects that staff members wanted to do anyway were presented in such a way that they could be sold to external contract partners as 'relevant' to them. Research was commissioned by, for example, the Macintosh Retail Group, the Limburg Savings Bank and the National Investment Bank, while work placements were created for students. In addition, Schreuder established the Foundation for Business Community Links with the Faculty of Economics, an entity which collected sponsorship money from businesses, among other things for the appointment of visiting professors, so that interesting lectures could be offered to both students and people from the business community. He also got involved with the establishment of the Centre for European Studies. Initially, this initiative more or less 'fell into his lap'. The mayor of Maastricht, Philip Houben, told Schreuder informally that there was friction between Tilburg University and the American partners involved in the Programme for European Studies. This successful programme had been providing American students in Tilburg with a foundation in economic, political and legal knowledge about Europe for years. Houben asked Schreuder how he felt about bringing this programme to Maastricht, in view of the Faculty of Economics' international ambitions. Schreuder, of course, considered this an excellent idea, and Queen's Commissioner Sjeng Kremers was on his side. Not only Houben, but Kremers too wanted to make Maastricht into 'a real showcase' with as many international knowledge centres as possible. With financial support from the local and provincial authorities, the Centre for European Studies (CES) did indeed end up coming to Maastricht, where it was immediately brought under the umbrella of the university. Schreuder and Molle became interim directors. The first director of the Institute was Pim Fortuyn, who later went on to become a well-known publicist and politician in the Netherlands, and was even then an unconventional man: 'He was recommended to us by Wil Albeda, who had worked with him in Rotterdam. I personally got on well with Pim', says Schreuder, 'but unfortunately we had to let him go after about a year and a half'.[18]

Schreuder was closely involved in the relocation of yet another institute to Maastricht. He responded positively to Kremers' suggestion of bringing the Netherlands International Institute for Management (RVB) from Delft to Maastricht. This non-profit organisation, which was supported by the government and had links with Delft University of Technology, focused on training managers in developing countries. When, in 1988, Kremers saw an opportunity to lure the RVB away from Delft, he took action immediately. He gave the institute a new building in Maastricht free of charge, which it moved into in 1989.[19] It was renamed Maastricht School of Management (MSM) in 1993. From the outset the idea was for the institute to become part of the Faculty of Economics, or at least of the university. Schreuder considers the fact that they never managed to do this – in spite of three attempts over the years – to be 'a bloody shame': 'both institutions would benefit from the combination. And the fact that attempts to make this happen fail time and again usually points toward the people involved'.

CAN I PRACTICE WHAT I PREACH? During his sabbatical at the Harvard Business School in 1990, there were multiple reasons for Schreuder to reflect on his future. To begin with, he received job offers from various different places, including from abroad, where he was offered a chair 'at a renowned business school'. In addition, he felt increasingly challenged by his object of study: would his knowledge and skills also prove valuable in the reality of the business world? The question 'can I practice what I preach?' became increasingly pertinent for him. The third reason had to do with the Faculty of Economics, which had entered into a more stable period; for Schreuder, with his enterprising personality, this meant it was time to look for the next challenge. Partly because of his family situation, he chose to remain in the Netherlands. He ended up moving on to Royal DSM, a chemistry giant based in Limburg which had suffered dramatic losses in the early 1990s. As a 'corporate strategist', Schreuder took on the task of helping DSM to develop activities that were less sensitive to economic fluctuations.[20] He ended up working there for twenty years, between 1991 and 2011. In this period, DSM adjusted to the new circumstances and transformed into an international Life Sciences & Material Sciences company.[21] When in 2011, at the age of 60, he left DSM, he was again 'ready for something new'. Looking back on his professional career, he considers himself 'lucky': 'of course, being able to help build the new faculty and make it into a success was a fantastic opportunity. Later on, at DSM, I was once again fortunate to be given responsibility for the strategy of a company that felt the need to transform itself, and was able to go through that transformation successfully. I'm grateful for the opportunities I've been offered. I now feel the need to "give back" to people and society: after the stages of "learning and earning", now my focus has shifted to "returning"'. That is why he has turned his attention to a broad array of meaningful activities in line with his interests and expertise, such as coaching and advising companies and individuals, heading up a range of different organisations and playing a supervisory role: 'It's great that my supervisory responsibilities have enabled me to turn my attention to education and research once again. With these roles, I've come full circle in my working life'.

13 *Gerard de Vries* A SERIOUS UNIVERSITY NOT ONLY OFFERS CAREER TRAINING BUT ALSO CULTIVATES ACADEMIC THINKING AND CULTURE

IN A MOMENT OF IMPETUOUSNESS In the summer of 1986 Gerard de Vries (born in 1948) travelled from the high north of the Netherlands to Maastricht for a job interview. The State University of Limburg was looking for a professor of Philosophy to strengthen the core unit (*basisvoorziening*) of Philosophy at the Faculty of General Sciences 'in formation'. The role of this faculty was to offer courses for students enrolled in the existing faculties. At that time De Vries was working at the University of Groningen and had never even visited Maastricht before. To his surprise he saw priests and members of religious orders walking around everywhere in the city, 'actually wearing habits!'[1] He found this Catholic atmosphere quite strange, as he had grown up in an atheist environment and was a member of left-wing intellectual circles with colleagues such as Lolle Nauta, Ger Harmsen and Pim Fortuyn. He felt startled by the fact that Catholicism was still so visible in Maastricht, and experienced quite a culture shock. The chairman of the Selection Committee was Bertus de Rijk, a professor emeritus of Philosophy from Leiden who specialised in ancient and mediaeval philosophy and who had now settled in Limburg and was a member of parliament for the PvdA (Labour) party. As De Vries recalls, Paul Thung also sat on the committee. Thung was professor of Medicine in both Leiden and Maastricht and right from the start he had helped the university with advice on launching new initiatives. Tannelie Blom, as a representative of the recently employed staff of the core unit of Philosophy, also formed part of the committee, as did Louis Boon, whom De Vries knew well. Boon had been employed as a professor of Philosophy in Health Sciences since the start of 1985 and had drawn De Vries' attention to the vacancy. They were both on the editorial board of the philosophy journal *Kennis en Methode. Tijdschrift voor wetenschapsfilosofie and methodologie* ('Knowledge and Method. Journal for Science Philosophy and Methodology').

The university was seeking a professor of Philosophy. The job description was fairly general but specified that the post included promoting a sense of social responsibility in science – a mandatory task for universities at the time. Specifically, Thung believed that in view of the ethical risks that science and technology could present to society, the prospective professor should be active in this area. De Vries soon proved to be the right candidate, and in a 'moment of impetuousness' he decided to relocate to Maastricht. Born in the Frisian town of Leeuwarden, De Vries was an engineer and had studied Applied Mathematics at the Technical University of Twente. But his chief interest lay in philosophy of science: 'in the development of science, and in the scientific and political problems involved in science'. In 1977 he earned his PhD with Nauta in Groningen with a thesis on *Sociale orde, regels en de sociologie: een wetenschapsfilosofisch onderzoek naar theorievorming in de sociologie* ('Social order, rules and sociology: a philosophy of science investigation of theory formation in sociology'). After serving for some years as a member of the academic staff in Twente, in 1981 De Vries was asked to move to Groningen to replace Nauta when the latter went to Zambia for three years to set up a philosophy institute in Lusaka.

During these years, Philosophy of Science as an academic subject was undergoing rapid development: increasingly, research was focusing on the empirical – sociological and historical – study of scientific practices and on the relationship between science and society, instead of further elaborating the more traditional philosophical ideas about science. This shift was reflected at some other Dutch universities as well (in particular Amsterdam, Twente and Leiden). De Vries introduced this 'empirical shift' to the Philosophy of Science department in Groningen. In addition to Philosophy students he also taught 'Engineering, Sociology and Science students' in Twente and Groningen. In 1984 this teaching led to a widely praised textbook that was used for decades at many universities: *De ontwikkeling van wetenschap: een inleiding in de wetenschapsfilosofie* ('The development of science: an introduction to philosophy of science').

De Vries did not feel it was a problem that in Maastricht he was required to teach courses to students in various faculties in order to 'give them some cultural baggage and academic education'. He had already acquired the requisite experience in Twente and Groningen. Another attractive factor was that he could take along two members of staff whom he held in 'high regard': the philosopher Rein de Wilde from Groningen and the engineer and technology researcher Wiebe Bijker from Twente. The fact that the faculty was in formation at that time also had positive aspects: it provided the opportunity to start something new. As part of his preparations for his Maastricht appointment, he travelled with Boon to the United States in October 1986 to gather ideas for a programme that would devote attention to the social implications of scientific and technological developments.[2] They returned with letters from Harvard, the Massachusetts Institute of Technology and Virginia Tech that expressed interest in closer collaboration in this field with the university in Maastricht. On 15 March 1987, two days before his 40th birthday, De Vries was appointed professor – something he really appreciated, such a short time before reaching middle age. At that time the Faculty of General Sciences 'in formation' consisted of two core units: Philosophy and History. Two further core units in the field of Mathematics and Information Science were also being planned.

THE FACULTY OF GENERAL SCIENCES: A SPRINGBOARD? His first experiences in Maastricht were extremely disappointing. After an introductory meeting with Karl Dittrich, the third member of the Executive Board, he was still unsure of what was expected of him. Dittrich told him that the new faculty had been wished for by the University Council, and also told him straight out that he, Dittrich, did not really know what a professor of Philosophy was doing at the State University of Limburg. Whatever the case, setting up a new study programme was not an option. De Vries thought: 'What in God's name am I going to do here?'. Had he, in his moment of impetuousness, made the right decision? The Faculty of General Sciences 'in formation' was, he now realised, a kind of trick that would enable the State University of Limburg to get a larger budget from the state education authorities.[3] The creation of the Faculty of Health Sciences in 1984 had, so to speak, paved the way for this new faculty – in the hope that this, just like its predecessor, would serve as a springboard for expansion initiatives. But it was doubtful whether these had a realistic chance of success. At the time that De Vries appeared in Maastricht, various attempts to set up new degree programmes in the fields of literature, chemistry, liberal arts, philosophy, education science, mathematics and history had all fallen by the wayside. Shortly before De Vries's arrival, two Canadians, Luis Branda and Barbera Ferrier, who were attached to McMaster University in Hamilton, had suggested an Arts and Sciences programme. The idea behind this was to train academically educated generalists on the basis of a wide variety of arts, science and social science courses. But this plan bit the dust at an early stage – for various reasons the four existing faculties did not want to cooperate.[4]

In the mid-1980s the State University of Limburg had not succeeded in supplementing its rather one-sided range of practically and vocationally oriented programmes with other courses that offered more general, broad-based training. It was simply impossible to set up Arts and Science programmes: the job market had no need for languages, and sciences were too expensive – which is what the State University of Limburg was told by the Ministry of Education and Science. Since 1984 the universities had been in the grip of a task allocation plan that involved hefty spending cuts. Moreover, in 1986 the Selective Shrinkage and Growth scheme played a role: in addition to further spending cuts, the Minister of Education, Deetman, now also introduced incentive measures to promote new and promising research programmes. In this time of economic recession the idea of a new degree programme seemed a sign of hubris. The 'other' universities preferred to keep the Maastricht newcomer as small as possible – or perhaps, even better, to see it disappear completely. Nonetheless, staff of the core units of Philosophy and History were engaged in making plans for a new Arts and Culture programme, in collaboration with higher professional education (the Maastricht arts programmes). They could count on the support of Executive Board President Rob van den Biggelaar, who attached strong value to the university's cultural influence in the region. Consequently he also tried to recruit Wiel Kusters, a Dutch-language specialist from Maastricht who was active in cultural affairs and, in 1986, happened to be engaged as a visiting professor in Berlin.[5]

A LOST CAUSE On his arrival in Maastricht, De Vries found a number of young, mostly pre-doctorate staff members in the faculty. The very first staff member in the Philosophy core unit was Blom, who had studied philosophy in Leiden and had been recruited by De Rijk back in 1984 to teach courses, such as Logic to Law students.[6] Other staff members in the faculty included the philosophers Maarten Doorman, Werner Callebaut and the philosophy educationalist Pieter Mostert. Chris den Hamer, originally also a philosopher, was the director of the faculty in formation. There were also a few historians such as Ton Nijhuis and Jeroen Dekker. Jo Wachelder was a theoretical physicist who had become involved in the State University of Limburg during his compulsory community service and began studying Philosophy of Science. Before the arrival of De Vries, Boon had been seen as the driving force, attempting to generate enthusiasm for the research themes in the field of medical ethics. The purpose of this faculty in formation – the faculty was formally founded in October 1987 – was to increase the focus on the university's ideal of cultural education. Blom and Doorman in particular made an effort to develop a new Arts and Culture degree programme, seeking close collaboration with the local art colleges. The Ministry of Education and Science strongly supported such an 'experimental alliance', but De Vries was sceptical. Of course, he had not come to Maastricht because of these expansion plans, but instead felt a greater affinity with the kind of research being conducted by Boon. Moreover, he had seen a similar experiment fail elsewhere in the Netherlands. According to De Vries, setting up an Arts and Culture degree programme in collaboration with higher professional education would be 'a lost cause' for the faculty. He felt that the gap between higher professional education and academic education was too wide: 'they are different degree

Gerard de Vries

programmes for different kinds of students'. And so De Vries did not really support this initiative either. He took part in the consultations with the Academy of Arts and the Theatre School but was unable to feel 'much enthusiasm' on these occasions, 'to express it diplomatically'. In consultation with civil servants of the Ministry he pointed out that if the Minister wanted serious collaboration between universities and higher professional education, he had to start by changing the law because it obstructed such collaboration in formal terms. From 1987 onwards the Arts and Culture plan was explored further, but it was ultimately set to fail. Besides this, there was little support within the State University of Limburg, and consultation with the institutes for higher professional education also proved to be difficult. Finally the Ministry rejected the idea – there were already various other universities that were aiming for comparable arts and culture studies.

'DELTA STUDIES' Right from the start De Vries was convinced that a faculty without students – one that would thus be largely financially dependent on other faculties – would not be viable in the long term. Such a 'club without its own clubhouse' ran the almost unavoidable risk of being scrapped at the next round of spending cuts. The sense that it was necessary to support the extremely precarious positon of the Faculty of General Sciences grew when he, as freshly appointed dean, was told that the faculty had to move to the Carré building on Tongerseweg; at that time the core units were accommodated in several buildings on Bouillonstraat, but now had to make way for Economics. He felt that the Carré building was 'the deathblow for everything, because you were distant there from everyone else'. After some negotiation he was able to convince the Executive Board to relocate the faculty to the Elisabethhuis on Abtstraat. This also provided space for Boon's Theory of Health Sciences Department with 'people like Klasien Horstman and Guy Widdershoven', who focused on research into the ethics, history and sociology of health care. Another advantage of this 'coming together' was of course that the research themes of Boon's group were in line with De Vries's interests. Indeed, an important part of his teaching would be focused on contributing to the creation of the Theory of Health Sciences course in the Health Sciences programme. The major impulse for this course was the 'empirical shift' that had not only taken place in the philosophy of science, but was now also impending in the field of medical ethics. This shift would also form the basis of the Foundation Day speech given by De Vries in January 1993.

The faculty now not only had a vigorous manager in De Vries, but also a creative thinker with a highly individual way of doing things, as demonstrated by the fact that as early as March 1987 he presented 'a proposal for further development' for a new degree programme.[7] Its name – 'Delta Studies' – reflected its focus on themes located in the 'alpha' (arts), 'beta' (sciences) and 'gamma' (social sciences) sectors. During his trip with Boon to the United States, De Vries had already gained inspiration for such a programme and he now further developed Branda and Ferrier's proposal for 'Arts and Sciences'. He sketched out a broad, multidisciplinary degree programme 'in which, besides specific subjects, space was also reserved for teaching regarding the overall development of a scientific, technical, cultural and societal nature'. The students would have to learn to evaluate the consequences of such developments in the longer term and from an international perspective. De Vries was convinced that these broadly trained generalists, who also had experience in science subjects, would be able to find their place in the job market. Delta Studies was set up as a non-aligned degree programme that would draw on the expertise of various faculties, and the students would thus be able to take various study tracks. De Vries felt that this programme would make the State University of Limburg 'a serious university'. At that time it had a legitimacy issue because it offered only practically and professionally oriented courses. He was not only concerned about the future of his 'own' faculty, but indeed he feared that the university as a whole could be abolished. According to De Vries, the State University of Limburg was known nationwide as a 'provincial joint' and suggestions had already been made in the press that its dissolution would remove the need for spending cuts at other institutions.

The staff of the Faculty of General Sciences felt rather taken by surprise by the 'Delta Studies proposal for further development', as De Vries had only just arrived. But, certainly as befits philosophers and historians, they were also open to discussion and new perspectives. The fact that the faculty staff were a 'makeshift and motley crew' was actually an advantage in this respect. De Vries's plan was certainly received with interest. However, the lawyers and economists were less enthusiastic about Delta Studies, while support from this quarter was essential if the programme was to have any chance of success. Hans Crombag, dean of the Faculty of Law, had difficulties with the proposal because he felt it was prompted too much by a search for 'the gap in the market'. He feared that such a concept would result in degree programmes that would be relatively short-lived, such as Business Studies. Furthermore, his own faculty was already training generalists; he did not want to invest in a competitor. Luc Soete – who according to De Vries was regarded within the university as 'an interesting thinker' – was also asked for his opinion and he was less worried about competition: the Faculty of Economics was actually facing a surplus of students. According to Soete, Delta Studies met an important criterion: the programme was 'ahead of the market'. He had no problems with the fact that there were elements in common between Delta Studies and the Faculty of Economics, where there was also a focus on technological developments. However, the teaching load at the Faculty of Economics was too great to permit collaboration in Delta Studies. Moreover, he preferred to further develop the area of international relations and technology, with an emphasis on information science and technology assessment.[8]

TOWARDS A FULL-FLEDGED UNIVERSITY? So the reactions from Law and Economics were not too encouraging; after all, they were working on their 'own survival strategies'.[9] However, De Vries continued his plans undeterred. He also took part in the debate on the profiling and expansion of the State University of Limburg, which was in full swing in the summer of 1987. It was the task of *Werkgroep 6000* to develop a strategy that would enable the university to have 6,000 students by 1990. In 1986 the number was still around 3,000. Expansion clearly was the major goal. Would the State University of Limburg remain viable if it did not have 6,000 students by 1990? Minister Deetman stated that on the basis of its existing faculties, the university should grow to accommodate 6,000 students. However, the Executive Board aimed for expansion towards Arts and Culture courses: only then could Maastricht really enjoy the status of a 'full-fledged university'. The driving force in *Werkgroep 6000* was the young secretary Gerard Korsten, an education sociologist from Nijmegen who had joined the State University of Limburg in the summer of 1986. He put the possibilities of strategic planning into perspective and at the same time advocated an 'independent reconsideration of the desired societal functions of the university'.[10] While Korsten stressed that strategic policy was not the same as strategy in line with market practice, Rector Vic Bonke enlisted an advertising agency for a national recruitment campaign to raise the profile of the State University of Limburg and to attract more students. This marketing campaign was met with a fair degree of scepticism – De Vries, for instance, felt that the campaign was rather mundane – but it proved effective. Korsten was concerned about the lack of vision and consistent ideas and was relieved that the new Executive Board President Loek Vredevoogd began to undertake the strategic expansion of the university from April 1987 onwards. Vredevoogd was an economist who originated from the Ministry of Education and Science, where he had been deputy director general for higher education. He knew how the Ministry worked, including the shortcuts. Convinced that the State University of Limburg was 'in a bit of a blind alley', he was enthusiastic about the opportunity to contribute to the development of this young institution.[11] Vredevoogd felt that the university had conducted an inconsistent policy up to that time and that it was vital to develop a strategy. The Ministry had not yet received many properly developed plans for new degree programmes, and as soon as Vredevoogd got to see De Vries's Delta Studies concept he responded positively: by putting the emphasis on the societal and cultural aspects of science and technology, De Vries had come up with an original and unusual plan.

Vredevoogd advised De Vries to continue development of Delta Studies, but also urged him to keep quiet about it for the time being. He was convinced that other universities would raise a commotion if they found out that plans were afoot in Maastricht to create a degree programme relating to cultural studies and liberal arts; that would make it difficult for the Ministry of Education and Science to grant the State University of Limburg a new programme. Deetman did indeed inform the State University of Limburg that he was receiving very many 'innovation proposals' in the field of culture: the universities in Utrecht, Amsterdam and Rotterdam also had plans for their own Arts and Culture programmes. And so the State University of Limburg was told by the Ministry that, due to its geographical location, an international orientation in education would be regarded as interesting. In the memorandum *Profilering en uitbouw van de Rijksuniversiteit Limburg. Aanzet tot een beleidsplan voor de lange termijn* ('Profiling and expansion of the State University of Limburg. Approach to a long-term policy plan'), published in late 1987, the expansion plans of the Faculty of General Sciences, which by now also included core units of Mathematics and Information Science, was discussed only in very general and strategic terms. However, it was clear that the university was now seeking to expand towards a strong international orientation, also in the area of culture and technology. This was also set out in the *Ontwikkelingsplan Rijksuniversiteit Limburg 1989-1992* ('Development Plan for the State University of Limburg 1989-1992'. The university decided to experiment with new degree programmes, but according to Vredevoogd the form that the new programmes would ultimately take largely depended on unpredictable factors and on government decisions.[12]

SHARPER FOCUS FOR DELTA STUDIES De Vries focused on further refinement of Delta Studies. He did this in secret and more or less alone. However, the Executive Board knew about it, as did De Rijk, Boon and Korsten. In the faculty De Vries, who was already fairly taciturn about this issue, now kept his mouth firmly shut. He carried out all his preparations at home and not even his secretary knew about it. He found he had to make major changes to Delta Studies, one reason being that the 'faculty thresholds' at the State University of Limburg were higher than he had thought. On the other hand he could count on support from Health Sciences.[13] Partly at the instigation of Vredevoogd he conducted secret consultations with other institutions in the region: the Open University in Heerlen and even the Theology programme at Rolduc Abbey. He was actually quite pleased that these consultations remained unfruitful, as he had doubts about the quality that the potential partners would be able to offer.

De Vries devised a new, independent education programme. Standing by his bookcase he asked himself: 'Well, what would I like to teach them, and what should I teach them?'. The first programme version was completed by the end of 1988: a Liberal Arts programme designed along American lines. It was about the intellectual tradition of the West and critical reflections on this, but it differed from established programmes by taking the 'Western intellectual tradition' to mean not only the literary and philosophical traditions, but also science and technology. De Vries believed that the students should at the very least become acquainted with philosophers like Thomas Kuhn, Martha Nussbaum and a sociologist such as Norbert Elias.[14] 'How do you discuss and how do you analyse the development of science and of technology; how do you deal with societal issues and relating controversies? And then I asked myself: what do these people need to know now? And to be quite honest, I simply followed my own interests here.'

However, Vredevoogd was warned by the Ministry of Education and Science that a Liberal Arts programme was bound to annoy the other universities, as in recent years the government had made strong spending cuts in faculties of literature and of social sciences. But Vredevoogd retained confidence in De Vries and arranged an informal meeting in a small upstairs room of a well-known Indonesian restaurant in The Hague in order to win over a few civil servants from his former Ministry. According to Vredevoogd, it was also time to mobilise support from the general public and to 'get high-level academics involved'. They considered asking De Rijk to serve as founding dean, but that was tricky from a strategic perspective – De Rijk was already on the Education Council tasked with advising the Minister about new degree programmes.[15] In any case, from now on De Vries had the backing of the committee appointed by the Executive Board, for which the members had been invited to sit in a private capacity, including Boon, Dekker and Nico Roos from the Faculty of Law. De Rijk and Wil Albeda acted as advisors. Albeda was a professor of General Economics, a prominent member of the CDA (Christian-Democratic) party and by now also the chairman of the Scientific Council for Government Policy (WRR). Korsten was the secretary, acting from his position in *Werkgroup 6000*. The committee worked fast and in secret.

ARTS AND CULTURE: AN EXPERIMENTAL DEGREE PROGRAMME The report *Cultuur- and Wetenschapsstudies* ('Arts and Culture') was completed in May 1989. With its new Arts and Culture programme the State University of Limburg aimed for 'greater intellectual depth' and a 'more balanced profile' as a university institution.[16] The report presented Arts and Culture as a degree programme with an 'innovative curriculum' in the field of the humanities: it was explicitly experimental and not a duplicate of any existing programme in the field of cultural studies and humanities. Arts and Culture focused on 'cultural problems of modern society' that were caused by developments in science and technology; with it, the university aimed to address current developments in science and society while at the same time increasing its international orientation. Of course, such goals were also viewed favourably by the Ministry of Education and Science. Contacts had already been established 'with renowned universities' in the United States that offered programmes in the fields of science, technology & society, and science, technology & values. The proposal was accompanied by the letters that De Vries and Boon had received at the end of 1986 from, among other bodies, Harvard University and the Massachusetts Institute of Technology in which these universities expressed their willingness to collaborate. Arts and Culture was about 'the fundamental issues and choices of an ethical, political and social nature' that resulted from 'the rapid rate of technological developments'. The idea was that the programme would not only have an academic-intellectual, but also a practical-societal dimension. This idea gelled with the basic principles of the State University of Limburg, which had its intellectual roots in the 1960s. The Arts and Culture programme was also to develop new visions 'of the development of society'. It is clear that Arts and Culture was not a degree programme structured by academic discipline: by focusing chiefly on these 'fundamental issues' it took a generalist, interdisciplinary approach with an open attitude to 'the confrontation of the various intellectual traditions'. This approach was suited to a problem-driven curriculum, as the report stated. The report briefly addressed the various education modules and requested permission from the Minister to begin on 1 September 1990. Minister Deetman had the report on his desk at the end of June 1989.

REACTIONS FROM WITHIN Deetman was not the only one to first see the plan in the summer of 1989. The staff of the Faculty of General Sciences saw it for the first time, too. Of course, they had already realised that De Vries was cooking something up, but this *modus operandi* created opposition. De Vries said that people 'justifiably felt completely taken aback'. In particular the staff members who had originally invested their energies in the now-abandoned Arts and Cultural Studies programme were outraged at the lack of communication. In his department, De Vries was applauded by his newly arrived staff members De Wilde and Bijker, but Mostert was very angry about his autocratic behaviour. Furious, Mostert tendered his resignation a year later.[17] Emotions ran high at History as well. The newly recruited staff member Joop de Jong, who sat on the faculty expansion committee, felt passed over. However, besides indignation about De Vries' 'solo action' there was also willingness to further discuss the plans. The mathematicians and information science specialists showed a lukewarm response to De Vries's plans. The relations between the core units of Philosophy and History on the one hand and the core units of Mathematics and Information Science on the other were strained. In this discussion Wiel Kusters, endowed professor of Literature on behalf of the Limburg University Fund (SWOL), refrained from adopting a pronounced position: he had only just been appointed and held a small, part-time post.[18] In response to the accusation that no 'decent discussion' had been conducted in the university, De Vries replied that he could not have acted in any other way. He had been forced to 'soil his hands' in order to eliminate the risk that other universities would start setting up their own Arts and Culture programmes as well.

POLITICAL LOBBY Vredevoogd was not completely confident that the Minister would approve the experimental degree programme. Together with De Vries and Korsten he organised a lobby to get 'important representatives of civil-society organisations and the business community' to put in a good word with Deetman. This resulted in positive responses from persons such as Jos van Kemenade (who, as Minister of Education and Science, had once oversaw the birth of the State University of Limburg) and Queen's Commissioner Sjeng Kremers. Kremers was convinced that the graduates would be successful in the job market if the international orientation of the programme really took shape and the quality was good, because: 'quality always wins!'[19] In order to gain political support, Job Cohen and De Rijk talked to the PvdA, while Vredevoogd and Albeda focused on the CDA. Co Greep, one of the founders of the Faculty of Medicine, was enlisted to win over the VVD (Liberal) party. Vredevoogd felt that this lobbying was necessary because the other universities were by definition against the State University of Limburg.[20] From November 1989 it was no longer Deetman, but Jo Ritzen (PvdA) who as Minister of Education and Science in the third Lubbers government (CDA and PvdA) would have to issue a verdict on the Maastricht application. He received negative recommendations from the Association of Universities in the Netherlands (VSNU) and from the Education Council. These were based on three objections: the learning objectives were formulated in overly general terms, the degree programme was too broad to achieve academic depth and there were doubts about the research potential.[21] The Limburg lobby was immediately mobilised. Thijs Wöltgens, leader of the PvdA group in parliament and a native of Limburg, was asked to talk to Ritzen and Kremers was given the task of explaining the importance of the new degree programme to the Minister. Ritzen then gave the State University of Limburg another chance to adjust the programme.

De Vries, in consultation with Korsten, quickly modified the Arts and Culture report, also taking into account the reactions from his own faculty. He now described the 'central thread' of the programme as follows: it aimed to provide insight into modern culture, which was formed by 'a heterogeneous network of diverse intellectual (artistic, political and religious as well as scientific) traditions'.[22] Science and technology were regarded explicitly as cultural phenomena, and as constitutive for modern society. In this version the students could choose from three tracks during their studies: Philosophy of Biomedical Sciences, Theory and History of Technological Culture, and Cultural History of the Modern Age.[23] De Vries also formulated twelve learning objectives. To give a few examples, the student should gain knowledge of 'the chief moments in the history of philosophy and of junctures in the cultural and societal history of modern Western society' and should also gain knowledge of 'science and technology as societal phenomena and of the genesis of the technological intervention culture'.[24] The new proposal also devoted more attention to the two ongoing research projects: 'Science and Technology Research' and 'Transformation, Intervention and Regulation in Culture and Society'. In the modified version, Arts and Culture was actually given a broader scope. Nonetheless, in May 1990 the Education Council approved the new proposal. One prominent member of this council was De Rijk, who had successfully defended it. At the end of May 1990, Ritzen decided that the Faculty of General Sciences could begin the experimental programme on 1 September 1991. However, extra staffing for History and Literature was required – subject to the caveat that any further development towards a faculty of literature was ruled out.[25] 1990 was a significant year, because this was also the year that the State University of Limburg admitted its six thousandth student.

A NEW FACULTY OF ARTS AND CULTURE De Vries was shocked when, in September 1991, he found almost 150 students at the doorstep. He recalls that the information days went well – 'the school pupils and their parents went back home in very high spirits'. But he had not expected so many students to register: 'We were completely overwhelmed, and they came from all over the country'. His idea had been to create a 'high-quality internationally oriented programme' with 25 or 35 students at most, and now 'the world had changed a bit,' because everyone was 'up to his neck in teaching work'. The six course textbooks for the first year were ready – The History of the Body, The Good Life, Experimental Physics, Enlightenment and Romanticism, Modernisation, and Evolutionary Thinking – but the textbooks for the higher years still needed to be created. Alongside these modules the students also received skills education in fields such as science and technology, argumentation training and computer skills. De Vries says that a huge amount of work went into the teaching because 'suddenly we were faced with a great number of students'. He was a major proponent of problem-based teaching, but also found it to be highly labour-intensive.[26] Moreover, new staff had to be brought in as quickly as possible, such as Joke Spruyt and Marietje Kardaun who were recruited by De Rijk. In 1992 Kusters was appointed full professor of General Literature and was given his own Department of Literature and Art. Shortly after this, Arnold Labrie was taken on as professor of Social and Cultural History. This rapid growth created its own dynamism: the new staff members all brought their own discipline-specific resources with them, which benefited the pluralism of approaches but also led to tensions, differences of opinion and sometimes fierce debates, which were not always fruitful. The basement of the Elisabethhuis saw frequent and heated discussions between staff members originating from sometimes highly disparate historical and philosophical traditions.[27] De Vries himself, so he says, had no problems with this – on the contrary, he liked the intellectual sparring.

The start of the Arts and Culture programme also brought De Vries new administrative worries. The huge influx of students led to 'a totally imbalanced whole' in the Faculty of General Sciences. The mathematicians and information scientists, says De Vries, formed their own separate little world. They did not yet have their own degree programme and were thus completely dependent on core funding, but they had ambitious growth plans. This imbalanced growth sparked off a conflict about the distribution of funds. De Vries needed little effort to persuade all involved parties that it would be better for them to go their separate ways – a standpoint fully backed by the Executive Board. At the end of 1991 posts were reassigned: De Vries stepped down as dean and went to Paris for a six-month sabbatical, and professor of Mathematics Koos Vrieze became the new dean of the Faculty of General Sciences. The splitting of the faculty came about under his leadership: Mathematics and Information Science continued as part of the Faculty of General Sciences, while the Departments of Philosophy, History, Literature and the recently created Department of Technology and Society Studies were grouped together under a new umbrella: the Faculty of Arts and Culture.

In 1994 the Faculty of Arts and Culture was officially instituted. The Faculty of General Sciences had served its function as a springboard for a new degree programme, and in turn the mathematicians and information scientists now made plans for a new course of studies. The first dean of the Faculty of Arts and Culture was the poet and man of letters Kusters.

SCIENCE AND TECHNOLOGY RESEARCH Following his period as dean and his sabbatical, De Vries shifted his attention to research within the research project Science and Technology Research. There he focused on research into the ethical and societal aspects of developments in medicine and health care. As research leader he liked to stimulate discussion; he saw the university as a place for 'creative scepticism'.[28] There is nothing more enjoyable than a hearty debate with multiple perspectives. As a 'typical' Northern Dutchman, he was a person who did not mince words – something that some people found hard to handle. Nonetheless, during his time in Maastricht he saw through a large number of PhD students: he supervised the PhD projects of cws staff and PhD candidates such as Sjaak Koenis, De Wilde, Doorman,

Blom, Ruud Hendriks and Karin Bijsterveld and more than ten PhD students working at other faculties or institutions. He not only presented sharp criticism, but was able to encourage and stimulate as well. When Bijsterveld (who, as the first female professor at Maastricht University, has recently become a member of the Royal Netherlands Academy of Sciences (KNAW)), wrote him a letter of resignation because she did not feel she could survive in the academic world, he refused to accept it and then encouraged her with substantive feedback.[29] In the foreword to her PhD thesis Bijsterveld wrote the words that De Vries regards as the finest compliment he has ever received: De Vries is able 'to talk about improvements [to submitted draft chapters] in such a way that even as you leave the room you think you came up with them yourself'. Of course, De Vries also regarded the development of an academic profile as being a prerequisite for legitimising the Arts and Culture programmes. He was one of the founders and the first scientific director of the Graduate School of Science, Technology and Modern Culture (WTMC), in which the universities of Groningen, Amsterdam and Twente also participated. The WTMC was recognised by the KNAW in 1995; this he regarded as a major milestone. By that time De Vries had been in Maastricht for more than seven years and was seriously beginning to feel the effects of 'the seven-year itch'. He always feels this sense of unrest once things are 'signed and sealed': 'I think I can say that I'm good at thinking up something, at starting something, at getting something up and running, but once everything is in place and working well, then I have to be on my way'. This opportunity presented itself when he was asked to shake things up in Amsterdam. In 1997 he left Maastricht and moved to the University of Amsterdam to contribute to the creation of a new Faculty of Humanities that would accommodate literature, philosophy and theology and where the Bachelor's/Master's system needed to be introduced. He has no problems with the fact that the Faculty of Arts and Culture then went in search of new themes in education and research, focusing on science and technology research, because 'once I'm gone, then I'm gone'.

14 *Wiel Kusters* WE WOULDN'T GET ANYWHERE WITHOUT SCIENCE, BUT WE'D BE NOWHERE WITHOUT THE ARTS

A DEAFENING EXPLOSION On 28 October 1983, a deafening explosion reduced the impressive towers at shaft III of the state-owned Emma mine in Hoensbroek to rubble. This was no mining accident, however: the explosion was a controlled demolition. A thundering step – and not the first – in the painful march towards a transformed mining region. South Limburg was set for change: a cleaner, more prosperous, modern area with better quality of life... Wiel Kusters was there to witness it all. Jacques Reiners of Studium Generale had asked him to collaborate on a film with images of the spectacular explosion. 'He asked me whether I'd attend the demolition and read something for the camera. They filmed it all, and you can actually hear a huge explosion in the background while I'm reciting a poem.'[1] Still moved by the experience as he recalls it years later, Kusters was startled to see a flock of birds fly out of the tower as it exploded. They reminded him of old paintings depicting a dying person's soul leaving his body in the form of a bird. Kusters had already been living in Maastricht for years at the time. In addition to making a name for himself as a poet and author, he was working as a journalist and creating television programmes for a regional broadcaster and the national KRO (Catholic Broadcasting Corporation) network. It was no surprise that he and Reiners had crossed paths. However, no one could have predicted that Kusters would end up becoming a professor or being appointed the very first dean of the Faculty of Arts and Culture.

FURTHER EDUCATION Born in 1947 in Spekholzerheide, near Kerkrade, Wiel Kusters was the third and youngest son in a mining family. He never knew his oldest brother, who died as an infant. The second child, Jo, suffered from rheumatism and was forced to spend the first few years of his life in hospitals far from home. Wiel, the youngest, was a good learner and followed his brother Jo to an extended primary education (ULO) school. Although the ULO offered excellent education, the resulting degree certificate did not grant access to higher education; nor did it help him get the job he wanted as a journalist in training at the *Maas en Roerbode* regional newspaper. To get a foot in the door, they told him, he would need a Higher Civic School diploma or more senior qualification.

He eventually managed to obtain the certificate by attending night school and taking a state exam. He wanted to write, and had already managed to get his first poems published. His future wife Tonie Ehlen and her sisters impressed upon him: 'Wiel, you should study Dutch literature'. First, though, he had to enter military service, which proved to be a depressing intermezzo in his life. 'I was deeply unhappy, I felt like my spirit was being crushed.' He served as a telex operator, and witnessed the international tensions surrounding the Russian invasion of Czechoslovakia in August of 1968. 'We'd get highly classified telexes on the Russian military build-up in the middle of the night. I'd think: oh dear, it's all about to kick off.' With his military service completed in the autumn of 1968, he finally took the leap and enrolled as a student at Nijmegen University's Dutch Language and Literature programme. He also familiarised himself with both Latin and Greek with the help of a classical languages student, and managed to pass the state exam at *gymnasium* (pre-university) level with flying colours just before taking his preliminary examination in Dutch Language and Literature. At the time, that diploma was a formal requirement for obtaining a degree certificate in language and literature.

DUTCH LANGUAGE AND LITERATURE STUDIES The Dutch Language and Literature programme fit him like a glove, offering an ideal opportunity to explore both modern-day and older literature. His thesis focused on eighteenth-century novels, a phenomenon that – with the exception of Aagje Deken and Betje Wolff, whose works were part of the official canon – had been largely overlooked in official literary history. It proved to be quite an experience: reading texts that had not seen the light of day for a hundred years; a real treasure hunt. Outside, a student revolt was unfolding: demonstrations and occupations were a daily occurrence. He watched it all from the sidelines. 'I just thought: guys, you've just finished grammar school and now you've suddenly decided you want a revolution – *I want to study*. I tried to enter the library, but they were all lying on the ground blocking the damn door...'

Although he never aspired to become a teacher, that is exactly what he ended up doing. First in Nijmegen, then Sittard, which proved more convenient: Tonie, a conservatory student, was living in Maastricht at the time. 'I moved to Maastricht from Nijmegen in 1972, and we got married that very same year; I should add that that's how things went in those days.' He obtained his degree in 1973. Kusters spent six years working as a teacher in Sittard, from 1972 to 1978. 'I resigned in 1978, to the rector's dismay. Tonie had since taken up a position teaching music at the conservatory. We thought: we'll manage.'

He started working as a freelancer for newspapers and broadcasters, and made documentaries. He also published poetry anthologies, became editor at *De Gids*, a literary magazine, and wrote his PhD dissertation on the poetry and poetics of Gerrit Kouwenaar. Shortly after having obtained his PhD in 1986, he was offered the opportunity to spend six months teaching Dutch Language and Literature in Berlin as a guest professor. He decided the opportunity was too good to pass up and left for Germany. Working in an academic environment agreed with him. 'I'd worked as a freelancer for quite some time and enjoyed it, but I was starting to yearn for a job, an environment around me, colleagues.'

In retrospect, the Studium Generale at Limburg University proved to be an ideal work placement. Kusters demonstrated his skills, and the university realised what it was missing. 'I told Jacques Reiners: you organise things here (I'd gone over their programme); why don't we hold about six or eight sessions where we read, interpret and discuss poetry?' He agreed, and the events proved popular. Reiners kept asking him to do more, and Kusters used the Studium Generale as a stage and launching pad. In the absence of the yet to be established Arts programme, he gave poetry, literature and the arts a place in both academic life and the city itself. The experience left him wanting more.

CULTURAL PROFILE Kusters' audience also included Ben Niessen, secretary of the Executive Board. Niessen was aware of the university's ambitions and plans for expansion. '"You should really talk to Van den Biggelaar", he told me.' President of the Board Rob van den Biggelaar placed great value on the university's regional cultural profile. Kusters learned that the university had ambitions in the area of literature, art and culture, possibly in the form of a new programme in collaboration with local art colleges. A literature faculty was not in the cards; such an initiative was not deemed innovative and would undoubtedly be blocked by language and literature faculties elsewhere in the country. So what form would it take?[2] As it turned out, 'something literary' did take shape before a definitive decision had been reached. The initiative was led by former Executive Board President Sjeng Tans, himself a Dutch language specialist. Sjeng and Wiel got along well. Tans also wanted 'his' university to raise its cultural profile; where he had once dreamt of a chair in Limburg dialect, Gerard de Vries – professor of Philosophy and dean of the

Faculty of General Sciences since early 1987 – had rejected the idea as 'provincial dabbling'.[3] At the time, Tans no longer had a seat on the university Board although he did hold a position on the board of the University Fund Limburg (SWOL). He exerted his influence and initiated an endowed chair in Language and Literature funded by SWOL.

PROFESSORSHIP After having responded to an advertisement and taken part in an open job application procedure, Kusters was appointed professor with an endowed chair in General and Dutch Language and Literature in the Faculty of General Sciences. It was no coincidence that the professorship's name started with the word 'general'. 'It seemed sensible to take the broadest possible approach, as this offered a lot of leeway.' Kusters' position initially felt 'somewhat lonely', as it had not been embedded in any department. He viewed his chair as a core unit for the university, along the lines of the History and Philosophy core units.[4] Kusters held his inaugural address entitled *Pooltochten* ('Arctic Explorations') on 12 October 1989. Instead of focusing on a single author, body of work or literary movement, he chose a subject that lent itself to both literary and non-literary perspectives. Surely Arctic explorers and poets both embodied the same heretic desire to break out of the quotidian, cross boundaries and explore unknown areas that had traditionally been deemed impenetrable? *Pooltochten* – a narrative with little relation to any specific programme or theory – proved to be Kusters's calling card in more ways than one: 'as far as I'm concerned, we should be constantly crossing the boundaries of our territory'. In addition to students, he aimed to keep focusing on interested parties outside of the academic world. He called upon the university to keep doing its part in 'improving the cultural and literary infrastructure in both the city and its surrounding region'. The chair was partly intended to encourage 'regional cultural emancipation'. Kusters had already established a southern branch of the Society of Dutch Literary Studies prior to his appointment, in an effort to lend 'an impulse' to local literary life.

CULTURAL EXPANSION? The university was all too eager to expand its cultural activities. De Vries had previously presented a Liberal Arts programme under the moniker 'Arts and Culture'. The Education Council initially deemed the initiative 'unscientific and too broad'. Maastricht's application seemed to have little chance of approval. Its ultimate success was attributable to political pressure.[5] A new, adjusted application was finally approved in May of 1990, offering Kusters an opportunity to expand the literature department's staff. Kusters' Faculty of General Sciences comprised a handful of historians, philosophers, mathematicians and information scientists, with De Vries as the only other Arts & Humanities professor. Philosophy and History were housed in the Sint Elisabethhuis on Abtstraat, while the mathematicians and information scientists were accommodated on Bredestraat. 'Despite being a Dutch language specialist, I was never meant to work here in that capacity. I was placed in the nascent Arts and Culture working group, an alliance with historians and philosophers. The group, which also included an economist, was chaired by Maarten Doorman.' Kusters joined just in time to contribute to the establishment of the Arts and Culture programme set to start in 1991, a contribution he is quick to downplay: 'I didn't have much influence on the process at the time. I was all alone and didn't have any staff'. He had a good rapport with the various historians and philosophers, and the feeling proved to be mutual. To his surprise, he soon received a phone call from Philosophy lecturer Rein de Wilde, who was eager to meet and talk. 'To my utter shock and surprise, he asked me whether I wanted to join the Faculty Board. He told me they would appreciate having me as a new member. I just thought: but I don't have any administrative experience. Is that why I'm here? Would I be any good at it? I want to be working on education.' The conversation in the garden of Kusters' home on Alexander Battalaan dragged on, and he eventually agreed.

A DEPARTMENT OF LITERATURE & ART Kusters' memories of those early days mainly consist of endless meetings in the basement of the Elisabethhuis. 'Drafting memoranda, that kind of thing. We started in September of 1991.' They had no way of knowing how many students they would attract. 'We really didn't know what to expect at all.' When it came to programmes such as Medicine, Law and Economics, most pupils had some idea what to expect in terms of content, but no one knew what to make of a programme in Arts and Culture at the time. Staff breathed a collective sigh of relief when close to 150 first-year students enrolled for the first year. The new programme proved to be a success. 'We started expanding and were eventually able to hire more people.' Kusters' endowed chair was converted into a regular professorship. History and Philosophy were supplemented with a third department. 'As soon as I was on board, I wanted my own department. Maybe it's just something that comes naturally to me: starting a theatre group at school, launching a school paper with an editorial staff...' This own department, initially referred to as 'Literary Studies in formation' was later renamed Literature & Art. It became a centre of expertise on subjects such as literature, theatre, cinema and visual arts. 'I wasn't looking for copies of myself. I wanted people who represented the things I wasn't.' His preference went out to candidates who could offer something in addition to their specific area of expertise; at minimum, prospective new staff members should have an affinity with the faculty's experimental, broad approach to culture. This applied to

Philosophy and History as well as to the Literature & Art Department. The newly established faculty was awash with people who represented at least two worlds and combined multiple disciplines. In addition to his knowledge of theatrical theory, Paul de Bruyne was active as an author and director. Eddy Houwaart combined medicine and history, while Jo Wachelder was at home in the fields of physics and history. Wiebe Bijker was both an engineer and technology sociologist. And the list went on. Efforts were made to appoint people in the habit of crossing disciplinary lines. 'Pretty much everyone we hired in those days was more than just a regular philosopher, historian or literary scientist.'

DEAN OF THE FACULTY OF ARTS AND CULTURE In the meantime, efforts to accommodate both information scientists and mathematicians in a single faculty despite their varying areas of interest were starting to cause resistance. Although collaboration between the sciences and humanities was certainly a commendable ideal, it seemed better to let both sides go their own way. On 1 January 1994, the Faculty of Arts and Culture officially opened its doors in a historic building on Kapoenstraat. Kusters was to be the faculty's very first dean: 'I was appointed from the ranks of the existing Board, and I can't say it was really what I wanted either'. Despite having gained no administrative experience prior to entering the academic world, Kusters proved to be a quick learner. Crucially, he discovered that university life was far more political than he ever would have expected.

Over the course of Kusters's first year as dean, Arnold Labrie was appointed professor of History and two new chairs were established. Bijker was appointed professor of Technology and Society and soon became the focal point of a new, internationally oriented Department of Technology & Society Studies. The faculty was soon supplemented with a professor holding an endowed chair in History and Monument Conservation Policy. The establishment of a fourth department around Bijker's chair was no matter of course. 'In our view, Wiebe's focus was too specific and narrow to warrant the establishment of a department along the lines of History, Philosophy and Literature Studies.' The university appeared to be witnessing the birth of a new discipline. 'We decided to ask Bertus de Rijk for advice, as he was well-respected and liked across the board. Bertus didn't initially support Wiebe's plan either; he was too much of a philosopher for that.' A compromise was eventually reached; the broad intentions were reflected in the new department's name.

The notions of either a broad approach or further specialisation had clashed before in the faculty's history. Social constructivism had taken flight in the wake of post-modernism, and seemed both an appealing and fruitful approach in terms of technology programmes. Kusters, who was no expert in either field, was naturally more inclined towards a phenomenological approach. In addition to differing views, conflicts of interest between and within the departments were becoming an increasingly pressing issue. The idea of building something new together gradually gave way to a competitive atmosphere.

By the time the first students received their degree certificates in 1995, various graduation tracks with the potential to evolve into separate degree programmes were already under development: Political Culture and Visual Culture, later to be renamed Media Culture. These projects were not always met with the greatest enthusiasm. Founding dean De Vries, for example, was not impressed. He used every argument at his disposal to counter the notion that 'image' or 'image-based culture' could ever offer a sound basis for new degree programmes. Other philosophers within the faculty took a more positive view, provided the new programme offered room for ample theoretical reflection, or 'meta-questions'.

Kusters, who some colleagues deemed 'too nice' to ever make an effective administrator, never used his position as dean to put his own discipline ahead of other fields. He wanted literature to have a real seat at the table, rather than an isolated existence: 'something relevant to the world, like philosophy and history'. He subscribed to the view that science and technology shape modern culture, and always strove to emphasise areas of overlap when developing new projects with colleagues. *Mines et Mineurs* ('Mines and miners'), a project financed with European funding and developed and implemented in close collaboration with research universities and universities of applied sciences in Hasselt, Aachen and Liège had technical, medical, cultural and literary dimensions as well as being strongly oriented towards the region. The initiative was close to Kusters's heart for several reasons: the lives of local miners had been an important source of inspiration for his poems and stories since the 1970s.

As mentioned, new employees in his Literature and Arts Department were partly selected on the basis of their willingness to collaborate with other disciplines. The fledgling department was also unique in another key area. Whereas the Philosophy and History Departments started out as male-dominated environments, Kusters could not seem to hire enough women. 'People would tease me about it: oh, it's Wiel and his girls again. Still, I simply felt they were the most qualified candidates.' A large number of his female appointees such as Lies Wesseling, Renée van de Vall, Ginette Verstraete and José van Dijck, would go on to become professors at Maastricht and other universities.

In his capacity as dean, Kusters made up part of the Interdisciplinary History Consultative Platform for Literature and History (DLG), a consultative body for deans of the various language and literature faculties. 'At first, they would only let me attend as an observer. They were apprehensive to say the least.' Their initial attitude was reflected in the response of Nijmegen University dean Hans Bots after Wiel Kusters politely introduced himself at the very first DLG meeting: 'Ah, yes, but I really object to you! We'd also get phone calls from staff at other language and literature faculties around the country. Typically, they'd go like this: "We're holding our Faculty Board meeting this afternoon, and we'll be discussing what you're doing in Maastricht – so what are you doing over there?" I'd always explain – in a somewhat superior tone of voice – that we did things *very differently*...'.

Setting up the new Department of Literature & Art, expanding the new faculty and defending it against its jealous counterparts – these activities took up a large part of Kusters's time in the mid-1990s. He also took every opportunity to raise his department's profile, using his own fame as a writer and poet. The university needed both the city and province. In his view, the effort to establish roots in the region and create goodwill in Maastricht and its surrounding environment was just as important as internationalisation.

The new faculty's pioneering spirit and appeal were reflected in its annual information days, which were yet to be streamlined under the influence of university policy. 'They were basically parties! We took plenty of time for those events, which were always marked by at least three lectures. Bertus de Rijk held a talk on philosophy and the audience simply ate it up. Wiebe held a fascinating talk on technological development on the basis of Mary Shelley's Frankenstein, while I explained how a Hans Christian Andersen fairy tale (*The nightingale*) was embedded in cultural history and philosophy. Attendance levels were always high. Obviously, our team was still relatively small at the time; everyone participated. People went home with the sense that they belonged here, a sense that interesting things were happening.' It was a stimulating period, partly due to the young faculty's warm ties with Rector Job Cohen and Executive Board President Karl Dittrich. 'I seem to recall we received five hundred thousand guilders to finance further expansion of the Humanities library, which was underfunded at the time. That sort of funding would be unthinkable nowadays.'

A DEVASTATING EVENT For many staff members, the stately mansion on Kapoenstraat was more than just a workplace: it was a warm nest where they felt at home. Paradoxically, this sense of belonging was most poignant on the day the building lost its innocence. On Monday, 29 January 1996, José de Groot, a staff member at the Faculty Office, died after being stabbed by her estranged husband in her office on Kapoenstraat. The faculty was in total disarray. 'I got everyone together in the Spiegelzaal', Kusters recalls, 'I had catering bring out big pots of coffee, and we all just talked and talked.' The next day, he held a carefully worded and sober speech in that very same Spiegelzaal expressing 'the incomprehensible, the sadness and horror we all felt (...) helping us to feel what we felt while offering comfort despite it all', in the words of Renée van de Vall, his successor as department chair.[6] 'We all took white flowers from a big bouquet of roses, and crossed the courtyard to the place where it had happened. The door to José's room was closed, covered in a colourful poster she had probably put up herself in better days. It had since been papered over with an official police notice stating that the room was off limits. A mountain of flowers piled up against the door. A sad procession, by any means. José de Groot was our colleague, not our property. And still there's that sense that she's been stolen from us.'[7]

FACULTY OF ARTS AND SOCIAL SCIENCES Before long, the name 'Arts and Culture' (*cultuurwetenschappen*) no longer felt appropriate. De Vries was especially vocal in his criticism. In his view, the name was too traditional. He felt it would lead people to believe that the emphasis was on art and culture, drawing them to the faculty with the wrong expectations. In order to address this situation, De Vries and others wanted to see the name changed to social and cultural sciences. Kusters opposed the measure: 'I felt that would be too great of a swing in the other direction, and would ultimately lead to the demise of arts and literature'. In the end, a compromise was reached in the form of Arts and Social Sciences. The faculty building was adorned with a neon sign in two colours proudly proclaiming the new name: Faculty of Arts *and Social Sciences*. When the time came to think of an English name, the term 'Humanities' seemed the most obvious choice. However, this term had already been appropriated by General Sciences. The university eventually settled on 'Arts and Social Sciences'.

In September 1997, the faculty bade farewell to Gerard de Vries as he took up a new position at the University of Amsterdam. De Vries seemed to have had his fill of Maastricht. Despite having gained recognition for his crucial initiatory role as the founding dean of Arts and Sciences, his critical attitude on various issues had not always been appreciated. At De Vries's farewell reception, Kusters – who had since been succeeded as dean by Bijker – recited a playful quatrain on the ups and downs in their relationship with De Vries. 'We genuinely got along, but had very different temperaments.'

Cooperation with Bijker, who would later succeed Kusters as dean in September of 1996, proved far easier. 'We were definitely a good team in administrative terms. If we had to get something done, Wiebe would always prepare the flip-over charts and diagrams; he was the engineer, while I was more of a storyteller.' The two supplemented each other, and were polar opposites in certain areas. 'Wiebe was more focused on his career, and achieved a great deal in that respect. I didn't, and never wanted to.' Many of the dissertations written under Kusters' supervision were the work of external PhD candidates.

Both of the expansion plans developed during Kusters's tenure as dean –

under the monikers of visual culture and political culture – were eventually realised. Political culture evolved into European Studies, an independent degree programme that immediately attracted such a large number of students that it threatened to eclipse the erstwhile flagship programme Arts and Culture. Visual culture was basically repositioned and ultimately introduced under the more modern-day name of media culture, despite a long and painful gestation period. New objections kept being raised. It even got to the point where Kusters, who was hardly known to run from confrontations or cause rifts, angrily stepped down from the Faculty Board chaired by Paul Tummers.

PROBLEM-BASED LEARNING It proved to be one of his rare 'line in the sand' moments. Solidarity with 'his' faculty was the rule, a sense of loyalty that also extended to problem-based learning. As a lecturer, he had mixed feelings. 'I'm one of those people (and not the only one at this faculty) who likes to tell a story. I've always enjoyed lectures. The same goes for tutorial groups, when they went well. Still, I often had great difficulty making sure they were both informative and meaningful. That was a much greater challenge than any lecture I ever held. If you're having difficulty with something and you repeatedly find yourself thinking: this isn't working, not in this group, or with this material, you need to be careful you don't develop an aversion to that format and those meetings.'

The effort to adjust problem-based learning to the subject at hand was not at odds with the basic ideology. An approach that works well in a concrete medical case study might not necessarily be optimal for every other area. Whereas medical professionals and lawyers are expected to solve problems, arts and culture are often about the opposite, turning a seemingly problem-free situation into a problem. 'One of the main things I've always tried to teach students is: how do you deal with texts, both literary and otherwise? What do you do while you're reading? What is interpretation? With the way problem-based learning sessions are structured, you can't really analyse a text in depth with the group in the way I used to with our early poetry groups at the Studium Generale. We'd read things together and comment on them. The word for lesson *(les)* is derived from the word for reading *(lezen)*. Although it's extremely archaic in a sense, it's also an essential form of education, and it's certainly indispensable in my field.' These are skills that students can only learn by doing. 'It's quite difficult to integrate that into problem-based learning tutorial group sessions. That might well be most frustrating thing I've encountered so far: the setting is basically least suited to teaching students new skills.' Within the context of problem-based learning, the use and application of texts becomes entirely utilitarian. The text does not have much significance in itself, it just serves as a 'shopping cart' for information.

'Our students are in danger of developing a rather superficial attitude to the written word.' Texts are reduced to a source of information. You only use the parts you need. 'You basically throw the text away after you've extracted all useful information... I don't really see a solution to be honest. That's unless you decide to introduce reading lessons alongside problem-based learning: *lectiones*. Reading, together with others who also want to read, using our own knowledge and experience, your ability to contextualise, and taking the time to do so: I feel I never had enough opportunity to do that.'

BILINGUALISM Speaking of downsides, we should also mention the de facto abolition of Dutch as the institution's language of instruction, despite Kusters's pleas to maintain a bilingual university. 'At some point, we agreed that English would be our second language, while the university would retain the name 'Universiteit Maastricht'. Jo Ritzen threw that idea out when he was appointed President of the Executive Board. I discussed it with him at one point. I told him: if you want to encourage internationalisation *in this region* you might want to consider French or German.' According to Kusters, Ritzen – who served as President of the Executive Board from 2003 to 2011 – had his own ideas about internationalisation. He felt it was about time the university let go of its focus on the Limburg region. 'Ritzen took the view that we had too many students from Limburg. I thought that was somewhat of a strange priority. In actual fact, we weren't that deeply rooted in the Limburg region, and I made that point at the time. A comparison of the figures showed a well-balanced mix of people from within and outside the region. In fact, we were one of the most nationally oriented universities in the country. Groningen was more regional than we were, and I'd even venture so far as to say that the same applied to Amsterdam! On the other hand, we were also striving to ensure that Maastricht University – which was also working hard to promote internationalisation – took root in the region. This was also prompted by practical considerations: we needed support, financial and otherwise, from the province and city. Amongst other purposes, such assistance would help fund Leonie Cornips's chair in 'Limburg Language Culture'. A university shouldn't be a stranger to its own town and region, and should be a source of pride for local residents!'

GROWTH With the success of European Studies and rapid growth in employee numbers, the building on Kapoenstraat soon became too small. The faculty relocated to Grote Gracht, where it set up new accommodations in both the renovated Hof van Tilly and Kanunnikenhuis (the 'Soiron building') and various structures behind and between these two monumental edifices. In view of the growing scale of operations and conflicts of interest between the various departments, it was deemed wise to abolish the practice of rotating the position of dean among the university's 'own' professors. Instead, a decision was made to recruit an experienced external administrator with no allegiance to any specific party: a professional dean. Tummers, a classicist affiliated with Nijmegen University, proved to be the ideal candidate. Nevertheless, the experiment failed to achieve the desired results and was discontinued. In 2006, Rein de Wilde (who had succeeded De Vries as professor of Philosophy) took up the position. He would remain dean for a period of ten years.

LOOKING BACK Looking back on his own time as dean, Kusters recalls a pleasant experience. 'I never really expected I'd enjoy it. Obviously, it wasn't my dream job, but I never hated it.' As regards the various phases of his career, he mainly recalls a sense of continuity. 'I started as a writer and subsequently pursued an academic education to remain involved with my areas of interest. Writing is very different from science, but the two also have something in common: the sense of wonderment. Arts and Culture attracted a lot of young prospective students because it encouraged them to see the world from a very different perspective. They learned to see the waters in which they were swimming, so to speak.' Kusters never perceived the transition from writer and freelancer to the academic world and cultural sciences as a schism. 'Arts and Culture starts with that sense of wonderment that precedes any questions.'

He occasionally wonders whether today's university would have welcomed him with the enthusiasm he experienced in 1989. 'I don't mean people would have anything against me, but we've become far more instrumental, more goal-oriented over time.' Research funding is increasingly organised through the Netherlands Organisation for Scientific Research (NWO). 'In my short time as dean, I never made much of an effort to mould the faculty into that model.' Kusters has little patience for efforts to streamline research lines and themes. 'That approach is diametrically opposed to the other educational ideology our department used to promote: the notion that universities should focus on the things that matter to them. This still poses a challenge during quality assurance assessments: our multifaceted and interdisciplinary nature often tended to be problematic.'

On 1 June 2012, his 65th birthday, Kusters received a warm farewell from the academic community. His farewell lecture, entitled 'Staging the Truth', held a few surprises for the audience. The speaker had scarcely commenced his speech when audience members suddenly saw Kusters's face appear on a large screen above the lectern. His voice seemed out of synch with itself. Most assumed some sort of technical malfunction, but the truth was very different. As it turned out, the entire thing had been staged in advance, as part of a video show. The speaker interrupted himself from the screen and took over his own lecture. As Kusters – dressed in his formal toga – sat in the front row next to his wife listening and watching the speech unfold, his informally attired alter ego addressed the audience from the screen in Dutch with English subtitles. His speech was interspersed with clips from the Nobel address by Harold Pinter, a unique collage of poetry, theatre and political diatribe. Both lectures explored politicians' misappropriation of language: the subtle use of words in an effort to obscure values and truths outside the realm of language. In Kusters' view, science and art are equally essential: 'We wouldn't get anywhere without science, but we'd be nowhere without the arts.'

15 *Hans Peters* AS AN EXPERIMENTAL, TRANSNATIONAL DEGREE PROGRAMME, KNOWLEDGE ENGINEERING SERVED TO STRENGTHEN OUR SCIENCES EDUCATION

FURTHER EDUCATION? Hans Peters started his career at the State University of Limburg in January 1984. He was one of the 'trailblazers' that helped establish the propaedeutic phase of the Economics programme launched in September 1984. A good three years later, in the late summer of 1987, he transferred to the Faculty of General Sciences' core unit (*basisvoorziening*) of Mathematics.[1] At the time, the faculty comprised four core units: Philosophy, History, Mathematics and Information Science.[2] Peters, who had obtained his PhD in Mathematics a year prior at Nijmegen University on the basis of a dissertation on *Bargaining Game Theory*, received an offer to become senior university lecturer. Koos Vrieze, who had been appointed professor of Mathematical Decision Theory in the spring of 1987, was seeking staff members capable of manning the Mathematics core unit – there simply were no female candidates at the time. Amongst other departments, Peters was expected to teach courses at the Faculty of Economics, where he had served as a member of the Quantitative Economics Department since 1985. The notion of launching a new degree programme did not come up during Vrieze and Peters' conversations at the time.

However, the dean of the Faculty of General Sciences, science philosopher Gerard de Vries, who had also joined Maastricht University in early 1987, was convinced that a faculty without students could never remain viable in the long term. He had already been considering this problem before joining the university.[3] De Vries sought to expand the institution's activities on the nexus between culture and technology; the launch of the Arts and Culture programme in 1991 was largely the result of his efforts. Peters was also quick to realise that a faculty 'entirely dependent of those other faculties' might not manage to stay afloat when the next round of cutbacks came along – a far from unlikely event given the economic recession of the 1980s. Although, as

Peters recalls, the four departments were intended to yield synergy, this ultimately proved 'too much to ask'.

While De Vries focused on establishing the Arts and Culture programme, which was mainly based around the Philosophy and History Departments, staff at the Mathematics and Information Science groups also realised that they would have to start a new programme in order to survive. Despite its long-standing desire to develop more traditional, sciences-based degree programmes, the State University of Limburg had never given these ambitions much credence. Although Peters realised the university had no claim to programmes in the area of fundamental mathematics, physics, biology or information science, 'we thought it might be interesting to develop a new type of degree programme'. From late 1987 onwards, the university's strategy was aimed at expanding its technology-related activities. The idea was to secure support from the business community and other regional knowledge institutions. Amongst other useful contacts, Maastricht University had been in touch with Shell's research director Harry Beckers since 1985, who advised the university on the possibilities for a technology-related initiative. With the support of the Limburg provincial authorities, Beckers advocated the establishment of a Research Institute for Knowledge Systems (RIKS) that would conduct research on knowledge engineering, artificial intelligence and cognitive information science.[4] At the time, both the State University of Limburg and Open University backed the plan. In the business community, DSM, OCE and Shell also pledged their support.[5]

FREE-WHEELING Hans Peters, originally born in Maastricht as Hendrikus Johannes Maria in 1953, had not expected to return to his place of birth in 1984. He had moved to Amsterdam in 1971 to study Economics at VU Amsterdam, having graduated from secondary school at *gymnasium* level with an exact sciences profile. Despite having no background in economics, the degree programme appealed to him due to its 'relatively left-wing leanings'. At the time, he felt 'you had to know something about economics if you wanted to change society'. However, he rapidly discovered, 'within the space of two months, actually', that he was not interested in economics at all and decided to terminate his enrolment within just a few months. One year later, he enrolled in the Philosophy programme at the University of Amsterdam. Despite his best intentions, he did not last more than a year. Although subjects such as Medieval Philosophy certainly interested him, philosophy as a whole simply did not offer the structure he needed. As he concluded at the time: 'philosophy has no beginning and no end'. He lacked the motivation and self-discipline to finish the courses. At the time, Peters explains, it was still relatively easy to transfer to another programme. The student grant system was less strict, and – unlike today's student population – students in the 1970s were not driven by the notion of building a CV. 'Free-wheeling' was viewed as normal, and students even tended to frown upon careerist ambitions. Peters fulfilled his compulsory military service and spent a period working for the PTT postal service. He eventually decided to study Mathematics in Nijmegen in 1974, a subject in which he had always excelled. He continued to explore various tangents over the course of his studies. For instance, he took a hefty minor in Philosophy of Science, followed by a teacher training course and 'spent at least six months doing something entirely different'. After eight years of studying, he obtained his PhD in Mathematics and was appointed Mathematics Department staff member at the Catholic University of Nijmegen (which today goes by the name Radboud University Nijmegen). However, with the number of Mathematics students rapidly declining, the chances of obtaining a permanent position were negligible.

RETURN TO A 'NICE LITTLE TOWN' Initially, Peters could not muster much enthusiasm for a job interview in Maastricht. Although he felt it was a 'nice little town', the place lacked dynamism and he had not expected to return until his retirement. Nevertheless, he applied for the position of university lecturer in 1983. The job was set to involve curriculum development for the new Economics programme. This notion did hold immediate appeal. Peters – 'somewhat grudgingly, of course' – moved to his new workspace on Tongersestraat in 1984. As he recalls, founding dean Wil Albeda spent most of the introductory meeting on 2 January looking out of the window. It was not until Peters mentioned he was writing a dissertation on game and negotiation theory that Albeda finally perked up – the subject seemed to hold his interest. Despite being responsible for Mathematics education, Peters felt the subject was basically impossible to teach within the predetermined framework of problem-based learning.[6] General Economics professor Joan Muysken and Business Administration professor Hein Schreuder joined the fold at a later stage to help develop the curriculum at Maastricht, and soon started to bicker amongst themselves. The arrival of Muysken and Schreuder certainly did not make the ongoing efforts to integrate General Economics and Business Economics any easier.

Regardless, Vrieze was impressed by Peters's research and convinced him to join his Department of Mathematics. Group staff also included Frank Thuijsman, Piet Boekhoudt and Christian Heij, of whom the latter two specialised in mathematical systems theory. The core unit, later to become the Information Science Department, was also being established at the time. Jaap van den Herik was appointed its professor of Information Science. Van den Herik had also studied Mathematics and made a name for himself in the area of computer chess and artificial intelligence. Van den Herik headhunted staff members such as Peter Braspenning and Jos Uiterwijk and managed to bring in a relatively large number of researchers for temporary research projects. Unfortunately, Vrieze and Van den Herik's shared passion for games – bridge and chess, respectively – did not bring the two men any closer together. Although Peters claims they initially got along quite well, tensions soon flared. Vrieze and Van den Herik simply did not see eye to eye, to put it mildly. The two men were both easily annoyed, and could not seem to muster a sense of humour or perspective. Dean De Vries mainly had difficulties with Van den Herik, who was constantly pushing for more research funds, better facilities and more spacious accommodations without which – he claimed – rapid scientific expansion could not be achieved. For example, Van den Herik felt his 'big plans' for collaboration with RIKS – which was yet to be established at the time, incidentally – simply could not be put off.[7] With Philosophy and History located in the Elisabethhuis on Abtstraat and the two other departments assigned to other accommodations (divided over Tongersestraat 53 and Bredestraat) any hope of 'synergy' within the Faculty of General Sciences was a mere illusion. Where such initial start-up periods were generally marked by a sense of camaraderie, the atmosphere at Mathematics seemed to be tarred by tensions between the two clashing professors' egos from the very beginning. Van den Herik was especially prone to conflicts with his employees, even those with less prominent egos. The only ones who managed to maintain good relationships with him were those who 'did exactly as he said or kept their heads down'. Despite having struggled to cope with the bad mutual relationships and arguing from the outset, Peters could not deny that Maastricht was proving to be more dynamic than he had expected.

KNOWLEDGE ENGINEERING Once it became clear that mathematicians and information scientists played a negligible role in De Vries's plans, discussions on the further expansion of technology activities were resumed. All hopes were pinned on efforts to strengthen the university's exact sciences activities. Whereas De Vries felt technology as a cultural factor was crucial to broader society, the mathematicians and information scientists felt the theme of technology should have an entirely different emphasis. *Werkgroep 6000* worked hard to spark debate on the issue. The group met with various key figures within the university, such as Luc Soete of MERIT, Hein Schreuder of Business Administration and Henk Schmidt, who had floated the idea of developing a new Cognitive Information Science programme in 1985 in conjunction with Gerard Kempen, professor of Psycholinguistics in Nijmegen. (at the time, Maastricht University had no interest in developing such an initiative).[8] It also canvassed the opinions of various external parties, including the aforementioned Beckers, DSM CEO Hans van Liemt and Queen's Commissioner Sjeng Kremers. The infrastructure at the State University of Limburg was deemed too weak to support further expansion in the realm of medical technology. Collaboration with Eindhoven University of Technology and the University of Leuven seemed to offer potential, but the two parties soon proved to be less than enthusiastic about helping Maastricht.

The period from 1987 through 1988 saw intensive debate between the mathematicians and information scientists, eventually resulting in a memorandum entitled *Kennistechnologie. Voorstel voor een studierichting aan de Faculteit der Algemene Wetenschappen* ('Knowledge Engineering. Proposal for a new degree programme at the Faculty of General Sciences') (April 1989). Vrieze and Van den Herik had left drafting of the proposal up to Peters and Braspenning. Although Peters no longer recalls the exact genesis of the term 'knowledge engineering', he does emphasise that the decision to use it was 'obviously a highly strategic matter'. Knowledge Engineering was becoming increasingly popular, and the new exact sciences programme – the first of its kind in the Netherlands – would undoubtedly raise the State University of Limburg's profile. Peters and Braspenning took a highly pragmatic approach when preparing the memorandum: 'What do we actually have here? We've got Mathematics and Information Science. What do we want? We can't develop new Mathematics and Information Science programmes against the wishes of the other universities, so we'll have to take a different approach. Effectively speaking, we also don't offer pure mathematics, or even pure information science. The people here are all on the fringes of the more applied fields, so the new programme should reflect that fact. If not, we'll end up proposing something we don't really know enough about.' Peters and Braspenning's proposal to set up a Knowledge Engineering programme was certainly ahead of the curve. However, the term itself was not new. In November 1985, the State University of Limburg had organised a seminar entitled 'Knowledge systems and artificial intelligence on the basis of applied knowledge engineering'. The event saw the 'father' of artificial intelligence, information scientist and Stanford University professor Edward Feigenbaum, hold a four-hour lecture.[9] Feigenbaum was one of the first to coin the phrase 'artificial intelligence' and used his time on the symposium stage to highlight the great future benefits of knowledge engineering.[10]

Peters and Braspenning viewed knowledge engineering as 'a scientific discipline centred around the acquisition, representation, processing and presentation of knowledge'.[11] Knowledge engineering thus occupied the nexus between information science and mathematics. The idea was promoted as a 'multidisciplinary approach to problems relating to the structuring and representation of knowledge', partly in an effort to highlight the innovative nature of this new exact sciences programme. Knowledge engineering had emerged in response to the growing focus on cognitive processes starting in the late 1970s and early 80s, and the potential for automating knowledge processing through the use of knowledge systems. The aim was to teach students how to apply knowledge from the fields of mathematics and information science. Information science was key to the storage (databases) and use (expert systems and artificial intelligence) of knowledge, whereas mathematics focused on processing (statistics) and application (mathematical decision theory, modelling). Peters and Braspenning thus viewed Knowledge Engineering as an application-oriented 'method-based programme'. Students learned to focus on practical problems such as the introduction of new manufacturing technologies, the robotisation of production processes and planning of long-term processes, such as processes in the area of cardiovascular disease and the greenhouse effect. They also highlighted the option of further 'internationalising' Knowledge Engineering: there might be potential to further develop the degree programme in collaboration with a foreign university. Peters and Braspenning emphasised that the State University of Limburg would have to hurry: Knowledge Engineering should be launched as a programme by 1990 at the latest in order to stave off competition from Twente, Amsterdam and Tilburg. They assumed an intake of 25 to 50 students would be feasible during the start-up phase, growing to 50 to 100 during the 'stable phase'.

A STRATEGIC MOVE: COLLABORATION WITH THE LIMBURG UNIVERSITY CENTRE Initial hopes of a launch in 1990 proved overly optimistic. The university was sceptical of Peters and Braspenning's proposal. It seemed unlikely the State University of Limburg would really be eligible for this exact sciences programme. Despite having aimed to strengthen its activities in this field for years, the institution's ambitions had been consistently thwarted. Executive Board chair Loek Vredevoogd and Board member Karl Dittrich – who had launched the concept of the 'learning region' – supported the idea of developing an expansion strategy based around further strengthening Maastricht University's exact sciences activities through collaboration with foreign universities. As they were already aware, the Ministry of Education and Science – more particularly Minister Ritzen – was interested in promoting internationalisation. In their view, collaboration with the Limburg University Centre, currently known as Hasselt University, seemed the most logical course of action. The institution was known for its wealth of knowledge on the exact sciences. The Limburg University Centre had launched in 1973 at Diepenbeek campus, offering a total of six programmes: Mathematics, Physics, Chemistry, Biology, Dentistry and Medicine. The launch was intended to compensate for the loss of local mining jobs. However, the Limburg University Centre was not authorised to offer full-fledged degree programmes. Students seeking to obtain a degree certificate were required to follow up by attending a 'real' university, with most students opting to transfer to the University of Leuven. Accordingly, Leuven regarded the Limburg University Centre as a de facto annex. A transnational degree programme in Knowledge Engineering would thus yield a 'win-win situation' for both Maastricht and Diepenbeek: the State University of Limburg would gain a new exact sciences programme, while the Limburg University Centre could offer a full four-year degree programme.

The Limburg University Centre and the State University of Limburg held frequent consultations over the course of 1990. Despite the various inevitable legal issues, the two institutions rapidly reached agreement on several key aspects of the collaboration. The aim was to establish a transnational programme offering a 'double degree': a licentiate in accordance with Belgian law, and a doctoral degree certificate in accordance with Dutch legislation. Although the parties did encounter practical problems in terms of the division of tasks and funding (proposal: fifty/fifty), the issues seemed 'solvable with effort and creativity'.[12] Vredevoogd was encouraged to see that both the Belgian and Dutch Ministers of Education were open to the experiment: this was crucial, as Leuven wanted to keep Diepenbeek under its thumb. Vredevoogd was also expected to consult Leuven on the issue, which he found 'somewhat challenging' in view of the fact that 'Leuven runs Belgium'.[13] Once the two Ministers had made it clear they had no objections to the cross-border programme, Leuven – as Vredevoogd recalls – finally acquiesced, 'without much of an effort, actually'. Despite not having been involved in these high-level meetings, Peters does recall being contacted out of the blue by Freddy Dumortier, professor of Mathematics and Statistics at the Limburg University Centre somewhere during 1990. Dumortier wanted to know whether he would be willing to help set up something new, a proposal Peters enthusiastically agreed to.

Although collaboration with Maastricht was a strategic move, Peters claims this did not mean 'we were doing it against our will, on the contrary'. However, he did discover that the Belgians had a somewhat different approach to meetings. Whereas the Dutch felt all agreements recorded in the minutes had been formally established, their Belgian counterparts tended to take a somewhat more flexible or indeed creative approach and did not hesitate to put matters up for discussion again at a later stage. Despite hailing from Maastricht himself, a city near the Belgian border, this approach did leave Peters feeling 'somewhat surprised'. He also 'realised that you had to spend more time talking to people on a one-on-one basis: everything tended to sort itself out again after a few lunches with the odd glass of wine'. Despite the Belgians' 'greater freedom of interpretation', Peters 'wouldn't go so far as to say their approach doesn't work, it just works differently'.

KNOWLEDGE ENGINEERING AS A CROSS-BORDER PROGRAMME Despite their different approach to meetings, the parties did manage to make progress over the course of 1990. By the end of the year, a lengthy and thorough report entitled *Experimentele transnationale studierichting Kennistechnologie*

('Knowledge Engineering: an experimental transnational degree programme') had been completed. The document was then submitted to the Belgian and Dutch Ministries in early 1991 following various minor amendments.[14] In addition to Dumortier, the Limburg University Centre Information Science professors Eddy Flerackers and Marc Gijssens had contributed, while Peters and Braspenning had received assistance from other State University of Limburg staff in the guise of Vrieze and information scientist Ton Weijters. Van den Herik and Soete were also involved in an advisory capacity. The report set out the Limburg University Centre and State University of Limburg's joint ambition to play a 'leading role' in the area of higher education with a view to the upcoming European integration process.[15] Despite being largely based on Peters and Braspenning's proposal, the document also contained more elaborated proposals on the programme's content. In accordance with the initial proposal, knowledge engineering was defined as a 'scientific discipline dedicated to study and application of the following aspects of knowledge: acquisition, processing, usage and presentation'. Despite the inevitable comparisons with Knowledge Engineering programmes in the US, the expansion strategy called for a focus on the unique character of this experimental programme with its strong mathematical leanings.

In addition to reflecting the trend towards international academic alliances and the prevailing spirit of European unification, plans for the Knowledge Engineering programme – and a possible future English-language version – were designed to meet the demand for vocationally-oriented programmes in the area of modern information technology. Knowledge engineers, it was suggested, would be able to find employment in any organisation facing complex planning, decision-making and management issues. The proposal outlined three potential profiles for knowledge engineers. Firstly, the model engineer trained to develop models for mainly technical and business-related knowledge domains. Secondly, the operations research-oriented knowledge engineer, equipped with comprehensive mathematical knowledge of models and oriented towards decision theory and systems theory. Thirdly, the knowledge system designer specialising in the development of artificial intelligence modules. In addition to these three main profiles, knowledge engineers would also have the option of pursuing an academic career in which they could contribute to the further development of knowledge engineering. The emphasis would then be on decision theory or knowledge system design.

In addition to the collaboration with Diepenbeek, Knowledge Engineering justified its image as a cross-border programme on the basis of its multidisciplinary nature. Students were offered subjects such as decision theory and systems theory, knowledge systems, network and graph theory, logic and modelling theory, knowledge theory, mathematics and computer science. The aim was to emphasise the interrelationships between each of these disciplines whenever possible. This integration effort would be further strengthened due to the programme's focus on practical applicability, whereby students learned how to solve real-world problems.

So how was the collaboration between the Limburg University Centre and State University of Limburg reflected in the degree programme's practical structure? The programme was offered at two locations, and lecturers had to travel back and forth between Diepenbeek and Maastricht. Students in the first two years studied at Diepenbeek, which emphasised the acquisition of basic knowledge in the area of mathematics and information science and their various sub-areas, as well as general physics. The last two years of the programme were taught at Maastricht, where students would opt for one of the three main profiles, carry out a work placement and write a thesis. The Dutch had failed to convince their Belgian counterparts of the need to adopt problem-based learning. Despite having expressed their interest in this approach, lecturers at the Limburg University Centre tended to stick by traditional lectures and practical training. As the somewhat cautiously worded mission statement emphasised, Maastricht would emphasise problem-based learning, insofar as this was 'possible and desirable'.[16]

POSITIVE RESPONSES Staff at the State University of Limburg responded enthusiastically. The transnational degree programme was viewed as 'an excellent example of interuniversity collaboration within the Euroregion'.[17] These positive sentiments were broadly shared, with the other Dutch universities expressing their appreciation for 'the sound nature of the report'. Knowledge Engineering was sufficiently innovative to justify this 'experimental degree programme'. The transnational approach in itself was viewed as 'an experiment' that effectively reflected 'the opening of the internal European borders in 1992'.[18] The Education Council issued a positive recommendation. The transnational nature of Knowledge Engineering met with approval: collaboration with the Limburg University Centre would eliminate the need for further investments in the area of mathematics and information science, while the programme was expected to attract more than enough students. The initiative was also expected to have a positive impact on the regional business communities in both the Netherlands and Belgium. Unfortunately, however, the Belgians failed to muster much interest for the notion of problem-based learning. More importantly, the Education Council expressed its concern about the statement that Maastricht would apply problem-based learning at the new Knowledge Engineering programme insofar as 'possible and desirable'. After all, this approach was surely fundamental to the State University of Limburg's philosophy? Following a positive recommendation by the Flemish Community Minister of Education, Ritzen finally granted his approval in September 1991 with the proviso that he wanted to see greater clarity and consensus on the issue of problem-based learning.[19] As Peters explains, the transnational programme undoubtedly gained approval with such relative ease due to the fact that the State University of Limburg would not be treading on the other universities' proverbial toes. At the time, no other institutions were offering a comparable transnational programme. The Ministry of Education and Science provided start-up funding to the tune of three million guilders.[20]

TEETHING PROBLEMS Despite the high level of interest during the information days, a mere 14 students ultimately signed up for the transnational experiment in September of 1992. The sense of disappointment was palpable: student numbers had been expected to total at least 50. Dutch students failed to see the appeal of the rather scholarly Belgian academic climate, and were less than enthusiastic about the prospects of spending their first two years in Diepenbeek. Although Maastricht and Diepenbeek are less than thirty kilometres apart, Diepenbeek was difficult to reach from Maastricht by public transport and the Dutch students were unwilling to find 'digs' in Diepenbeek. Peters recalls initial plans to organise a shuttle bus service that would transport students to Diepenbeek. However, a large portion of the few Dutch students to actually enrol – Knowledge Engineering attracted a total of 22 students in 1993 – dropped out prematurely after it became clear that their knowledge of mathematics paled in comparison to that of their Belgian counterparts. As Peters explains, the level of abstract mathematics taught at Belgian secondary schools was especially high in comparison.

This situation was compounded by another practical problem on the side of the Dutch lecturers. Belgium applied a point-based system, whereby all students were discussed 'in great detail' at the end-of-year meeting. 'The teachers would take stock of every student's development.' Peters 'didn't like the idea at all'. He also got the impression that the university's higher organisational levels had failed to take account of the practical problems and cultural differences between the Dutch and Belgians from the outset. As was to be expected, the problems surrounding Knowledge Engineering had a detrimental effect on morale at the Faculty of General Sciences. When Vrieze outlined his vision for a yet-to-be-established 'Sciences Faculty' spearheaded by the Mathematics and Information Science Departments during a meeting on the faculty's future in early 1993, De Vries's response was somewhat cynical: how did Vrieze expect to play a pioneering role at such a faculty when the Knowledge Engineering programme only had 'about ten Dutch students'?[21] Vrieze had expected a greater show of solidarity from De Vries, and made it clear that he felt the Arts and Culture programme might turn out to be a passing fad. De Vries, who regarded that programme as his personal brainchild, had 'little patience' for such notions. In his view, Arts and Culture had been keeping the entire faculty afloat since introduction of the student-based grant system. This, he emphasised, was a historical event: science activities had not been funded by the humanities 'since Galilei's time'.[22] Although there was no immediate rupture in early 1993, the meeting did result in a 'highly unpleasant situation'. The separation of ways following the launch of the Faculty of Arts and Culture in 1994 came as no surprise to any of the parties involved.

WHAT NEXT? Peters spent another two years teaching, but jumped at the opportunity to become professor of Quantitative Economics at the Faculty of Economics in 1993. He turned down Vrieze's offer a professorship at the Mathematics Department. Not only did he feel ideally suited to the chair in Economics – with its emphasis on mathematical economics – he had also had his fill of the endless bickering between Vrieze and Van den Herik. As he explains, people were 'leaving all the time, in those days'. One of the founding fathers of Knowledge Engineering, Braspenning, was even sidelined following a conflict with Van den Herik, and subsequently decided to leave of his own accord. Peters watched the developments at Knowledge Engineering unfold from a distance after 1993.

Those tumultuous developments managed to rack up a remarkable number of column inches in university magazine *Observant*.[23] An externally appointed dean, Kasper Boon, also failed to get the ship running smoothly, as did a hired consultant. The viability of Knowledge Engineering repeatedly came under question. Up until the year 2000, the number of first-year students averaged around 25.[24] However, the Executive Board was committed to sustaining the university's only exact sciences programme, and wanted to maintain its transnational collaboration model at all costs. Although the Educational Sciences programme launched in 2001 with just 14 students was discontinued after just one year due to poor intake levels and high financial risks, the Executive Board continued to invest in Knowledge Engineering and collaboration with the Limburg University Centre.[25] 2002 even saw the launch of the much heralded transnational University Limburg. The new institution's name was abbreviated to tUL at the request of the Flemish – the acronym TUL was too reminiscent of the Flemish word for catamite.[26]

Knowledge Engineering was the first degree programme to be offered by the transnational University Limburg. However, that university did not prove to be the 'appealing testing ground within the European higher education area' so many had been hoping for.[27] The tUL's embroilment in Knowledge Engineering complicated matters further still: from that point onwards, Dutch students stopped turning up almost altogether. However, discontinuation was still not on the table, not even after Maastricht University was forced to bear the brunt of a multi-million euro deficit in 2003.[28] In an effort to 'save' Knowledge Engineering, the programme was largely transferred from the tUL and assigned to the newly established Faculty of Humanities and Sciences in the period around 2005, where it was also repositioned as a new English-taught programme. The departure of Vrieze and Van den Herik introduced a new period of stability for the knowledge engineers. The experimental introduction of the project-based education system developed at Aalborg University (a proposal by Kasper Boon) turned out well for the new Sciences programme; like Maastricht, the Danish university established in 1974 had built its profile around educational innovation from the very start. In addition to lectures and practical training, the emphasis was on project-based education. Students would jointly elaborate specific themes within the framework of projects such as 'building a rule-based knowledge system for the establishment of alert levels during potential flooding of the Meuse'.[29] Such large-scale and complex project tasks proved to be closer to day-to-day practice than the smaller issues in problem-based learning course books, and had a positive effect on student motivation. As of 2010, intake levels remained relatively stable at around 50 students a year; a significant number for any Sciences programme.[30] Peters now has enough distance to look back on his pioneering days with a sense of self-depreciation: 'Knowledge Engineering eventually did quite well for itself after Peters's departure'.

16 *Louis Boon* THE MOST INTERESTING THEMES ARE FOUND AT THE INTERFACE OF THE SOCIAL SCIENCES AND NATURAL SCIENCES

A LONG PROCEDURE Louis Boon was working as an academic staff member at the Sub-faculty of Psychology in Utrecht when, in 1983, he stumbled across a job opening in Maastricht in the newspaper. The General Faculty of the University of Limburg had established a professorship with 'the embryonic title' of chair in Philosophy and Ethics.[1] The new professor was to help develop the Health Sciences Theory specialisation. It was largely the student members of the Faculty Council who had insisted on greater theoretical depth at Social Health Science. They wanted to know more about the principles and ethical aspects of the discipline. What did the concept of social health science actually entail? Plans were being forged to establish a new Faculty of Health Sciences with seven specialisations. The field of health sciences attracted Boon, as he was interested in the areas where the natural sciences and social sciences overlapped. He applied for the position in August 1983 but – in what turned out to be a small complication – he had not yet obtained his PhD. However, his dissertation had already been accepted and he had authored numerous publications. That was still possible in those days, Boon says thirty year later. 'It would be completely unimaginable now'. All the other key figures mentioned in this book arrived at the university via connections in one way or another, but not so with Boon. Boon knew no one in Maastricht. He hardly knew where the city was, never mind having heard about problem-based learning. In fact, he 'really didn't have the foggiest idea what it was'. But starting something new was not a problem for him; in fact, the opposite was true.

The selection procedure became a drawn-out affair. According to Boon, chance would have it that the composition of the committee changed frequently. For example, the director of the faculty was suddenly appointed head of human resources of the university, on account of his predecessor de-

parting 'just like that'. The dean also disappeared halfway through the procedure to make way for medical biologist Foppe ten Hoor. Founding father Co Greep initially sat in the committee, only to exit later after he had been deposed as dean of the Medical Faculty. Boon remembers the only committee member to remain throughout the entire procedure was professor Paul Thung. Thung, who was trained as a pathologist, was affiliated with Leiden University and had also been involved with the State University of Limburg from its inception. He was very interested in medical education reform and found himself fascinated by the experiment going on in Maastricht. He was allowed to determine the theme of his chair and described his post as – 'he could be quite outrageous in that way' – professor 'of the Relationship between Medicine and the Natural Sciences'. It was not long before Boon and Thung discovered they got along very well. Things got exciting towards the end of the selection procedure: a tour of the other Dutch universities revealed that not everyone thought Boon would make a suitable professor. Besides, he had competition from Groningen in the form of Theo Kuipers, a classically trained philosopher of science. The fact that Boon was eventually appointed in February 1985 and could start three months later was largely thanks to Thung's support.

ALOYSIUS JOHANNES Boon had never thought he would end up in science: he came from an environment that was totally unfamiliar with the world of universities. Boon was born into a middle-class Catholic family in Breda in 1948. His parents named him Aloysius Johannes after his grandfathers. Before the arrival of little Louis, his father had had a farm, but shortly after the war he exchanged a piece of land in order to start a shop. Boon's strong affinity with nature is probably due to his family's farming background – he would get up at any time of the night to help a badger in danger, or any other animal for that matter. His father and mother worked in their shop, where they sold a wide range of goods: from household articles, haberdasheries, hardware and crockery to toys and petrol. His parents had only completed elementary school and were not especially thrilled when Louis informed them that he wanted to attend *gymnasium* (pre-university secondary education). The 'idea of wanting to develop yourself' was not something they could appreciate, says Boon. But he loved reading, and especially read 'lots and lots of novels'. Boon's parents eventually let him have his way and he started pre-university education: 'the first and, for a very long time, the last' in his family to do so. During his secondary school years, Boon acquired a taste for French literature. One of favourite novels was *Voyage au bout de la nuit* (1932) by Louis-Ferdinand Céline. Boon become fascinated by the lyricism full of bitterness, cursing and swearing, the nihilism and the author's cynical view of mankind. He still rereads that novel every three or four years. That penchant for the French language turned out to be his salvation after his French teacher came to his defence just as he was about to be expelled from school during a 'fairly unmanageable period'. Boon eventually scored high marks in his final examinations with a focus on social sciences and modern languages.

SOCIOLOGY AND PHILOSOPHY Boon began studying Sociology and, after a while, also Philosophy at the University of Amsterdam in 1967. Though that was 'during the left-wing period', Boon was not especially interested in politics. As he says himself, he was something of a loner, an individualist, who did not fit into groups very easily. To his amazement, an article of his was selected for publication in a scientific journal during his studies. An academic career attracted him because, at a university, you were 'actually paid' to read and write. Immediately after graduation in 1974, he left for Mannheim to teach Mathematical Logic at the university there. A year later, he was hired as an academic staff member at VU Amsterdam's Faculty of Science, where he could work on the history of the natural sciences. It was 'a truly wonderful time,' Boon recalls. 'It was the only period in which I was totally left in peace and had almost no teaching responsibilities.' Boon became involved in the launch of two journals: the *Amsterdams Sociologisch Tijdschrift* ('Amsterdam Journal of Sociology') and, somewhat later, *Kennis en Methode. Tijdschrift voor wetenschapsfilosofie en methodologie* ('Knowledge and Method: Journal for the Philosophy of Science and Methodology'). The editorial boards of both publications proved inspiring company and included the sociologists Christien Brinkgreve and Dick Pels and science philosopher Gerard de Vries, who would later go on to establish the Arts and Culture degree programme at Maastricht in around 1990.

In 1978, Boon left for the Sub-faculty of Psychology at Utrecht University. Psychology fascinated him, owing to the common ground this social science shared with the natural sciences. His 1982 textbook on the history of psychology, *Geschiedenis van de psychologie* ('History of Psychology'), was reprinted no fewer than eight times. In Utrecht, Boon had many teaching duties, which is why he says it took him a fairly long time before he obtained his PhD with a dissertation titled *De list der wetenschap. Variatie en selectie: vooruitgang zonder rationaliteit* ('The Ruse of Science. Variation and Selection: Progress without Rationality'). In his dissertation, Boon applied the theory of evolution to explain the growth of knowledge. According to Boon, scientific progress is not so much the result of rational intentions of individual researchers as of 'the ruse of science': only those ideas and theories that are selected as useful are able to develop further. By highlighting the selection function of a research community, Boon called for attention for the social development of science. This view appealed to Thung, who found Boon to be 'an extremely interesting person' with a very broad intellectual horizon. Boon easily found his place in the newly established Faculty of Health Sciences, a faculty that was unique in the Netherlands, which with its Humanities, Sciences and Social Sciences departments was responsible for seven degree programmes.[2]

HEALTH SCIENCES Boon started work at the young faculty in the spring of 1985. His department was initially called 'Health Ethics and Philosophy', a 'ridiculous name', he thought. It was as if 'health ethics did not already come under philosophy'. That name was the invention of professor of Medical Ethics Paul Sporcken, also a priest and moral theologian, who had been working at the university since 1974; he was a man whom Boon recalls warmly because he represented a non-dogmatic type of Catholicism. In the mid-1980s, the faculty was undergoing major changes. The three existing specialisations (Health-care Policy and Management, Health Education and Education and Nursing Science) were supplemented by four new ones: Health Sciences Theory, Mental Health Sciences, Biological Medicine and Movement Sciences. With 16 departments, the faculty's heterogeneity was considerable. How did it all hold together? Boon says that, at Health Sciences, 'Philipsen's triangle' was viewed as a totem, like 'a kind of flag on the battlefield around which people could congregate'. He adds that the triangle did not play a strong conceptual role. The advantage of this arrangement was that it placed health sciences activities in a comprehensible framework.

Boon initially focused on research. He tried to get a seat on the Science Committee, but was unsuccessful when Gerjo Kok, then professor of Health Education, secured the seat for himself. Boon then entered the Faculty Board, where he became the member responsible for education. Foppe ten Hoor, professor of Human Biology, had just been appointed dean at that time. From the beginning, Boon had been very impressed with the education system at Maastricht. He observed 'with surprise how refreshing problem-based learning was for the students' and became a strong advocate of this approach. Boon recalls how, in that period, students still disliked tutors who tried to involve themselves with their group too much. Whenever that happened, students would respond indignantly: 'Come on, that's not what we're here for!' As the member responsible for education, Boone faced the challenge of revising the core curriculum, which required changes due to the new degree programmes. The revision had a high priority. Boon started with the structure of the new curriculum – he benefited from the fact that he 'was new and therefore carried no baggage'. In his opinion, the curriculum contained 'a ridiculous amount of health sciences philosophy and theory', and that was therefore the first thing he wanted to cut back to more normal proportions, thereby freeing up space for new subjects. The revision prompted a lot of discussion and, for a short while, it looked as though the faculty would not survive. Boon recalls how Mental Health Sciences staff disagreed with the plans and threatened to go their own way. Boon believes that the only reason the faculty remained intact was because there were always sufficient numbers of students. For example, in 1986 the faculty welcomed 300 first-year students.[3] Consequently, there was never time for anyone to get bored.

Another major problem that the faculty faced was how to divide its funding. The issue was that not all specialisations were funded in the same way. As Biological Medicine and Movement Sciences received sciences funding, they had more money to spend per student than the other five specialisations. This allocation of funds excited envy. Tensions rose high when financial problems occurred in early 1987. Dean Ten Hoor tried to implement a reorganisation which financially favoured the Natural Sciences degree programmes, and according to Boon 'that cost him his job.' The Faculty Council dismissed Ten Hoor and Boon was appointed the new dean in the summer of 1987. It was a post he gladly accepted since 'all that fiddling around in the faculty had to be put to a stop'.

Boon remembers his deanship as 'an exciting time'. The faculty seemed to be facing 'financial disaster', so new reorganisation plans were drawn up. But by the time the plans were ready, they were no longer needed, Boon says. The financial pressure on the faculty had dissipated. What had happened? The Executive Board, and particularly Karl Dittrich, had pressured the Faculty of Health Sciences to abandon the enrolment quota of 300 students. The Executive Board was determined that the State University of Limburg would continue to grow. It had failed to meet the target of 6,000 students in 1990 as set out in the Deetman motion. At the Health Sciences Faculty, they were terrified of having to deal with a huge increase in student numbers, but in the end the faculty succumbed to the pressure. In 1987, there were suddenly 400 first-year students at the gates, and that did not include the more than 80 first-year part-time Nursing Science students. One year later, student numbers were still growing strongly. 'That was another massive blow for the organisation', but this growth also meant that the faculty no longer needed to cut back or reorganise. However, the faculty was bursting at the seams: it was housed in a number of buildings and had to relocate temporarily to Kapoenstraat 2 until the new building in Randwyck was ready.

As faculty dean, Boon also had to deal with a second curriculum overhaul, prompted by the findings of a 1986 External Review Committee which had levelled a fair amount of criticism at the degree programme. Henk Schmidt, education psychologist and Faculty Council member responsible for education, would play an important role in this curriculum review. The curriculum was completely redone: thanks to differentiation programmes, the students we given far more options in choosing their own learning pathways from the start. According to Boon, the renewed curriculum was a case of 'no one was happy, but everyone was satisfied'. As dean, he continued to have a heavy teaching workload: 'at least 600 hours'. He did not need a lot of sleep.

EXPANSION PLANS The price that Boon had to pay for all these activities was that he could not be involved in research to the extent that he had hoped when he chose Maastricht. He was too impatient and his intellectual interest too broad to specialise as a scientist. Consequently, he was not interested in specialising. There were 'always other things' that he wanted to learn, whether it was 'more mathematics or more history or more philosophy or more biology'. Boon tried to maintain that breadth of interest, but at a certain point he had to admit that he was 'too broad and did too much' to be a good researcher. Looking back at his career, he says: 'You can't pursue a career in research if you're engaged in evolution biology and psychology, and also dabble in history and snippets of philosophy while you're actually most interested in cognitive psychology or cognitive neuroscience. It just won't work because your grasp will be superficial'.

Boon's broad interest and preference for intellectual adventures, combined with his drive, served him well when drawing up expansion plans. In fact, he was involved with the Faculty of General Sciences from its establishment in 1986. This faculty included philosophers, historians, mathematicians and information scientists who supported the other faculties. However, the idea was that this faculty would also serve as a launchpad for new degree programmes.[4] Boon was vice-chair of the General Sciences Committee and had 'something of a free hand' there because the chairman, Rector Vic Bonke, often had other worries. He was also chair of the application committee which appointed De Vries as professor at the Philosophy Department in late 1986. He still knew De Vries well from the editorial board of *Kennis en Methode*. In October of that year, they had travelled together to the United States to visit several renowned universities in New York and Boston: New York University, Columbia University, Harvard University and the Massachusetts Institute of Technology. The ideas that De Vries picked up on that trip would eventually help shape the basis of a new degree programme: Arts and Culture.

SOCIAL SCIENCES? Boon had been toying for some time with the idea of the further expansion of the university in the area of the social sciences. In the summer of 1990, he got a discussion going about this in the Board of Deans. The deans were asked to consider the possible launch of degree programmes in Educational Sciences and Policy Sciences. Boon argued for the establishment of a 'real' academic discipline and suggested exploring the possibilities of starting a degree programme in the social sciences. The Executive Board still favoured an expansion strategy focusing on the domains of culture and technology. The deans eventually sided with Boon and his idea of 'exploring the area of the social sciences'. According to Boon, the Board of Deans involving themselves with the expansion of the university was 'a serious five-fingered salute to the Executive Board.'[5]

Boon worked closely with Gerard Korsten on this exploratory mission. As secretary of *Werkgroep 6000*, Korsten had previously worked for the Arts and Culture degree programme and was fetched by Boon to Health Sciences to get involved with internationalisation. Both men considered the State University of Limburg too limited in its breadth and scale, even after the establishment of the Arts and Culture degree programme, although the university student population would reach 6,000 in the autumn of 1990.[6] Furthermore, Boon and Korsten believed the university's expansion should not be geared to offering yet more competencies – i.e. highly vocational degree programmes – but to traditional scientific disciplines. Boon and Korsten 'went about talking to almost everyone at the institution' to exchange thoughts and ideas and so outline a plan. At that time, Boon had been dean for three years and his work had been growing increasingly routine: another budget, another open day. The idea of setting up something new gave him fresh energy. And he was especially drawn to the idea of a degree programme in Psychology, still recalling with fondness his years working in that field in Utrecht. Korsten was more interested in a Sociology degree programme.

Other than the top-down strategy for expansion at Arts and Culture – De Vries had drawn up his plans in consultation with the Board in relative isolation – Boon and Korsten opted for a bottom-up method that was aligned with what staff wanted. In the late summer of 1990, they knew from speaking with staff members that there was enough support to pursue two tracks: a socio-cultural degree programme and a degree programme in the behavioural sciences. In early 1991, they issued an interim report containing two more detailed options. The first was a cluster of degree programmes designated International Social Studies whose focus was to be on international developments, relations, differences and comparisons. The second entailed a Psychology degree programme which would not offer the full range of specialisation options, as was the case elsewhere, but would be designed around the theme of 'cognition and learning'.[7] Both degree programmes would be promoted, within the university and beyond, as 'distinctive' programmes with an international accent; their intention was of course to attract new categories of students, and not to compete against existing Maastricht programmes. Boon and Korsten's strategy was based on 'optimum use of the expertise available at the State University of Limburg', since they knew in-house expertise would be indispensable to any new initiative launched without external resources.

Initial reactions from both the Board of Deans and the Executive Board were favourable enough for Boon and Korsten to steam ahead. They sought and received specialist input from all the faculties; most ideas came from psychologists such as Jelle Jolles, Harald Merckelbach, Henk Schmidt, Marcel van den Hout and Anita Jansen, all working at the Faculty of Medicine or the Faculty of Health Sciences.[8] In the summer of 1991, the *Verkenning sociaal-*

wetenschappelijke studierichtingen ('Exploration of possible social sciences degree programmes') was complete: the degree programmes in International Social Studies and Psychology had been further fleshed out, the curricula were in the pipeline, including learning outcomes and an overview of social sciences expertise at the university, which was calculated to be 176 FTE. Boon and Korsten published the report in a personal capacity. The tone of the reactions was largely positive, though the Executive Board favoured Psychology above International Social Studies, which they considered too vague and certain to fail in The Hague, as it would only lead to unemployment. Belief in social engineering seemed to be on the wane.[9] Moreover, there were organisational questions about any new degree programme: which faculty should it be assigned to: Health Sciences or General Sciences?

In short, there was plenty to discuss for the Psychology and International Social Studies degree programme committees, which with support from 'the powers that be' were tasked with presenting concrete plans in the autumn of 1991. In *Observant* of 7 November 1991, Boon explained the expansion proposals which were to elevate 'the impoverished intellectual climate of the university'. In the same article, Rector Job Cohen said that he welcomed any plan that broadened the university's base, but that these plans were far from finalised. According to Cohen, the *Exploration* 'had been written during a spare moment', and it was uncertain whether the university actually possessed the required expertise. It did not surprise him that the plan was the idea of Health Sciences, since their student numbers had been falling for a while. Boon felt offended and complained angrily about Cohen's 'stupid move' to Executive Board President Loek Vredevoogd. How could a rector betray the expansion initiative like this? Boon had turned to Vredevoogd since he was the Board member actually responsible for university expansion. It was also Vredevoogd who, due to his excellent connections with the Ministry of Education and Science, understood better than anyone how the Ministry viewed Maastricht's ambitions – as far as he was concerned, they would certainly be willing to discuss a new experiment in Maastricht. He saw a 'gap in the market' and was pragmatic enough to seize the opportunity, even though he had to admit that these two social science degree programmes did not fit in the strategy he advocated for the university.[10]

In 1992, the Psychology committee appointed a programme advisor, Rob de Vries, a psychologist and science philosopher whom Boon knew from his Utrecht days. De Vries was tasked with identifying what exactly distinguished the Maastricht curriculum from other Psychology degree programmes in the country and what would be required under the University Statute (*Academisch Statuut*) to adopt the programme. According to De Vries, both a dynamic and an opportunistic attitude were required.[11] The members of the Psychology committee were immensely enthusiastic. According to Boon, the committee included people who 'saw their future in the new Psychology degree programme', people such as neuropsychologist Jelle Jolles, experimental psychologist Merckelbach, education psychologist Peter Bouhuijs, knowledge engineer Peter Braspenning and Boon himself of course. A large part of their motivation was because they were from Medicine, Health Sciences or General Sciences and liked the idea of working at a 'real' Faculty of Psychology; after all, Health Sciences remained 'just an application area'. Boon made himself chair of the International Social Studies committee in order to 'keep the fire hot', though he remembers the lack of enthusiasm from committee members Gerard de Vries, Hans Philipsen, Luc Soete and Chris de Neubourg – who, according to Boon, could not see any future for themselves in this new degree programme. Moreover, Soete and De Neubourg, especially, were far too busy promoting internationalisation at their own Economics Faculty. During the course of 1992, Boon and Korsten therefore decided to mainly devote their time and energy to the Psychology degree programme.

TOWARDS A DISCIPLINARY PSYCHOLOGY DEGREE PROGRAMME The goal of establishing an academic discipline like psychology was remarkable for a university which, from its inception, had emphasised the crucial importance of multidisciplinary collaboration and interdisciplinary research. This was not lost on the Psychology committee, which presented its plans in the summer of 1992. There was something paradoxical about the *Psychologie in Maastricht* ('Psychology in Maastricht') report, with its overwhelmingly monodisciplinary curriculum, having been born of interfaculty cooperation. The Psychology degree programme did not just mean a broadening of the university's academic base, it was also to serve as a counterbalance to the generally vocational, multidisciplinary degree programmes that the State University of Limburg had hosted since the 1980s by focusing on the 'niches' in Dutch higher education. It was now of course essential to avoid resembling Psychology degree programmes elsewhere in the country. For that reason, the Maastricht degree programme would not focus on clinical psychology – an area that also had the highest unemployment – but seek its distinctive signature in a specific profile with a focus on cognitive psychology and biopsychology. The dominant theme of the former was 'acquisition, representation and use of knowledge', while that of the latter was 'brains and behaviour'. Maastricht psychologists already had an international reputation in these areas and, moreover, interest in biopsychology and cognitive psychology was gaining ground, especially in the United States. The *Psychologie in Maastricht* report, complete with a – fairly detailed – proposed curriculum, was well received at the State University of Limburg. Minor adjustments were made to the report in the autumn, including a greater emphasis on its international character: the degree programme was to include a track offered fully in English.[12] The Minister of Education and Science, PvdA (Labour) party member

Jo Ritzen was known to be enthusiastic about the State University of Limburg's international ambitions. Yet the fiercest discussion did not concern the programme's curriculum, but its place within the university organisation, i.e. the debate was more political than anything else. No fewer than three faculties were vying for the Psychology degree programme. To Boon and Korsten's dismay, the Medical Faculty was suddenly embracing Psychology, which they were dead against. They believed that Psychology – their brainchild! – belonged to Health Sciences; after all, it had been their initiative. However, after much deliberation, the Executive Board decided that Psychology should in due course be part of the 'expansion faculty', the Faculty of General Sciences, assuming that the degree programme was actually launched. In late 1992, the second version of *Psychologie in Maastricht* was ready to be sent to the Ministry of Education and Science for approval. Vredevoogd found it 'a truly excellent proposal' and lent it his full support.[13]

ALL HELL BROKE LOOSE In early 1993, *Psychologie in Maastricht* was on the desk of Ritzen, who liked the plan, according to Boon. But as soon as the other universities got wind of it, 'all hell broke loose', Vredevoogd remembers well. The *Kamer Psychologie* (Psychology Association) of the consultative body for the social sciences, part of the Association of Universities in the Netherlands (VSNU), was alarmed by the plans from Maastricht. While there was appreciation for the initiative, the degree programme was viewed as too narrow and specialist, in a time when job prospects for psychologists did not look particularly good. And, most alarming of all, the country already had eight Psychology degree programmes, so how 'efficient' would it be to have a ninth? Representatives from Nijmegen, who feared competition, were especially critical: 'another programme offering what we do already should not be permitted and it will not see the light of day'. Vredevoogd would not be fazed and continued to support the Maastricht proposal. When Ritzen announced in May that the VSNU's Psychology Association had advised against the degree programme, the disappointment in Maastricht was palpable. Crisis talks were held immediately. Was there any point continuing with the Psychology degree programme? Yet the university remained hopeful: the Education Council still had to consider the application. Not long after, however, the council also advised Ritzen against the programme. Things looked bleak for Maastricht, as it was impossible for the Minister to ignore these negative opinions. Vredevoogd had maintained intensive contact with the Minister and understood his dilemma. On the one hand, Ritzen found the specifics of the Maastricht proposal interesting but, on the other, he could not, certainly as a native of Limburg, give preference to the State University of Limburg by ignoring the negative advice. It was a tough dilemma. Vredevoogd was not yet prepared to give up, especially as he knew from his contacts with civil servants at the Ministry that there was no anti-Maastricht sentiment there.[14]

Boon had the idea of having a number of renowned professors of Psychology write to Ritzen and, as experts, make the argument for a Psychology degree programme in Maastricht. One of the advisers to the Psychology committee, Nico Frijda, a well-known emeritus professor of Experimental Psychological at the University of Amsterdam, was happy to take the lead. He was on good terms with Merckelbach and Jansen. Together with five other prominent Dutch professors of Psychology, he argued in favour of the original, solid Maastricht degree programme that was supported by 'excellent' research groups.[15] Ritzen was not surprised by the letter. Vredevoogd had already liaised with the Minister on the matter, giving the Minister an argument to delay a decision on Maastricht. According to Vredevoogd, the letter was not published, so that the Minister would have sufficient room to manoeuvre. In the meantime, Ritzen instructed the deputy director general for science policy, Diana Wolff-Albers, to investigate whether the report was really up to standard. Wolff-Albers was quickly able to respond that that was indeed the case.[16] It was now a question of waiting for the Education Advisory Committee (ACO), which had been delegated the advisory task of the Education Council. The ACO was expected to be less biased. Boon was able to get along with the chairman who, like Boon himself, 'was mad about dachshunds' – which immediately created a bond between the two. Ritzen urged the State University of Limburg to lend even more international cachet to Psychology by seeking collaboration with the Limburg University Centre in Hasselt in Belgium. In the new application, the university 'obediently complied with the Minister's wishes'.[17] It did not matter that there was no Psychology degree programme in Hasselt. That barrier was soon overcome in a written declaration confirming the institution's willingness to collaborate. For Boon himself, a lot hung on the eventual decision about Psychology. He had not been dean of Health Sciences since mid-1993. His demand for a year off to go on a sabbatical had precluded him from a second term. In hindsight, he now views that demand as an overestimation of himself. His departure was partly influenced by the fact that staff at the Faculty of Health Sciences frowned at his unflagging efforts for Psychology. His academic ambitions lay of course in the field of Psychology, where he wanted to be dean.

PSYCHOLOGY IN MAASTRICHT The situation was saved in early 1994. Having received a positive recommendation from the ACO, Ritzen granted permission for Maastricht to commence a Psychology degree programme, on the condition that it would not be based in its own faculty. The universities of Nijmegen and Tilburg continued to protest against the Maastricht Psychology degree programme, but to no avail. Ritzen freed up funds so that the programme could get going in September 1995. It was a miracle that the State University of Limburg succeeded in acquiring a discipline like Psychology, given the opposition it faced from multiple sides. Though Boon views chance as a determining factor in history, it is clear that together with Korsten and Vredevoogd – not to mention the dachshunds – he had been able to nudge chance in the right direction. Of course, the outcome had only been possible due to the quality of the degree programme, to which especially Jolles, Schmidt, Merckelbach and Rob de Vries had contributed. Soon after the good news, Boon went to Indonesia for a year, where he was a guest lecturer at Gadjah Mada University in Yogyakarta. All attention now went to setting up the Psychology degree programme, which was based in a wooden shed in Randwyck. As chair of the Psychology committee, Boon could now call himself dean. For the time being, however, Psychology was part of the Faculty of General Sciences. Boon ensured that Psychology remained fully independent at General Sciences as a kind of 'pseudo-faculty'. Not only could he style himself dean, he also had a seat on the Board of Deans.

The transformation from 'golden idea' to implementation, i.e. a well-run Psychology degree programme, placed high demands on staff.[18] They set to work with much enthusiasm, despite the heavy workload. Since many staff brought in expertise from other faculties, the degree programme could get off to a flying start. Merckelbach and Rob de Vries, especially, worked hard on behalf of the programme in the first year. In September 1995, 170 students enrolled, far more than the 75 that had been expected. It had been assumed that the sciences profile would probably deter students, but that was not the case. On the contrary, cognitive and biological psychology turned out to be very popular. Students believed that these tracks offered good employment opportunities. Furthermore, the international orientation and the small-scale, problem-based education increased the programme's appeal. It was structured in thematic blocks, such as Social Behaviour, Memory and Differences between People, which drew on knowledge from multiple disciplines and sub-disciplines. For example, Differences between People involved genetics, differential psychology, social psychology and psychometrics. During the first two years, students were introduced to the full breadth of the field of psychology, after which they had to choose between cognitive psychology and biological psychology. Cognitive psychology came in two variants: cognitive ergonomics and education psychology. Biological psychology also had two variants: neuropsychology and development psychology. Also, both specialisations allowed students to choose the psychopathology variant. From the first year, Boon was involved in another course: History and Theory of Psychology.[19]

Psychology was a success, and garnered much appreciation among the students. After one year, Psychology at Maastricht was the number one degree programme in the Options Guide for Higher Education.[20] In 1996, more than

200 first-year students enrolled, and those numbers would continue to increase. The psychologists also scored well in the area of research. The Experimental Psychopathology research school and the Brains and Behaviour institute were vital to the image of the degree programme, even though they were established at other faculties. Psychology set up a research programme into memory function, which produced three sub-programmes. Schmidt pushed the research towards the 'performance of everyday memory'. Merckelbach, professor of Experimental Psychology from 1996, focused on research into 'disorders in everyday memory', working particularly in the area of forensic psychology. Jolles played a central role in the sub-programme 'memory-related processes: biological versus environmental factors'.

The work of the Board, on which the four founding fathers Boon, Jolles, Schmidt and Merckelbach had to collaborate, was beset by difficulties, however. Tensions between Boon, Jolles and Schmidt especially ran high. There were arguments about complying with working agreements and future lines of research, but the difficulties mainly came down to a clash of egos. The personal relationships between the Board members had become extremely strained. In the summer of 1997, things got very messy. Jolles, Schmidt and Merckelbach withdrew their confidence in Boon. He was accused of unacceptably coarse behaviour. Boon's emotional fervour in his work was now working against him. The Executive Board intervened. A split into two camps, i.e. those in favour of Boon and those against, was imminent. Boon had no choice but to step down as dean. Executive Board member and known troubleshooter Hans Philipsen tried to smooth things out as interim dean. In the end, Boon remained on the Board as the member responsible for the budget and organisation. The Psychology degree programme was scheduled to relocate to a new building on Universiteitssingel in 1999. Looking back on the conflict, Boon fully blames himself for that fall from grace: his undiplomatic actions had been guided too much by hubris. The relationship between Boon and his former friend Schmidt suffered permanent damage. Boon says that sheer bad luck also played a part in the conflict. The *Wet modernisering universitaire bestuursorganisatie* (University Government (Modernisation) Act (MUB)) had just taken effect. This Act introduced vertical relationships to the university: the professor was accountable to the dean, the dean was accountable to the Executive Board and the Executive Board was accountable to the Supervisory Board.[21] Boon says that it was Karl Dittrich, then President, who told him that the Executive Board had acted resolutely in order to make a good impression on the Supervisory Board.

Thus came an end to Boon's short-lived deanship of a 'pseudo-faculty'. The Faculty of Psychology was formally opened in September 1997, in a move made possible by the MUB, which granted greater independence to the universities vis-à-vis the government. Boon retained his professorship of History and Theory of Psychology at the faculty. He took a sabbatical in São Paulo in

Brazil, where he helped introduce problem-based learning at the *Escola Paulista de Medicina*, and thus remained a potential disruptive factor in the path of the new dean, Gerjo Kok. Kok was professor of Health Education at the Faculty of Health Sciences and transferred to Psychology. Founding fathers Jolles and Schmidt also stepped down in due course, with Jolles departing for VU Amsterdam and Schmidt going to Erasmus University Rotterdam. In Rotterdam, Schmidt started a degree programme in Psychology based on 'the Maastricht model', i.e. with a problem-based curriculum for which Schmidt himself had provided the theoretical foundation. In 2009, he was appointed Rector at Rotterdam.

UNIVERSITY COLLEGE MAASTRICHT In late 1999, Boon was suddenly asked by Dittrich if he saw any merit in developing a broad-based, English-language bachelor's degree programme akin to the liberal learning tradition found in the English-speaking world. Dittrich pointed to the successful initiative in Utrecht, where professor of Sociology Hans Adriaansens had founded University College Utrecht with a Liberal Arts and Sciences degree programme. Could Maastricht University, with its internationalisation ambitions, learn something from this example? And would Boon be willing to go to Utrecht to make inquiries? The idea of an English-language college tied in with recent developments in higher education. Indeed, the Bologna Declaration, which had taken effect in June 1999, was an agreement between 29 European countries to create an open European higher education system within 10 years, with the introduction of a Bachelor's/Master's system allowing for comparable degrees and accredited diplomas. The idea was that the unstoppable forces of globalisation would make different demands of graduates in the 21st century: broad employability, greater flexibility and mobility as well as a willingness to adopt lifelong learning. Consequently, according to the Minister of Education, Culture and Science Loek Hermans of the VVD (Liberal) party, higher education needed to become flexible with as few restrictive rules as possible. Though Boon had been damaged in the conflict at Psychology, Dittrich saw in him a person who approached a new project with a 'pioneer's mentality'.[22] He knew how to surround himself with the right people and would 'break down barriers' to achieve his goal.

Boon 'thoroughly enjoyed' University College Utrecht. Adriaansens had set it up entirely according to the American model: a selected group of national and international students on campus took an intensive, broad-based bachelor's programme in Liberal Arts and Sciences. Though Boon also advocated a college along these lines, he did not think much of the residential character: university students were 'not supposed to be in boarding school', but living among 'everyday people and other students'. Nevertheless, the students were certainly enthusiastic about the small-scale, intensive education offered in combination with the responsibility they had for choosing their own path in the curriculum. When working on the social sciences expansion plans, Korsten and Boon had entertained the idea of establishing a more flexible school instead of a faculty, with the school attracting lecturers from various faculties; the plan received no support at the time, however.

Dittrich was not the only Executive Board member who was positive about University College Maastricht; the enthusiasm was shared by Rector Arie Nieuwenhuijzen Kruseman, who believed that the university should focus more on students' academic development.[23] Whereas Boon in 1990 initially got involved with the plans to expand social sciences at his own initiative, he now had the support of the Executive Board as soon as he set to work. In the spring of 2000, Dittrich asked him if he would be willing 'to lead the efforts' to establish a university college. To Boon's surprise, Nieuwenhuijzen Kruseman introduced a second 'leader' to the project: Louk de la Rive Box, director of the European Centre for Development Policies in Maastricht. Boon was also able to enlist Korsten's participation, albeit his half-committed participation this time, since Korsten wished to focus on research during a sabbatical. Korsten had been director at Psychology, and was later made student adviser at his own request. It was not long before friction developed between De la Rive Box and Boon. Boon informed the Executive Board that he was willing to back down, but after approximately nine months it was De la Rive Box who departed to take up a professorship at Arts and Culture. With new energy, Boon again focused on the plans for a university college. He had the backing of the Executive Board, but for a University College Maastricht to succeed it was of course vital to have sufficient support among the institution's academic community.

In the course of 2001 and 2002, discussion meetings were organised to find this support and discuss course proposals, which were put forward by lecturers from all faculties. While a number of lecturers from the Faculty of Arts and Culture wished to participate, there was also opposition from this faculty. Paul Tummers, dean since October 2000, was particularly critical. He feared competition: the Arts and Culture programme was already involved in the Liberal Arts tradition as well. Moreover, the faculty offered an English-taught Arts and Culture track and was developing a new European Studies degree programme. Indeed, the idea of a Liberal Arts and Sciences programme designed to produce critical intellectuals by offering them a broad academic and cultural education was nothing new. But the college aimed to inject new life into this old ideal. To avoid encroaching in Tummers's territory, Boon realised that the college would need 'its own identity', and a scope that extended beyond the social sciences and humanities and also encompassed the natural and life sciences.

Boon and Korsten eventually developed a bachelor's programme that offered a broad range of 'disciplinary courses'. The entire English-language curriculum was ready in the autumn of 2001. The college offered three 'concentrations': Social Sciences, Humanities and (Life) Sciences. On commencing the second year, students had to definitively choose one concentration. Within a concentration, students furthermore had the choice to specialise in a discipline or theme or to choose a combination of disciplines and themes. The college therefore offered something new: a 'demand-based' rather than a 'supply-based curriculum'. By being able to largely compile their own curricula independently, students could focus on their preferences and develop their talents to their full potential. University College Maastricht promoted its small-scale, problem-based learning (within groups of no more than 12 students), but also experimented with learning communities and project-based education, in which students applied academic skills. The college was an Honours programme that targeted particularly motivated students who were willing to work 40 hours a week. Initially, students were not selected but were advised on whether or not to participate following an introduction – which advice was almost always followed. Student intake started at 100, later grew to 150 and was eventually limited to 200 students. Boon hoped that a kind of 'intellectual community' would develop between students and lecturers, characterised by ongoing discussions about their discipline and about novels and films. He had insisted that University College Maastricht operate as an independent unit under the responsibility of the Executive Board. The college was to transcend all the faculties, as it were. Incorporation into any faculty would be fundamentally wrong. In early 2002, the Executive Board consented to the establishment of the college, following the approval of the University Council. Boon became its first dean.

Looking back at that period, Boon says that it was mainly the Ministry of Education and Science that kept up the momentum. Boon recalls that the Ministry was truly wildly enthusiastic about the phenomenon of a university college. Anything that might work to reverse the compartmentalisation in education, as it was referred to in The Hague, could count on the Ministry's support. According to Boon, the Ministry actually approved the launch of University College Maastricht in September 2002 without first having received a detailed plan, and even without having seen an application. 'It really was like cycling downhill with the wind in your back; it couldn't have gone better', Boon remembers. After around a year, University College Maastricht received a hefty investment from the Ministry, aimed at stimulating the experiment.

From the outset, the college attracted large numbers of students, with relatively many coming from abroad. The programme received high marks from the students, and the small building on Bouillonstraat 8 was soon exchanged for the specially renovated Nieuwenhof monastery. The success of the Maastricht College would not remain a one-off: other universities soon followed suit. The idea of selection did not deter students. By the early 21st century, there was no longer a taboo at universities against 'distinction and excellence'. In fact, students were prepared to sacrifice much – also in financial terms – to attend a university college. The prestigious character, the small-scale structure, the rich learning environment, the open curriculum, the individual supervision and the international orientation had considerable appeal.

A NEW 'ROGUES FACULTY' AND A SECOND UNIVERSITY COLLEGE As dean of University College Maastricht, Boon was disappointed to be excluded from the Board of Deans, with the argument that he was not a dean of a faculty but of an Institute for Education. On further examination, incorporation of the college into a faculty seemed to Boon to offer advantages, such as more opportunities to claim research time. During a discussion on the future of the General Faculty – apparently the name Faculty of General Sciences merely elicited laughter abroad – he proposed that the Executive Board establish a new faculty as the successor of the Faculty of General Sciences: the Faculty of Humanities and Sciences. This new faculty would then be able to accommodate all kinds of independent institutes and degree programmes, while probably also serving as a suitable base for new expansion initiatives. Boon envisioned a kind of 'rogues faculty' that would 'attract every kind of misfit'. In 2005, he became founding dean of the Faculty of Humanities and Sciences. This faculty not only accommodated University College Maastricht, but also Knowledge Engineering, the School of Governance (an institute established in 2004 to promote good governance around the world) and the International Centre for Integrative Assessment & Sustainable Development. By that time, Boon had acquired a reputation as an initiator of new degree programmes. The university derived considerable prestige from its University College Maastricht. To Boon's 'surprise and reasonable bewilderment', the Executive Board asked him in the spring of 2008 to examine whether the university ought to expand into the natural sciences. Jo Ritzen, President of the Executive Board since February 2003, was particularly optimistic. He wanted to reinforce ties with companies such as DSM, Philips and Sabic: a strong Limburg economic infrastructure was in need of more specifically trained 'knowledge workers'. Boon saw it as a challenge. Since its establishment, the university had always desired a Sciences degree programme, but no avail: the other universities had always opposed any such overtures. Boon was instructed to expand Maastricht University with a range of natural sciences; the idea was to first introduce a bachelor's and later a master's programme. It was clear that the existing system of universities offered no room for another classic degree programme in the Natural Sciences. The university therefore had to come up with 'something new' by linking up with the region's existing research infrastructure. DSM was an obvious choice.[24]

Together with Johan Dijkema, a man with a broad perspective and an eloquent style, Boon immediately thought of the successful formula of the American College model, which would allow the university to stand out from the rest. Nowhere else was there a Science College where students could chart their own, individual learning pathways through a wide range of Natural Sciences courses. The focus of the college would, however, lie on areas such as biology and chemistry. According to Boon, it was 'time to market a personalised bachelor's programme in the Natural Sciences'. He says that the idea of a Science College immediately aroused enthusiasm among lecturers who were involved with the Natural Sciences at his faculty and at University College Maastricht. Support also came from the Faculty of Medicine, and staff from the universities in Aachen and Hasselt also indicated their willingness to participate. Boon followed the same procedure as for the establishment of the first college. It was now also easier to get the ball rolling internally, because the new college involved fewer diverse degree programmes. The programme for the new college was soon ready for implementation. The Science College followed the same pattern as the first college. 'Fully in the Liberal Arts and Sciences tradition', it had an open curriculum. Each semester, the students were free to choose the courses and skills training that appealed to them. The offering was broad and included biology, chemistry, mathematics, physics, neurosciences and a subject titled 'entrepreneurship'.

The plan was sent to the Minister of Education and Science in the autumn of 2009. It failed however 'at the first hurdle': the Higher Education Efficiency Committee (CDHO) – the ACO no longer existed – considered 'the specifics of the plan to be completely worthless'. Boon suspected a political move aimed at denying Maastricht this degree programme in the Natural Sciences; other universities also had plans to establish Science Colleges. At the same time, however, it emerged that Maastricht University in fact already had permission to establish such a college because University College Maastricht had been entered in the CROHO register under the code of a Liberal Arts *and Sciences* degree programme.[25] The situation was therefore uncertain. It was decided to make full use of the opportunities provided by this code, as it allowed Maastricht University maximum flexibility. According to Boon, that was 'pushing the edge of the envelope' – it 'really was seeking out the limits of what was legally possible'. His successor at Maastricht University College, Harm Hospers, who had been responsible for education at the Faculty of Psychology, considered it a risky move: he preferred to see the two colleges remain independent of one another. Eindhoven University of Technology expressed indignation: Maastricht University had violated existing agreements! Boon went on the offensive. Using coarse and insulting language, he berated the quality of education at Eindhoven – everyone involved had to be calmed down – and pointed out that at least half of the students enrolling in the Science College would come from abroad.[26] By the time that Maastricht Science College opened its doors to 100 students in September 2011, Boon had already departed. Thomas Cleij, professor of Chemistry at Hasselt University, was appointed the college's first dean. In an acknowledgement of the sensitivities of other universities, the college was subsequently renamed the Maastricht Science Programme.

A THIRD UNIVERSITY COLLEGE AT CAMPUS VENLO In 2010, Boon stepped down as dean of the Faculty of Humanities and Sciences, handing over responsibility to Hospers. Boon had already indicated that he would stand down in 2010 and go on a sabbatical. Furthermore, there had been a number of conflicts at the faculty, involving the School of Governance, Knowledge Engineering and 'problem professor' Jaap van den Herik, among others. Boon went on a two-year sabbatical at Columbia University's Teachers College in New York, where he focused on education reform and the emergence of agriculture. Shortly after his return in the autumn of 2012, Boon was approached by Nick Bos and Executive Board President Martin Paul to investigate the suitability of an expansion of Campus Venlo. Up until that point, Campus Venlo had housed just two small master's programmes. The Board wanted to see the development of more programmes and more research. Again, Boon was surprised that he was being approached, but thought it an interesting plan owing to the areas of overlap with the theme of 'health'. Though he was now 64 years of age, he wanted to continue working, particularly in the area of teaching. The Executive Board saw opportunities to work with the province and business sector to 'push up' Venlo. A bachelor's programme seemed the obvious way to go, but it did not seem likely that such a programme would get CDHO approval. Both Wageningen and Nijmegen were sure to oppose any plans. Boon's idea was to establish a branch of University College Maastricht in Venlo, and thus use the University College's CROHO code for a third time. Even with this trick up Maastricht's sleeve, it was not certain that the CDHO would give its blessing. Nevertheless, there was an opportunity to get a university college launched in Venlo.

The idea of a University College Venlo was part of an ambitious initiative that had existed for some time: based on 'the power of mutual knowledge development', Maastricht University, together with other knowledge institutions, the government and the business community, sought to strengthen the Limburg economy and, more importantly, the province's 'entire social structure'.[27] A mutual commitment on the parts of the university and the province had always featured strongly in Limburg. The university's establishment and expansions were largely responses to the need for economic restructuring following the mine closures. It was part of this university's DNA. Since the late 1980s, expectations of universities, including Maastricht University, had increased: 'knowledge transfer for the benefit of society' had become a statutory duty. In addition to education and research, the university was expected to produce practical, useful knowledge that could be applied to improve the region's economic infrastructure and business climate. Ritzen saw potential partners in companies such as DSM and Sabic. If Maastricht University wanted to promote itself as a regional and international knowledge centre, it would have to cooperate with the business community. That was good for 'work placements, jobs, research and innovation'.

Boon retired on 1 November 2013 and re-entered full-time employment on 2 November to work on the continued expansion of Campus Venlo, of which University College Venlo was a key component. In a welcome development, the Province of Limburg was willing to co-finance the college as part of a stimulation policy for the northern part of the province. Funding for the college therefore seemed guaranteed. Boon also did not need to 'start from scratch' in Venlo, since the Faculty of Health, Medicine and Life Sciences and the School of Business and Economics already offered two master's programmes there: Health Food Innovation Management and Global Supply Chain Management.[28] Venlo was referred to as a logistics hotspot and was known for both its domestic and international operations in the area of 'food, fresh and flowers'.[29] As was the case with his previous projects, Boon worked in consultation with lecturers – this time with lecturers from the Faculty of Health, Medicine and Life Sciences and the School of Business and Economics – on developing a new bachelor's programme. It was of course the intention from the start for the study programme to key in to Venlo's economic activities. Consequently, University College Venlo offers a broad range of courses in two major domains: 'food-nutrition-health' and 'logistics and services'. The theme of nutrition ties in completely with Boon's penchant for seeking out interesting subjects – the theme of 'taste' for example – in the interface of the social sciences and natural sciences. As it happens, he has less affinity with 'logistics', and is less enthusiastic about networking with the business community. Based on University College Maastricht, University College Venlo is referred to as a Liberal Arts and Sciences programme owing to its open curriculum. It is a miracle that the college in Venlo was approved at all. The Higher Education Advisory Board had issued a negative advice to Minister Jet Bussemaker, but she allowed the statutory term to lapse, resulting in the branch being automatically approved.

University College Venlo has a strong practical focus, with a curriculum that devotes considerable attention to 'the transition from knowledge to application and from research to valorisation and entrepreneurship'.[30] The degree programme started with 20 students in 2014. Boon hopes that 40 first-year students will start in 2016. An annual inflow of 150 was the initial expectation, but that ambition has been adjusted significantly.[31] According to Boon, Campus Venlo needs time to develop. Resources also need to be allocated so that it can conduct its own research, which it needs to be able to attract good lecturers and foster an academic climate. At the time of writing

– the spring of 2016 – Boon is increasingly counting down the days, also in view of his age. The end is relatively close now, he says. By his own admission, he did probably take on more projects than he should have. His ambition now is to lay a solid foundation in Venlo for his successor.

He dares not make any predictions about the future of Maastricht University. In any event, its development is largely a contingent process. It is the task of the next generation to take advantage of new opportunities that spring up as the university continues to 'grow and blossom', and to respond nimbly to new developments in the world. Through to the end of 2016, he will remain dean at Campus Venlo for three days a week and will continue teaching two days a week at University College Maastricht. He also intends to keep on teaching for a year or two after January 2017, before 'passing into oblivion'. Boon finds 'comfort in the idea that Maastricht University' will survive him.

NOTES

Introduction

1. Dittrich, *Van ivoren toren naar glazen huis*, 153
2. For the sake of legibility, in this introduction the name 'State University of Limburg' will be replaced by 'Maastricht University', as the university started calling itself in 1996. Since 2008, the university has primarily been referred to by its English name even in a Dutch context.
3. Between 1954 and 1971, the number of students quadrupled. In 1970, there were more than 103,000. By late 2015, the Association of Universities in the Netherlands (VSNU) put the total at nearly 260,000 enrolled students.
4. Rupp, *Van oude en nieuwe universiteiten*, 1. Oddly enough, the State University of Limburg/Maastricht University is not discussed anywhere in this book.
5. Rüegg (ed.), *A History of the University in Europe*, vol. IV, 575 ff. This book gives very short shrift to the period after 1945, and it barely discusses Maastricht University at all. The author calls for the establishment of an international study group of university historians who, taking an international comparative approach, will focus on the fate of the universities that were established in Europe after around 1970, often legitimised under the banner of 'educational reform'. The core question here should be: what became of the planned reforms? Are there also universities that foundered? How did the universities manage to position themselves in a national and international context?
6. See Dorsman, L.J. and Knegtmans, P.J., *Het universitaire bedrijf. Over professionalisering van onderzoek, bestuur en beheer*. Hilversum, 2010.
7. Griffioen and Van Winden, 'Decademia. Studeren aan de Potemkinuniversiteit', 21. Compared to other countries, the Netherlands is falling behind where the required volume of investments in education and research is concerned. *Differentiëren in drievoud omwille van kwaliteit en verscheidenheid in het hoger onderwijs*, 93.
8. *NRC Handelsblad* newspaper, 16 May 1994.
9. See Collini, S., *What are Universities For?* London, 2012. See also: Dijstelbloem, H., Huisman, F., Miedema, F. and Mijnhardt, W., 'Wetenschap in transitie. Zeven zorgen voor de universiteit', in: Verbrugge, A. and Baardewijk, J. van (eds.), *Waartoe is de universiteit op aarde? Wat is er mis en hoe kan het beter?* (Amsterdam, 2014), 111-124.

10 One notable constant amid these high expectations is the fact that the rate per funded student made available by the Ministry of Education, Culture and Science for Dutch university education has been falling for years. In 2017, too, the amount per student in the Ministry's budget will fall to €3,587, compared with €3,707 in 2016. *Nieuwsbrief VSNU, 17 October 2016*. Incidentally, the amount for research funding will also decrease in the 2017 budget.

11 Dittrich, *Van ivoren toren naar glazen huis*, 159-160. At an anniversary conference organised by the University of Groningen, Ernst Heinrich Kossmann made the following statement, putting things into perspective in the way that is so typical of him: 'The university betrays its past and jeopardises its future if it aspires to be there only or primarily for the exceptionally gifted. If the university – like any other educational institution, in fact, more so than any other – has a duty to maintain cultural continuity, it must make those of moderate ability a key priority.' (*Observant*, 31 August 1989). See also: Dijstelbloem, Huisman, Miedema and Mijnhardt, *Wetenschap in transitie. Zeven zorgen voor de universiteit*, 11-124. And see: http://www.vsnu.nl/files/documenten/Domeinen/Strategie-PA/Toekomststrategie/Vizier%20vooruit.pdf

12 '*Differentiëren in drievoud omwille van kwaliteit en verscheidenheid in het hoger onderwijs.*' 37 ff.

13 A number of publications that directly relate to the history of Maastricht University are: Caljé, P., 'Maastricht en zijn universiteit. Interacties tussen universiteit, stad en regio', in: Royen, E. van (ed.), *Maastricht kennisstad. 850 Jaar onderwijs en wetenschap*. Nijmegen, 2011. Herraets, J. (ed.), MCMLXXVI-MMI *Universiteit Maastricht: 25 jaar jong in 2001*. Maastricht, 2001. Klijn, A. *Onze man uit Maastricht. Sjeng Tans 1912-1993*. Nijmegen, 2001. Knegtmans, P.J., *De medische faculteit Maastricht: een nieuwe universiteit in een herstructureringsgebied, 1969-1984*. Assen, 1992.

14 See Dorsman, L.J. and Knegtmans, P.J., *De menselijke maat in de wetenschap. De geleerden(auto)biografie als bron voor de wetenschaps- en universiteitsgeschiedenis*. Hilversum, 2012.

15 See the chapter on Louis Boon.

16 Frijhoff, *Keuzepatronen van de universiteit in historisch perspectief. Herziene en gedeeltelijk herschreven versie van een lezing, gehouden te Maastricht op 12 februari 1987 ter gelegenheid van het tweede lustrum van de Rijksuniversiteit Limburg*, 26. See also: *Differentiëren in drievoud omwille van kwaliteit en verscheidenheid in het hoger onderwijs*.

17 The task of writing a comprehensive historical overview may end up falling on the shoulders of those who are given the opportunity to delve into the university's history and do extensive archival research as part of Maastricht University's 50-year anniversary. After all, it is the fate of university historians that universities tend not to be interested in their history in an ongoing, structural way, but only on those occasions that anniversaries are celebrated. Incidentally, it would be unwise to put off the start of this kind of research for too long. It may also be a good idea to follow the example of other universities and make certain parts of this university history available online while the project is under way in order to promote historical awareness.

18 See Drenthe-Schonk, A. et al., *Vrouwen in onderwijs en onderzoek aan de Rijksuniversiteit Limburg. Een rapport van de emancipatiecommissie januari 1995*', Maastricht 1995. See also: Smelik, A.M. and Bosch, C.W. *Beelden van vrouwen, mannen en wetenschap: een onderzoek naar beeldvorming en sekse aan de Universiteit Maastricht*. Maastricht, 1998. Perhaps Maastricht University continued to be male-dominated for a long time *because* it was a young university. The shared experiences of the first generation of men who were in charge here reinforced their sense of being part of an old boys' network. Women simply were not on their radar. One of the interviewees, for example, recounted that 'it

simply didn't occur to [him] to look for women' when hiring academic staff. Over the past few years, Maastricht University has tried to catch up where this is concerned: a sign of its maturity.
19 See the photo taken by Harry Heuts of the procession during the opening of the academic year in September 2016 on the flyleaf of this book. The number of female professors has visibly risen compared to the cover image, which is from 2008.
20 See the chapters on Wynand Wijnen, Coen Hemker, Wiel Kusters, Hans Peters and Louis Boon. The chapter on Hans Peters briefly discusses the fate of Educational Sciences, a degree programme which only ran for a year and was cancelled due to a lack of interest from students.
21 Van Berkel, *Academisch leven*, 52.
22 See *Differentiëren in drievoud omwille van kwaliteit en verscheidenheid in het hoger onderwijs*. The Hague, 2010 and *Vizier vooruit. 4 Toekomstscenario's voor Nederlandse universiteiten*. VSNU, 2016.
23 Recent figures on the cohorts of students from 2007 to 2010 reveal that the percentages of both Dutch students and international students who successfully obtained their bachelor's degree at Maastricht University within the allotted study time or in the subsequent year are the highest and the second highest respectively of all Dutch universities. See Claassens, *Studiesucces Nederlandse versus internationale studenten. Notitie ten behoeve van de VSNU Stuurgoep Internationaal*, 30 September 2016.
24 See publications by university historians such as Klaas van Berkel on the University of Groningen, Jan Brabers on Radboud University Nijmegen, Leen Dorsman on Utrecht University, Ab Flipse on VU Amsterdam, Péjé Knegtmans on the University of Amsterdam and Willem Otterspeer on Leiden University. See also the following important article: Frijhoff, W., 'Honderd jaar universiteitsgeschiedenis in Nederland', *Studium*, 6 (2013) 3-4, 197–206.

25 Incidentally, this book is not the fruit of contract research in the strict sense, as the author took the initiative of writing it herself. She did, however, seize the opportunity of the university's anniversary to get it published. See also: Hansen, E., 'The Uses and Abuses of Contemporary University History in Denmark': in: Eckhardt Larsen, J. (ed.), *Knowledge, Politics and the History of Education* (Münster, 2012) 137-150.
26 Oral history emerged in the 1970s as part of the sociocritical and emancipatory motivation to give a voice to those people who were at risk of disappearing in the maelstrom of history. The method was a manifestation of the need for 'history from below'. One of the pioneers of oral history was Paul Thompson, who in 1978 published *The Voice of the Past* (Oxford, 1978). This book became a classic and was reprinted multiple times. The many publications about this method have come to fill entire libraries. In the Netherlands, Selma Leydesdorff in particular did ground-breaking work with her studies on, among other things, the country's Jewish past and Jews who had survived the Holocaust. See also: Leydesdorff, S., *De mensen en de woorden*. Amsterdam, 2004. Other important works on this subject are: Kurkowska-Budzan, M. and Zamorski, K., *Oral History. The Challenges of Dialogue*. Amsterdam-Philadelphia, 2009. Perks, R and Thompson, A. (eds.), *The Oral History Reader*. New York, 2000. Ricoeur, P., *Memory, History, Forgetting*. Chicago-London, 2004. Samual, R. and P. Thompson (eds.), *The Myths We Live By*. London, 1990. Tumblety, J. (ed.), *Memory and History*. London-New York, 2013. Nowadays, the method has become widespread in the academic world and appears to be on the rise, as there is growing appreciation for the role of the individual, and for individual stories and individual memories in the larger historical picture. See also the theme issue 'De herinnering aan het woord', *Ex Tempore*, 31 (2012) issue 3.
27 Brodsky, *Loflied op Clio*, 16.

28 Nijhof, *Levensverhalen*, 22.
29 Samual and Thompson phrase this as follows: 'Any life story, written or oral, more or less dramatically, is in one sense a personal mythology, a self-justification'. Samual and Thompson (eds.), *The Myths We Live By*, 10.
30 Draaisma, *De heimweefabriek*, 78 ff.

1 Wynand Wijnen

1 In 1972 the *numerus fixus* was introduced, an enrolment restriction. Admission of first-year students was linked to a maximum number set in advance, with a lottery system determining who would be admitted to the Medical degree programme. Later a system of weighted draws was introduced.
2 Between 1954 and 1971 the number of students quadrupled; by 1970 there were over 103,000 students. Knegtmans, *De Medische Faculteit Maastricht*, 8. This rise in numbers was due to the post-war baby boom, the general increase in prosperity and the expansion of the student grant system.
3 Klijn, *Verlangen naar verbetering. 375 jaar academische geneeskunde in Utrecht*, 229 ff.
4 Griffioen, *Gezonderwijs in Nederland en Vlaanderen*, 1 ff.
5 Klijn, *Verlangen naar verbetering. 375 jaar academische geneeskunde in Utrecht*, 236 ff.
6 Maastricht had faced strong competition from Twente and Eindhoven in particular.
7 Knegtmans, *De Medische Faculteit Maastricht*, 2.
8 Schmidt, *De tovenaar van Bunde*, 5.
9 Ibid. See also: Van der Vleuten and Van Berkel, *Wynand Wijnen (1934-2012) – een man van betekenis*. In memoriam, 5. Wijnen's PhD supervisor Wim Hofstee saw little merit in this relative assessment and feared that the method would lead to lowering the norm, because students would work less hard as a group in order to keep the average mark low.
10 Klijn, *Onze man uit Maastricht. Sjeng Tans*, 256 ff.
11 Knegtmans, *De Medische Faculteit Maastricht*, 76.
12 Conversation with H. Snellen-Balendong on 7 August 2014.
13 See the chapter on Henk Schmidt. Conversation with H. Schmidt on 14 October 2015.
14 Wijnen, 'Fundamentele beschouwingen over onderwijsvernieuwing', in: Herpen, K. van et al. *Onderwijsvernieuwing*. Tilburg, April 2012.
15 Schmidt, *De tovenaar van Bunde*, 7.
16 Conversation with H. Snellen-Balendong on 7 August 2014.
17 Ibid.
18 Ibid.
19 Quoted in: Herraets, *Het onverstoorbare gelijk van Wynand Wijnen*, 14.
20 Conversation with H. Schmidt on 14 October 2015.
21 Ibid.
22 *Sociale gezondheidkunde. Plan voor de ontwikkeling van onderwijs en onderzoek aan de algemene faculteit*, 14.
23 The Van Agt cabinet (a CDA and VVD coalition) was in office from 1977 to 1981.
24 See the chapter on Hans Philipsen for the further developments.
25 *Observant*, 30 January 1981.
26 Wijnen was present at the meeting in Kingston where the organisation was founded and recalled that 'after some bickering, because the American sphere of influence could not have the secretariat, nor could the Russian one' the decision was made to base the secretariat in 'politically neutral' Maastricht.
27 *Observant*, 17 July 1981.
28 *Observant*, 22 January 1982.
29 From the mid-1970s, the terms 'problem-oriented learning' and 'problem-based learning' were often used to refer to the same thing, but in the early 1980s 'problem-based learning' became dominant. See the chapter on Henk Schmidt for more information about the differences between problem-oriented and problem-based learning.

2 Wim Brouwer

1. Unless otherwise stated, the quotes are derived from an interview with W. Brouwer on 10 June 2014.
2. See Aulbers B.J.M. and G.J. Bremer, *De huisarts van toen: een historische benadering*, Rotterdam, 1995.
3. Klijn, *Verlangen naar verbetering. 375 Jaar academische geneeskunde in Utrecht*, 257-258.
4. Only one in five graduate doctors in the Netherlands chose to set up as a GP.
5. In 1988 the training programme lasted two years, as of 1994 it lasts three years.
6. 'Basisfilosofie van de Medische Faculteit Maastricht. Consequenties voor opleiding en praktijk', *Medisch Contact*, (1974) 29, 227.
7. Brouwer, *Medische Faculteit Maastricht en huisartsgeneeskunde*, 230-231.
8. Ibid.
9. Interview with G. Blijham, 15 November 2014 and 7 February 2015.
10. Interview with L. Lodewick, 6 April 2014.
11. Brouwer and Romme, *Faculteit en eerste lijn*, 122.
12. Interview with E. Steur, 8 January 2014. Interview with L. Lodewick, 6 May 2014.
13. Tiddens, *Toespraken gehouden bij gelegenheid van de eerste dies natalis,* 3, 5, 7. Tiddens: 'In doing so, we need to free ourselves of the idea that primary health care is just a copy of hospital health care. An indistinct copy of limited significance. An increase in referrals, an increase in hospital admissions, an increase in the number of specialist operations is caused by insufficient use being made of the possibilities that good general medical practice can offer'.
14. Bouhuijs, *De ontwikkeling van het Praktisch Medisch Onderwijs in de huisartspraktijk*, 20. See also: Bouhuijs, Brouwer and Mol, *Praktisch medisch onderwijs in de huisartspraktijk*, 10.
15. Knegtmans, *De Medische Faculteit Maastricht*, 130.
16. Brouwer and Romme, *Faculteit en eerste lijn*, 123.
17. Interview with H. Crebolder, 27 March 2014 and 1 April 2014.
18. Brouwer and Romme, *Faculteit en eerste lijn*, 1-3.
19. Knegtmans, *De Medische Faculteit Maastricht*, 176.
20. Undated cutting from *Observant*. Personal archive of C. Hemker.
21. Metsemakers was among the first generation of Medical students in 1974 and would later become professor of General Medical Practice.
22. *Observant*, 31 March 1983.
23. Interview with H. Crebolder, 27 March 2014.
24. Brouwer, *Vallen en opstaan*, 14.

3 Marius Romme

1. Unless stated otherwise, the quotations are derived from interviews with M. Romme that took place on 1 November, 12 November, 4 December and 17 December 2013.
2. Knegtmans, *De Medische Faculteit Maastricht*, 77.
3. Klijn, *Vijverdal Maastricht: psychiatrie en huisvesting*, 34-40.
4. Ibid., 31 and 39-40. Central government wanted to exert more influence on health care and be more actively involved in its planning, which is why a law on the construction of hospitals was being drafted. The *Wet ziekenhuisvoorzieningen* (Hospital Provision Act) came into effect in 1971.
5. Ibid., 40-41.
6. Ibid., 206-207.
7. In his journey towards becoming a neurologist, Romme owed a lot to professor of Psychiatry Piet Kuiper, who was 'an excellent teacher'. Romme describes Kuiper as an 'intelligent man', 'very informed by psychoanalysis', and 'a neurotic': 'he never rode the lift with a woman'.
8. Oosterhuis en Gijswijt-Hofstra, *Verward van geest*, I, 461.
9. Romme, *Doel en middel*, 226 ff.
10. Romme, *Regionalisatie en integratie in de geestelijke gezondheidszorg*, 50.
11. RIAGG: Regional Institution for Outpatient Mental Health Care. RIAGGs are

non-denominational and organised by region. Within these institutions, different professional groups work together – mainly psychiatrists, psychologists, social psychiatric nurses and social workers – focusing on a wide range of mental health-related issues. The establishment of the RIAGGs was completed in 1982.

12 Maastricht University Archive, Interview by J. van den Boogard with H. Tiddens, 29 January 1985.

13 The eight core staff members: Wim Brouwer (General Medical Practice), Co Greep (Surgery), Coen Hemker (Biochemistry), Harry Hulsmans (Internal Medicine), Jos Lemmens (Surgery), Marius Romme (Social Psychiatry), Harmen Tiddens (Chairman of the Faculty and professor of Paediatrics) and Roelof Willighagen (Histopathology); Wynand Wijnen became head of the Educational Development Office.

14 Knegtmans, *De Medische Faculteit Maastricht*, 80.

15 Sierksma, *Ambulant en academisch*, 90 ff.

16 Klijn, *Vijverdal Maastricht: psychiatrie en huisvesting*, 84.

17 http://www.canonsociaalwerk.eu/nl/ Retrieved 29 February 2016. The other instigators were Hans van der Wilk, former patient and former chairman of the Dutch Patients' Union (*Cliëntenbond*), and Egbert van der Poel, Director of the Pandora Foundation.

18 Oosterhuis and Gijswijt-Hofstra, *Verward van geest en ander ongerief*, II, 823-824.

19 See Romme et al., *Het psychiatrisch ziekenhuis in diskussie*, Amsterdam, 1985. The instigators were ultimately unsuccessful in their efforts; the campaign did not result in a change in policy.

20 Ibid., 825.

21 The members of this committee were Jos Diederiks, Hans Philipsen, Hein Wellens and Harry Struyker Boudier.

22 See Herraets, J. 'Proefschrift te licht bevonden', *Observant*, 22 November 1983 and Herraets, J. 'Afwijzing proefschrift wekt woede van betrokkenen', *Observant*, 8 December 1983. See also: *Universiteit Maastricht. 25 Jaar jong in 2001*, 35-36.

23 Email from M. Romme to A. Klijn, 10 February 2016.

24 *De Telegraaf* newspaper, 24 November 1983.

25 Brouwer and Romme, *Faculteit en eerste lijn*, 134.

26 Interview with J. Bremer, 2 September 2014.

27 *Universiteit Maastricht. 25 Jaar jong in 2001*, 36.

28 http://www.observantonline.nl/Home/Artikelen/articleType/ArticleView/articleId/10268/WaargebeurdObservant Retrieved 29 february 2016 This account of the story is by Hemker, who considered Romme's coup to be 'a real shame for the faculty'. Interview with C. Hemker, 16 July 2013. Incidentally, Hemker said that he had heard the story from Frans Verheij, who was then director of Vijverdal and who himself was in conflict with Romme at the time about the construction process for Vijverdal, which had got out of hand. In other words, the rumour cannot be verified but serves to exemplify the overall atmosphere in the Faculty of Medicine at the time.

29 A host of publications began to come out, written – among others – by Romme and Escher. Just a small selection: *Omgaan met stemmen horen* (1988), *Stemmen horen accepteren* (1993), *Omgaan met stemmen horen, een gids voor hulpverlening* (1999), *Kinderen die stemmen horen: over stemmen horen gesproken: wat moet je weten en wat kun je doen?* (2000), *Leven met stemmen* (2012), *Psychosis as a personal crisis: an experience-based approach* (2012). For more information, see http://www.hearing-voices.com/ Retrieved 29 February 2016.

30 Statement by M. Romme to A. Klijn, 10 February 2016.

4 Ine Kuppen

1. Unless indicated otherwise, all quotes are derived from a conversation with I. Kuppen held on 23 June 2014.
2. *Protocol promoties. Rijksuniversiteit Limburg, college van Decanen – CvD 002.76 IK.* Maastricht, 20 April 1976. Peter Cuypers, personal archive.
3. Conversation with W. Wijnen, 13 June 2012.

5 Coen Hemker

1. Unless stated otherwise, all quotes are derived from conversations with C. Hemker on 16 July 2013, 26 August 2013 and 3 September 2013.
2. Hemker, H.C., *Tekst uit te spreken door promotor bij uitreiking bul, 4-12-1981.* Personal archives of H.C. Hemker.
3. Hemker, H.C., *Het Nederlandse stollingsonderzoek. Rede ter gelegenheid van het twintig jarig bestaan van de Nederlandse Vereniging voor Haemostase en Thrombose*, 2009. Personal archives of H.C. Hemker.
4. Loeliger, *In de greep van de protrombinetijd*, 40.
5. Hemker et al., 'Nature of prothrombin biosynthesis: preprothrombinaemia in vitamin K-deficiency', *Nature*, 1963, 200, 589-590.
6. *Concept-advies over benoeming hoogleraar in de biochemie*, 5 March 1973. Personal archives of H.C. Hemker.
7. Conversation with G. Majoor, 18 August 2014.
8. Although the basic philosophy referred to 'problem-oriented learning', the term 'problem-based' took over in the 1980s. See also Chapter 1, note 29.
9. Hemker, *Critical perceptions on problem-based learning*, 270.
10. Speech by Hemker at his farewell reception, undated. Personal archives of H.C. Hemker.
11. Conversation with G. Majoor, 18 August 2014.
12. Knegtmans, *De Medische Faculteit Maastricht*, 139.
13. Hemker, *Wat heet volwaardig?*, 8.
14. Conversation with R. Reneman, 29 July 2015.
15. Most of the medical psychologists and medical sociologists who initially participated in the multidisciplinary Cardiovascular Diseases research project withdrew from the project fairly quickly. Reneman noted that the pace of research was much slower among those specialists and that 'it's true, nothing was getting published, nothing was being achieved'. Conversation with R. Reneman, 31 August 2015.
16. Gerard Majoor: 'There was, of course, money for the medical facilities and they couldn't spend that on the clinics, so those guys saw vast sums of money for the taking and, as a result, they were constantly trying to get more funding for physiology and biochemistry... and Willighagen wanted to prevent that, really; he felt that that money should be reserved for clinical work and for education, and yes, with those forces at play around him, he was no match... Willighagen was a very dear man, but he didn't have enough backbone'. Conversation with G. Majoor, 18 August 2014.
17. Conversation with E. Steur, 6 January 2014.
18. For a historical overview see: CARIM *Annual Report 2013. School for Cardiovascular Diseases.* Maastricht, sa. In 2013, there were over 250 employees working under the auspices of the CARIM organisation.
19. *Limburgsch Dagblad* newspaper, 10 September 1981. 'The Coupe Alliance, in which amateur cooks from all across the Netherlands compete for top honours, was decided in Castle Wittem yesterday: a contestant from Maastricht claimed the prize. The only male finalist among four women, Prof. M.C. Hemker – a 47-year-old biochemist from the State University of Limburg – defeated the other contestants by literally suiting the jury's taste best in the cooking challenges. Jury members Wina Born, Michiel van der Plas, Alfons Stevens, Laurent Savelkoul and chair Hans Belterman

deemed the preparation, creativity, flavour, colour and presentation of the candidate from Maastricht's dishes worthy of the crystal Coupe Alliance trophy.'
20 The Executive Board (consisting of President Rob van den Biggelaar, Rector Wijnen and third member Hulsmans) had informed the Board of Deans that they opposed Hemker's appointment as Rector on the grounds that as an 'eminent scientist', he was simply too valuable to science to distract himself with other matters. The deans, however, considered this a 'singular point of view' and maintained their support of Hemker's candidacy. Letter from the Board of Deans to the Executive Board, 7 July 1981. Personal archives of H.C. Hemker.
21 *Observant*, 22 January 1982.
22 Hemker, *Waar een W.I.L. is...*. Speech delivered by Prof. H.C. Hemker, Rector of the State University of Limburg, on the occasion of the University's seventh Foundation Day on 14 January 1983, 12.
23 Letter from H.C. Hemker to L. Vroman, 29 March 1983. Personal archives of H.C. Hemker.
24 Letter from H.C. Hemker to L. Vroman, 9 April 1984. Personal archives of H.C. Hemker.
25 Hemker, *Wat heet volwaardig?*, 7.
26 Knegtmans, *De Medische Faculteit Maastricht*, 194.
27 Hemker, *Wat heet volwaardig?*, 5 ff.
28 *Observant*, 30 August 1983.
29 Hemker, *Waar een W.I.L. is...*, 24.
30 Hemker, H.C. 'Samenwerking tussen industrie en universiteit in stroomversnelling', *LAB/ABC*, March 1985, 6-7.
31 Hemker, *Waar een W.I.L. is...*, 22.
32 Letter from H.C. Hemker to W. Brouwer, 31 May 2000. Personal archives of H.C. Hemker.
33 Hemker, *Thrombin*, 5 ff. For a historical overview see also: Hemker, H.C., 'Recollections on thrombin generation', *Journal of Thrombosis and Haemostasis*, 6 (2007), 219-226.

6 Geert Blijham

1 Unless stated otherwise, all quotes are derived from conversations with G.H. Blijham on 15 November 2014 and 7 February 2015.
2 To learn more about the progress tests, see the chapter on Wynand Wijnen.
3 Conversation with A.J. van der Linden, 14 October 2014.
4 For more on this discussion, see Knegtmans, *De Medische Faculteit Maastricht*, 64 ff.
5 See Hillen et al., *Interne Geneeskunde Maastricht*, 46 ff.
6 Conversation with A.J. van der Linden, 14 October 2014.
7 See Knegtmans, *De Medische Faculteit Maastricht*, 104 ff. and 177 ff.
8 Report of events as experienced by Ton van der Linden, 2014.
9 Ibid.
10 During discussion of the Memorandum on the Prospects for South Limburg with the cabinet on Friday 16 November 1979, Kremers laid out a number of the province's demands. VVD party member Arie Pais, Minister of Education, Culture and Science, became so annoyed that he stormed out of the Trêves Room in a rage. With Pais out of the room, Kremers managed to garner sufficient support for the construction of a new university hospital – thanks in part to chair Dries van Agt, the Prime Minister at the time, as well as fellow CDA member and personal friend of Kremers'. When Kremers thinks back on all the Ministers who made a contribution to the Province of Limburg, and by extension, to Maastricht, Van Agt is 'by far number one' on the list. The very next day, early on a Saturday morning, Kremers received a phone call from Til Gardeniers, the Minister of Health. As Kremers recalls, the Minister offered him ƒ200 million to 'do other things', assuming hospital construction did not move forward. Kremers was deeply indignant and did not respond to the suggestion. 'Til, I'm furious. I am truly furious', he said, and hung up the phone. Conversation with J. Kremers, 16 February 2014.

11 In 1978, the unemployment rate in South Limburg had reached 10%, while the national average in the Netherlands was only 5%. See Elmpt, H.J.P.G. van, *Een besef van eigen kracht. Limburgse provinciale politiek in de periode 1962-2007*, Maastricht, 2011.
12 Kremers approved a reduction in the number of beds without a struggle, as he assumed that, once the planned hospital had been built, there would be a readjustment phase anyway. As Kremers remembers it, Deetman was not out to eliminate 'the eighth faculty' in the name of budget cuts at all – something the State University was on guard against. For that reason, Kremers still 'feels quite positively towards' Deetman, with whom he never had a difference of opinion in matters of principle. Conversation with J. Kremers, 16 February 2014.
13 For more about this episode in the history of Internal Medicine, see Hillen et al., *Interne Geneeskunde Maastricht*, 54 ff.
14 His inaugural lecture was entitled *Het geheim van de ontaarde crypt* and addressed the 'search for prevention, occurrence and treatment of colon cancer'.
15 Klijn, *Verlangen naar verbetering. 375 Jaar academische geneeskunde in Utrecht*, 307.
16 In 2009, when Blijham was offered the chance to become first a member and then chair of the Supervisory Board of the Maastricht University Hospital (azM), he welcomed the opportunity.

7 Hans Philipsen

1 Unless stated otherwise, all quotes are derived from conversations with H. Philipsen on 12 July 2012, 14 June 2012, 22 June 2012, 12 July 2012, 24 August 2012, 18 September 2012 and 9 October 2012.
2 VARA: *Vereeniging Arbeiders Radio Amateurs* (Association of Worker Radio Amateurs).
3 Philipsen graduated in both Sociology and Anthropology.
4 TNO: Netherlands organisation for applied scientific research. TNO's aim is to make knowledge practicable for businesses and government bodies. It has several branches.
5 See Philipsen, H., *Toespraken gehouden bij gelegenheid van de opening van het academisch jaar 1977/1978*. Maastricht.
6 *Ontwikkelingen voor de Algemene Faculteit van de Rijksuniversiteit Limburg*. Maastricht, 1976.
7 Costs rose quickly: at the beginning of the 1960s, 4.3% of GDP went to health care. In 1973 that figure was already 7.2%, and it continued to rise to 14.3% by 2014.
8 *Ontwikkelingen voor de Algemene Faculteit van de Rijksuniversiteit Limburg*, 5 ff.
9 Key roles in this ten-man working group were played especially by Jan Kuiper, professor of Social Medicine at VU Amsterdam, Paul Thung, professor of Medicine at Leiden University and – of course – Philipsen.
10 *Sociale Gezondheidkunde. Plan voor de ontwikkeling van onderwijs en onderzoek aan de algemene faculteit. Rapport van de Werkgroep Algemene Faculteit*. Maastricht, 1978.
11 *Ontwerp voor een studie Sociale Gezondheidkunde aan de Rijksuniversiteit Limburg*, 10.
12 Drop was a contemporary of Philipsen; she passed away in 2002.
13 By the time that Social Health Science was launched in 1980, the term 'problem-oriented learning' was beginning to lose currency in favour of 'problem-based learning'.
14 Philipsen, H., Lecture on 7 January 1981. Personal archive of H. Philipsen.
15 Until 1987, enrolment restrictions applied to Social Health Science and later to Health Sciences. In 1981 the degree programme admitted 150 students and in 1985 it admitted 250, including students doing a part-time programme in Nursing Science. After 1987, the number of first-year students exceeded 500.
16 Thung and Volder, *Het eerste jaar. Rapport over de propaedeuse Sociale Gezondheidkunde 1980/1981*, 24 ff.

17 Philipsen, Sociale gezondheidkunde, 7 ff.
18 *Gezondheidswetenschappen in Maastricht*, 10-11.
19 Deetman probably wished to support his own Deetman motion. In late 1983, the State University of Limburg had a total of just under 2,000 students, while the aim was to have 6,000 by 1990. Moreover, his decision fitted in with the role allocation plans that he wanted to get on with in 1984.
20 See the article by H. Philipsen, 'Een bouwsteen voor de geschiedschrijving. Gezondheidswetenschappen, eenheid en verscheidenheid', in: *Universiteit Maastricht. 25 Jaar jong in 2011*, 75 ff.
21 See Van den Bergh-Braam, A.H.M., *Verplegingswetenschap in Nederlands perspectief. Rede uitgesproken bij de aanvaarding van het ambt van buitengewoon hoogleraar in de verplegings-wetenschap.* Leiden, 1986.
22 Pasch, T. van de, 'Als de verplegingswetenschap het niet bestudeert, doet niemand het', *Tijdschrift voor Verpleegkundigen* (2003) 9, 25.
23 Cohen was given a guarantee that he could return as a professor. On his return in 1995, he wished to be reappointed as Rector. Faced with a choice between Cohen and Philipsen, the Board of Deans chose Cohen.
24 *Observant*, 8 June 2000. See the chapter on Louis Boon for the role of Philipsen as dean *ad interim* during a conflict involving the Psychology study programme in 1997.
25 Since 2008 the university has been referred to by its English name ('Maastricht University') even in Dutch in order to emphasise its international character.
26 Philipsen, *Op zoek naar zorgland*, 50.

8 Henk Schmidt

1 Unless otherwise stated, the quotes are derived from an interview with H. Schmidt on 14 October 2015.
2 Adriaan de Groot became known for the 'empirical cycle', which consists of five stages: the observation of empirical facts; the formulation of a general hypothesis based on those observations; the formulation a specific hypothesis; the testing of that hypothesis by means of an experiment, and evaluation through falsification or verification. His work on assessing student performance is less well-known, but perhaps even more significant, and culminated in the book *Vijven en zessen: cijfers en beslissingen: het selectieproces in ons onderwijs*. Groningen, 1966.
3 See the chapters on Wynand Wijnen and Wim Brouwer.
4 http://www.kec-um.nl/erfgoed/personen
5 Bremer, J., *Handleiding voor tutoren (= begeleiders van onderwijsgroepen).* Maastricht, August 1975. J. Bremer's personal archive. Interview with J. Bremer held on 2 September 2014.
6 Schmidt, H.G. and Bouhuijs, P.A.J., *Het tutorensysteem*. Maastricht, 1977.
7 Schmidt, H.G. and Bouhuijs, P.A.J., *Onderwijs in taakgerichte groepen*. Utrecht, 1980. With thanks to Virginie Servant, who earned her PhD at Erasmus University Rotterdam in 2016 with a dissertation entitled *Revolutions and Re-iterations. An intellectual history of Problem-based Learning.*
8 Verwijnen, G.M.G., Van der Vleuten, C. & Imbos, T., 'A comparison of an innovative medical school with traditional schools: An analysis in the cognitive domain', in: Nooman, Z., Schmidt, H.G. & Ezzat, E. (eds.), *Innovation in medical education, an evaluation of its present status.* New York, 1990, 40-49.
9 Schmidt, H.G., Cohen-Schotanus, J. & Arends, L.R., 'Impact of problem-based, active learning on graduation rates for 10 generations of Dutch medical students.' *Medical Education*, 43 (2009) 3, 211-218.
10 Schmidt, H.G., 'Leren van problemen, een inleiding in probleemgestuurd, in: Vroon, A. (ed.), *Handboek voor de Onderwijspraktijk*. Deventer, 1979.

11 Schmidt, H.G., Van der Arend, A., Moust, J.H.C., Kokx, I. & Boon, L., 'Influence of Tutors' Subject-Matter Expertise on Student Effort and Achievement in Problem-Based Learning', *Academic Medicine*, 68 (1993) 10, 784–791.
12 Schmidt, H.G. & Moust, J.H.C., 'What Makes a Tutor Effective – A Structural-Equations Modeling Approach to Learning in Problem-Based Curricula', *Academic Medicine*, 70 (1995) 8, 708–714.
13 See the chapters on Wynand Wijnen and Ine Kuppen.
14 Schmidt, H.G., Neufeld, V.R., Nooman, Z.M. & Ogunbode, T., 'Network of Community-Oriented Educational-Institutions for the Health-Sciences', *Academic Medicine*, 66 (1991) 5, 259–263.
15 Norman, G.R. & Schmidt, H.G., 'The Psychological Basis of Problem-Based Learning – A Review of the Evidence', *Academic Medicine*, 67 (1992) 9, 557–565.
16 Schmidt, *Activatie van voorkennis,* 132–139.
17 Schmidt, H.G. (ed.), *Probleemgestuurd onderwijs,* 9 ff. Schmidt, *Hoe goed is ons geheugen?* 224–228.
18 Schmidt, H.G., Rotgans, J.L. & Yew, Y.E.H., 'The process of problem-based learning: what works and why', *Medical Education,* 45 (2011) 8, 792–806.
19 See the chapter on Geert Blijham. See also: Klijn, *Verlangen naar verbetering. 375 jaar academische geneeskunde in Utrecht,* 305–310.
20 See also the chapter on Louis Boon.
21 De Pinho, A.L., Mota, F.B., Velloso, M., Conde, F., Alves, L.A. & Lopes, R.M., 'Mapping Knowledge Produced on Problem-Based Learning between 1945 and 2014: A Bibliometric Analysis', *Creative Education,* 6, (2015) 576–584. Azer, S.A., 'The Top-Cited Articles in Medical Education', *Academic Medicine,* 90, (2015) 1147–1161. Schmidt, H.G., Vermeulen, L. & Van der Molen, H.T., 'Long-term effects of problem-based learning: a comparison of competencies acquired by graduates of a problem-based and a conventional medical school', *Medical Education,* 40 (2006) 6, 562–567. Schmidt, H.G., Van der Molen, H.T., Te Winkel, W.W.R. & Wijnen, H.F.W., 'Constructivist, problem-based learning does work. A meta-analysis of curricular comparisons involving a single medical school', *Educational Psychologist,* 44 (200) 4, 227–249. Schmidt, H.G., Muijtjens, A.M.M., Van der Vleuten, C.P.M., & Norman, G.R., 'Differential Student Attrition and Differential Exposure Mask Effects of Problem-Based Learning in Curriculum Comparison Studies', *Academic Medicine,* 463–475. doi: 10.1097/ACM.0b013e318249591a
22 In 1996 Schmidt received an honorary doctorate from the Université de Sherbrooke, in Quebec, Canada for his work in the field of problem-based learning and his later research into the development of medical expertise, and in 2004 he became the first winner of the Karolinska Institutet Prize for Research in Medical Education. In 2006 he received the Distinguished Career Award from the American Educational Research Association.

9 Job Cohen

1 Unless stated otherwise, all quotations are derived from an interview with J. Cohen held on 1 September 2015.
2 See Griffioen, C. et al. (eds.), *Gezonderwijs in Nederland en Vlaanderen. Veertig jaar Nederlandse Vereniging voor Medisch Onderwijs*. Houten, 2012.
3 Interview with C. Flinterman, 26 May 2015.
4 Cohen and Crombag, *De nieuwe medische faculteit in Maastricht en de juridische opleiding,* 355.
5 The question was: what was the best way to work on case studies? According to Crombag, Cohen and Joan de Wijkerslooth, those skills had to be practiced in a practical. See *Een theorie over rechterlijke beslissingen* (1977) by Crombag, De Wijkerslooth and Cohen.
6 See *Toespraken gehouden bij gelegenheid van de officiële opening van de Rijksuniversiteit Limburg, 9-1-1976*. Maastricht, 1976.

7 Interview with J. Kremers, 16 January 2014.
8 For more on the Deetman motion, see the chapter on Wynand Wijnen.
9 See *Schets van een juridische studierichting aan de Rijksuniversiteit Limburg*. Maastricht, 1979.
10 Maastricht University Archives, 07.11 cba10.0369 *Oprichting faculteiten. Oprichting Faculteit der rechtsgeleerdheid; reacties op eerste schets juridische opleidingen uit 1979* and *Eindrapport Rechten in Maastricht* by the preparatory committee for the Law degree programme (1981), folder 2.
11 Maastricht University Archives, 07.11 cba 10.0369 *Oprichting Faculteiten. Oprichting Faculteit der Rechtsgeleerdheid; reacties op eerste Schets juridische studierichting, reacties alsmede aanpassing aan bemerkingen Academische Raad. 1-1-1979 tot en met 31-12-1983.*
12 Interview with J. Balkema, 22 June 2015.
13 Interview with C. Flinterman, 30 April 2015.
14 Maastricht University Archives, 07.11 cba 10.0369 *Oprichting Faculteiten. Oprichting Faculteit der Rechtsgeleerdheid; reacties op eerste Schets juridische studierichting, reacties alsmede aanpassing aan bemerkingen Academische Raad. 1-1-1979 tot en met 31-12-1983. Rechten in Maastricht. Plan voor een juridische studierichting aan de Rijksuniversiteit Limburg te Maastricht.* Report by the preparatory committee for the Law degree programme, issued to the Faculty Board of the General Faculty.
15 Interview with K. Dittrich, 8 June 2015.
16 Alma van Bers (Interdisciplinary Study of Law), Hans Lensing (Criminal Law), Gerard Mols (Criminal Law) and Jan Willems (International Public Law).
17 Wim Beurskens (Private Law) and René de Groot (Private Law).
18 Interview with K. Dittrich, 8 June 2015.
19 Interview with R. de Groot, 23 April 2015.
20 Interview with K. Dittrich, 8 June 2015.
21 Maastricht University Archive, 5.3.02.1 fdr/0289 *Onderwijsaangelegenheden 1985 – 1991.*
22 Cohen, *Over het denken van juristen*, 10.
23 Interview with K. Dittrich, 8 June 2015.
24 Herraets, *Cohen, de eerste jurist in Maastricht*, 24-25.
25 Interview with C. Flinterman, 30 April 2015.
26 Herraets, *Cohen, de eerste jurist in Maastricht*, 25.
27 Interview with C. Flinterman, 30 April 2015.
28 Maastricht University Archives, 5.3.02.1 fdr/0289 *Onderwijsaangelegenheden 1985 – 1991.*
29 *Doorgaan, maar beter*, 2.
30 Interview with K. Dittrich, 8 June 2015.
31 Interview with R. de Groot, 23 April 2015.
32 Beurskens, W. and Verhey, N., 'Thematisch onderwijs', in: *Ervaringen met probleemgestuurd juridisch onderwijs*, 45.
33 See the chapter on Wynand Wijnen.
34 *Observant*, 2 May 1986.
35 See Beurskens, W. and Verhey, N., 'Thematisch onderwijs', in: *Ervaringen met probleemgestuurd juridisch onderwijs*, 35-58.
36 See Cohen, M.J. and Elzinga, W.E., 'Vaardigheden in het juridisch onderwijs, in: *Ervaringen met probleemgestuurd juridisch onderwijs*, 71-88.
37 Maastricht University Archives, 5.3.02.1 fdr/0289 *Onderwijsaangelegenheden 1985 – 1991. Brief van A. Claessens en H. Crombag aan het Faculteitsbestuur*, 27 February 1989.
38 Interview with C. Flinterman, 26 May 2015.

10 *Ria Wolleswinkel*

1 Unless stated otherwise, all quotes are derived from conversations with R. Wolleswinkel on 12 February 2015, 26 February 2015 and 2 April 2015.
2 Psychologist and education reformer Van Calcar advocated an education system that focused on equal opportunities for everyone. He dedicated himself to helping children from deprived backgrounds.

3   Freire published his book in Portuguese in 1970. English and Dutch translations followed one and two years later, respectively.
4   Klijn, *Vijverdal: psychiatrie en huisvesting*, 88.
5   See R. Wolleswinkel, 'Studeren in een probleemgestuurd curriculum', in *Ervaringen met probleemgestuurd onderwijs*, 21-34.
6   Moust, J.H.C., R.E. Bakker and H.J.P. Nuy, 'De rol van de docent in probleemgestuurd onderwijs', in *Ervaringen met probleemgestuurd onderwijs*, 59-70. Moust did not think a tutor necessarily had to be an expert on a particular subject.
7   See R. Wolleswinkel, 'Studeren in een probleemgestuurd curriculum', in *Ervaringen met probleemgestuurd onderwijs*, 29.
8   Ibid., 30.
9   *Observant*, 5 February 1987.
10 See https://openaccess.leidenuniv.nl/bitstream/handle/1887/14639/V+2006-5+In+memoriam+Ad+Geers.pdf;jsessionid=CC55A120FDD4A38514A83176AD45D52B?sequence=2, retrieved on 30 May 2016.
11 *Opzij* is a Dutch feminist magazine.
12 For University College Maastricht, see the chapter on Louis Boon.
13 Conversation with R. de Groot, 23 April 2015. Incidentally, this career path had already been assumed when he applied for a position at the university in 1981.
14 Wolleswinkel, *Gevangen in moederschap*, 340.
15 Kelk, C. 'Gevangen in moederschap', *Nederlands Juristenblad*, 72 (1997) 43, 1990 – 1992.
16 The European Action Research Committee on Children of Imprisoned Parents has since developed into a large non-governmental organisation. See http://childrenofprisoners.eu/.
17 In 1998, Flinterman made the move to Utrecht to become director of the Human Rights research school. This research school is supported by the following organisations: the T.M.C. Asser Institute in The Hague, Erasmus University Rotterdam, Leiden University, the University of Tilburg, Utrecht University and Maastricht University. The University of Amsterdam, the University of Louvain (KU Leuven), Utrecht University and Maastricht University participate in Ius Commune.
18 See also: the chapters on Hans Philipsen and Job Cohen.
19 See also: the chapter on Louis Boon with regard to the Bologna Declaration.
20 See https://www.eiuc.org/.
21 This book is now in its fifth edition. Schlössels was a PhD student in Maastricht and is now professor of Administrative Law in Nijmegen. Hage was senior lecturer and is now professor of General Legal Theory.
22 In the first year, groups numbered 14 members, later 19.
23 *Draaiboek Onderwijs 2015 – 2016. Faculteit der Rechtsgeleerdheid Maastricht*. The education method (still) places a strong emphasis on students' own responsibility for their learning process, self-motivation and self-direction. These guidelines were drawn up under Wolleswinkel's responsibility. It is clear 'that working in small groups of students yields better study results and returns; that working from concrete case material and a certain level of prior knowledge results in a stronger anchoring of that knowledge; that working with assignments leads to more efficient use of study time and to better study results; that the exam forms should preferably dovetail with the education method to achieve optimum results; that variation in education and exam methods prevents students from becoming demotivated; that the acquisition of study skills and professional skills is not an automatic process, but one which needs to be planned out and worked on'.

11 Joan Muysken

1   Unless otherwise stated, all quotations are derived from conversations with J. Muysken held on 23 September 2014, 29 September 2014 and 9 October 2014.

2 *Limburgs Dagblad* newspaper, 15 May 1981.
3 Statement by Tom van Veen, 18 December 2015.
3 Ibid.
4 *De Limburger* newspaper, 20 January 1983.
5 See *Economie in Maastricht. Plan voor een studierichting economie aan de Rijksuniversiteit Limburg te Maastricht.* Maastricht, 1983.
6 *Observant*, 13 January 1984.
7 *Observant*, 13 September 1984.
8 *Universiteit Maastricht 25 jaar jong*, 129.
9 Interview with J. Kremers held on 14 February 2014. According to Kremers, the distinction from the Vatican that he had brought along especially for the occasion was found to be particularly impressive.
10 Interview with H. Schreuder, 22 October 2014.
11 See Keizer, P. and Soeters, J. (eds.), *Economie, sociologie en psychologie: visies op integratie*. Assen/Maastricht, 1987.
12 Muysken and Schreuder, *Economische wetenschappen: eenheid in verscheidenheid?*, 35–36.
13 Ibid., 158.
14 Muysken, *Van Reaganomics tot de Eurocrisis*, 37–38.
15 In 1988, 20% to 30% successfully completed the first year of their degree on their first attempt. *Observant*, 22 April 1988.
16 In 2016, this figure is an impressive 4,000.
17 See the chapter on Schreuder. Hofstede later went on to hold a second partial chair at the State University of Limburg, as well as becoming professor of Comparative Culture Studies of Organisations.
18 *Observant*, 7 October 1993.
19 *Universiteit Maastricht 25 jaar jong*, 121 ff.
20 *Observant*, 22 November 2009.
21 See *3 Decades of Economic Diversity. Essays on Labour, Technology and Monetary Economics in honour of prof. dr. Joan Muysken*. Maastricht, 2013.
22 Muysken, *Van Reaganomics tot de Eurocrisis*, 6.

12 *Hein Schreuder*

1 Unless otherwise stated, all quotations are derived from conversations with H. Schreuder held on 22 October 2014 and 3 December 2014.
2 *Economics in Maastricht*, 32.
3 This report was translated into 37 languages, and more than 12 million copies were sold.
4 Schreuder is currently Chairman of the Supervisory Board of Ecorys, the legal successor to the Netherlands Economic Institute. With this, he feels things have 'come full circle'.
5 Schreuder, H., 'Onderwijsdoelstellingen: een organisatorisch-theoretisch menu', in: Keizer, P. (ed.) *Probleemgestuurd onderwijs in de economische wetenschap*, 33–51.
6 Albeda, W. and H. Schreuder, *Business School*. Maastricht, 5 September 1984. H. Schreuder's private archive.
7 The Faculty of Law would pull out in the end. See the chapter on Joan Muysken. Molle, W.T.M., *Informatie Europese Studies. Conclusies en aanbevelingen*. State University of Limburg, Faculty of Law/Faculty of Economics. Maastricht, December 1985. H. Schreuder's personal archive.
8 Confidential. Brief summary of meeting held on 27 March 1985 on the establishment of a business school as part of the curriculum of the Faculty of Economic Sciences. 1 April 1985. H. Schreuder's personal archive.
9 Combining an endowed chair with a regular post as professor is no longer possible nowadays, but still was at the time.
10 Letter from H. Schreuder to R. Verspeek. Maastricht, 22 April 2002. H. Schreuder's private archive.
11 International Management later (1993) became part of the International Business degree programme, under the impetus of John Hagedoorn. In 1993, the

General Economics Department launched the International Economic Studies specialisation, with Chris de Neubourg as the driving force, though by that time Schreuder had already left the university.
12 For more on MERIT, see the chapter on J. Muysken. Schreuder used the terms 'locals' and 'cosmopolitans' in reference to the university in his speech 'Het universiteitsleven in bedrijf', given on the occasion of the State University of Limburg's fifteen-year anniversary in 1991 and published in *Universiteit & Hogeschool*, year 38, No. 4, April 1992.
13 Muysken, J., *Hoe algemeen is de algemene economie?* Speech (condensed version, in Dutch) given upon acceptance of the professorship in General Economics at the State University of Limburg. Assen/Maastricht, 1985.
14 See the chapter on J. Muysken. Schreuder, H. *Economie (en) bedrijven. Over de bedrijfseconomie als discutabel, spannend en eigen-aardig onderdeel van de economische wetenschappen.* Assen/Maastricht, 1985. This speech can also be found in Muysken & Schreuder (1985).
15 Business economics first became part of higher education in 1909, when a professor of Business Economics and Accounting was hired at Delft University of Technology. In 1913, the Netherlands School of Commerce (the precursor of Erasmus University) was established in Rotterdam. See Schreuder, *Economie (en) bedrijven*, 4-5.
16 The book *Economic Approaches to Organizations* (London, Prentice-Hall) was also translated into Chinese, Danish, Japanese, Korean, Portuguese and Spanish.
17 *Observant*, 11 September 1986.
18 See also: *Observant*, 26 October 1989.
19 Interview with J. Kremers held on 14 February 2014.
20 After moving on to DSM, Schreuder continued to be part of the Faculty of Economics for some time as honorary professor.
21 He reflects on this period in the book *From Coal to Biotech: The Transformation of DSM with Business School Support* (2015), co-authored with Jean-Pierre Jeannet.

13 Gerard de Vries

1 Unless specified otherwise, all quotes are derived from an interview with G.H. de Vries on 19 September 2015.
2 See the chapter on Louis Boon.
3 Caljé and Wachelder, 'Cultuur- en Wetenschapsstudies in de traditie van de Europese universiteit', in: *Universiteit Maastricht 25 jaar jong in 2001*, 150.
4 People at the Faculty of Law were worried about competition from within: the Faculty of Law was already training generalists. Moreover, the degree programme turned out to be far too expensive, being based on a ratio of one lecturer to four students. The economists also opposed it, believing that the State University of Limburg would do better to focus on international management, business studies and international business studies. It was also moot whether there was actually a demand for generalists in the job market. Asked for their opinions, Tannelie Blom, Maarten Doorman and Chris den Hamer were not enthusiastic either. Personal archive of Gerard Korsten, Documents relating to *Werkgroep 6000*.
5 See the chapter on Wiel Kusters.
6 Interview with T. Blom, 2 September 2015.
7 G.H. de Vries, State University of Limburg. Faculty of General Sciences. *Delta Studies, een voorstel tot nadere uitwerking*. Draft. 23 March 1987. Personal archive of G. Korsten.
8 *Verslag eerste bijeenkomst Delta Studies, 14 August 1987.* Personal archive of G. Korsten. Luc Soete was busy setting up the research institute MERIT: Maastricht Economic Research Institute on Innovation and Technology.
9 Interview with K. Dittrich, 12 October 2015.

10 Korsten, G., *Naar een strategie voor de verdere uitbouw van de RL*, eerste interimrapport *Werkgroep 6000*. Maastricht, October 1986. Personal archive of G. Korsten. *Observant*, 27 November 1986.
11 Interview with L. Vredevoogd, 19 September 2015.
12 *Verslag bilateraal overleg College van Bestuur Board en faculteit der Gezondheidswetenschappen over de nota 'Profilering en uitbouw van de RL, on 21 October 1987'*. Personal archive of G. Korsten.
13 *Verslag bilateraal overleg College van Bestuur Board en faculteit der Gezondheidswetenschappen over de nota 'Profilering en uitbouw van de RL, on 21 October 1987'*. Personal archive of G. Korsten.
14 Caljé and Wachelder, 'Cultuur- en Wetenschapsstudies in de traditie van de Europese universiteit', in: *Universiteit Maastricht 25 jaar jong in 2001*, 159.
15 Letter from Gerard Korsten to Gerard de Vries, 24 February 1989. Personal archive of G. Korsten.
16 *Cultuur- en wetenschapsstudies. Rijksuniversiteit Maastricht*. Maastricht, May 1989. Personal archive of G. Korsten.
17 *Observant*, 22 March 1990.
18 See the chapter on Wiel Kusters.
19 Caljé and Wachelder, 'Cultuur- en Wetenschapsstudies in de traditie van de Europese universiteit', in: *Universiteit Maastricht 25 jaar jong in 2001*, 160.
20 Interview with Vredevoogd, 20 November 2015.
21 Letter from A.M.P. Knoer, chair of the Education Council, to J.M.M. Ritzen, Minister of Education and Science, The Hague, 29 December 1989. Personal archive of G. Korsten.
22 *Cultuur- en wetenschapsstudies. Rijksuniversiteit Maastricht*. Maastricht, April 1990. Personal archive of G. Korsten.
23 Apparently the historians had gained in influence. The first version of the report did not mention a third track 'Cultural History of the Modern Age', but instead 'Symbols in Modern Society'.
24 *Cultuur- en wetenschapsstudies. Rijksuniversiteit Maastricht*. Maastricht, April 1990. Personal archive of G. Korsten.
25 Letter from J.M.M. Ritzen to the Executive Board of the State University of Limburg, Zoetermeer, 31 May 1990. Personal archive of G. Korsten.
26 De Vries: In this method the students were, so to speak, thrown in at the deep end and learned to swim by themselves – and then would 'gradually learn the difference between breaststroke and backstroke'.
27 Oral statement by Maarten Doorman to Annemieke Klijn, 16 June 2016.
28 Schuyt, *De universiteit als verzamelplaats van creatieve scepsis*, 129.
29 Statement by K. Bijsterveld, 15 June 2016.

14 Wiel Kusters

1 Unless specified otherwise, all quotes are derived from conversations between A. Klijn and W. Kusters on 12 August 2015 and 17 August 2015.
2 Caljé and Wachelder, 'Cultuur- en Wetenschapsstudies in de traditie van de Europese universiteit', in: *Universiteit Maastricht 25 jaar jong in 2001*, 154-156.
3 Conversation with G. de Vries, 19 September 2015. Tans had obtained his PhD in *Isoglosses around the Maastricht area in the Belgian and Dutch South-Limburg dialects* (Maastricht, 1938).
4 *Observant*, 23 February 1989.
5 See the chapter on Gerard de Vries.
6 *Ik woon in duizend kamers tegelijk. Opstellen voor en over Wiel Kusters* (Nijmegen 2012), 255.
7 In the words of Wiel Kusters at a meeting in the Spiegelzaal on 30 January 1996.

15 Hans Peters

1 Unless indicated otherwise, the quotes below are derived from a conversation with H.J.M. Peters held on 5 September 2016.

2   The Faculty of General Sciences was formally established in October of 1987.
3   See the chapter on Gerard de Vries.
4   Maastricht University Archives, 5.3.02.4cba00011 *Opleidingen FdAW Kennistechnologie, transnationale experimentele studierichting, samenwerking met LUC Diepenbeek. Map 1-1-1987 – 31-3-1991. Notitie van G. Korsten, secretaris Werkgroep 6000* 'Voorbereiding en aanpak overleg met de heer Beckers op 12 augustus 1987'.
5   *Limburgsch Dagblad* newspaper, 29 June 1985.
6   Peters: 'We were incorporating practical applications in the first-year course books, but the mathematics teaching itself was very traditional: holding lectures and solving equations. Still, once the first year of Economics was on track – we had developed all the assignments – we saw the emergence of a new phenomenon: the expert. As an expert, you were expected to be waiting at your desk while the tutorial groups were underway. You could be called in to provide assistance if the tutor was having problems, which tended to happen quite often in our case. There were about ten tutorial groups during the first year. I remember we had to keep showing up to explain all our assignments to the tutor, who had a harder time grasping them than the students themselves. Some of the students were smart enough to get it, but that didn't apply to the tutors. As you can imagine, we started to get the sense problem-based learning wasn't all that suited to these types of fields'.
7   *Observant*, 9 December 1988. Van den Herik and his group relocated to a building on Bredestraat. The plans to establish RIKS date back to 1985. The official opening took place in 1989.
8   Maastricht University Archives, 5.3.02.4cba00011 *Opleidingen FdAW Kennistechnologie, transnationale experimentele studierichting, samenwerking met LUC Diepenbeek. Map 1-1-1987 – 31-3-1991. Cognitieve informatica. Een voorstel tot het inrichten van een nieuwe studierichting aan de Rijksuniversiteit Limburg. RL, Maastricht, 1985.*
9   *Limburgsch Dagblad* newspaper, 9 October 1985. Amongst other organisations, the seminar was sponsored by DSM and Open University. Feigenbaum was a member of the advisory board at the US-based Sperry Corporation, a centre for knowledge systems. Sperry helped to secure a computer system for the application of artificial intelligence on behalf of the yet-to-be-established RIKS, pressuring then Minister of Education and Science Wim Deetman to structure RIKS as a para-academic institution.
10 *De Telegraaf* newspaper, 5 November 1985. See: E.A. Feigenbaum, *Knowledge Engineering: The Applied Side of Artificial Intelligence.* Stanford University, 1980.
11 Maastricht University Archives, 5.3.02.4cba00011 *Opleidingen FdAW Kennistechnologie, transnationale experimentele studierichting, samenwerking met LUC Diepenbeek. Map 1-1-1987 – 31-3-1991. P.J. Braspenning (vakgroep informatica) en H.J.M. Peters (vakgroep wiskunde), Kennistechnologie. Voorstel voor een studierichting aan de faculteit der algemene wetenschappen. 26 april 1989.*
12 Maastricht University Archives, 5.3.02.4cba00011 *Opleidingen FdAW Kennistechnologie, transnationale experimentele studierichting, samenwerking met LUC Diepenbeek. Map 1-1-1987 – 31-3-1991. Kennistechnologie in samenwerking tussen LUC en RL, 22 mei 1990.*
13 Conversation with L. Vredevoogd, 20 November 2015.
14 The University Council had proposed various amendments in January 1991.
15 Maastricht University Archives, 5.3.02.4cba00011 *Opleidingen FdAW Kennistechnologie, transnationale experimentele studierichting, samenwerking met LUC Diepenbeek. Map 1-1-1987 – 31-3-1991. Experimentele transnationale studierichting kennistechnologie. Rijksuniversiteit Limburg, Maastricht, Nederland en Limburgs Universitair Centrum, Diepenbeek, België. Maastricht/Diepenbeek, februari 1991.*
16 Ibid.

17 Maastrcht University Archives, 5.3.02.4cba00011 *Opleidingen FdAW Kennistechnologie, transnationale experimentele studierichting, samenwerking met LUC Diepenbeek. Map 1-1-1987 – 31-3-1991. Brief van M.J. Cohen, voorzitter van het college van decanen, aan het college van bestuur en de universiteitsraad. Maastricht, 17 januari 1991.*
18 Maastricht University Archives, 5.3.02.4cba00011 *Opleidingen FdAW Kennistechnologie, transnationale experimentele studierichting, samenwerking met LUC Diepenbeek. Map 1-1-1987 – 31-3-1991. Brief van J. Ritzen aan het college van bestuur van de Rijksuniversiteit Limburg, 6-9-1991. Brief van C. Boerman, plaatsvervangend voorzitter VSNU aan de minister van onderwijs en wetenschappen J. Ritzen. Utrecht, 4 juni 1991.*
19 Maastricht University Archives, 5.3.02.4cba00011 *Opleidingen FdAW Kennistechnologie, transnationale experimentele studierichting, samenwerking met LUC Diepenbeek. Map 1-1-1987 – 31-3-1991. Brief van J. Ritzen aan het college van bestuur van de Rijksuniversiteit Limburg, 6-9-1991.*
20 NRC newspaper, 12 September 1991.
21 *Observant*, 21 January 1993.
22 Ibid.
23 *Observant*, 29 November 2012.
24 With thanks to Patricia Meertens of the Student Services Centre, who pointed out that it is impossible to retrieve the exact figures. Email to A. Klijn, 5 September 2016.
25 The Education Sciences programme was launched in 2001 and was vociferously supported by then Rector Arie Nieuwenhuijzen Kruseman in line with the university's 'Leading in Learning' initiatives. The preparatory committee consisted of education scientists Cees van der Vleuten, Wim Gijselaers and Els Boshuizen. Education Sciences was assigned to the Faculty of Psychology, which had no desire to accommodate it. When intake levels proved limited to around 15 students, the realisation dawned that there was no sufficient 'market' for the new programme. The Faculty of Psychology refused to bear the resulting financial risks and called for discontinuation of the programme, a measure that was eventually taken within the space of a year. The students who had already started were offered an opportunity to finish their studies. Memorandum from E. Boshuizen to A. Klijn, 13 September 2016 and 14 September 2016.
26 *Trouw* newspaper, 12 January 2001.
27 Conversation with K. Dittrich, 12 October 2015. In addition to the cultural differences between Dutch and Flemish staff members, the tUL was also blighted by the politics of power: for example, the University of Leuven opposed the institution, and Maastricht University's Faculty of Medicine did not want to cooperate as it also had eyes on the new Science programmes.
28 *Observant*, 13 March 2003.
29 See Perrenet, J. en T. Weijters, 'Projectgeoriënteerd onderwijs bij Kennistechnologie aan de UM', in: *Tijdschrift voor informatica-onderwijs* (1997), 5, 168-169. Uiterwijk, J., 'Van probleem- naar projectgestuurd onderwijs. Kennistechnologie, anders dan andere', in: *Universiteit Maastricht 25 jaar jong in 2001*, 169-175.
30 We would like to thank Patricia Meertens of the Maastricht University Student Services Centre for providing this information, 5 September 2016.

16 *Louis Boon*

1. Unless stated otherwise, all quotes are derived from conversations with L. Boon on 8 and 23 March 2016.
2 See the chapter on Hans Philipsen.
3 *Onderwijs in de Gezondheidswetenschappen. Een zelfstudie*, Appendix Table 2.2.
4 See the chapter on Gerard de Vries.
5 Until the adoption of the University Government (Modernisation) Act (MUB) in 1997, the deans were appointed by the Faculty Council and not by the Executive Board. Consequently, the Council of Deans could operate relatively independently of the Executive Board.

6 Korsten, G. and L. Boon, *Kanttekeningen voor de discussie over een Faculteit Sociale Wetenschappen aan de Rijksuniversiteit Limburg*, August 1990.
7 Korsten, G. and L. Boon, *Tussenrapportage Sociaal Wetenschappelijke Opleidingen*. Maastricht, 1991.
8 Harald Merckelbach, Marcel van den Hout, Anita Jansen and Arnoud Arntz, *Een biopsychologisch curriculum in Maastricht*, April 1991. Jelle Jolles, *Een curriculum neuropsychologie en psychobiologie* in, 14 April 1991. Personal archive of G. Korsten.
9 See also: Boon, 'Psychologie in Maastricht, een persoonlijke prehistorie', in: *Universiteit Maastricht 25 jaar jong in 2001*, 181-188.
10 Conversation with L. Vredevoogd, 20 November 2015.
11 Email from Rob de Vries to A. Klijn, 25 April 2016. Psychology degree programmes were already being offered by the University of Amsterdam, VU Amsterdam, Leiden University, the University of Groningen, Utrecht University, Tilburg University, Radboud University Nijmegen and the Open University of the Netherlands.
12 See Psychologie in Maastricht, July 1992 and Psychologie in Maastricht, January 1993.
13 Conversation with L. Vredevoogd, 20 November 2015.
14 Ibid.
15 Letter from N.H. Frijda, professor of Experimental Psychology at the University of Amsterdam, G. Kempen, professor of Cognitive Psychology at Leiden University, G. Mellenbergh, professor of Psychological Methodology at the University of Amsterdam, N.E. van de Poll, professor by special appointment of Comparative and Physiological Psychology of Emotions at the University of Amsterdam, P.A. Vroon, professor of Theoretical Psychology at Utrecht University and W.A. Wagenaar, professor of Experimental Psychology at Leiden University to J. Ritzen, Amsterdam, 9 June 1993. Personal archive of G. Korsten.
16 Conversation with L. Vredevoogd, 20 November 2015.
17 *Limburgsch Dagblad* newspaper, 3 February 1994.
18 Conversation with H. Philipsen, 24 August 2012.
19 *Onderwijsvisitatie Psychologie. Zelfstudie*. Maastricht, 2000.
20 *Observant*, 28 August 1997.
21 Willems, *Overheid en universiteit: een langdurige relatie*, 327 ff.
22 Conversation with K. Dittrich, 12 October 2015.
23 Arie Nieuwenhuijzen Kruseman was professor of Internal Medicine and Rector of Maastricht University (UM) from 1998 to 2003.
24 Boon and Dijkema at the time also suggested a master's programme with an emphasis on 'bio-based materials' and 'systems biology of ageing, health and nutrition': two lines of research that were closely aligned with existing interests in the region, certainly at a company like DSM.
25 CROHO: Central Register of Higher Education Degree Programmes. A degree programme must be entered in CROHO with a specific code to be eligible for government funding of education institutions, to award student grants/loans and to confer degrees and titles.
26 http://web.tue.nl/cursor/internet/jaargang53/cursor08/nieuws/index.php?page=n1, retrieved on 22 April 2016.
27 *Kennis-As Limburg Groeimotor van de regio*. Maastricht, April 2013. This strategy could also accommodate Maastricht Health Campus and Chemelot Campus Sittard-Geleen.
28 From 2016, Maastricht University intends to focus primarily on the theme of nutrition.
29 *Kennis-As Limburg Groeimotor van de regio*, 29.
30 http://cdho.nl/page/downloads/Bijlage_2._Samenvatting_van_de_aanvraag_bacheloropleiding_Liberal_Arts_and_Sciences_University_College_Venlo.pdf. Retrieved on 25 April 2016.
31 *Observant*, 8 November 2013.

LITERATURE AND SOURCES

CONSULTED LITERATURE

Ament, A., Arkel, P. van, and J. Boots, *Proceedings of the Workshop on Hospitals, Health Care and Medical Education. New Solutions for the Eighties*. Rijksuniversiteit Limburg, Maastricht, 1977.

'De Achtste Medische Faculteit', *Medisch Contact*, 27 (1972), 33, 873-878.

'Basisfilosofie Achtste Medische Faculteit', *Medisch Contact*, 27 (1972), 33, 879-884.

'Basisfilosofie van de Medische Faculteit Maastricht. Consequenties voor opleiding en praktijk', *Medisch Contact*, (1974) 29, 227.

Bergh van den-Braam, A.H.M., *Verplegingswetenschap in Nederlands perspectief. Rede uitgesproken bij de aanvaarding van het ambt van buitengewoon hoogleraar in de verplegingswetenschap aan de Rijksuniversiteit Limburg op vrijdag 31 oktober 1986*. Leiden, 1986.

Berkel, H. van, et al. (ed.), *Lessons from Problem-based Learning*. Oxford: 2010.

Berkel, K. van, *Academisch leven. Over geschiedenis, karakter en veerkracht van de Nederlandse universiteit*. Amsterdam, 2009.

Bleyen, J. and L. Van Molle, *Wat is mondelinge geschiedenis?* Leuven - The Hague, 2012.

Blijham, G.H., *Het geheim van de ontaarde crypt. Rede, uitgesproken bij de aanvaarding van het ambt van hoogleraar in de inwendige geneeskunde, in het bijzonder de medische oncologie, aan de Rijksuniversiteit Limburg te Maastricht op vrijdag 29 juni 1990*. Maastricht, 1990.

Blok, A., *De vernieuwers. De zegeningen van tegenslag in wetenschap en kunst, 1500-2000*. Amsterdam, 2013.

Bouhuijs, P.A.J. and H.G. Schmidt, *Effekten van taakverdeling binnen onderwijsgroepen op leerresultaat en satisfaktie bij studenten*. Maastricht, 1977.

Bouhuijs, P.A.J., H.G. Schmidt, R.E. Snow & W.H.F.W. Wijnen, 'The Rijksuniversiteit Limburg, Maastricht, Netherlands: Development of Medical Education', in: Katz, F.M. & T. Fülop (eds.), *Personnel for Health Care: Case Studies of Educational Programmes* (Geneva, 1978) 133-151.

Bonke, F.I.M., M.J. Cohen and P.M.E.M. van der Grinten, *Opening academisch jaar 1985/86 2 september 1985*. Maastricht, 1985.

Boon, L. et al., *Disciplines, kundes en de kwaliteit van wetenschap. Onderwijskunde, Gezondheidsvoorlichting en -opvoeding in internationaal perspectief*. Maastricht – Groningen, 1989.

Boon, L. and G. Korsten, 'De universiteit: organisatie en variatie', *U & H. Tijdschrift voor wetenschappelijk onderwijs*, 38 (1990-1992) 4, 158-166.

Boon, L., Korsten, G. and R. de Vries, *Psychologie in Maastricht. Commissie Psychologie*. Maastricht, 1992.

Bouhuijs, P.A.J., W. Brouwer and A.H.M. Mol, 'Praktisch medisch onderwijs in de huisartspraktijk', *Huisarts en Wetenschap*, (1980) 23, 8-12.

Bouhuijs, P.A.J. et al., 'The Rijksuniversiteit Limburg, Maastricht, the Netherlands. Development of Medical Education', in: Katz, F.M. and T. Fulop (eds). *Personnel for health care: case studies of educational programmes*. Public health papers, No. 70, WHO. Genève, 1978.

Bouhuijs, P.A.J., *De ontwikkeling van het Praktisch Medisch Onderwijs in de Huisartspraktijk*, Maastricht, 1983.

Brodsky, J., *Loflied op Clio*. Amsterdam, 1991.

Brouwer, W., 'Medisch Faculteit Maastricht en huisartsgeneeskunde', *Medisch Contact*, (1974) 29, 230-231.

Brouwer, W. and M.A.J. Romme (red.), *Faculteit en eerste lijn*. Utrecht/Antwerp, 1981.

Brouwer, W., Kerkhof, P.D. and P. Pop, *De relatie 1e- 2e lijn in ontwikkeling. Evaluatie van het experiment Diagnostisch Centrum Maastricht*. Maastricht. 1983.

Brouwer, W., *Vallen en opstaan*. Afscheidsrede Rijksuniversiteit Limburg. Maastricht, 1986.

Caljé, P., 'Maastricht en zijn universiteit. Interacties tussen universiteit, stad en regio', in: E. van Royen (red.), *Maastricht kennisstad. 850 Jaar onderwijs en wetenschap*. Nijmegen, 2011.

Campagneresultaten 1987. Belangstelling voor de RL gestegen. Dienst Voorlichting RL, Maastricht, sa.

CARIM *Annual Report 2013. School for Cardiovascular Diseases*. Maastricht, sa.

Claassens, A., *Studiesucces Nederlandse versus internationale studenten. Notitie ten behoeve van de* VSNU *Stuurgoep Internationaal 30 september 2016*. sp, 2016.

Claessen, H., Moust, J.H.C. e.a., *Werkboek studievaardigheden: probleemgestuurd doornemen van studiemateriaal*. Maastricht, 1982.

Cohen, M.J. and H.F.M. Crombag, 'De nieuwe medische faculteit in Maastricht en de juridische opleiding ', *Nederlands juristenblad*, 53 (1978) 19, 355-360.

Cohen, M.J. et al., *Hoger onderwijs in de jaren negentig. Een sociaal-democratische visie op het stelsel van hoger onderwijs en wetenschapsbeoefening*. Published by the Wiardi Beckman Stichting. Amsterdam, 1990.

Cohen, M.J. and G.H. de Vries, *Redes gehouden op de 16 Dies Natalis van de Rijksuniversiteit Limburg 10 januari 1992*. Maastricht, 1992.

Cohen, M.J., *Over het denken van juristen*. Maastricht, 1992.

Cohen, M.J. and R.S. Reneman, *Redes gehouden op de 17e Dies Natalis van de Rijksuniversiteit Limburg, 8 januari 1993*. Maastricht, 1993.

Cohen, M.J. and B.E.F.M. de Witte, *Redes gehouden op de 20ste Dies Natalis van de Rijksuniversiteit Limburg 12 januari 1996*. Maastricht, 1996.

Cohen, M.J., *Wetenschap en wetenschapsbeleid. Toespraak ter gelegenheid van de eenentwintigste dies van de Universiteit Maastricht uitgesproken op vrijdag 10 januari 1997*. Maastricht, 1997.

Cohen, M.J. and A.C. Nieuwenhuijzen Kruseman, *Redes gehouden op de 22e Dies Natalis van de Universiteit Maastricht, 9 januari 1998*. Maastricht, 1998.

Collini, S., *What are Universities For?* London, 2012.

Corduwener, J., *Een vreemdeling op Justitie. Het asielbeleid van Job Cohen*. Amsterdam-Antwerpen, 2001.

Curriculum vitae: stichting, groei, huidige situatie en perspectieven van de Rijksuniversiteit Limburg. Maastricht, 1986.

Differentiëren in drievoud omwille van kwaliteit en verscheidenheid in het hoger onderwijs. Advies van de Commissie Toekomstbestendig Hoger Onderwijs Stelsel. The Hague, 2010.

Dijstelbloem, H., Huisman, F., Miedema, F. and W. Mijnhardt, 'Wetenschap in transitie. Zeven zorgen voor de universiteit', in: Verbrugge, A. and J. van Baardewijk (ed.), *Waartoe is de universiteit op aarde?*

Wat is er mis en hoe kan het beter? (Amsterdam, 2014), 111-124.

Dittrich, K.L.L.M. et al., *Redes gehouden tijdens de opening van het Academisch jaar 1998/1999 op 7 september 1998 en de 23e Dies Natalis op 8 januari 1999.* Maastricht, 1999.

Dittrich, K.L.L.M., et al., *Redes gehouden tijdens de opening van het Academisch Jaar 1999/2000 op 6 september 1999 en de 24ste Dies Natalis op 7 januari 2000.* sp, sa.

Dittrich, K.L.L.M., et al., *Redes gehouden tijdens de opening van het Academisch Jaar 2000/2001 op 4 september 2000 en de 25ste Dies Natalis op 12 januari 2001.* sp, sa.

Dittrich, K.L.L.M., et al., *Redes gehouden tijdens de opening van het Academisch Jaar 2001/2002 op 3 september 2001 en de 26ste Dies Natalis op 11 januari 2002.* sp, sa.

Dittrich, K.L.L.M., et al., *Redes gehouden tijdens de opening van het Academisch jaar 2002/2003 op 2 september 2002 en de 27ste Dies Natalis op 10 januari 2003.* Maastricht, 2003.

Dittrich, K., 'Van ivoren toren naar glazen huis', in: Verbrugge, A. and J. van Baardewijk (red.), *Waartoe is de universiteit op aarde? Wat is er mis en hoe kan het beter?* (Amsterdam, 2014), 151-162.

De doelstellingen van Ziekenhuis Maastricht. Signalement van een ontwikkeling. Maastricht, 1979.

Doelstellingen ziekenhuis Maastricht. Maastricht, 1979.

Dorsman, L.J. and P.J. Knegtmans, *Het universitaire bedrijf. Over professionalisering van onderzoek, bestuur en beheer.* Hilversum, 2010.

Dorsman, L.J. and P.J. Knegtmans, *De menselijke maat in de wetenschap. De geleerden(auto)biografie als bron voor de wetenschaps- en universiteitsgeschiedenis.* Hilversum, 2012.

Draaisma, D., *De heimweefabriek: geheugen, tijd & ouderdom.* Groningen, 2008.

Drenthe-Schonk, A. et al., *Vrouwen in onderwijs en onderzoek aan de Rijksuniversiteit Limburg. Een rapport van de emancipatiecommissie januari 1995.* Maastricht 1995.

Economie in Maastricht. Rapport van de werkgroep economie als voorbereidingscommissie voor de studierichting economie aan de Rijksuniversiteit Limburg, uitgebracht aan het faculteitsbestuur van de Algemene Faculteit. Maastricht, 1983.

Eertwegh, E. van, M. de Volder and V. Dubois, *Over de mogelijke rol van hoorcolleges binnen taakgericht groepsonderwijs geïllustreerd aan de hand van ervaringen in een onderwijsblok.* Onderzoek van onderwijs, Rijksuniversiteit Limburg. Maastricht, 1983.

Ervaringen met probleemgestuurd juridisch onderwijs. Opstellen ten behoeve van de conferentie van 15 januari 1988, 1ste lustrum van de Faculteit der Rechtsgeleerdheid, Rijksuniversiteit Limburg. Deventer, 1989.

Frijhoff, W.T.M., *Keuzepatronen van de universiteit in historisch perspectief. Herziene en gedeeltelijk herschreven versie van een lezing, gehouden te Maastricht op 12 februari 1987 ter gelegenheid van het tweede lustrum van de Rijksuniversiteit Limburg.* Rotterdam, 1987.

Frijhoff, W., 'Honderd jaar universiteitsgeschiedenis in Nederland', *Studium*, 6 (2013) 3-4, 197–206.

Gezondheidswetenschappen in Maastricht. Maastricht, 1983.

Griffioen, C. et al. (ed.), *Gezonderwijs in Nederland en Vlaanderen. Veertig jaar Nederlandse Vereniging voor Medisch Onderwijs.* Houten, 2012.

Hansen, E., 'The Uses and Abuses of Contemporary University History in Denmark': in: Eckhardt Larsen, J. (ed.), *Knowledge, Politics and the History of Education* (Münster, 2012) 137-150.

Hemker, H.C., J.J. Veltkamp, A. Hensen and E.A. Loeliger, 'Nature of prothrombine biosynthesis: preprothrombinaemia in vitamin K-deficiency', *Nature*, (1963) 200, 589-590.

Hemker, H.C., *"Waar een W.I.L. is..."* Rede, uitgesproken door prof. dr. H.C. Hemker, rector magnificus van de Rijksuniversiteit Limburg, bij gelegenheid van de zevende Dies Natalis van de universiteit, op 14 januari 1983. Maastricht, 1983.

Hemker, H.C., *Een zachte machine*. Rede uitgesproken door prof. dr. H.C. Hemker, rector magnificus van de Rijksuniversiteit Limburg, bij gelegenheid van de achtste Dies Natalis van de universiteit, op 13 januari 1984. Maastricht, 1984.

Hemker, H.C. et al., *Redes uitgesproken bij gelegenheid van de negende Dies Natalis van de Rijksuniversiteit Limburg, op 11 januari 1985*. Maastricht, 1985.

Hemker, H.C., 'Critical perceptions on problem-based learning', *European Review*, 9 (2001) 3, 269-274.

Hemker, H.C., 'Recollections on thrombin generation', *Journal of Thrombosis and Haemostasis*, 6 (2007), 219-226.

Hemker, H.C., *Trombine*. Maastricht, 2013.

'De herinnering aan het woord', *Ex Tempore*, 31 (2012) No. 3.

Herraets, J., 'De lichting 1982', *Continuüm. Kwartaalblad van de Universiteit Maastricht*, 2 (1998) 3, 6-21.

Herraets, J., 'Job Cohen. De eerste jurist van Maastricht', *Continuüm. Kwartaalblad van de Universiteit Maastricht*, 2 (1998) 3, 23-25.

Herraets, J., 'Karl Dittrich. De man die eigenlijk alleen maar voorzitter van MVV wilde worden', *Continuüm. Kwartaalblad van de Universiteit Maastricht*, 2 (1998) 3, 26-30.

Herraets, J., 'het onverstoorbare gelijk van Wynand Wijnen, onderwijsvernieuwer', *Tijdschrift voor hoger onderwijs,* 17 (1999), 1, 10-19.

Hillen, H. et al. (ed.), *Interne geneeskunde Maastricht. Eenheid én verscheidenheid 1910-2014*. Maastricht, 2014.

Integraal plan voor universitaire participatie in de regionale gezondheidszorg. Maastricht, november 1982.

Internationalisering van de Rijksuniversiteit Limburg. Een beleidskader voor de periode tot en met 1994. Maastricht, June 1991.

Internationalisering aan de Rijksuniversiteit Limburg. Een rapportage over de ontwikkeling van het internationaliseringsproces in het onderwijs tot 1993. Maastricht, 1993.

'10 Jaar academisch ziekenhuis Maastricht', *Traject*, 11 (1996) 4, special issue.

Job Cohen: betrokken beschouwer. Interview en verzamelde Uitlegcolumns t.g.v. het afscheid van Job Cohen als staatssecretaris van O&W. The Hague, 1994.

Kasper, J.D.P. and L.E.H. Vredevoogd (ed.), *Marketing van universiteiten. Noodzaak of modeverschijnsel?* Maastricht, 1991.

Keizer, P. and J. Soeters (ed.), *Economie, sociologie en psychologie. Visies op integratie*. Assen/Maastricht, 1987.

Keizer, P. (ed.), *Probleemgestuurd onderwijs in de economische wetenschap*. Assen/Maastricht, 1989.

Kennis-As Limburg. Groeimotor van de regio. Maastricht, April 2013.

Klijn, A., *Onze man uit Maastricht. Sjeng Tans 1912 – 1993. Een biografie*. Nijmegen, 2001.

Knegtmans, P.J., *De Medische Faculteit Maastricht. Een nieuwe universiteit in een herstructureringsgebied, 1969-1984*. Assen-Maastricht, 1992.

Korsten, G. and P. Frissen, *Actuele ontwikkelingen in het hoger onderwijsbeleid; trends, perspectieven en problemen. Onderzoek van Onderwijs*. Rijksuniversiteit Limburg, nummer 33. Maastricht, February 1987.

Korsten, G. and L. Boon, *Verkenning Sociaalwetenschappelijke Studierichtingen Rijksuniversiteit Limburg*. Maastricht, July 1991.

Kurkowska-Budzan, M. and K. Zamorski (eds.), *Oral History. The challenges of dialogue*. Amsterdam-Philadelphia, 2009.

Kusters, W., *Pooltochten. Inaugurele rede Maastricht*. Amsterdam, 1989.

Kusters, W. and J. Perry, *Versteende wouden: mijnen en mijnwerkers in woord en beeld*. Amsterdam, 1999.

Kusters, W., *In en onder het dorp: mijnwerkersleven in Limburg*. Nijmegen, 2013.

Kusters, W., *Pierre Kemp: een leven*. Nijmegen, 2010.

Leydesdorff, S., *De mensen en de woorden. Geschiedenis op basis van verhalen*. Amsterdam, 2004.

Loeliger, E.A., *In de greep van de protrombinetijd. Een persoonlijke visie op 45 jaar orale antistollingsbehandeling*. Leiden, 1985.

Loon, P.J.J.M. van, *De Economische Faculteit in Maastricht: een intentie in praktijk gebracht. Diesrede gehouden door prof. dr. P.J.J.M. van Loon ter gelegenheid van het tweede lustrum van de Rijksuniversiteit Limburg 10 januari 1986*. Maastricht, 1986.

Maarseveen, H. van, 'Rechten in Maastricht', *Nederlands Juristen Blad*, 29 August 1981, No. 29, 777-779.

Made in Maastricht. Instellingsplan RL 1996-1999. Maastricht, 1995.

Moust, J.H.C., M.P.J. van den Broek and A. Swaans, 'De probleemgestuurde onderwijsbenadering van de Faculteit der Rechtsgeleerdheid te Maastricht', *Ars Aequi: juridisch maandblad*, 44 (1995) 12, 942-948.

Muysken, J., *Hoe algemeen is de algemene economie? Rede in verkorte vorm uitgesproken bij de aanvaarding van het ambt van hoogleraar in de Algemene economie aan de Rijksuniversiteit Limburg*. Assen/Maastricht, 1985.

Muysken, J. and H. Schreuder (ed.), *Economische wetenschappen: eenheid in verscheidenheid*. Maastricht, 1985.

Muysken, J., *Van Reaganomics tot de Eurocrisis: 30 jaren in Maastricht*. Afscheidsrede Prof. dr. Joan Muysken, hoogleraar Algemene Economie School of Business and Economics. Maastricht, 29 November 2013.

Nijhof, G., *Levensverhalen. Over de methode van autografisch onderzoek in de sociologie*. Amsterdam, 2000.

Onderwijs in de Gezondheidswetenschappen. Een zelfstudie. Faculteit der Gezondheidswetenschappen. Maastricht, 1991.

Onderwijskundige uitgangspunten. Nota van de Onderwijscommissie in het kader van de onderwijsdiscussie. Faculteit der Rechtsgeleerdheid, Rijksuniversiteit Limburg. sp, 1987.

Onderwijsvisitatie. Geneeskunde en Gezondheidswetenschappen, VSNU. Utrecht, 1992.

Onderwijsvisitatie Psychologie. Zelfstudie. Maastricht, 2000.

Onderzoek. Rijksuniversiteit Limburg. Maastricht, sa. [1984].

Ontwerp voor een studierichting Sociale Gezondheidkunde aan de Rijksuniversiteit Limburg. Rijksuniversiteit Limburg/Al-gemene Faculteit. Maastricht, 1979.

Ontwikkelingen voor de Algemene Faculteit van de Rijksuniversiteit Limburg. Maastricht, 1976.

Oosterhuis, H. and M. Gijswijt-Hofstra, *Verward van geest en ander ongerief. Psychiatrie en geestelijke gezondheidszorg in Nederland (1870-2005)*. 3 volumes. Houten, 2008.

Pasch, T. van de, 'Als de verplegingswetenschap het niet bestudeert, doet niemand het', *Tijdschrift voor Verpleegkundigen* (2003) 9, 24-27.

Perks, R and A. Thomson (eds.), *The Oral History Reader*. New York, 2000.

Perrenet, J. and T. Weijters, 'Projectgeoriënteerd onderwijs bij Kennistechnologie aan de UM', *Tijdschrift voor informaticaonderwijs* (1997), 5, 168-169.

Philipsen, H. *Toespraken gehouden bij gelegenheid van de opening academisch jaar 1977/1978 op september 1977*. sp, sa.

Philipsen, H., *Sociale gezondheidkunde*, Rijksuniversiteit Limburg. Maastricht, 1981.

Philipsen, H. and W. Kusters, *Redes gehouden op de 18e Dies Natalis van de Rijksuniversiteit Limburg, 14 januari 1994*. Maastricht, 1994.

Philipsen, H. and M.J. Cohen, *Redes gehouden op de 19e Dies Natalis van de Rijksuniversiteit Limburg, 13 januari 1995*. Maastricht, 1995.

Philipsen, H., *Op zoek naar zorgland. "De WAO, de thuiszorg en de Bijlmerramp: randgebieden rond het medisch centrum van gezondheidszorg"*. Maastricht, 2000,

Plas, M. van der, *Zonen en dochters*. Baarn, 1989.

Profilering en differentiatie. Naar een samenhangend stelsel van opleidingen aan de Rijksuniversiteit Limburg. Maastricht, September, 1984.
Profilering en uitbouw van de Rijksuniversiteit Limburg. Aanzet tot een beleidsplan voor de lange termijn. Maastricht, September 1987.

Rapport inzake de organisatorische ontwikkeling van de Rijksuniversiteit Limburg. Published by Raadgevend Bureau Ir. B.W. Berenschot bv. Utrecht, 1974.
Rapportage 1987 vernieuwingsfonds extramurale profilering. Faculteit der Geneeskunde RL, January 1988.
Rechten in Maastricht. Plan voor een juridische studierichting aan de Rijksuniversiteit Limburg te Maastricht. Maastricht, 1980.
Rechten in Maastricht. Verkenning van een nieuwe opleiding Nederlands Recht aan de Rijksuniversiteit Limburg. Maastricht, 1981.
Reorganisatieplan, vastgesteld door het Bestuur van de Fakulteit der Geneeskunde in zijn vergadering d.d. 29 mei 1990, Rijksuniversiteit Limburg. Maastricht, 1990.
De Rijksuniversiteit Limburg in ontwikkeling. Een schets van beleidslijnen en uitbouwplannen. Maastricht, September 1988.
Rijksuniversiteit Limburg: stichting, groei, huidige situatie, perspectieven. Maastricht, 1985.
Rijksuniversiteit Limburg. Cultuur- en Wetenschapsstudies. Maastricht, 1989.
Rijksuniversiteit en regio. De financieel-economische betekenis van de Rijksuniversiteit Limburg voor de regio. Maastricht, 1982.
Ricoeur, P., *Memory, History, Forgetting.* Chicago-London, 2004.
Ritchie, D.A. (ed.), *The Oxford Handbook of Oral History.* Oxford, 2011.
RL en regio. De financieel-economische betekenis van de Rijksuniversiteit Limburg voor de regio. Uitgave Dienst Voorlichting. Maastricht, 1982.
Roder, J. de (ed.), *Ik woon in duizend kamers tegelijk. Opstellen voor en over Wiel Kusters.* Nijmegen, 2012.

Romme, M.A.J., *Regionalisatie en integratie in de geestelijke gezondheidszorg. Verslag van een bezoek aan 8 mental health centra. Studiereis WHO fellowship 1972.* The Hague, 1974.
Romme, M., 'Gedragswetenschappen met betrekking tot onderzoek, opleiding en gezondheidszorg', *Medisch Contact,* (1974) 29, 232-234.
Romme, M.A.J., *Doel en middel. Een bijdrage tot de medische economie door middel van een sociaal geneeskundige exploratie van de selectie voor opname van psychiatrische patiënten.* sp, 1967.
Romme, M.A.J. and D.M.J. Bauduin, *Psychiatrische epidemiologie: een onderzoek naar de spreiding van geesteszieken. Een literatuurstudie.* Baarn, 1976.
Romme, M.A.J. et al. (ed.), *Voorzieningen in de geestelijke gezondheidszorg. Een gids voor consument en hulpverlener.* Alphen aan den Rijn, 1978.
Romme, M.A.J., H.F. Kraan and R. Rotteveel, *Wat is sociale psychiatrie? Een inleiding.* Alphen aan den Rijn, 1981.
Romme, M.A.J. et al., *Het psychiatrische ziekenhuis in diskussie. Verslag van de actie Moratorium Nieuwbouw APZ'en.* Amsterdam, 1985.
Romme, M.A.J., A. Escher et al. (ed.), *Stemmen horen accepteren.* Maastricht, 1990.
Royen, E. van (ed.), *Maastricht kennisstad. 850 jaar onderwijs en wetenschap.* Nijmegen, 2011.
Rupp, J.C.C., *Van oude en nieuwe universiteiten. De verdringing van Duitse door Amerikaanse invloeden op de wetenschapsbeoefening en het hoger onderwijs in Nederland, 1945-1995.* The Hague, 1997.

Samuel, R. and P. Thompson (Eds.), *The Myths We Live By.* London – New York, 1993.
Schets van een juridische studierichting aan de Rijksuniversiteit Limburg. Maastricht, 1979.
Schmidt, H.G. and P.A.J. Bouhuijs, *Het tutorensysteem.* Maastricht, 1977.
Schmidt, H.G. and P.A.J. Bouhuijs, *Probleemgeoriënteerd onderwijs.* Maastricht, 1977.

Schmidt, H.G. and P.A.J. Bouhuijs, *Onderwijs in taakgerichte groepen*. Utrecht, 1980.

Schmidt, H.G. and J.H.C. Moust, *Hoe ervaren Maastrichtse medische studenten hun opleiding?* Maastricht, 1980.

Schmidt, H.G., *Activatie van voorkennis, intrinsieke motivatie en de verwerking van tekst: studies in probleemgestuurd onderwijs*. Apeldoorn, 1982.

Schmidt, H.G. (ed.), *Probleemgestuurd onderwijs. Bijdragen tot de onderwijsdagen 1981*. Harlingen, 1982.

Schmidt, H.G. *Activatie van voorkennis, intrinsieke motivatie en de verwerking van tekst: studies in probleemgestuurd onderwijs*. Maastricht, 1982.

Schmidt, H.G., 'De tovenaar van Bunde', *Tijdschrift voor hoger onderwijs,* 17 (1999), 1, 3-9.

Schmidt, H.G., *Hoe goed is ons geheugen? Toespraak ter gelegenheid van de vierentwintigste Dies Natalis van de Universiteit Maastricht op 7 januari 2000*. Maastricht, 2000.

Schmidt, H.G., 'Hoe goed is ons geheugen?' *De Psycholoog,* (2000), 224-228.

Schmidt, H.G., L. Vermeulen & H.T. van der Molen, 'Longterm effects of problem-based learning: a comparison of competencies acquired by graduates of a problem-based and a conventional medical school', *Medical Education,* (2006), 40, 562-567.

Schmidt, H. G., H.T. Van der Molen, W.W.R. Te Winkel & W.H.F.W. Wijnen, 'Constructivist, problem-based learning does work. A meta-analysis of curricular comparisons involving a single medical school'. *Educational Psychologist,* 44 (2009) 4, 227-249.

Schmidt, H.G, A.M.M. Muijtjens, C.P.M. van der Vleuten & G.R. Norman, 'Differential Student Attrition and Differential Exposure Mask Effects of Problem-Based Learning in Curriculum Comparison Studies'. *Academic Medicine,* 87 (2012) 4, 463-475. doi: 10.1097/ACM.0b013e31824 9591a

Schmidt, H.G., J.I. Rotgans & E.H.J. Yew, 'The process of problem-based learning: what works and why', *Medical Education,* (2011), 45, 792-806.

Schreuder, H., *Maatschappelijke verantwoordelijkheid en maatschappelijke berichtgeving van ondernemingen*. Leiden/Antwerp, 1981.

Schreuder, H., *Economie (en) bedrijven. Over de bedrijfseconomie als discutabel, spannend en eigen-aardig onderdeel van de economische wetenschappen*. Rede in verkorte vorm uitgesproken bij de aanvaarding van het ambt van hoogleraar in de Bedrijfseconomie aan de Rijksuniversiteit Limburg op vrijdag 6 september 1985. Assen-Maastricht, 1985.

Schuyt, K., 'De universiteit als verzamelplaats van creatieve scepsis', in: Verbrugge, A. and J. van Baardewijk (ed.), *Waartoe is de universiteit op aarde? Wat is er mis en hoe kan het beter?* (Amsterdam, 2014), 125-140.

Sierksma, P., *Ambulant en academisch. 60 Jaar GGZ in Maastricht en omgeving, van Riagg tot Virenze*. Voerendaal, 2016.

Smelik, A.M. and C.W. Bosch, *Beelden van vrouwen, mannen en wetenschap: een onderzoek naar beeldvorming en sekse aan de Universiteit Maastricht*. Maastricht, 1998.

Sociale gezondheidkunde. Plan voor de ontwikkeling van onderwijs en onderzoek aan de Algemene Faculteit. Maastricht, 1978.

Studeren aan de Rijksuniversiteit Limburg. Een inleiding in de medische studie en in de studie sociale gezondheidkunde. 1980/1981 Algemene Faculteit/Medische Faculteit. Maastricht, 1980.

De studie in de economie. Rijksuniversiteit Limburg Algemene Faculteit. Maastricht, 1983.

Terugblik en vooruitzien. Vijf jaar vakgroep gezondheidsrecht, september 1982 – september 1987. Maastricht, 1987.

Themadag, georganiseerd ter gelegenheid van de start van de studierichting Nederlands Recht aan de RL op 7 september 1982. Maastricht, 1982.

Thompson, P., *The Voice of the Past. Oral History*. Oxford, 2009 (3rd ed.).

Thung, P.J. and M.L. de Volder, *Het eerste jaar. Rapport over de propaedeuse sociale gezondheidkunde 1980/1981*, Rijksuniversiteit Limburg, Algemene Faculteit. Maastricht, 1981.

Tiddens, H.A, Willighagen, R.G.J. and W.H.F.M. Wijnen, 'Medisch onderwijs in ontwikkeling. Studiejaar 1974 - 1975 Medische Faculteit Maastricht'. *Medisch Contact*, 30 (1975) 1077-1085.

Tiddens, H.A., *Toespraken gehouden bij gelegenheid van de eerste dies natalis van de Rijksuniversiteit Limburg.* sp, 1977.

Tiddens, H.A., *Rede uitgesproken bij gelegenheid van de tweede dies natalis van de Rijksuniversiteit Limburg op 13 januari 1978.* Maastricht, 1978.

Toespraken gehouden bij gelegenheid van de officiële opening van de Rijksuniversiteit Limburg, 9-1-1976. Maastricht, 1976.

Tumblety, J. (ed.). *Memory and History. Understanding memory as source and subject.* Oxon/New York, 2013.

Tumblety, J. (eds.), *Memory and History.* London-New York, 2013.

Universiteit Maastricht, MCMLXXVIMMI, 25 jaar jong in 2001. Maastricht, 2001.

De universiteit, een vitaal organisme. Een uitgave ter gelegenheid van het afscheid van Ed d'Hondt als voorzitter van de Vereniging van Universiteiten VSNU. The Hague, 2006.

Verbrugge, A., 'De universiteit en de hoogste zorg voor kennis', in: Verbrugge, A. en J. van Baardewijk (ed.), *Waartoe is de universiteit op aarde? Wat is er mis en hoe kan het beter?* (Amsterdam, 2014), 207-226.

Verslag van het congres "Universiteit & Maatschappelijke Betekenis" gehouden ter afsluiting van het 2e lustrum van de Rijksuniversiteit Limburg op 12 februari 1987 te Maastricht. Maastricht, 1987.

Vizier vooruit. 4 Toekomstscenario's voor Nederlandse universiteiten. VSNU, 2016.

Vleuten, C. van der and H. van Berkel, 'Wynand Wijnen (1934-2012) – een man van betekenis. In memoriam', *Examens*, (2013) 1, 5-6.

Volder, M.L. de, and P.J. Thung, *Implementing a problem-based curriculum: a new social health programme at the University of Limburg, the Netherlands,* Rijksuniversiteit Limburg. Maastricht, 1982.

Wachelder, J.C.M., *Universiteit tussen vorming en opleiding. De modernisering van de Nederlandse universiteiten in de negentiende eeuw.* Hilversum, 1992.

Wetenschappelijk onderzoek. Organisatie en projecten. Dienst Voorlichting Rijksuniversiteit Limburg. Maastricht, 1982.

Wijnen, W.H.F.W., et al., *Sociale gezondheidkunde. Plan voor de ontwikkeling van onderwijs en onderzoek aan de Algemene Faculteit. Rapport van de werkgroep Algemene Faculteit aangeboden aan het College van Bestuur van de Rijksuniversiteit Limburg op 22 mei 1978 te Maastricht.* Maastricht, 1978.

Wijnen, W.H.F.W., 'Hoe verder na Dijsselbloem?', in: *Thema Hoger Onderwijs*, (2008) 3, 1-7.

Wijnen, W.H.F.W., 'Fundamentele beschouwingen over onderwijsvernieuwing', in: Herpen, K. van (ed.), *Onderwijsvernieuwing*, Tilburg, April 2012.

Willems, G.C.M., *Overheid en universiteit: een langdurige relatie.* Nijmegen, 2013.

Willighagen, R.G.J. and Hemker, H.C., 'Wetenschappelijk onderzoek in relatie met de praktijk van de gezondheidszorg', *Medisch Contact*, (1974) 29, 235-236.

Witte, B. de & C. Forder, *The Common Law of Europe and the Future of Legal Education. Le droit commun de l'Europe et l'avenir de l'enseignement juridique.* Deventer, 1992.

CONSULTED PERIODICAL SOURCES

Observant: information and news magazine of the State University of Limburg, 1980-

Observant: independent weekly of Maastricht University, 1998-

CONSULTED ARCHIVES

Maastricht University Archives

Private collection of Joost Bremer, Maastricht

Private collection of Coen Hemker, Maastricht

Private collection of Gerard Korsten, Maastricht

Private collection of Hein Schreuder, Maastricht

Private collection of Wynand Wijnen, Bunde

PHOTO CREDITS

Cover and end paper (front) — Professorial cortège at the opening of the 2016 academic year – photo Harry Heuts ©

2 — Queen Juliana arrives at St. Servaas Church to attend the dies natalis of the State University of Limburg on 9 January 1976. Photo Jos Nelissen – Maastricht University Archives

20 — Announcement of the early inauguration of the country's eighth medical faculty in the chapel of the former Jesuit monastery in Maastricht, 16 September 1974. From left to right: Wynand Wijnen, Harmen Tiddens, Sjeng Tans and Antoine Rottier – Maastricht University Archives

22 — Wynand Wijnen, around 1986. Photo Coen van der Gugten – Maastricht University Archives

23 — Wim Brouwer, 1980. Photo Coen van der Gugten – Maastricht University Archives

24 — Marius Romme, around 1990. Photo Hans van Dijk, Maastricht University Archives

25 — Ine Kuppen, 1991. Photo Hans van Dijk – Maastricht University Archives

26 — Coen Hemker, around 1980. Photo Coen van der Gugten – Maastricht University Archives

27 — Geert Blijham, mid-1980s – collection Geert Blijham

28 — Hans Philipsen, around 1984. Photo Hans van Dijk – Maastricht University Archives

29 — Henk Schmidt trying out a card-index system designed to guide students through medical case studies, 1979. In practice, the system proved unworkable, 1979. Photo Coen van der Gugten - Maastricht University Archives

30 — Job Cohen 1982. Photo Coen van der Gugten - Maastricht University Archives

31 — Ria Wolleswinkel, 2015. Photo Joey Roberts – collection Ria Wolleswinkel

31 — Joan Muysken, 1993. Photo Hans van Dijk – Maastricht University Archives.

33 — Hein Schreuder, 1985. Photo Hans van Dijk – Maastricht University Archives

34 — Gerard de Vries, 1996. Photo Hans van Dijk, Maastricht University Archives

35 — Wiel Kusters 1996. Photo Frits Widdershoven ©

36 — Hans Peters, 1993. Photo Joey Roberts – Maastricht University Archives

37 — Louis Boon 1987. Photo Franco Gori © – Observant archives

38 — Spot the female professor! Riet Drop, professor of Medical Sociology, 1994. Photo Nelis Tutkey © – Observant archives

40 — Queuing up for the first course books, September 1974 – Maastricht University Archives

54 — Skills lab. Photo Hans van Dijk – Maastricht University Archives

64 — The core group. From left to right, front: Ben Niessen (secretary), Wynand Wijnen, Roelof Willighagen, Co Greep, Wim Brouwer and Harry Hulsmans; in back: Harmen Tiddens, Jos Lemmens, Marius Romme and Coen Hemker – collection Ghislaine Niessen

76 — Ben Wijers and Ine Kuppen, Building and Information Services Team, 1991 – Maastricht University Archives

84 — Coen Hemker in the lab – collection Coen Hemker

96 — Graduation ceremony in 1979 – Maastricht University Archives

106 — Social Health Science information day, 1979. Photo Hans van Dijk, Maastricht University Archives

122 — Henk Schmidt and Peter Bouhuijs at the book launch for Onderwijs in taakgerichte groepen ('Educartion in Task-Oriented Groups'), 1980. Photo Coen van der Gugten - Maastricht University Archives

132 — First meeting of the committee set up to develop a Law programme at the State University of Limburg; clockwise around the table, starting from the mantelpiece: Loek Hulsman, J.F.T. Becker, Ewoud Hondius, Cees Flinterman, Albert Koers, Rob van den Biggelaar, Tim Koopmans, Max Rood, J.J. van Wessem, Wynand Wijnen, E. Backerra, Paul Thung and Sjeng Tans, 11 September 1980 – Maastricht University Archives

152 — Law group picture, 1988. From left to right: Geert van den Heuvel, Josta Mommertz, Hans Lensing, Vivienne ?, Gaby van den Biggelaar, Leo Hendriks, Agnes Martijn, Jürgen Wösetshofer, Miet Stijnen, ?, Taru Spronken, Jan Klifman, Ria Wolleswinkel and Joop Beckers – Maastricht University Archives
164 — Student tutorial, early 1990s. Photo Hans van Dijk – Maastricht University Archives
180 — Lecture. Photo Hans van Dijk – Maastricht University Archives
194 — The almost complete General Sciences Faculty, 1986. From left to right: Chris den Hamer, Tannelie Blom, Marleen Vara, Maarten Doorman, Jo Wachelder, Ton Nijhuis and Paul Galestin; below: Jacques Reiners, Pieter Mostert, Marty Heuvelman, Helen Keasberry and Anja Cuppens. Photo Franco Gori © – Observant archives
210 — Lies Wesseling during a tutorial, 1993. Photo Hans van Dijk – Maastricht University Archives
224 — Knowledge Engineering Information Brochure, 1992. The geologist engaged in conversation with the knowledge engineer – Maastricht University Archives
236 — In front of the hut where Psychology started. From left to right: Willie Schipper, Gerard Korsten, Louis Boon, Henk Schmidt, Peter Vermeer, Rob de Vries, Huub Aretz, Anouk Cuijpers and Wil Hoenjet – collection Willie Schipper

End paper (back) — Louis Boon waves farewell to students of University College Maastricht – photo Philip Driessen © – Observant archives

Photo credits

INDEX OF PERSONS

Adriaansens, Hans 249
Agt, Dries van 136, 165, 167
Albeda, Wil 91, 165-171, 181, 182, 184-188, 191, 202, 204, 225
Andersen, Hans Christian 216

Baan, Pieter 65, 66, 68, 70, 71
Backhaus, Jürgen 176
Bal, Peter 161,
Balkema, Jeppe 19, 133, 137, 139, 140, 141, 145, 155, 156, 158
Barend, Sonja 75
Bauduin, Dorine 71
Beckers, Harry 224, 226
Béguin, Suzette 95
Bell, Norman 124
Bergh-van den Braam, Anneke 117
Bers, Alma van 139, 155
Beurskens, Wim 139, 144
Biggelaar, Rob van den 52, 135, 136, 167, 187, 197, 211
Bijker, Wiebe 195, 203, 214, 217
Bijsterveld, Karin 207,
Blijham, Geert 7, 15,16, 19, 27, 58, 97-104, 128
Blom, Tannelie 19, 193, 197, 207
Boekhoudt, Piet 226
Bollen, Claire 19
Bonke, Victor 89, 94, 126, 128, 146, 147, 187, 200, 241
Boon, Louis 8, 14, 15, 19, 37, 129, 193, 195, 197-198, 199, 201-203, 213, 235-256
Boon, Kasper 233, 234
Bos, Nick 254
Bots, Hans 216
Bosshardt, Aleida 154
Bouhuijs, Peter 49, 60, 98, 123, 124, 127, 139, 141, 172, 244
Boven, Theo van 140, 159, 162
Bradt, Meredith 19
Branda, Luis 196, 199
Braspenning, Peter 225, 227, 228, 230, 233, 244
Bremer, Joost 19, 74, 108, 124
Brinkhorst, Laurens Jan 112,
Brinkgreve, Christien 238
Brouwer, Wim 7, 13, 19, 23, 46, 47, 55-63, 72, 108
Brünott, Loes 155, 156, 158, 159
Bruyne, Paul de 214
Bussemaker, Jet 255

Calcar, Co van 151
Callebaut, Werner 197
Cassell, John 69

Castro, Fidel 80
Cleij, Thomas 254
Cohen, Dolf 134
Cohen, Job 8, 14, 19, 30, 91, 97, 118, 131-151, 155-157, 159, 168, 204, 216, 243
Coenegracht, Jef 98, 100, 101, 103
Cornips, Leonie 219
Crebolder, Harry 19, 61, 63
Crombag, Hans 131, 133-136, 145, 146, 167, 199
Cuypers, Peter 79, 88

Deetman, Wim 51, 63, 91-93, 103, 112, 116, 135, 168, 170, 197, 200, 201, 203, 204, 240
Deken, Aagje 210
Dekker, Jeroen 197, 202
Derickx, Mieke 18
Diederiks, Jos 108
Dijck, José van 216
Dijkema, Johan 254
Dittrich, Karl 5, 11, 19, 82, 118, 137-139, 146, 151, 196, 216, 228, 240, 248-250
Doorman, Maarten 197, 206, 213
Dorsman, Leen 19
Dostojevski, Fjodor 155
Douma, Sytze 190
Driehuis, Wim 165
Drift, Koen van der 167
Drop, Riet 80, 108, 114, 160
Duijn, Jaap van 165, 168
Dumortier, Freddy 229, 230
Dzon, Marijke 19

Ehlen, Tonie 210
Elders, Jacques 140
Elias, Norbert 202
Elzinga, Wendelien 159
Es, Jan van 55, 56
Escher, Sandra 74

Feigenbaum, Edward 227
Ferrier, Barbera 196, 199
Fijten, Mieke 41
Flendrig, Guus 103, 104
Flerackers, Eddy 230
Flinterman, Cees 19, 137, 139, 140, 142, 143, 145, 146, 155, 156, 159, 161, 162, 168
Fortuyn, Pim 191, 193
Foucault, Michel 155
Foudraine, Jan 154
Franssen, Jean 19
Freeman, Chistopher 171

Freire, Paolo 8, 31, 151, 153, 162
Frijda, Nico 246

Gijsel, Peter de 176, 177
Gijssens, Marc 230
Goldschmidt, Jenny 159
Gori, Franco 19
Goudzwaard, Bob 184
Greep, Co 46, 51, 52, 56, 61-63, 69, 72-74, 79, 80, 81, 90, 100-103, 128, 204, 237
Groot, Adriaan de 44, 121
Groot, José de 216, 217
Groot, René, de 19, 139, 146, 155, 157, 160, 162
Groot, Wim 108

Habermas, Jürgen 155
Hage, Jaap 162
Hage, Patsy 75
Hamer, Chris den 197
Harmsen, Ger 193
Harzing, Anne-Wil 189
Heertje, Arnold 167
Heijltjes, Mariëlle 189
Hemker, Coen 7, 13, 19, 26, 46, 47, 52, 56, 62, 73, 78, 79, 83-95, 98
Hendriks, Ruud 207
Herik, Jaap van den 225-227, 230, 233, 234, 254
Heij, Christian 225
Hicks, John 174, 179
Hofstede, Geert 176, 177, 187
Hoor, Foppe Ten 237, 239, 240
Horstman, Klasien 198
Hospers, Harm 253
Houben, Philip 191
Hout, Marcel van den 242
Houwaart, Eddy 214
Hove, Mark ten 170
Hulsmans, Harry 46, 52, 78, 83, 85, 100, 103

Imbos, Tjaart 123

Jansen, Anita 242, 246
Janssens, Marion 19
Jolles, Jelle 242, 244, 247
Jong, Frits de 166
Jong, Joop de 203
Jonge, Freek de 122
Joosten, Jan 108

Kardaun, Marietje 205
Keizer, Piet 168, 170, 173
Kemenade, Jos van 46, 50, 101, 110, 111, 204

Kempen, Gerard 226
Klein, Ger 46
Knottnerus, André 63
Koenis, Sjaak 206
Kok, Gerjo 239, 249
Kok, Wim 149, 150
Koopmans, Tim 137, 138
Korsten, Gerard 19, 200-202, 204, 242-245, 247, 250
Kouwenaar, Gerrit 211
Kraan, Herro 71
Kremers, Sjeng 19, 61, 102, 103, 112, 135, 167, 168, 170, 186, 187, 191, 204, 226
Kuhn, Thomas 202
Kuiper, Jan Piet 115
Kuipers, Simon 165, 166
Kuipers, Theo 237
Kunst, Paul 170
Kuppen, Ine 13, 19, 25, 77-82
Kusters, Wiel 14, 19, 35, 197, 203, 205, 206, 209-221

Labrie, Arnold 205, 214
Lathouwer, Ingrid 19
Lelkens, Jan 101
Lemmens, Jos 46
Lensing, Hans 139, 144
Letschert, Rianne 13
Liemt, Hans van 182, 226
Linden, Ton van der 19, 100
Lindenberg, Siegwart 190
Lodeweges, Lidie 133
Lodewick, Léon 19, 58
Loeliger, Fredi 85
Londen, Joop van 62, 71
Loog, Myra 19
Loon, Paul van 170, 181, 188

Macfarlane, Robert Gwyn 85
Majoor, Gerard 19, 86, 88, 123
Marres, Edmond 99
Marshall, Alfred 174
Meijers, Jan 59
Melchior, Léon 66
Mellenbergh, Don 121
Merckelbach, Harald 19, 242, 244, 246-248
Metsemakers, Job 62
Mitchell, William 178
Mol, Tonja 60
Molle, Willem 176, 186, 187, 191
Mols, Gerard 139, 142, 155
Mostert, Pieter 197, 203
Moust, Jos 123, 139
Mulder, Karel 168
Muysken, Joan 14, 19, 32, 165-179, 181, 184, 185, 188, 225

Nauta, Lolle 193, 195
Neubourg, Chris de 166, 177, 244
Neufeld, Vic 127
Niessen, Ben 211
Nieuwenhuijzen Kruseman, Arie 250
Nijhuis, Ton 197
Norman, Geoff 127
Nussbaum, Martha 202

Os, Jim van 75

Pais, Arie 50, 101, 112-114, 135, 138, 158, 167
Palm, Franz 19, 175, 184
Paul, Martin 254
Pels, Dick 238
Perry, Jos 19
Peters, Hans 19, 36, 170, 223-234
Philipsen, Hans 13, 19, 28, 50-52, 90, 105-119, 149, 244, 248
Pielet, Jean-Pierre 19
Pinter, Harold 221
Praag, Herman van 75
Prakken, Ties 159

Querido, Arie 66, 67, 69

Reiners, Jacques 209, 211
Reneman, Rob 19, 88, 89
Richartz, Mark 70
Rijk, Bertus de 193, 197, 201, 202, 204, 205, 214, 216
Ritzen, Jo 204, 205, 219, 228, 231, 245, 246, 252, 255
Rive Box, Louk de la 250
Romme, Carl 67
Romme, Sjoerd 189
Romme, Marius 13, 19, 24, 46, 47, 56, 65-75, 108, 124, 133
Roos, Nico 142, 202
Roosjen, Menno 19
Rotteveel, Rob 71
Rottier, Antoine 109, 110
Rouwenhorst, Wilhelmina 115
Rutgers, Victor 138, 155
Rutten, Frans 168

Saive, Michel 19
Schipper, Willie 19
Schlössels, Raymond 162
Schmidt, Henk 14, 19, 29, 48-50, 80, 98, 121-130, 139, 141, 172, 226, 240, 242, 247-249
Schreuder, Hein 14, 19, 33, 170, 173-175, 181-192, 225, 226
Schreuder, Paul 181
Servais, Anja 19
Simon, Tiny 19, 77, 78
Slangen, Brigitte 19

Slangen, Linda 19
Snellen-Balendong, Hetty 49
Snijders, Jan 41, 42
Soete, Luc 19, 171, 188, 199, 226, 230, 244
Soeters, Jo 170
Sorge, Arndt 189
Soulier, Jean-Pierre 85
Spoormans, Huub 159
Sporcken, Paul 239
Spruyt, Joke 205
Steur, Edward 19
Stevens, Ineke 19
Sturmans, Ferd 74
Struyker Boudier, Harry 89

Tak, Twan 140
Tans, Sjeng 44-46, 49, 57, 65, 66, 68, 79, 86, 109, 110, 128, 135, 211, 212
Tempelaar, Dirk 170
Thuijsman, Frank 225
Thung, Paul 42, 50, 113, 131, 135, 137, 138, 168, 193, 195, 237, 238
Tiddens, Harmen 13, 42, 43, 45-47, 49-51, 56-59, 61, 65, 68, 69, 77-80, 85, 88-90, 99, 104, 105, 108, 109, 114, 122, 123, 136
Traas, Lou 184
Trimbos, Cees 67, 72
Tummers, Paul 218, 220, 250

Uiterwijk, Jos 225
Uyl, Joop den 46, 68

Vall, Renée van de 215, 217
Veder-Smit, Els 113
Veen, Tom van 170
Veld, Roel in 't 94, 149, 171
Veringa, Gerard 109
Vermeulen, Bram 122
Verspeek, René 19, 168, 176
Verstraete, Ginette 215
Verwijnen, Maarten 123
Vorst, Fred 115
Voskamp, Chris 124
Vredevoogd, Loek 19, 146, 148, 200-202, 204, 228, 229, 243, 245-247
Vries, Gerard de 14, 19, 34, 193-207, 211, 212, 215, 217, 220, 223, 224, 226, 232, 238, 241, 242, 244
Vries, Rob, de 243, 247
Vrieze, Koos 206, 223, 225-227, 230, 232-234
Vroman, Leo 92, 95
Vroman, Tineke 92
Wallage, Jacques 97
Wachelder, Jo 197, 214

Weijters, Ton 230
Wellens, Hein 89, 101
Wesseling, Lies 215
Widdershoven, Guy 198
Wijnen, Wynand 13, 16, 19, 22, 41-53, 57, 60, 78, 80, 85, 87, 90, 97-99, 108, 110-115, 121-128, 131, 133, 141, 168, 185
Wijmen, Frans van 19
Wilde, Rein, de 18, 19, 195, 203, 206, 213, 220
Willems, Jan 139
Willighagen, Roelof 46, 47, 56, 78, 86, 98
Wilmes, Ronald 18
Winden, Frans van 168
Witteloostuijn, Arjen van 189
Wolff, Betje 210
Wolff-Albers, Diana 246
Wolleswinkel, Ria 14, 19, 31, 151-163
Wöltgens, Thijs 204
Woltjer, Geert 170

Zeguers, Jacques 89
Ziesemer, Thomas 176
Zwaal, Rob 89

COLOPHON

This publication was realised thanks in part to support from the Limburg University Fund/SWOL.

Translation Translation and Editing Service, Maastricht University
Design Brigitte Slangen, Nijmegen
ISBN 978 94 6004 310 9

© 2016 Annemieke Klijn, Maastricht; Vantilt Publishers, Nijmegen commissioned by Maastricht University

Cover illustration — Professorial cortège at the opening of the 2016 academic year – photo Harry Heuts © – Maastricht University Archives

No parts of the publication may be reproduced and/or made public by means of print, photocopy, microfilm or in any other manner without the publisher's prior consent. Every effort has been made to trace copyright holders and obtain their permission for the use of copyright material in accordance with the statutory requirements. The publisher apologises for any errors or omissions in the list of illustrations and would be grateful if notified of any corrections.

MIX
Paper from responsible sources
FSC www.fsc.org FSC® C004472